A GAMBLING MAN

Charles II and the Restoration
1660–1670

JENNY UGLOW

faber and faber

First published in 2009
by Faber and Faber Limited
Bloomsbury House
74–77 Great Russell Street
London WC1B 3DA
This paperback edition first published in 2010

Typeset by Faber and Faber Limited
Printed in England by CPI Bookmarque, Croydon

A CIP record for this book
is available from the British Library

ISBN 978–0–571–21734–2

For Steve

3 5 7 9 10 8 6 4 2

Contents

IV HEARTS / *coeurs*

V SPADES / *piques*

VI THE CLEARANCE / *la fin*

A Note on the Text

In quotations, style follows the source cited, hence the variations in spelling and capitalisation.

The spelling of names follows that in the *Oxford Dictionary of National Biography*, and these change as people receive new titles and ranks (Hyde to Clarendon, Monck to Albemarle, Palmer to Castlemaine etc.)

Charles II ruled three kingdoms – England and Wales, Scotland, and Ireland. Where the interests of all three are combined, I have occasionally used the term 'Britain'.

With regard to dates, until 1753, the English used the Julian calendar and the rest of Europe the revised Gregorian calendar, which was ten days ahead (eleven in the next century). I have given the dates used in British documents and diaries.

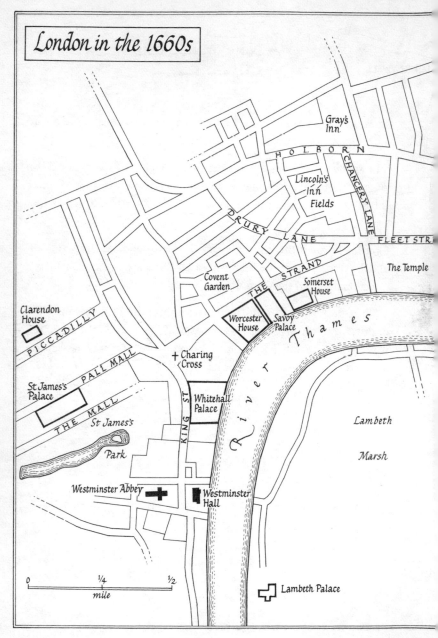

London in the 1660s

Gray's Inn

HOLBORN

Lincoln's Inn Fields

CHANCERY LANE

DRURY LANE

FLEET STR

The Temple

Covent Garden

THE STRAND

Somerset House

Clarendon House

PICCADILLY

Worcester House

Savoy Palace

River Thames

+ Charing Cross

St James's Palace

PALL MALL

KING ST

Whitehall Palace

Lambeth

THE MALL

St James's Park

Marsh

Westminster Abbey

Westminster Hall

0   ¼   ½
mile

Lambeth Palace

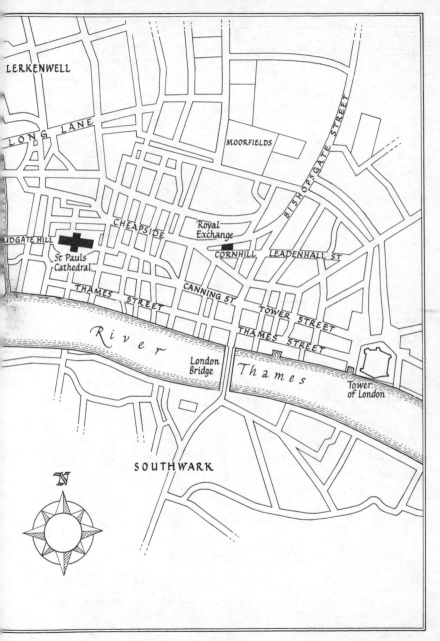

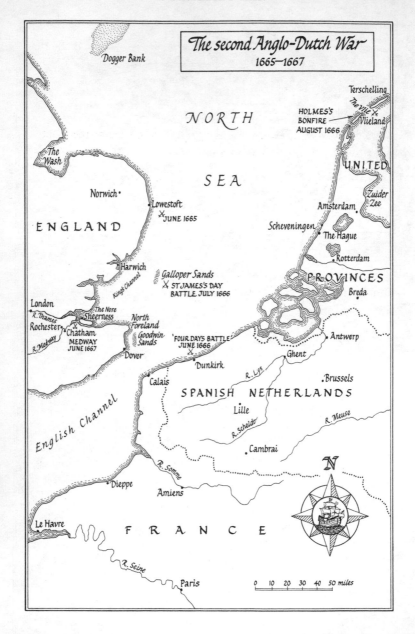

The second Anglo-Dutch War
1665–1667

'A King in a Commonwealth is like the Heart in a Body, the Root in the Tree . . . the Sun in the Firmament.'

THOMAS REEVE, *England's Beauty in seeing King Charles restored*, 1661

'A pox on all kings!'

AN OLD WOMAN, watching Charles's entry into London, 1660

'It is in the Lawes of a Commonwealth, as in the Lawes of Gameing; whatsoever the Gamesters all agree on, is Injustice to none of them.'

THOMAS HOBBES, *Leviathan*, 1651

DIEV ET MON DROIT.

Cross Faithorne Sculp.

The Second Charles, Heire of y.ᵉ Royall Martyr,
who, for Religion and his Subiects Charter,
spent the best Blood, y.ᵉ uniust Sword ere dy'de,
since the rude Souldier pierc'd our Sauiours side:
who such a Father hadst; art such a Son;
redeeme thy people and assume thy Owne.

J. T.

Prologue: The Republic Trumped

> Hazard is the most bewitching game that is played on the Dice; for when a man begins to play, he knows not when to leave off; and having once accustomed himself to play at Hazard, he hardly, ever after, minds anything else.
>
> attrib. CHARLES COTTON, *The Compleat Gamester*, 1674

CHARLES II WAS A GAMBLING MAN. He was not a wild player at dice or cards – he left the big stakes to his courtiers. But he took risks, judged odds and staked all, including his kingdom. He kept his cards close to his chest and made it hard to guess his hand. He borrowed to cover his bets. Some said his soul was in hock to the French king, the Pope, or the Devil. Many asked whether Charles was playing for himself, or for the nation. And who were the winners and losers?

This book is about the first ten years of the Restoration, from 1660 to 1670, looking at the life of Charles II through the lens of these years, glancing back at what formed him and forwards to what followed. In his hazardous game, sometimes he lost, sometimes he won and sometimes he was at the mercy of events, charting his way through opposing factions or riding his luck, living for the moment and being ruled by his desires. At the end of the decade the die was cast. From then on he would rule in a different way. It was an extraordinary decade, marked by struggles for power in state and Church and by blows like the Plague, the Great Fire and the Dutch war. But it had an exhilarating bravado and energy, embodied in talented, flamboyant women as well as clever and sometimes unscrupulous men. It saw the founding of the Royal Society, the return of the theatre, the glamour, fashion, gossip and scandal of the court, and the resurrection of London, rising like a phoenix from the ashes.

No single person makes 'history', the intricate, national and international shuffle and roar of events, personalities, ideas and beliefs, grinding through human time like the shifting of tectonic plates. But people sometimes make decisions that tip subsequent events in a particular direction. Charles II was one such person. His return in May 1660 was a crucial turning point, and although the Stuart dynasty would soon lose the crown, the way that Charles played his hand is part of the reason that Britain is still a monarchy today: we call the Commonwealth and Protectorate the 'Interregnum', as if it was a gap in an accepted sequence.

Every regime change that is held to express the will of the people holds out the hope of lives transformed. A tired, demoralised nation calls out for change. There are petitions, riots, demonstrations, candle-lit processions. A young, charismatic man is called to power, greeted in his capital by vast cheering crowds. But what happens when the fireworks fade and the euphoria cools? Can he unite the divided nation, or will he be defeated by vested interests, entrenched institutions and long-held prejudices?

The reign of Charles II had a distinct atmosphere that set it apart from what had gone before and what followed after. The two rulers before him, his father Charles I and the Great Protector, Oliver Cromwell, had both been men of single-minded principle, and this contributed in part to the collapse of the regimes they tried to impose. Charles I's belief in the authority of king over parliament and subjects led to his death; Cromwell's strength forged a unity that fractured when he died. Charles II, by contrast, was pragmatic and sceptical. He had principles, but was ready to bend them to keep his throne safe, protect the Stuart line and create space for his own pleasures. The problem was that for a king at this point in European history there was no private space. Every aspect of his life, his mistresses, his theatre-going, even his choice of clothes was a reflection on his state. The king literally embodied his kingdoms.

And while Charles had the common touch, and liked to present himself as a kind of folk-hero, heir to the Tudors, and close to his people, he was in fact closer to the old cousinship of European monarchs. The tall man who claimed the English throne by divine right and by blood had Scottish and Danish grandparents on his father's side, and French and Italian on his mother's. From his maternal grandmother, Marie de Medici, he derived the dark hair and olive-skinned Italian looks that won him the name of the 'Black Boy'.

It is a challenge for someone like me, whose sympathy lies with the radicals and artisans protesting against abuse of power, to venture into the centre, the heart of that power. Yet it is alluring. And while I have written about artists and writers, inventors and scientists, what if a person's art is also his life, his role simply 'being the king'? For anyone interested in the relationship between the public and private self, there are few more intriguing characters than Charles II. The first puzzle is simply how did Charles manage to stay on the throne? His father was executed and his brother James lasted less than three years before he was ousted by William of Orange in 1688. Yet Charles stayed in place for twenty-five years. What balancing skills did he have that his father and brother lacked?

The bare facts suggest a man who needed to create a carapace to survive, to protect any coherent sense of self. He was loved by his parents, brought up as the adored eldest son in a luxurious court, entertained by masques of gods and goddesses, until jolt after jolt shattered this idyll. At twelve he stood by his father when the standard was raised at Nottingham, marking the beginning of the Civil War, the unthinkable turning of subjects against their king. He saw the palaces abandoned, the capital closed. At Edgehill a cannonball narrowly missed him. At fifteen, he was sent west as general of the Western Army; at sixteen he fled to the Scilly Isles, then Jersey, then to France. He was nineteen when his father was executed. In the years that followed he scoured foreign courts for aid, broke and hopeless.

In exile he devised a strategy based on charm, outward compliance and private evasion. He escaped the competing demands of his mother Henrietta Maria and his anxious senior courtiers, not in books but in wild bodily release: riding, tennis, sailing, gambling and sex. He knew what it was to cadge loans and dodge creditors. He kept up all the structures of court life, appointing Privy Councillors and arranging presence chambers for audiences, even while living in cold rented rooms. To hide hurt, or hope, he practised looking as if he took nothing seriously, especially not work or religion. He found an inner life by absenting himself, mentally. He knew too, what it was to fail. 'Those who will not believe anything to be reasonably designed, except it be successfully executed,' he wrote when he was twenty-five, 'had need of a less difficult game to play than mine is.'[1]

The Restoration was an age of performance, from the triumphal processions of the court and the City to the plays in the theatres and the festivals of the streets. Charles was a supreme performer, a leading player in a huge cast. As 'Charles II', he was both a man and a function, a wayward, clever individual and a king, whose actions were constrained by his parliament and his vast band of followers and hangers-on. He acted through others. He knew it too, hence his quick riposte to this verse of Rochester's:

> We have a pritty witty king,
> And whose word no man relys on:
> He never said a foolish thing,
> And never did a wise one.

When Charles found this pinned to the door at Whitehall, he is supposed to have remarked, with typical laconic evasion, 'This is very true: for my words are my own, and my actions are my ministers'.'[2]

As king he inhabited a construct, constantly trying to shape it to his own desires. Charles-king was split into three entities. As 'the crown', he was the head of three countries – England and Wales, Scotland, and Ireland – ruling through his ministers, gathering revenues, declaring war, laying down religious policy as Defender of the Faith. As patron, he used his kingly power to promote certain movements or groups and to turn a cold shoulder towards others, granting charters to trading companies, fostering the Royal Society, awarding patents to the theatres. And then, as if he flung his crown onto a chair and tugged on comfortable boots, he became the suave courtier, the merry monarch. Yet crown, patron and courtier are all performances. It is hard to find the secret, non-performative self.

Charles was clever, affable and courtly. Yet he was also a cynic, with a reserve and unpredictability fostered by his wandering youth. He found it hard to give his full assent to any commitment or spiritual doctrine. He was physically restless and easily bored, sensual and sentimental, prone to unthinking acts of generosity and sudden infatuations. He loved to be entertained, to be made to laugh. This is why he adored the theatre, but also partly why he forgave his childhood friend Buckingham so often, despite his dangerous manoeuvres, and pardoned the brilliant young Rochester for his wildness and disrespect. Whenever a new scandal occurred, or an old story was told, Charles would lean forward, asking to hear all the details. His court, with its endless intrigues, was like a private menagerie: he indulged his courtiers like pet animals. In a world of backbiting, he was among the few kind figures, 'tender and generous', one observer said, but this very generosity could make him seem a fool. Not everyone liked Charles's act, but they admitted that the mask was superb. So good, in fact, that it was hard to work out if he was cunning or naïve, clever or lucky.

Our modern obsession with the inner self was alien to the people of the Restoration, except in terms of the soul's relationship with God, something that Charles does not discuss. His wit and flashes of anger appear in notes he scribbled at the Privy Council, but no diaries survive, and few letters. Even the intimate letters to his sister Henriette-Anne, 'Minette', leave out vital parts of his life. But others watched him. Spreading out from the court, the king's actions affected everyone, traders and dancers, farmers and doctors, seamen and schoolchildren. They made their own narratives to explain what was happening and used their own modes of description – Pepys's busy diary, Aubrey's scattered gossip, Hamilton's quasi-fictional memoirs of the comte de Gramont, the stoical rebuttals of Bunyan and Milton. Their facts may err, but the telling is true to what they believed they saw. This is the weather in the streets.

Charles thus appears to us reflected and refracted in the accounts of others, distorting mirrors where the image is bent by the writer's own stance. John Evelyn, trying to be fair, praised through negatives: 'A Prince of many Virtues, & many greate Imperfections, Debonaire, Easie of accesse, not bloudy or Cruel'.[3] Clarendon, who had known him since he was fifteen, wrote sadly in his last exile of Charles's great abilities, his laziness, his bad companions. Halifax, who served him towards the end of his reign, drew him as a brilliant dissembler, a man of pleasure with a vacuum where principle should lie, while Bishop Burnet saw him as a cynic whose experience had convinced him that no one served him out of love: 'And so he was quits with all the world, and loved others as little as he thought they loved him.'[4]

This was written long after the Glorious Revolution of 1688. By then Charles's dealings with France and his deathbed conversion to Catholicism were known, and the horrified Burnet, to whom these were the worst possible deceptions – 'a chain of black actions, flowing from blacker designs' – re-read the king as an arch conspirator. But in 1683, in Charles's lifetime, Burnet made no such judgement. He saw Charles as having a 'softness and gentleness with him, both in his air and expressions that has a charm in it'.[5] And, like Halifax, Burnet found that the king's most frustrating characteristic was that he was impossible to judge at all:

The King has a deal of wit, indeed no man more, and a great deal of judgment, when he thinks fitt to employ it; he has strange command of himselfe, he can pass from pleasure to business and business to pleasure in so easy a manner that all things seem alike to him; he has the greatest art of concealing himself of any man alive, so that those about him cannot tell, when he is ill or well pleased, and in private discourse he will hear all sorts of things in such a manner, that a man cannot know, whether he hears them or not, or whether he is well or ill pleased with them.[6]

This is the mask of the gamester, looking at his cards, giving nothing away. Charles had the typical gambler's tendency to compartmentalise his life, and ignore the way that extravagance in one area might bring destruction in another. He had the gambler's belief, too, that he could outwit his opponents, that the next play would make everything right, in a single stroke. He was not always cool and calculating. Sometimes he dithered. Sometimes he underestimated others at the table and misread the run of play. But he had a streak of ruthlessness that saw him through.

With the death of Charles I in 1649, the sanctity of monarchy had vanished. Monarchs had died violently before in wars and coups, but this death was particularly shocking because the king had been tried like a common felon, and executed by his own people. The appeal to law, and the implication that some kind of contract existed, in which a king was bound to protect his people and if he broke this they had a right to dethrone and even kill him, was new, and startling. His son had no blank page on to which he could inscribe his own ideas of kingship. Instead he had to negotiate his way through a welter of battling interests.

The post-Restoration government, where the monarch was theoretically head of state yet parliament held the purse-strings and passed the laws, was unique in Europe. And while the continent offered a great range of models, none provided an answer as to how this new, uneasy balance might evolve. At one extreme were the autocracies of the Ottoman Empire and Russia and the absolutist monarchies of Spain, Austria and France. (Charles's long stay in France, some people thought, had induced a leaning towards absolute power, and brought him to feel that 'a king who might be checked, or have his ministers called to account by a parliament was but a king in name'.[7]) At the opposite end of the spectrum lay the republics of the United Provinces, Venice and Poland–Lithuania, the loose confederation of Switzerland and a host of smaller states and city governments. There was no 'natural' state.

The execution of Charles I, 30 January 1649

In 1660 the chance of a republic vanished for ever, but time did not curve backwards. The waters did not close over the eighteen years since the civil wars began, as though they had never been. The constitutional fracture, wrought by the execution of the king and the brief republic, coincided with marked shifts in ideas of men and women's relation to society. In all areas of life, from experimental science to personal belief, people searched for new philosophies to explain the world. Contrary to myth, the years under Cromwell had not all been dank and drab. The maypoles, fairs and festivals largely disappeared but victories were won, trade boomed and luxuries flooded into the capital. The achievements of Charles II's reign built on the energy and intellectual ferment of the Interregnum. But in the late 1650s the mood had soured, and while dissenters and republicans lamented, the mass of people called for the return of a king.

Everyone over twenty-five had some memory of the two civil wars, of 1642–6 and 1648, when thousands of ordinary citizens had died and families had been torn apart. No one, high or low, wished to return to such a state. Many royalists changed sides in the early 1650s simply for self-preservation. Now many who had served parliament changed back again. The Commonwealth had, however, given the common people a stronger view of their rights. When the London apprentices issued a 'Remonstrance' calling for the king's return, they stated that they would defend with their 'Lives and Fortunes the Laws of this Land and the Liberty of the Subject'.[8] The radical sects had also taught people to look inwards, to consider conscience as the true authority, often in defiance of the state. The newsletters, pamphlets and broadsheets, and the discussions in taverns and early coffee-houses, began to create a new forum for public opinion. At the same time, the power of the merchants and goldsmiths who had bankrolled Cromwell brought a new relationship between the City and the state that was hard to roll back. The idea of contract and exchange as the basis of social relations, rather than authority and command, was widely discussed.

As Archbishop Tillotson would later say, 'The fashion of the age is to call every thing into question.'[9] This questioning was applied to the very make-up of the universe and the nature of man. While some people still believed in portents and prodigies and the mysteries of alchemy, others were pondering the mechanical theories of Descartes and imbibing the scepticism of Montaigne. Indeed many people did both at the same time. One best-selling book of the late seventeenth century was Richard Allestree's *Whole Duty of Man*, published in 1658, which assumed a world guided by Providence and advocated pious, sober living and respect for authority. It was almost rivalled, however, by the translations of Lucretius' *De rerum natura*, which put the philosophy of Epicurus into seductive verse, denying divine design and depicting the universe as a whirl of atoms, in a perpetual state of flux.[10] In a witty poem, Margaret, Duchess of Newcastle, substituted a new puzzle for the scholastic conundrum of how many angels could fit on the head of a pin – how many atoms, or separate worlds, existed within the earrings of a court beauty?

> For millions of these atoms may be in
> The head of one small, little, single pin.
> And if thus small, then ladies well may wear
> A world of worlds as pendents in each ear.[11]

This world-view did not preclude belief in God. But for some adherents it led logically to a philosophy of living for the moment, through the senses. Lucretius challenged ideas about the immortality of the soul and the superiority of man to beast, while his materialism fostered secular, as opposed to spiritual, theories of the state.

A generation younger than his advisers, Charles was attuned to these new ideas as well as to the regal ceremonial of court life. Thomas Hobbes, who was briefly his mathematics tutor in Paris, had sent ripples of controversy through the intellectual, religious and political worlds with his *Leviathan*, in 1651. His description of the 'state of nature', when men are driven by strong primal drives 'without a common Power to keep them in awe', conjured up a chaos that must have seemed terrifyingly vivid to those who remembered the civil wars:

there is no place for Industry; because the fruit thereof is uncertain: and consequently no Culture of the Earth; no Navigation, nor use of commodities that may be imported by Sea; no commodious Building; no Instruments of moving, and removing, such things as require much force; no knowledge of the face of the earth; no account of the Time; no Arts; no Letters; no Society; and which is worst of all, continuall feare, and danger of violent death; and the life of man, solitary, poore, nasty, brutish and short.[12]

The cure for this terror was for the people to submit to the strong ruler who could make them safe, the 'Leviathan' sucking power into himself. Although Hobbes allowed for some vague deity to keep this all-powerful leader in check, the state was a man-made construct, based on force. 'Because the major part hath by consenting

voices declared a sovereigne', wrote Hobbes, 'he that dissented must now consent with the rest; that is, be contented to avow all the actions he shall do, or else be justly destroyed by the rest.'[13] In 1651, *Leviathan* appeared to justify submission to Cromwell as the de facto ruler and Hobbes was damned by the royalists. But could his doctrine of submission now also apply to the nation under Charles?

Almost more influential than his authoritarian vision was Hobbes's relativism, his insistence that language and moral judgements were not given by God but constructed by societies: '*True* and *False* are attributes of Speech, not of Things.'[14] Good and evil, said Hobbes, were merely names that signified inclination or aversion, and these differed between men and societies, according to their different customs and opinions.[15] Once again, everything came into question, including the virtues of reason and language, the capacities held to separate man from beasts.

Charles swam among such uncertainties. The sober historical accounts that chart the political intricacies and cultural shifts of his reign inevitably focus on particular institutions, events and theories. Perhaps, by looking at his life from many perspectives, we can get a different view of the real choices he made, the risks and chances he took when faced with an almost impossible situation. Charles had few great ambitions, thought Halifax when he wrote his memoirs in his disillusioned last years, apart from living an easy life. No more exile, no more bowing and scraping and smiling, no more shabby clothes and quarrelling, hungry followers. Little enough, were it not that this meant staying on the throne and amassing enough income to maintain his kingdom and his court – two of the hardest things in the world.

This book charts Charles's game in his first decade on the throne. His first task is to assume the mantle of king, settle outstanding problems and make his mark, and from the start the manners of his followers signify a new era. The next round follows ideas in action: the conflicts of faith, the discoveries of science, the mentality of the court, and the expression of conflict through performance, on stage and off. The third brings crisis, war with the Dutch, plague and fire. At the end of the decade, Charles fends off blame, deals with factions and takes his great gamble, the secret alliance with France. The period was dramatic and mixed, and any story that follows its fortunes has the air of a grand tragi-comedy, the favourite genre of the Restoration stage. Merchants whisper in a corner, a royal mistress sulks, a man pores through his microscope at a flea. Angry MPs push forward, rowdy courtiers brawl, Quakers are hustled into gaol, shrouded plague victims fade into the wings. The scenery shifts to rolling waves, with a line of warships, cannon blazing. Or a cityscape appears, red with fire. There are crowd scenes, tender duets, harsh betrayals. In the centre, from first to last, is a solitary hero, playing a game. He shuffles the cards, deals, looks at his hand and lays down his bets.

I THE DEAL / *la donne*

Habit de Cartier, by Nicolas de Larmessin, *c.*1690

1 Sailing

At length, by wonderful impulse of fate,
The people call him back to help the State;
And what is more, they send him money, too,
And clothe him all from head to foot anew
    ANON., 'A Historicall Poem'[1]

IT WAS LATE SPRING, with a fair May breeze in the Channel. Ahead lay England, the hollow lanes of Kent heavy with hawthorn, the hedgerows dusty with chalk. Behind lay Holland: Delft, with its bridges and canals and poor-boxes in every theatre; the neat houses of the Hague where maypoles stood outside each door. Behind lay wintry exile; before lay summer and glorious return.

All afternoon Charles paced the deck in his new clothes. As he walked with long, fast strides, the sailors examined their king. At twenty-nine, he was tall and dark, his face strong, with a long nose, heavy jaw and brown eyes slanting under thick, arched brows. He wore his own dark hair, and bore a hint of a moustache above full lips. His mouth could curl in amusement, purse in thought, tighten in anger. A mobile, sensual face. Today he smiled and cracked jokes to the audience that scuttled behind him, weaving between barrels, tripping over ropes.

The very ship shouted his triumph. Until the evening before, 23 May 1660, when it was still moored off Scheveningen, the port of the Hague, it had been the flagship *Naseby*, named after the battle of 1645 when Cromwell routed the royalist forces. It was built ten years later, a powerful three-decker, bulging with tiers of guns behind square portholes. When it was launched John Evelyn and his brother went to see 'the greate Ship, newly built, by the Usurper

Oliver, carrying 96 brasse Guns, & of 1000 tunn: In the prow was Oliver on horseback trampling 6 nations under foote, a Scott, Irishman, Dutch, French, Spaniard & English'. A statue of Fame 'held a laurell over his insulting head, & the word God with us'.[2]

God and the people, it seemed, had now made a different choice. Before the fleet weighed anchor the king and his brother James, Duke of York – who had been reinstated by parliament as High Admiral of the Fleet, a role his father had given him when he was nine – amended the names of the ships. The *Naseby*, which had trumpeted the royalists' humiliation, became the *Royal Charles*. The *Richard* (son of Cromwell) took the Duke's name, *James*, while the *Dunbar*, also marking defeat in battle, became the *Henry*, named after Charles's younger brother, Henry, Duke of Gloucester. The *Speaker*, voicing the power of the Commons, became the feminine *Mary*, for his sister the Princess of Orange, and the *Lambert*, honouring the brave republican general, took the name shared by Charles's mother and youngest sister, *Henrietta*. This family flotilla was surrounded by maritime cheers: the *Winsley* became the *Happy Return*; the *Cheriton* the *Speedwell*; the *Bradford* the *Success*, and with them sailed the *London* and the *Swiftsure*. The flotilla was blessed, as with an amulet, with a necklace of names.

Over the past month, when the *Royal Charles*-to-be had stood at anchor in the Downs off Deal, carpenters, sail-makers and chandlers rushed to refurbish it. The insulting figurehead of Cromwell was ripped down and replaced by Neptune flourishing his trident, riding on a sea-shell drawn by horses rising from the waves.[3] Edward Montagu, who was in charge of the fleet, asked his twenty-six-year-old assistant Samuel Pepys to order silk flags and 'scarlett waistcloathes' – the painted canvas covering the hammocks when they were stowed away – and to arrange for a special barge to bring the king on board, with trumpets and fiddlers. The ship was stocked with provisions, including a hundred pounds of beef, and silver plate for the royal table. Montagu had been in secret communication with Charles for the past month and on 10 May he received a message from General Monck saying that 'the King's friends thought his Majesty's present repair to London was absolutely necessary and therefore wished me to sail and waft the King over as soon as I could'.[4] Two days later he set sail for the Dutch coast, leaving the rest of his small fleet to follow. Even so, the ship was not quite prepared. On the voyage tailors and painters hastily cut yellow cloth into the shape of a crown and 'C.R.' and sewed it onto a fine sheet, which they tacked onto the flag instead of the State's arms.[5] They arrived in Dutch waters two days later. For the next week a gale rocked the ships at their anchors, in winds so violent that any thought of leaving was set aside. The time was spent in diplomatic gatherings, exchanges of courtesies, banquets and feasts.

At last the storms calmed. On Tuesday 22 May, the Duke of York – tall, thickset, handsome and stubborn – boarded the *Naseby*, so soon to be renamed, accompanied by the Duke of Gloucester. With a bevy of dignitaries the two dukes toured the ship and feasted off sides of beef on Montagu's silver plate. It was an eve of celebration and firing of cannon (Pepys fired his own gun outside his cabin and gave himself a black eye).[6] Next morning streams of people poured on board including the eighteen Lords Commissioners, sent to bring Charles home, and the royalist courtiers and their families. Chief among these was Edward Hyde, Charles's adviser since his youth, his guide in exile and architect of his return. Hyde was now a corpulent fifty, often wincing from the gout he had suffered since his thirties, when he accompanied the fifteen-year-old Charles to the West Country. Since then he had been the leading figure in his entourage, exhorting the prince to stay sober, avoid women and be more diplomatic to his hosts, in whatever country they were drifting through. He also orchestrated affairs at home through a system of spies, penning endless letters from icy rooms, when candles and food were running low. In recent weeks he had organised audiences, received petitions, dealt with volumes of correspondence. Now, with his three sons also on board, he might expect some relief.

The boarding parties were swollen by lawyers and priests, actors and poets, equerries, hairdressers, pages and cooks. The decks and gangways were jammed with men elbowing past each other, squeezing into corners, cramming into the cabins. Mid-morning, Charles arrived in his coach and stepped into a small boat, decked with garlands and crowns of flowers, which took him to the admiral's barge where Montagu waited in his finest clothes, glittering with silver and gold braid. As the king embraced him, kissing him on both cheeks, the sailors huzza'd and threw their caps in the air, into the sea, 'and even their doublets and waistcoats'.[7] Over fifty thousand people thronged the shoreline to see Charles leave and the water was black with boats. Torches and flares lit the sky. Guns fired in a chaos of noise. The smoke swirling through the rigging was so thick that for a moment it hid the ships completely from the watchers on the shore.

Following Charles and the Dukes of York and Gloucester, the women swept on board. First came their sister, Mary, with her ten-year-old son William, Prince of Orange, and then Charles's aunt Elizabeth of Bohemia, sister of Charles I, 'a very debonaire, but plain lady', thought Pepys. Almost half a century ago, in 1613, Elizabeth had married the German Elector Palatine, Frederick V. Six years later he was offered the crown of Bohemia but he ruled for less than a year before Catholic armies drove him from Prague in the winter snows – hence Elizabeth's title of 'the Winter Queen'. Having lost both Bohemia and the Palatinate, they settled in the Hague where they brought up their large family, including Prince Rupert, the dashing Cavalier general. (Rupert was a baby when they fled Prague and was almost left behind in the panic, being thrown at the last moment into the boot of the coach.)[8] A huge influence on her nephew Charles, the indomitable Elizabeth of Bohemia was the oldest of this Stuart family to learn the lessons of exile.

The royal party dined in state in the 'coach', a cabin on the quarterdeck which was usually the officers' wardroom. After Elizabeth, Mary and Prince William went ashore, the anchors were weighed and the sails were raised, their heavy cream canvas crackling and soughing in the breeze. Easing out of the harbour, tacking past the shallows and sandbanks, 'with a fresh gale and most happy weather', they sailed south and west, for Dover.

Charles was returning in peace to a land he had left in conflict. He had fought since the age of twelve, when his childhood of dignity and ceremony, tutors and music was shattered by the outbreak of the first civil war in 1642. The close, loving family was separated. In February that year Charles I took Henrietta Maria and their daughter Mary from Windsor to Dover, and put them on board ship. As they sailed, he galloped along the cliffs, waving to his wife and daughter, until their ship was lost to view.

Prince Charles himself left five years later, in June 1647, in the dying days of the royalist cause, yielding to his father's entreaties to quit England. Aged seventeen, he went first to the Scilly Isles, then Jersey and finally to France, to stay with his mother. In April 1648, his brother James also reached the continent, escaping from St James's Palace during a carefully staged game of hide-and-seek, disguised as a girl, and then boarding a Dutch ship. Eventually he arrived at the court of his sister Mary and her husband William II, Prince of Orange. That summer, when part of the parliamentary fleet mutinied and sailed to the Hague, Prince Charles came from Paris to see James. But instead of letting his fifteen-year-old brother be admiral in fact as well as name, he gave the command to his cousin Prince Rupert, a snub that James never forgot.

At the end of 1648, when rumours spread of plans to put his father on trial, Charles lobbied the courts of France and Spain and the Dutch republic with angry, but fruitless, persistence. The trial began on 20 January 1649. A week later Charles I was sentenced, and on the 30th, famously wearing two shirts so that he would not shiver and appear to show fear, he stepped through the window of the Whitehall Banqueting House, onto the platform prepared for his execution. The news reached his son on 5 February. His chaplain, Stephen Goffe, entered the room and hesitated, before addressing him slowly as 'Your Majesty'. Charles could not speak, but wept, furiously. Some reports say he dismissed Goffe with a wave, others that he rushed from the room. All agree that for the next few hours, he remained alone.

During the year that followed, all the European powers accepted Cromwell's authority, while Charles vainly begged for their support. By 1650 he seemed desperate, seeking distraction and choosing as his companion George Villiers, the mercurial Duke of Buckingham, five years his senior. After the violent stabbing of his father, the first duke, hated favourite of James I and Charles I, the baby George and his brother Francis, born after his father's death, were made royal wards. The Villiers brothers had thus grown up with the royal children but during the civil wars they toured the continent with their tutors, lingering in the Florence of Lorenzo de' Medici, studying amid Rome's baroque splendour, dallying in Venice and Geneva. On their return to England in 1649 they joined a reckless uprising in which Francis was killed, trapped with his back pinned against an oak tree. Buckingham fled to the exiled court. Both he and Charles had known tragedy, but to Charles, at nineteen, his friend's life seemed glamorous in contrast to his own shifting existence. In the words of Gilbert Burnet, Buckingham was then 'a man of noble appearance and of a most lovely wit, wholly turned to mirth and pleasure . . . the pleasantness of his humour and conversation, the extravagance and sharpness of his wit, unrestrained by any modesty or religion, drew persons of all affections and inclinations to like his company.'[9] But in Burnet's view, his scepticism and propensity to ridicule was dangerous, 'he possessed the young king with very ill principles both as to religion and morality, and with a very mean opinion of his father, whose stiffness was with him a frequent subject of raillery'.

The charismatic Buckingham played his part in the next disastrous move, when Charles, whose armies in Ireland had now been defeated, turned to the Scots. This was a painful choice. The Scottish rebellion against his father's imposition of the Anglican prayer book, and their signing of the National Covenant to uphold the presbyterian principles of the Scottish kirk, had spurred the course towards war in the late 1630s. And although they had later changed sides to support the king, they had finally handed him over to the parliamentary forces, and thus to his death. In approaching the Scots Charles was urged on by Buckingham, the Marquess of Argyll, the dominant figure in the kirk regime, and the Earl of Lauderdale, a Covenanter who nevertheless in 1648 had negotiated the 'Engagement' that secured Scottish support for the defeated Charles I. At last, after weeks of fraught negotiations, Charles agreed to accept the authority of the kirk. If his protestant French grandfather Henry IV had thought Paris worth a mass, Argyll reminded him, then perhaps Britain was worth a covenant. He was too late, however, to stop the Earl of Montrose, whom he had previously ordered to invade Scotland. By the time Charles's message arrived, Montrose's small army had been slaughtered in a Highland glen. Montrose himself was executed in Edinburgh, proclaiming his loyalty to the last.

After a long and stormy North Sea passage Charles landed at Garmouth, on the Spey, and on 3 July 1650, still aboard ship, he swore the solemn oath to uphold the National Covenant, and promised to follow the presbyterian form of worship approved by the General Assembly of the Kirk, 'and shall never make any opposition to any of these, nor endeavour any alteration therein'.[10] It was a cynical oath, sworn in desperation. The Scots knew this, and gloried in their power. When Charles travelled south down the coast to Aberdeen, he found the hand of Montrose nailed to the Tolbooth across the road from his lodgings. He said nothing, but he would never forget nor forgive. Although he was taken with great ceremony to Edinburgh and then to Perth, he was virtually the prisoner of the kirk, enduring long sermons and humiliating lectures.

Within a month of his arrival, Cromwell invaded, and in September the Scots army was defeated at Dunbar. The setback was made worse by the news that his sister Elizabeth, a prisoner at

From thy afflicted Vaile, that Cypresse Bower
still Watere'd fresh by thy Celestiall shower
Come forth, come forth, Bright Captive, & Declare
With a Full Orb the Innocent, and Faire.

Princess Elizabeth, portrayed in the frontispiece of Christopher Wase's
translation of Sophocles' *Electra*, 1649. This was dedicated to the princess,
thus casting Charles II as Orestes.

Carisbrooke Castle, had died of consumption, at the very point that she and his young brother Henry were given leave to go to France. In early October Charles used the pretext of a hunting trip to escape, hoping to raise royalist support in the Highlands, but he was soon overtaken, found exhausted in a peasant's cottage, and brought back to Perth. The Scots tried to make amends in January by crowning him King of Scotland in Scone, but as the months passed he grew increasingly bitter and when parliamentary troops crossed the Firth of Forth in July, he burst into action. With twelve thousand troops, he marched south. He hoped England would rise to greet him, but the people were sick of war and few would march with their old enemy the Scots. Buckingham sulked when Charles refused to let him lead the troops and when they were deep in England, with no chance of turning back, Cromwell caught up with them at Worcester. With twice the number of soldiers, on 3 September 1651, fighting through the narrow streets, he destroyed the Scottish army.

Everyone present praised Charles's courage. 'Certainly a braver Prince never lived,' said one of his officers, 'having in the day of the fight hazarded his person much more than any officer of his army, riding from regiment to regiment.'[11] His escape, too, was quick, decisive and bold. Now, nine years later, as he strode the deck of the *Royal Charles*, this was the story he returned to. 'All the afternoon the King walked here and there, up and down (quite contrary to what I thought him to have been), very active and stirring,' wrote Pepys.[12]

Upon the quarterdeck he fell into discourse of his escape from Worcester, where it made me ready to weep to hear the stories that he told of his difficulties that he had passed through, as his travelling four days and three nights on foot, every step up to his knees in dirt, with nothing but a green coat and a pair of country breeches on, and a pair of country shoes that made him so sore all over his feet, that he could scarce stir.

Although a huge reward of £1,000 was on his head, and all were asked to watch out for 'a tall black man, over two yards high', Charles dodged his pursuers with the help of the royalist network and his own wits and charm. He took refuge with Catholic gentry in Shropshire and Staffordshire before cutting his long black hair short and working his way across the West Country as a servant of Jane Lane, a colonel's daughter travelling to help her sister-in-law in childbirth. As a servant should, he rode on horseback with her, doffing his cap to his betters, overseeing the shoeing of a horse, fumbling with a kitchen jack, joking with ostlers and grooms. Finding no chance of a boat from Bristol or Bridport in Dorset, both bristling with Commonwealth troops, Charles turned east, along the south coast. People guessed who he was, but no one betrayed him. In Brighton, as he stood with his hands on the back of a chair near the fire, an innkeeper knelt down and kissed his hand, 'saying, that he would not ask him who he was, but bid God bless him whither he was going'.[14]

Colonel Wilmot escorting Charles and Jane Lane.

At last, after nearly six weeks, he found a passage in a collier brig from Shoreham in Sussex to Fécamp in Normandy. In a final scare, just off the French coast, the crew spotted a boat nearby that looked like a privateer and Charles and his companion Henry Wilmot, who had stayed by his side since Worcester at constant risk of his life, slipped into a small cock-boat manned by the ship's mate, a Quaker named Carver. As they neared the shore, Carver hoisted Charles onto his shoulders and carried him through the surf. By the time he reached Rouen he was so exhausted and ragged that the innkeepers took him for a vagrant and before he left they checked his room to see if anything was stolen.

In gratitude, the following year Charles created Wilmot Earl of Rochester, and when Wilmot died in 1658 he made his ten-year-old son John his foster son, the small boy who would grow up to be poet, satirist and tragic libertine. For years Charles stayed quiet about these adventures for fear of reprisals against his helpers, but now, on board ship, he could speak, and later he would shower them with honours. The escape from Worcester became a favourite story, soon embellished with the account of his day in the great oak at Boscobel, spying through the branches on the searchers below. The story was a reminder, to himself and to others, of what he could achieve. He had been cool and quick-thinking in sudden danger; he had enjoyed the variety, the disguise, the challenges, the fast pace. He had been courteous, never rattled, getting on easily with men and women he would not normally meet, from country matrons to soldiers, merchants and servants. Perhaps, too, he returned to these days so often because the help of the common people had given him a sense that he was loved, something he rarely felt in the flattery of the court.

When he told his story in mid-Channel in May 1660, his hearers were astounded, just as he intended. That evening he ate alone in his newly gilded cabin, treading luxurious Turkey rugs, slipping between fine linen sheets, pulling up the covers with their gold and silver fringes. But late into the night, in less comfortable quarters, Pepys and his friends were still talking of the king's escape, 'as how he was fain to eat a piece of bread and cheese out of a poor boy's pocket; how, at a Catholique house, he was fain to lie in the priest's hole a good while'. It was a calm night, with the waves lapping against the hull under a full moon, and the stars and flaring torches on the boats reflected in the inky Channel deeps. So calm, indeed, that wherries took excited groups back and forth, visiting their friends in the other ships into the early hours. Finally the company broke up. Under sail all night, the ships were quiet except for the cry of the watch.

2 Landing

And welcome now, great monarch, to your own;
Behold th' approaching cliffs of Albion;
It is no longer motion cheats your view,
As you meet it, the land approacheth you.
       JOHN DRYDEN, 'Astraea Redux'

AS DAY DAWNED, the company on the *Royal Charles* rose early.
Pepys dressed up in his best stockings and showed off the new wide
tops to his boots. 'Extraordinary press of Noble company, and great
mirth all the day . . . Walking upon the decks, where persons of
Honour all the afternoon.'[1] Among the crowd was the playwright
Thomas Killigrew, now in his late forties, who had been a page to
Charles I and a favourite of Henrietta Maria. He had followed their
son into exile, acting as Charles's agent in Venice (sent back after
complaints of his debauchery), and had then married a wealthy
Dutch wife and settled in Holland, fighting for the Friesland army.[2]
The Killigrews had been a court family since the time of Elizabeth I,
and Thomas's elder brothers, William and Henry, were a diplomat
and a royal chaplain. But while they were university-educated,
Thomas was not. The most exuberant of twelve children of a lively
musical and intellectual family, he made his way by his wits. On
board ship he told risqué stories and composed a song about the
cut-purse Moll Frith, 'which he sang to Charles II till tears of laughter ran down the merry monarch's cheeks'.[3]

To Lady Fanshawe, who had been by her husband's side all
through the hard years of exile, this was a voyage of 'joy and gallantry'. She rejoiced in the vessels sailing before the wind, 'with vast
cloths and streamers, the neatness and cleanness of the ships, the
strength and jollity of the mariners, the gallantry of the command-

ers, the vast plenty of all sorts of provisions. Above all, the glorious majesties of the king and his two brothers were so beyond man's expectation and expression!'[4]

The new king was well aware how great those expectations were. When he told the tale of Worcester, he did not carry the story forward from his landing in the surf. In 1650 he had landed on the shores of a continent devastated by decades of religious conflict. The Thirty Years War, which had begun with the Czech protestant rebellion in Bohemia that placed his aunt Elizabeth briefly on the throne, had ended only two years before. The rich lands of Bohemia and Bavaria and northern Germany had been stripped of crops and trees, their peasants strung up, their nobles decapitated, their castles razed. Sweden had been drawn into the war, then Denmark, France and Spain. In the exhausted aftermath Spain clung to the remnants of its empire under its crumbling Habsburg dynasty. In the Netherlands, after eighty years of resistance, William II of Orange wrested freedom from Spain for the seven United Provinces in 1648. For decades to come France and Spain would wrangle over the southern provinces of Flanders, the Spanish Netherlands.

Charles's own royal relations, born of a scattering of dynastic marriages across Europe, were in trouble. In 1641 his sister Mary, then nine years old, had married the fourteen-year-old Prince William of Orange. At the start of the civil war she crossed to the Hague. But although the House of Orange supported the royalist cause, it was locked in a struggle with the States General of the United Provinces – the most powerful province being Holland, a name that the English often gave the whole country. As well as having its own assembly, each province also elected a stadtholder, a governor, and this post was usually held simultaneously in all the states by the current Prince of Orange, since the family were revered by the common people for leading them in their war of independence. But when William II died of smallpox in 1650, eight days before his son was born, the republican government immediately reduced his family's power. Republicans in England rejoiced. 'God taketh away our enemies abroad viz the Prince of Orange,' wrote the puritan Essex vicar Ralph Josselin, 'which is great work as things stood there and here.'[5] When Charles fled from Worcester Mary was fighting her own battles. She could not know then that her son would survive to become one of the most powerful monarchs of Europe, as William III of England.

Nor could Charles expect much from the family of his mother, Henrietta Maria. France was not only fighting Spain but suffering its own civil war, the Fronde, the uprising of the great nobles and the *parlements* of Paris and the provinces. (In Paris gangs of old soldiers hardened by fighting in Germany used their *frondes*, or slings, to hurl stones through the windows of the royal palaces.) Charles's cousin Louis XIV was only six and until he came of age France was ruled by the Queen-Regent, Anne of Austria, and her adviser Cardinal Mazarin, who smiled on the English exile when it suited him and ignored him coolly when it did not.

Charles camped with Henrietta Maria in her quarters in the Louvre and St Germain, skulking in the freezing corridors, bored and poor. Soon all the family were in exile, as parliament finally gave the youngest brother, Henry, leave to cross the Channel in February 1653. In Britain, any uprisings were badly planned and soon routed. The exiled court quarrelled constantly, with the Queen's party opposing that of Hyde and James Butler, Marquess of Ormond, while the 'Swordsmen', loyal to Prince Rupert, veered between the two. Everywhere Charles went, he tried to keep up the appearance of a royal prince, dining off good plate, playing tennis, dancing. But for years he turned and turned and turned again, trailing his shabby band from court to court, palming royal pensions, smiling and bowing, learning to keep his counsel. In 1654, when Mazarin was making overtures to the Commonwealth and Charles was no longer welcome in France, he moved to Cologne as a pensioner of the Imperial court. His hopes rose when the Dutch were at war with England in the mid-1650s, and the Orange party flourished briefly again, but he was still unwelcome in Holland.

He was watched at every turn. From Cologne he wrote to Elizabeth of Bohemia, 'my sister and I goe on Sunday in the afternoone towards frankeforde . . . tis so great a secret that not above half of the town of Collen knows of it . . . I hope we shall be furnished with some good storyes before the ende of our voyage.'[6] When the German welcome ran out, he approached Spain, and in 1656 settled his court in Bruges, in the Spanish Netherlands, promising to help fight any French advance. By now he was adept at making promises he could not keep. In June 1658 the Anglo-French army defeated the Spanish and as a reward, Dunkirk was ceded to Cromwell's Britain. In exile many of Charles's supporters lost all they possessed. In the bitter March winds of this year the elderly Lord Norwich was wearing a cut-down coat, singed in a fire. 'Wonder not at my silence,' Norwich wrote in one letter, 'for I have been dull, lame, cold, out of money, clothes and what not.'[7]

Then came a glimmer through the clouds. In September 1658, on the seventh anniversary of the Battle of Worcester, Oliver Cromwell died, after a summer of storms and portents. His corpse, decaying too fast and badly embalmed, was stored away and a doll-like wax effigy of the Great Protector, robed like a king with a crown on his head, was propped up amid a blaze of candles in Somerset House for the people to file past. Two months later, the effigy was cloaked in black velvet and carried in state in an open chariot to Westminster Abbey. John Milton, Cromwell's Latin secretary, and his assistants, Andrew Marvell and the young John Dryden, marched in the great funeral procession.

When Cromwell's son Richard, 'Tumbledown Dick', was forced to resign by the New Model Army in May 1659, royalists in Britain at last saw a chance of action, planning risings across the country. But these were designed to coincide with a Spanish attack, and when Spanish support failed to come, many groups dispersed. The last hope lay with Sir George Booth, who was fighting a surprisingly successful campaign in Cheshire. Charles rode to Calais, only to learn, just as he was about to set sail for England, that Booth's men had been defeated and the leaders imprisoned. In his frustration, he made one last effort to wring help from France and Spain. The two powers were now allies again, and their representatives were to meet in October on the Spanish border to settle the marriage of Louis XIV to the Spanish Infanta, Maria Teresa. Charles sailed down the French coast to the port of Fuentarrabia in the Basque country, but although he impressed all present with his charm, intelligence and drive, he won nothing. While he was there, however, news came from London that turned his thoughts in a different direction. Visiting his mother and sister in Paris on the way, he sped back to Brussels.

The news that drove him north came from England, where old animosities had flared between the republican New Model Army and the Rump Parliament, which failed to meet one of the conditions on which the army had restored it to power, namely to give the troops their arrears of pay. In October, General John Lambert marched to London and summarily dismissed the Rump. Power now lay with the army council, and government broke down. Taxes went uncollected and the goldsmiths took their hoard out of the capital. The army itself was split by faction and on Boxing Day – when Charles arrived back in Brussels – the Rump Parliament reassembled and ordered Lambert to disband his forces. He refused. The resolution of the impasse lay far to the north, on the Scottish border, where George Monck, supreme commander of the army in Scotland, had massed his troops. For weeks, Monck gave no hint which way he would jump. Then on New Year's Day 1660, he crossed the border. In a cold January with great falls of snow, he marched south. He claimed that he was coming to the capital to demand pay for his troops, but he was besieged on all sides by petitioners asking that he press for a 'full and free Parliament', a newly elected body. Everyone knew that such a parliament would vote for the king's return.

In York, Lord Fairfax, the greatest of the early parliamentarian generals, who had resigned at the time of Charles I's trial, brought his volunteer forces to join Monck's parade. With him came Buckingham, who had spent much of the Interregnum trying by devious means to regain his sequestered estates – half of which had been given to Cromwell and half to Fairfax – and had married Fairfax's daughter Mary, an alliance that stunned royalists and Cromwellians alike. On 3 February Buckingham and Monck reached the capital. Within days of Monck's arrival, wrote Pepys, 'Boys do now cry "Kiss my Parliament!" instead of "Kiss my arse!" so great and general a contempt is the Rump come to among all men, good and bad.'[8]

General Monck, Duke of Albemarle

On 11 February, with the support of the Common Council of the City of London, Monck forced the Rump Parliament to admit the moderate MPs who had been excluded by 'Pride's Purge' in 1648, and arrange for a 'free' election. Excited citizens plied Monck's soldiers with drinks and money. Church bells pealed. Bonfires blazed along Cheapside, down Fleet Street and the Strand and in St James's. Rumps of beef were roasted in the street and the butchers made music with their knives.

A few brave spirits tried to stem the tide flowing so strongly towards a restoration. Among them was John Milton, who dashed into print with *The Ready and Easy Way to Establish a Free Commonwealth*. England should press on, Milton argued, not leaving a task unfinished, but fighting for a perpetual republic. 'What I have spoken', he wrote solemnly, 'is the language of that which is not called amiss the Good Old Cause.'[9] But everywhere the cry was for the return of the king.

Meanwhile, spies and emissaries dashed between London and Brussels, as royalist courtiers made contact with the presbyterian leaders of the now fully restored Long Parliament, trying to guess Monck's next move. Simultaneously Charles was approached, daily, from all sides. Even members of Cromwell's old Council of State like Anthony Ashley Cooper, who had so far spurned all royalist approaches, began corresponding with Charles's advisers. He stayed cool, evenly friendly to all. One of these advances, however, now paid off. This came from Sir John Grenville, who had been one of Charles's first appointments as a Gentleman of the Bedchamber in the West Country fifteen years before, had defended the Scillies for the Crown, and then stayed quietly in England during the Interregnum. Grenville also happened to be Monck's cousin. The previous autumn he had suggested that he might contact the General on Charles's behalf. At the end of March Charles wrote diplomatically to Monck, sending his letter through Grenville:

You cannot but believe, that I know too well the power you have to do me good or harm, not to desire you should be my friend . . . And whatever you have heard to the contrary, you will find to be false as if you had been told that I have white hair and am crooked . . .

However I cannot but say, that I will take all the ways I can, to let the world see, and you and yours find, that I have an entire trust in you, and as much kindness for you, as can be expressed by

Your affectionate friend, Charles R.[10]

In accepting, after some hesitation, this very personal letter, Monck at last showed his hand, telling Grenville that he hoped the king would forgive what was past. He had always been faithful to him at heart, he said, but never able to serve him until now. He laid down no conditions that would curtail royal power but merely demanded the guarantees he needed to win the army's support: a general indemnity, religious toleration, payment of arrears of pay, and security of possession in the lands bought from sequestered estates.

Monck also hinted that Charles might find it wise not to remain in Brussels, in the Spanish Netherlands, when Britain and Spain were technically at war. Taking this advice, Charles moved to his sister Mary's court at Breda. From here, on 4 April, advised by Hyde, he issued his Declaration of Breda, a dashingly confident statement. It met all Monck's demands: a full pardon to all who appealed to the king within forty days, the only exceptions being those who had signed Charles I's death warrant; 'liberty to tender consciences', unless differences of religion threatened the national peace; and payment of arrears of army pay. Charles also declared, cunningly, that all questions regarding the complicated property deals since 1649 should be resolved by the new parliament.

On the same day Charles wrote a clever, startling letter to the Speaker of the House of Commons. The liberties and powers of both king and parliament, he wrote, were 'best preserved by preserving the other'. Although he was anxious, he said, to avenge his father's death, he appealed to MPs as 'wise and dispassionate men and good patriots'.[11] And, he ended humbly, not minimising the pain of exile, 'We hope that we have made that right Christian use of our affliction, and that the observations and experience we have had in other countries hath been such as that we, and we hope all our subjects, shall be the better for what we have seen and suffered.'

Charles's followers in Breda held their breath. Sir William Killigrew, Thomas's brother, who had known Charles I well, spoke for many when he wrote a long letter, begging him to accept any terms for his return, 'at a time when the Nation call alowde for you! As the only cure for all their Evells.'[12] Killigrew's advice, that he should accept Parliament's conditions and 'putt on such golden fetters frankly', was pragmatic and prophetic. It would be impossible, he wrote, to compensate all those who had served the royalist cause, and all those who were now coming over to his side; half the revenues of England would not suffice. It would be impossible too to satisfy papists seeking toleration, presbyterians, Independents, Congregationists, 'and all the severall sorts of violent sectaries . . . whereas if your Majesty be tyed up by Articles none of all these can blame you for not answering their expectations'. If he agreed to their terms and let parliament deal with the detail, he could carry the day: 'A little honest Arts, Sir, this way, would bring you to more greatness and power than any of your Predecessors ever had.'

The old parliament was dissolved on 17 March and the Convention Parliament (so called because it was a 'free convention' rather than a proper parliament as it had not been summoned by a king) met the following month. The new MPs were ready to accept all Charles's 'honest Arts'. The House of Commons contained at least fifty Cavaliers, men who had fought for Charles I, or their sons, plus a hundred royalist MPs and many moderate presbyterians. On May Day the House heard the king's letter and Declaration and immediately passed a resolution to ask for his return. The news flashed round the country. 'To-day I hear they were very merry at Deal,' wrote Pepys, 'setting up the King's flag upon one of their maypoles, and drinking his health upon their knees in the streets, and firing the guns, which the soldiers of the Castle threatened; but durst not oppose.'[13] Maypoles were suddenly everywhere, a huge one in the Strand in London, so tall that sailors had to pull it up with ropes like a mast, and another in Oxford 'set up on purpose to vex the Presbyterians and Independents'.[14] A week later both houses of parliament proclaimed Charles II as king.

Why did the people of Britain – or the majority, at least – want a king so badly? Cromwell's regime had promised peace, but had plunged the country into war with Spain and with the Dutch, and although the wars brought victories, they were still far from popular. The trade that had flourished was stifled and the merchant ships that ventured out were attacked by privateers. Parliament quickly ran through the funds from the sale of confiscated lands, and slapped on constant, heavy taxes. At Cromwell's death the government was two million pounds in debt. The team that took over after his death were bitterly divided between the moderate parliamentarians and the holy warriors of the army and there seemed no hope of finding good management. Even more disturbing was the realisation that the country now had a standing army, of around forty thousand men, who were being used to control not only Scotland and Ireland but England as well.[15] The army was doubly hated, first because it was paid for by the deeply resented taxes, and secondly because it was dominated by sectarians, whose beliefs and strident moral strictures spoke only to a fraction of the population. Royalists wanted their land, money and jobs back; country gentry on both sides wanted the old local administration; many parishes wanted the familiar services of the abolished Church order; merchants wanted a trade revival; the apprentices whose enthusiasm rocked London wanted a better chance in life. Everyone wanted less tax and fewer soldiers. All these discontents paved Monck's road south. But they also set challenges for a new king.

In the weeks before parliament's decision was known, English and Scottish supplicants and place-seekers flooded Breda. Some came to seek pardons for friends and family, paying as much as £1,000; others brought gifts 'in good English gold', hoping to be remembered as being among those who first helped the king, after, as Clarendon put it tartly, managing to forget him for so many years. The cash helped Charles pay his debts and give his servants their arrears of wages, with an extra bonus 'to raise their spirits after so many years of patient waiting for delivery'.[16]

On 14 May he sailed downriver from Breda, accompanied by gaily decorated yachts. As they reached Dort every cannon in the town was fired, but when they tied up for the night, Sir John Grenville told Charles how parliament had voted, and that Montagu was here to take him home. Immediately, the yachts sailed on to Delft, where huge crowds cheered on the quayside in the dawn. The whole entourage then piled into seventy-three coaches and bowled along roads lined with soldiers to the Hague. Next day, Charles received the parliamentary commissioners, six from the House of Lords and twelve from the Commons, including General Fairfax, of whom he took special notice. He acknowledged their speeches in the friendliest manner, and – with admirable restraint – thanked them politely for their notes of credit for £50,000, plus an additional £10,000 for James and £5,000 for Henry. One highlight was the arrival of a trunk brimming with £10,000 in sovereigns. The messengers who brought it found the king looking down at heel: his best clothes, someone sneered, were not worth forty shillings. When he saw the money he became 'so joyful, that he called the Princess Royal and Duke of York to look upon it as it lay in the Portmanteau before it was taken out'.[17] A trunk full of coins was a blessing, since it was tricky to cash the huge letters of credit from parliament. By now Charles was used to the cautious Amsterdam merchants and knew that it was not easy, even in such an opulent city, to collect such a sum in ready money. In the end he took at least £30,000 back to London in bills of exchange.

The City of London had sent its own representatives to the Hague and Charles was confident that their goldsmiths would honour his bills. Other deputations were less welcome. He spurned an envoy from the judges who had tried his father. And when the presbyterian clergymen raised the question of the hated covenant and claimed that the Book of Common Prayer had been so long out of use that they hoped the king would not reinstate it, he responded 'with some warmth, that whilst he gave them liberty, he would not have his own taken from them'. He would stick to the prayer book he had used all his life, even 'in places where it was more disliked than he hoped it was by them'.[18]

In his week in the Hague, waiting for the storms to calm so that he could set sail, the diplomats of France and Spain who had formerly shunned him held feasts in his honour. The Dutch government, who had been hostile for so long, served a banquet on gold plate which they then presented to him. They then added a gift of a magnificent bed and a gallery of splendid works of art, which would set the style for his own art collecting. He read petitions, he went among the crowds. Men knelt to be blessed, and women seemed to find him irresistible.

The Great Feast the Estates of Holland made to the King and to the Royal Family, 1660, showing a marked contrast between the cavaliers on the right and the sober Dutch on the left.

Finally the calm came and the ships sailed. After the story-telling and night of rejoicing on the sea, by the morning of 25 May Charles's fleet was close to the coast of Kent. When Charles and the Dukes of York and Gloucester took breakfast, they found that some-one had put out the sailors' rations to show them what a ship's diet was, so they sat down and ate it: pease pudding and pork and boiled beef. Having identified thus with his sailors, Charles handed over £500 to be distributed among the ships' officers and men. As they neared the shore, and anchored in the Dover roads, the sheets were lowered and the topsails furled. The cliffs were black with people, cheering and shouting.

Early in the afternoon, to the thunder of a five-round salute from the ship's guns, answered by the cannon of Dover Castle, Charles climbed down the side of the *Royal Charles*. He rejected the gilded brigantine sent by parliament, and stepped instead into Montagu's barge.[19] Pepys was in one of the smaller boats in his wake, with a royal footman and 'a dog that the King loved (which shit in the boat, which made us laugh and me think that a King and all that belong to him are but just as others are)'.[20]

When he stepped on shore around three o'clock Charles knelt and thanked God. Monck was the first to greet him and bow in homage, and the king thanked him soberly, calling him 'Father'. They walked together up the beach with a canopy of state held over their heads. In front of a marquee filled with nobility and gentry, graciously making the first of his dead-pan equivocations, Charles accepted a Bible from the Mayor of Dover, declaring it 'the thing he loved above all things in the world'. Onlookers wept. Bonfires flared. Guns boomed and fires sprang from beacon to beacon, lighting him home.

Sailing from Holland, Charles II laid down the beginnings of a myth: the hero of the escape from Worcester, the people's king, who was 'just as others are'. Yet if he would bend his ear to all his sub-jects, as the Declaration of Breda had suggested, he would still tower over them all. Towards the end of the voyage he knocked his head against a low beam, as William Blundell remembered:

I was present on the ship (about five miles from Dover) two or three hours before King Charles II landed in England . . . when the King (by reason of an accident) took his own measure, standing under a beam in the cabin, upon his place he made a mark with a knife. Sundry tall persons went under it, but there were none that could reach it.[21]

It was a joke but it made its point. After Charles had landed, Montagu was ecstatic, amazed that he had brought the whole thing off without mishap and sure that honours lay ahead. He came back late to the ship, wrote Pepys,

and at his coming did give me orders to cause the marke to be gilded, and a Crown and C.R. to be made at the head of the coach table, where the King to-day with his own hand did mark his height, which accordingly I caused the painter to do, and is now done, as is to be seen.

O liver seeking God while the K.
is murthered by his order

Cromwell and Charles I, from *Cavalier Playing Cards*, designed by John Lenthall, 1660–2

3 How to Be King

Make hast (Great Sir) to our Arcadian Plain
And blesse this Island with your beams again . . .
May the Sun's influence of thy fair beams
Give store unto our Plains, life to our Streams.
So shall our Flocks yield us a good encrease
When Plenty's ushered in by welcome Peace.
Long may you live king of th'Arcadian land
And we learn to obey what you command.
ANON., *The Countrey-Man's Vive le Roy*, 1660

IN DOVER, Charles and Monck climbed into the royal coach and
sat facing forward, towards London. James and Henry sat opposite.
All was sedate and correct. But then Buckingham, whom Charles
had greeted coolly on the shore, leapt into the boot, the great cover
over the back wheels with its single seat. When Charles and James
changed to horseback, he rode on behind them, a devil at their
heels.

As they rode, labourers flung down their rakes and raced to the
roadside, village boys clambered on roofs, old men whistled and
women cheered, country girls with laced bodices and wide-sleeved
smocks hitched up their skirts and ran to throw flowers. It was a
strange, delirious greeting, like a moment from some dimly remembered myth. The old king had been killed in the winter chill at the
dead, dark turn of the year; the new king had come in the warmth
of spring, like life revived. He was a king of the May, the month of
his birthday, the month of his return. He was young and virile; he
would make the land fecund, bring plenty and peace. On the way,
as in a folk-tale, he summoned and conquered armies, but with
smiles, not with swords. On windy Barham Downs, where the local

races were held, Charles reviewed the troops gathered by Buckingham and the Earls of Oxford, Derby and Northampton, with the soldiers of Viscount Mordaunt, Ashley Cooper and the foot regiments of Kent. The men were ranked with drawn swords and as the king approached they kissed their sword-hilts and waved their glittering blades over their heads before marching in his train into Canterbury. The cathedral bells rang, the streets were strewn with flowers, and the Mayor presented 'a tankard of massy gold'.[1]

The courtiers who returned in Charles's wake after their long exile could hardly believe it. When the elderly Marquess of Newcastle landed at Greenwich, his supper, he said, 'seem'd more savoury to him, than any meat he had hitherto tasted'.[2] Was it still a dream? 'Surely?' he thought, 'I have been sixteen years asleep and am not thoroughly awake yet.'

Not everyone was so happy. To the old republicans it was as if they saw England dancing round an idol, a debauched crew, drinking and swilling their way around a false king. Two days after Charles landed, the governor of Windsor Castle was handed a note reporting that Thomas Lawrence, a dismissed soldier, had said 'that he was hired of Mr Jenkin of Bishopsgate to kill the king'.[3] Dismay spread long before Charles stepped ashore. A Captain Southwold declared that if he got hold of Charles he would dice him up 'as small as herbs in a pot' and a Lincolnshire vicar, on 'the night when bonfires were made for proclaiming the King . . . kicked the fire about and said, "Stay! The rogue is not yet come over"'.[4] Now the rogue had come. While some feared the worst, people in their thousands hoped their lives would change for the better.

From Canterbury Charles wrote to his sixteen-year-old sister Henriette-Anne – Minette, to her family – who was still with her mother in Paris. 'My head is so prodigiously dazed', he wrote, 'by the acclamation of the people and by quantities of business that I know not whether I am writing sense or no.'[5] He had plenty of business. He and Hyde both knew that one reason for the warmth of the cheers was that the restoration had been achieved without an armed invasion, without the help of foreign powers, and without loss of life. To keep this peaceful mood Charles must embrace powerful figures from the previous regime, both the ex-Cromwellian republicans and the moderate presbyterians who had fought against his father but had opposed his execution and had been in opposition for most of the Interregnum.

The work of fusing past and present power began straight away in Canterbury, so that the king's intentions might be clear before he reached London and had to face the Lords and Commons. On Saturday 26 May, after a service in the cathedral – which was almost collapsing into ruins after years of neglect – Charles appointed four new members of the Order of the Garter. The first was General Monck, and Charles told him pointedly that the honour was for 'your famous actions in military commands, and above all that by your wisdom, courage and loyalty, you have acted principally in our restoration without effusion of blood – acts that have no precedent or parallel'.[6] The next was Montagu, also a former servant of Cromwell, and soon made Earl of Sandwich, who received the honour from a herald on board his ship. To balance the two Cromwellians, Charles honoured two royalists, the Marquis of Hertford and Thomas Wriothesley, the Earl of Southampton.

From the moment he landed, as in his last days abroad, Charles faced a flood of requests. In his two days in Canterbury petitions poured in and people crowded round asking for an audience, some begging for pardon, others hoping for rewards. The Venetian ambassador, Francesco Giavarini, who raced on horseback from London, was impressed that Charles spoke to him in Italian, and impressed too by his patience as 'at great personal inconvenience he remained standing many hours to receive the great numbers who came on purpose to kneel and kiss his hand, according to the custom of the country'.[7]

He stopped here for two days before the procession set off up Roman Watling Street. All the way, the road was lined with cheer-

Wenceslaus Hollar, *The long view of London from Bankside*, 1647.
The London Charles would have known as a boy had hardly changed
when he crossed London Bridge in May 1660.

ing people, said Lady Fanshawe, as if it were a single street. At
Rochester, morris dancers swirled around the king, and at
Chatham, the ships in the dockyard fired echoing rounds. The
navy's loyalty declared, now Charles had to face the army. On 29
May, his thirtieth birthday, he set off for London. But before he rode
down the hill into his capital he had to cross Blackheath, where thirty thousand soldiers of the parliamentary army waited, summoned
by Monck, perhaps as a silent reminder of his power. Roundheads
gazed across at Cavaliers: at James, Duke of York, all in white, at
Henry, Duke of Gloucester, in green silk, at Charles in his silver
doublet, with gold lace on his cloak and a plume of red feathers in
his hat. After a pause the Commonwealth troops laid their arms on
the ground. Then they picked them up again as, technically at least,
soldiers of the king.

From there on it was buoyant pantomime. In Deptford, '100 Maydens Cloathed in White' scattered flowers and herbs in their way. At St George's Fields in Southwark tents were erected and a banquet held. The Lord Mayor, Thomas Allen, knelt and handed the king the sword of the city, and was knighted in return.[8] The king rode bareheaded between the old shops on London Bridge, and into the City.

This was still the medieval London, with bells pealing from its hundred old churches, loudest of all from St Paul's, crouching like a weather-beaten Gothic lion at the head of Ludgate Hill. The procession passed through narrow streets of gabled houses, with their upper storeys, or 'jetties', hanging out over the cobbles. Great arches of blossoming hawthorn curved over the way, and huge swags of green oak leaves were nailed to the house-beams. Flags crowned the roofs, and silken banners and rich Turkey carpets were draped from the windows. The sun shone, and the light flashed off swords and spurs, trumpets and cornets, reflected in a thousand glittering window panes. Aldermen, liverymen from the London companies, freemen and apprentices, trumpeters in scarlet, jugglers, heralds and soldiers joined the procession. As it snaked from the Guildhall to Westminster the numbers swelled to twenty thousand, taking many hours to pass. The parade wound down Ludgate Hill, across the Fleet river, past the thieves' dens and alleys of Alsatia, past the lawyers' chambers in the Temple and on into the Strand, with its golden-crowned maypole and its great old mansions with their gardens running down to the river. 'I stood in the Strand, & beheld it & blessed God,' wrote John Evelyn.

And all this without one drop of bloud, & by that very army, which rebell'd against him: but it was the Lord's doing, *et mirabile in oculis nostris*: for such a Restauration was never seene in the mention of any history, antient or modern, since the return of the Babylonian Captivity, nor so joyfull a day, & so bright, ever seene in this nation.[9]

Charles II arriving at the Banqueting House in 1660, after his triumphal procession through the city.

The king had conquered his city.

At every point Charles was studiously diplomatic. Replying to speeches of welcome at Whitehall, he addressed the House of Lords in casual, heartfelt tones – who could doubt his sincerity?

My Lords

I am so disordered by my journey, and with the noise still sounding in my ears (which I confess was pleasing to me, because it expressed the affections of the people), as I am unfit at the present to make such a reply as I desire. Yet thus much I shall say unto you, that I take no greater satisfaction to myself in this my change, than that I find my heart really set to endeavour by all means for the restoring of this nation to freedom and happiness; and I hope by the advice of my Parliament to effect it.[10]

Finally he sat through a ceremonial dinner, viewed by an awed public. Turning at last to leave, he quipped, famously, that he now realised it must have been 'my own fault that I have been absent so long – for I see nobody that does not protest he has ever wished for my return'.[11]

For the first few weeks Charles was circumspect, careful to present the sober aspect of the healing king. If he was to be trusted, he had to make his kingship visible, physically and personally, as well as felt in his actions as the 'Crown'.

When he took the throne he wanted passionately to be seen as the healer of his people's woes and the glory of his nation. Royal propaganda drew on religion and myth, custom, law and magic. Even before he landed, Samuel Tuke's *Character* had described him as 'handsome, graceful, serious, learned, shrewd, and of good morals for some time'.[12] Tuke knew Charles well and his portrait, though idealised, does suggest some vital aspects of his charm, his physical ease and his gift of attentivenes, which made people feel they were special when he talked to them:

His motions are so easy and graceful that they do very much recommend his person when he either walks, dances, plays at pall mall, at tennis, or rides the great horse, which are his usual exercises. To the gracefulness of his deportment may be joined his easiness of access, his patience in attention, and the gentleness both in the tune and style of his speech; so that those whom either the veneration for his dignity or the majesty of his presence have put into an awful respect are reassured as soon as he enters into a conversation.[13]

This ease and accessibility helped his cause, which was furthered by the press, the newsbooks and newsletters. News was disseminated across a vast web, with both formal and informal strands. Sheets of news had been printed and sold since 1641, and had proliferated during the Commonwealth. They were eagerly read in the coffee-houses and taverns, carried by the chapmen to the provinces, and sold in the city streets by 'flying stationers' and 'mercuries', boys and women who cried their hot news aloud, like hot pies, and often drew large crowds.[14] The journalist Henry Muddiman, who had been producing twice-weekly newsbooks for the Rump Parliament, now worked with the royalist Sir John Birkenhead, licenser of the press, to bolster the king's image in the new official newsbook *Mercurius Publicus*. In addition, local officials and men and women in country districts, or in Ireland, Scotland and the American colonies, relied on manuscript newsletters written by professional news-writers, to keep up with events and gossip.

Books and pamphlets, woodcuts and prints also spread the word. Within a year, works like Thomas Blount's *Boscobel: or the history of His Sacred Majestie's . . . preservation* appeared, retailing the dramatic flight from Worcester, as exciting as a chap-book legend. The painter Isaac Fuller produced a series of huge canvases, like a set of tapestries, turning classical and courtly poses into a crude, colourful drama of the king in disguise, the folk-hero of the people.[15] One of the pageants at the next Lord Mayor's show, staged outside the Nag's Head in Cheapside, also represented the 'great Woode, with the royal Oake, & history of his Majesties miraculous escape'.[16]

At the same time, *Eikon Basilike . . . or the true pourtraiture of Charles II* summoned the ghost of Charles's martyred father, sanctified after his death in a book of the same name. Closely echoing Tuke's words, the 'true portraiture' displayed the king to readers who had not seen the tall dark man riding on horseback in the London pro-cessions. He was, it explained, 'so exactly formed' that

from the crown of his head to the soule of his foot the most curious eye could not discern an error or a spot . . . Until he was near twenty years of

Isaac Fuller, *Charles II and Colonel Careless Hiding in the Boscobel Oak*

age, his face was very lovely but of late he is grown leaner with care and age; the dark and night complexion of his face, and the twin stars of his quick and sharp eyes sparkling in that night; he is most beautiful when he speakes, his black shining locks normally curled with great rings . . . his motions easie and graceful, and plainly majestick.[17]

To add to the fervour, city priests and country vicars preached lengthy sermons, whose message was clear: 'God's command is – Fear God, Honour the King.'[18] Kingship was more than an office of state. A king was the heart that pumped blood and gave life to the nation: through his representatives his will flowed through all institutions of state and Church. He created peers and bishops, gave charters to boroughs, appointed judges, directed the army and navy, made war and declared peace. If he wished, he could confiscate all land, and he could levy taxes on all who walked upon it, on the crops and cattle in the fields, the fish in the rivers, the riches in the mines. It was treason to curse him, and to wish, or even imagine, his death. He carried his subjects, as Hobbes said, like Jonah in the belly of the great Leviathan.

The potency of royalty was almost magical, and Charles did not hesitate to exploit it. Of the many portraits painted of him, all except a handful showed him in ceremonial robes or in armour, rather than as a mere mortal in everyday dress.[19] Within a week of his landing, queues built up of people begging to be touched for 'the King's Evil', a tradition that went back to Edward the Confessor, the holy king. The evil was scrofula, a tubercular disease of the lymph nodes, but the trail of supplicants usually contained sufferers from many other ailments. Charles himself was sceptical and wary, but more than ready to exploit the mystique.

To begin with the touchings took place in the open air, but after a deluge in June, when the sick waited for hours in the rain, ceremonies were held in the Banqueting House. In the first two months Charles touched around seventeen hundred people – stroking their faces with both hands, while his chaplain intoned, 'He put his hands upon them, and he healed them.' A thousand more waited. Exhausted, he announced that while he was 'graciously pleased to dispatch all that are already come', he would have to defer the rest 'to a more reasonable opportunity'. Patients could get tickets at the sign of the Hare in Covent Garden for Wednesday and Friday, 'which two days His Majesty is pleased to set apart for this so pious and charitable work'.[20] The stream never stopped, running on average to between three thousand and four thousand a year. Many proclaimed themselves cured, perhaps the result of auto-suggestion, perhaps because a disease like scrofula naturally waxed and waned. It was an expensive magic – Charles placed round the neck of each supplicant a gold coin, an angel, strung on a white ribbon – but it was money well spent. To some sufferers, the royal magic was innate in his person and needed no ceremonial trappings. According to John Aubrey, the visionary Arise Evans had 'a fungous nose and had said that the King's hand would cure him, and on the first coming of Charles II into St James's Park, he kissed the King's hand and rubbed his nose with it; which disturbed the King, but cured him'.[21] The power of touching, like the extravagant rituals and processions,

tied Charles's person to medieval ideas of divine kingship, and reinforced the link to the chivalric orders of romance. But it also
brought Charles into close physical contact with the poorest of his
people and he managed this with ease. His time roaming the streets
of foreign cities, and even his wanderings from Worcester, had made
Charles less formal than his father, or other European monarchs.
Observers were staggered by his lack of pomp. He stood bareheaded, gasped the Venetian resident, a style not used by any other
crowned head in Europe, 'but adopted by this king with everyone,
whatever his character, for he excels all other potentates in humanity and affability'.[22]

Charles touching for the King's Evil, with his chaplains on his left,
courtiers on his right and Yeomen holding back the crowds.

Yet Charles wanted it both ways. He gambled on his personal
power, and in doing so staked his reputation as a sober king. He
wanted the magnificence and ceremony, but he also wanted to show
that his court was not hidebound by antique custom, but young,
exciting, European in outlook. Although he rarely seemed hurried,

in the months after his return he worked like a demon, but work done, he enjoyed himself. In the years of exile, Hyde had often lamented that he could not control the leisure of Charles and his circle, and the same was true now. Charles was already establishing a rival image to that which his advisers were engineering so carefully, and one that would prove harder to control. A brilliant, witty and sometimes wild court was beginning to form around him.

Schooled by Hyde, Charles began with good intentions as regards the behaviour of his court. The Establishment Book for Whitehall in 1660 is entitled 'Regulations for the better service in the household', and declares its aim simply and solemnly, 'to establish good government and order in our Court, which from then may spread with more honour through all parts of our kingdom'.[23] Immediately, however, it gives a sense of what Whitehall was really like, when it decrees that in future there should be 'no Houses, Tents, Booths, or places to be employed for Tipling, selling or taking Tobacco, Hott waters or for any kind of Disorder'. The marshals must remove vagrants, rogues, beggars, idle and loose people and the porters keep out 'stragling and Masterless men, any suspitious Person or Uncivill, uncleanly and Rude People'. There must be no profanity, swearing or fighting. The sense of incipient chaos even touched the Chapel Royal. There had been, declares the little rule book, 'a very great Indecence and irreverence here . . . a throng of persons talk aloud & walk in time of divine service'. In future, all those guilty would be banned. As if primed for trouble, the rules insisted, too, that the Yeomen in the quasi-public Great Chamber who controlled the press of people bringing petitions or having business at court should be tall, strong and 'of manly Presence'. These royal bouncers apart, there were an infinity of roles to be performed and rooms and corridors to be supervised.

The new court set a very different style from the formality of Charles I. In the summer of 1660 rakes swaggered in velvet coats and high-heeled shoes, flocking around Charles as he walked in Hyde Park. Courtiers crowded into skiffs in the evening cool, following the royal barge and watching the fireworks fly. Charles was restless and energetic. (Several of the formal portraits suggest how much he disliked sitting still.) He rode, he swam in the Thames, he played bowls on the Whitehall green, and even on a large barge moored near the palace, where a spiral staircase led from the deck to a bowling green on the roof, covered with green cloth. 'It is level like a green in the open air,' noted one amazed spectator, 'with wooden tubs all round planted with all kinds of flowering plants and trees.'[24]

And wherever he was, Charles played tennis. First he refitted the tennis court at Hampton Court, and then installed a new court at Whitehall, the first for a hundred years. In this great room, with a court 118 feet long, lit by windows high in the wall, Charles played constantly. It was a hard, physical, sweaty game, played with cork and felt balls hit with heavy wooden rackets that had scarcely changed since Tudor times, their head about the size of a hand (this is the French *jeu de paume*). The ball rocketed off the high walls and the penthouse roof, and was served, fiendishly fast, at the opponent at the 'hazard end'. Unlike some kings, Charles did not always expect to win. In 1662 Pepys watched him play with Sir Arthur Slingsby, 'beating three and loosing two sets against my Lord of Suffolke and my Lord Chesterfield'.[25] And he did not mind an audience. A few years later, the Italian visitor Lorenzo Magalotti noted, 'He usually plays there three times a week in a doublet; the guards stand at the street door, but do not refuse entry to anyone who has the face or attire of a gentleman'.[26] Crowds came to watch him too as he dined in public, three times a week, in the Banqueting House or the presence chamber, where the crush was so great that a balustrade was erected in front of the table.

Charles seemed to need to fill every minute, from dawn to dusk. Ten days after his arrival a newsletter reported, 'His Majesty's only recreation as yet is at tennis by 5 o'clock in the morning for an hour or two.'[27] In mid-August Pepys hurried to Whitehall to find Sandwich, only to discover that the king had 'gone this morning at five in the morning to see a Dutch pleasure boat below bridge, where he dines and my Lord with him. The King do tire all his people that are about him with early rising since he come.'[28] The boat Charles had gone to see was the *Mary*, presented to him by the Dutch East India Company. Sailing, which he had learnt as a youth in Jersey, became another of his great passions. It was an exhilarating relief from the stifling court, fighting the river currents and harnessing the wind, hearing the slapping of the water and the cries of the crew. The following year he had an even finer yacht, the *Catherine*, built for him at Deptford. The Duke of York also had a yacht built, the *Anne*, and the brothers raced from Greenwich to Gravesend, tacking past wharves and warehouses out into the estuary, past the mud-flats and sand-banks and marshes. The wager was £100 and Charles lost sailing downstream against a contrary wind, but saved his stake on returning. The large yachts, each around a hundred tons, were a rare sight on a river crowded with traffic, their sails billowing among the forest of masts.

Charles also had a smaller Dutch pleasure boat, the *Bezan*, which

The royal yacht *'Bezan'*, 1661

was often used by members of the Navy Board to take them up and down to Deptford and Greenwich.[29] He lavished money on his yachts, fitting them out and making them luxurious. Account books over the years are full of entries such as 'carpett in the Henrietta yacht', or 'one fine Turkey carpet for the King's yacht Isabelle'. The *Isabelle* had walnut armchairs and stools, a walnut bed with a carved end and a very large strong table with twisted pillars for legs, which would fold down on both sides.[30] On his yachts, as on the tennis court, Charles showed off his sporting ability, his keen eye and love of speed.

This physical power was part of his allure, his presence as a strong, youthful king. He packed work into the mornings to leave the rest of the day free. One day in October he dashed off a note to Hyde at eight o'clock:

I am going to take my usual Physique at tennis. I send you heere the letters which my Ld Aubigny desires me to write, look them ouer, and if there be no exceptions to them returne them by twelue a clock, for I would willingly dispatch them this afternoone.[31]

In the afternoons, after the Council's work was done and Hyde had hobbled home, the king was free. Now was the time for entertainments, high and low. In August 1660, in the Great Hall where his parents had staged their elegant masques, he watched a show with tight-rope dancers. The skill of the dancers was legendary on the continent and now they, and three new court acrobats, entranced the English court. The next month, in a very different venue, he went to the Lady Fair across the river in Southwark. The fair, which had been subdued during the Interregnum, now burst into life again in a fortnight of riotous entertainment, with freak shows, and monkeys dressed as court gallants, turning somersaults on the wire, carrying lighted candles or balancing cups of water, 'without spilling a drop'. All the court went to see 'the Italian Wench daunce to admiration, & performe all the Tricks of agility on the high rope', and to admire her father, who could lift enormous weights by the hair of his head alone.[32]

Charles, however, wanted to bring smarter entertainment to London, and soon began negotiating with an Italian opera company and with foreign musicians. At Whitehall he had the old Cockpit theatre fitted with a new stage floor and pavilions in the gallery for musicians and players. Men worked through the nights to get it ready for the first performance on 19 November. In the same month, in a disdainful gesture at puritan restraint, Charles granted an exclusive patent to Thomas Killigrew and Sir William Davenant to build two playhouses and create new theatrical companies. They opened in converted tennis courts, Killigrew's King's Company, with experienced actors and the rights to many old plays, in Gibbon's Tennis Court in Vere Street, and Davenant's Duke's Company, patronised by James, in Salisbury Court near Whitefriars. Davenant was the most innovative, with a young, dynamic company and new writers, and in 1661 he moved to a newly built theatre in Lincoln's Inn Fields, complete with movable scenery. Both troupes lavished money on costumes, sets and music.

The most startling attraction was seeing women on stage, as in continental theatres. To begin with boys still played female roles. The current darling was the seventeen-year-old Edward Kynaston, 'a Compleat Stage Beauty', whom the ladies of quality swept off in their coaches to Hyde Park, still in his costume, as if he were one of them.[33] But Kynaston's reign was now over. The royal patent turned puritan disapproval on its head, declaring, tongue in cheek, that since it had been 'scurrilous' and unnatural to see men taking the parts of women, from now on all female parts should be acted by women, so that the plays would be 'not only harmless delights but useful and instructive representations of human life to such of our good subjects as shall resort to the same'.[34] Court women, including Henrietta Maria, had acted in the royal masques, and in 1656 an actress, Mrs Coleman, had appeared in a private performance before Cromwell of Davenant's own opera, *The Siege of Rhodes*. But the first time a woman stepped onto the public London stage was as Desdemona with the King's Company on 8 December 1660.

Within a year every play was sporting dancing, fast jigs, and cross-dressing roles to show off the actresses' fine legs.

Charles's other new public passion was the park. He and James often walked with their courtiers and their dogs in St James's Park, and in his first autumn three hundred labourers were called in to dig a new canal. He planted trees and groves and fruit trees and added to the exotic animals and birds that had been in the royal menagerie since the time of his grandfather James I. Foreign ambassadors and English trading companies brought new additions, from the Russian ambassador's pelican from Astrakhan to eighty-two ostriches from Morocco. There were deer of all kinds and flocks of wild fowl, for whom Charles created a decoy, 'which for being neere so great a City, & among such a concourse of Souldiers, Guards & people, is very diverting'.[35]

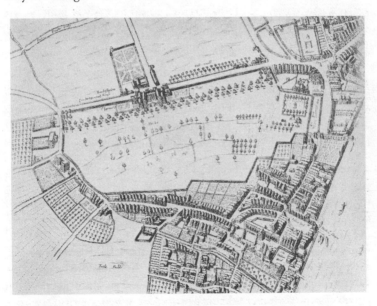

St James's Park, in Faithorne's map of 1658, before the new canal was dug, showing the road curving round from Charing Cross to Whitehall, and Berkshire House opposite St James's Palace. To the north, Piccadilly is an open country road.

Here too Charles was on display, showing off his physical grace by playing pell-mell on the new court he had built (on the site of the present Pall Mall), over eight hundred paces long, modelled on one at Utrecht. Here, enthused the poet Edmund Waller,

> . . . a well-polished Mall gives us the joy
> To see our prince his matchless force employ:
> His manly posture and his graceful mien,
> Vigour and youth in all his motions seen;
> His shape so lovely and his limbs so strong
> Confirm our hopes we shall obey him long.
> No sooner has he touched the flying ball
> But 'tis already more than half the Mall;
> And such a fury from his arm has got,
> As from a smoking culverin 'twere shot.[36]

In Waller's rapturous verse he is the emobodiment of martial force, as well as youthful beauty, his game a warning to the nation as well as a diversion.

The court itself was diverting, as if dressed for a play. The very cut of court clothes spoke defiance and proclaimed a new age. Only two years before, Sir John Reresby had arrived in London after brawling and seducing his way round Europe, to find that his clothes and his black servant immediately marked him out as a target:

The citizens and common people of London had then soe far imbibed the custome and manners of a Commonwealth that they could scarce endure the sight of gentlemen, soe that the common salutation to a man well dressed was 'French dog' or the like. Walkeing one day in the street with my valet de chambre, who did wear a feather in his hatt, some workemen who were mending the street abused him and threw sand upon his cloaths, at which he drew his sword, thinking to follow the custome of France in the like cases. This made the rabble fall upon him and me, that had drawn too in his defence, till we got shelter in a house, not without injury to our bravery and some blowes to ourselves.[37]

Now these French fashions were flaunted in the face of the people. The men were peacock-fine from top to toe, from their shallow-brimmed beaver hats, trimmed with ostrich feathers, to their be-ribboned shoes or loose-topped boots, with boot hose tumbling over the top. Their short doublets covered floppy linen shirts, which flowed down to wide-legged trousers called 'Rhinegraves' or 'petti-coat breeches', hanging loosely from the hips, and garnished with yards of ribbons.[38] Some had legs so wide that Pepys wrote of one man who 'put both his legs through one of his Knees of his breech-es, and went so all day'.[39]

From France came a new vogue for wigs (Louis XIV had forty wigmakers). This too was new and unsettling. 'Counterfeit hair', wrote the author Randle Holme, is 'a thing much used in our days by this generation of Men, contrary to our forefathers, who got Estates, loved their Wives, and wore their own hair'.[40] Soon wigs, like the new silk handkerchiefs that men waved nonchalantly as they walked, became a target for London thieves, tweaked off the head by a clever dog or by a small boy carried on another's shoul-ders. Many courtiers adopted black tumbling locks, mimicking the king, but there was a considerable choice. You could have simple locks to cover the ears and neck, fixed to a cap under your hat; a short bob; a 'campaign wig', complete with knots, bobs and a curled forehead; or a *frise*, full of small crisped curls. It was in fashion to comb the hair in public with large combs, a nicety to be cultivated, like taking snuff.

Clothes could cost a fortune. Buckingham allegedly spent £30,000 on his jewel-encrusted suit for the coronation. Although Charles's own coronation clothes were ordered from Paris at great expense, in daily life he was less flamboyant. One day in 1661 he turned up to see the Chancellor in a plain riding-suit and velvet cap, 'in which he seemed a very ordinary man to one that had not known him'.[41] But however casually he acted, he stayed stylish and cool, a pattern of good breeding. He dressed elegantly and formally, following Ormond whom he had always revered as a model. Ormond wore his hat stiff 'as the king did, without a button and uncocked', and had waistcoats laid out for him every morning –

'satin, silk, plain and quilted' – to choose according to the weather. In winter-time people were allowed to come to court with double-breasted coats, a sort of undress. 'The Duke would never take advantage of that indulgence; but let it be ever so cold, he always came in his proper habit; and indeed the king himself, the best judge of manners of his time, always did the same, though too many neglected his example.'[42]

In these early months, magic and ceremony and archaic formality collided at court with colour and fashion, liberty and licence. Charles was at once formal and engagingly human. A month after his arrival an urgent personal appeal appeared in *Mercurius Publicus*, asking help in finding his dog. It was black,

between the greyhound and a spaniel, no white about him only a streak on his breast, and tayl a little bobbed. It is His Majesties own dog, and doubtless was stolen. Whoever finds him may acquaint any at Whitehall for the dog was better known at Court than those who stole him. Will they never leave robbing His Majestie? Must he not keep a dog?[43]

The urgent but witty tone was not that of a self-important monarch. 'So affable was he in the galleries and park,' wrote one courtier of Charles's later days, 'he would pull off his hat to the meanest.'[44] But this very affability meant that when he chose to 'take on Majesty', his dignity was even more striking and effective. Charles understood the language of gesture and the old forms of kingship, but it was clear to all who watched him that his personal style was something quite new.

4 Three Crowns and More

Nor gold, nor Acts of grace; 'tis steel must tame
The stubborn Scot: a prince that would reclaim
Rebels by yielding, doth like him (or worse)
Who saddled his own back to shame his horse . . .
No more let Ireland brag her harmless nation
Fosters no venom, since the Scots plantation.
JOHN CLEVELAND, 'The Rebel Scot'

IT WAS A HUGE TASK to re-establish monarchical government, while taking into account, as Charles had promised, 'the advice of my Parliament'. He and his advisers had to remake the administration, bringing in leading figures from the past regime, while ensuring that the king was surrounded by people he could trust. The structure inherited from medieval times remained the model.[1] Power flowed from the king through the administration, divided between the Privy Council, the Exchequer and the Chancery. These were headed respectively by the two Secretaries of State, the Lord Chancellor and the Lord Treasurer. The Secretaries were responsible, among other duties, for representatives abroad, and for the Signet Office, which dealt with royal letters and grants; the Chancellor was head of the legal side of government and authorised grants of privileges and royal charters under the 'Great Seal'.

Charles held his first Privy Council meeting in Canterbury, within a couple of days of landing. He had already appointed Hyde as Lord Chancellor in exile, in 1658. Now, continuing his careful policy of conciliation, he chose as one of his two Secretaries of State, not the loyal Sir Richard Fanshawe who had shared his exile and expected the post, but Monck's secretary William Morice, who was, Fanshawe complained, 'a fierce Presbiterian, and one that never saw the King's face'.[2] Morice was balanced by Sir Edward Nicholas, who had served Charles I and given loyal service in the dark days abroad, while another royalist, the old Earl of Southampton, became Lord Treasurer. These men, with Ormond and Monck – now made Duke of Albemarle – were the innermost circle, 'the Secret Council', officially the Committee for Foreign Affairs, sometimes described as the forerunner of the cabinet. They were joined by Southampton's ambitious nephew by marriage, Anthony Ashley Cooper, a former member of the Protectorate's Council of State. After speaking eloquently on behalf of the crown in the House of Commons, as MP for Wiltshire, he was made Lord Ashley, and became Chancellor of the Exchequer in the spring of 1661.

Charles's full Privy Council numbered about forty men. It included his brothers James and Henry and seven of his councillors in exile, but the central pillar was Hyde. As a young man, Edward Hyde had been a brilliant lawyer and politician, the shrewdest of Charles I's advisers. At that stage, as he said himself, he had been proud and passionate, 'of a humour between wrangling and disputing, very troublesome'.[3] He had mellowed into affability, he thought, and he knew that his integrity was above temptation and that he was 'firm and unshaken in his friendships'. But many found him stern, unable to see another's point of view, stubborn and unchanging in his opinions. In 1660, judged Burnet, he was the 'absolute favourite, and the chief or the only minister, but with too magisterial a way. He was always pressing the King to mind his affairs, but in vain.'[4]

His lectures would later cause friction but for now Charles listened. Among Hyde's papers are bundles of scribbled notes, pushed across the table in their private meetings before Privy Council sessions, or slipped across to Whitehall by messenger. And outside the chamber Charles and Hyde talked through delicate business where no one could hear them, walking on the 'leads', the roof of the low Whitehall apartments by the river, which formed a sort of terrace. They discussed many things, among them what should be done with one of Montrose's Scottish judges, who had come down to

London and was, said Charles, 'undoubtedly doing all the mischieue he can, why he should not be layd up I can not tell'.[5]

Scotland was much on Charles's mind. He had three separate kingdoms. England and Wales formed one, with Scotland, and Ireland, which had an unusual semi-colonial status. Each required different treatment.[6] Although his grandfather James I of England and VI of Scotland had hoped to unite the kingdom, following the union of the two crowns in his own person when he succeeded to the English throne, Scotland had remained a separate nation. Her parliament was dominated by the crown through royal nominees, the Lords of the Articles, but her presbyterian Church resisted all efforts to bring it under state control. Charles I's fatal mistake had been to try to impose a full hierarchy of bishops and the Anglican prayer book, which Kirk leaders saw as a weapon of Rome. By 1638 they were in revolt. In the twists and turns of the civil wars, they turned back to supporting the king. Finally, three years after their army's defeat at Worcester, they were subdued by the short-lived Cromwellian Union of 1654.

The Prayer Book riots in Scotland, 1637

Ninety per cent of Scots lived on the land, a third of them above the Highland line. Most of these were crofters and landless labourers, dependent on their tenant-in-chief, their clan lord. The smaller lairds, holding land from the tenant-in-chief, were poor in comparison. And in the towns, especially in Edinburgh, a new middle class was growing, consisting of lawyers for Scotland's separate legal system, and merchants, who traded their linen, wool and salt, fish, coal and grain, with England and Ireland, Holland, France, Germany and Scandinavia. When the Scottish parliament was restored in 1660, it was dominated by the sons of hereditary noblemen and Highland chieftains. In June, when Scots aristocrats and gentry came to London, Charles asked them to advise him on the course he might take and as an interim government he restored the old Committee of Estates.

As his highest officers Charles appointed the Scots who had been loyal to him in exile, balanced by the more moderate leaders of the kirk. The Earl of Middleton was declared High Commissioner, responsible for summoning the parliament and raising troops, with his ally the Earl of Glencairn as Chancellor. But he gave the vital post of Secretary of State to the former Covenanter John Maitland, Earl of Lauderdale, who had been imprisoned ever since his capture at Worcester and had crossed to Breda on his release, just before the Restoration. Six foot five, with bristling red hair, violently outspoken, Lauderdale could launch into tirades in English, Latin, Greek or Hebrew. At court he was over-exuberant and dared to help himself to the royal snuff – altogether 'uncouth, boisterous, shaggy, ugly and cunning'.[7] Burnet knew him well, to his cost:

He made a very ill appearance: he was very big: his hair red, hanging oddly about him: his tongue was too big for his mouth, which made him bedew all that he talked to: and his whole manner was rough and boisterous, and very unfit for a Court . . . He was a man, as the Duke of Buckingham called him to me, of a blundering understanding. He was haughty beyond expression, abject to those he saw he must stoop to, but imperious to all others. He had a violence of passion that carried him often to fits like madness, in which he had no temper.[8]

Lauderdale was supported in the English court by Sir Robert Moray, whose easy tact and knowledge of chemistry and astronomy endeared him to Charles. Lauderdale himself never entirely won Charles's affection (the joke was that Charles stopped him coming to dinner by serving horse piss instead of syllabub), but he saw him as the man to push measures through the Scottish parliament and to keep the nation quiet.

The Scots had no intention of keeping quiet. In August, a group of leading kirk ministers met, to remind the king of his promise at Stirling to uphold the covenant, decrying him for restoring the bishops and following the Book of Common Prayer, 'upon which they made terrible denunciations of heavy judgements from God on him, if he did not stand to the Covenant, which they called the oath of God'.[9] The ministers were clapped in prison. Although they were soon released and the outcry in their sermons was silenced, 'they could not hold from many sly and secret insinuations, as if the ark of God was shaking and the glory departing'. Middleton's arrival in Edinburgh as High Commissioner in late 1660 made things worse. He outraged the Kirk ministers with his magnificence and extravagance, and his entourage shocked the people by drinking through the night and fighting in the streets.

The Scottish parliament, however, were generous when they met in January, voting Charles £40,000 per year to raise troops, from an excise on beer and ale. In 1661 Middleton also managed to force them to pass the drastic 'Act Recissory' that wiped the slate clean of all legislation passed by the covenanters' parliaments in almost thirty years, and another act replacing the presbyterian kirk by the episcopal church. The heated debates in the Scottish parliament boded ill for Charles's hopes of peace: 'It was a mad roaring time,' Burnet remembered, 'full of extravagance.' Exhilarated, Middleton then began trying to consolidate his power, passing acts that demanded the renunciation of the covenant, and imposing penalties on leading figures in the Scottish regime of the 1650s. This was clearly designed to target Lauderdale, and tensions were bound to arise. Far from benefiting from the Restoration, Scotland faced an era of bitter frustration, its government a nest of rivalry, its merchants restricted in their trade, and its national church under attack.

During the Interregnum, Ireland too had been forced into union with England and had lost its own assembly. Twenty years before, in 1641, the Irish Catholics had rebelled in a furious and bloody uprising against the domination of the English and the protestants. The Catholic gentry then ran the country until the end of that decade, and in 1649, after the execution of Charles I, Ormond had reached an agreement with the Catholic lords, promising toleration of their religion, before he attempted, in vain, to put together an effective royalist army. This was brutally crushed by Cromwell. Under his regime all Catholic lands were confiscated and settled by protestant veterans of the New Model Army, members of the Merchant Adventurers and Scottish Covenanters.

Charles was, in fact, restored to the throne in Ireland almost before he reached England. At the end of 1659, a group of parliamentary officers, led by the renegade royalist Roger Boyle, Lord Broghill, began talks with Charles and in February 1660 they had called a convention in Dublin, which declared in his favour. He was proclaimed king there on 14 May. Once in power, he restored the Irish assembly and chose Monck as his Lord Lieutenant, perhaps to reassure the Irish protestants. But since Monck stayed in London, and his deputy, the morose presbyterian Lord Robartes, made himself so unpopular with the Irish commissioners that he was dismissed before he set foot in Ireland, the running of the nation was effectively left with a committee of three Lords Justices, including Roger Boyle.

Boyle's grandfather had acquired his Irish land under the Tudors, while his father Richard, the 'upstart earl', was an unscrupulous opportunist who bought the title of Earl of Cork from James I and became Lord Justice and Treasurer of Ireland. (The Earl did everything on a large scale: he owned over forty thousand acres in

Munster and had eight daughters and seven sons. The oldest son, Richard, Lord Burlington, would inherit the title and the youngest, Robert Boyle, would become the famous chemist.) Instead of going into exile Roger, the third son, served the Cromwell regime in the hopes of regaining the family estates. In May 1660 he came to London, arguing loudly for the protestant landholders against the Catholics and Old Irish. Charles liked his style and energy – and his talent for writing plays. In September he created him Earl of Orrery and made him president of his home province, Munster.

A difficult, interminable process of negotiation began, in an attempt to return lands obtained by the Cromwellian planters to their old owners. In July 1662 Charles replaced Monck as Lord Lieutenant with his loyal supporter Ormond, whom he had now raised to the status of duke. In contrast to the Boyles, Ormond's family had been in Ireland since the fourteenth century, and were linked in an intricate mesh of kinship with the old Catholic families. With his stylish manner and mane of fair hair that won him the nickname 'James the White', Ormond borrowed cash and velvet coats and shining swords to make a suitably impressive return. He then moved into Dublin Castle, where he lived in grand vice-regal style, despite his massive debts.[10] Intensely nettled, Orrery was left with nothing except his presidency of Munster. From now on, beneath their co-operation, ran a tense rivalry.

With regard to the land disputes, Ormond negotiated a complex Act of Settlement, which was pushed painfully through the Dublin parliament. Charles – who upset the protestants by often intervening in individual cases, and seeming to favour the old Catholics – set up a court of claims to hear grievances. The Commissioners were bombarded with competing claims. In 1665 Ormond put through an Act of Explanation, by which Cromwellians had to surrender a third of the lands they held at the Restoration, but the court of claims was still sitting two years later and many of the original proprietors were still unsatisfied. The Catholics now owned less than a quarter of the land, as opposed to almost two

Peter Lely's portrait of Ormond in armour, celebrating the Restoration in 1660

thirds before the civil wars. The problems seemed intractable. 'I confess I am not able to see through the end of a settlement,' Ormond sighed to Hyde. If all the claims were accepted, 'there must be new discoveries made of a new Ireland for the old will not serve to satisfy these engagements'.[11] It was in connection with

Irish deputations that Charles said flippantly to Clarendon in 1661, 'For my part, rebell for rebell, I had rather trust a papist rebell than a presbiterian one' – only to have Clarendon remind him forcibly that he had forgotten the earlier rebellion against the English in 1641.[12]

Over the next fourteen years Ormond strengthened the Anglo-Irish governing class and re-established the Irish Episcopal Church. Even before he arrived, he wrote from London to reassure a truculent Orrery 'that there may be no apprehension but that a true Protestant interest is the immoveable foundation upon which his Majesty intends to build his security and the happiness of his Kingdoms'.[13] Yet Ormond's own strong Catholic connections and his friendship with presbyterian dissenters led him to treat both kinds of nonconformity as mildly as he could. Honour and duty and a practical faith seemed more important to him than details of doctrine. He steered a pragmatic course that avoided the worst whirlpools of controversial policy, but a deep animosity ran beneath the surface, waiting to spill over as soon as Charles was dead.

The colonies too were part of Charles's realm, integral to his dream of creating a great trading nation. Since the founding of Virginia in 1606–7, settlements had spread up the eastern seaboard of North America, from Maryland and Baltimore to Newfoundland. The New England confederation – of Massachusetts, Plymouth, Connecticut and New Haven – was by now almost independent, entering a period of prosperity and growth despite constant Indian wars. In defiance of a delegation from Charles these states clung stubbornly to their Commonwealth constitutions and nonconformist faith. After 1660 Charles's courtiers came forward with their claims: Lord Baltimore was restored to his position as proprietor of Maryland, to find his Catholic colony overrun by puritans, and in 1663 a group of courtiers became the first Lords Proprietors of the Carolinas, among them Clarendon, Albemarle and the Lords Craven and Ashley.

Ashley was also part-owner of a plantation in Barbados. In the West Indies, planters were turning their land over to sugar, while tobacco-growing moved to the mainland.[14] And with sugar came the terrible demand for slave labour: in a few years' time it was reckoned that Barbados alone had around twenty thousand planters and forty thousand slaves. The favourite Caribbean island for new ventures was Jamaica, which had been captured from Spain by William Penn in 1655, and whose warm climate was good for sugar, coffee, ginger, pepper and cinchona. But in all the islands, as the land was cleared for the plantations, the native forests disappeared. In the mid-1660s, the governor of Barbados reported that thirty years of cultivation had leached the soil and heavy rains on the hillsides were now washing it away. By 1665, only one small patch of woodland survived. Two years later, the Privy Council heard that 'the land is almost worn out, the thickets where cotton and corn are planted so burnt that the inhabitants are ready to desert their plantations'.[15] Another report noted that in Barbados, 'all the trees are destroyed, so that wanting wood to boyle their sugar, they are forced to send for wood to England'.[16]

As the crown's representative in the West Indies, Charles reinstated Francis, Lord Willoughby, who had been governor of the 'Caribees' in the early 1650s. Autocratic and unpopular, he governed with a council and island representatives, pouring his own fortune into colonisation schemes. His territory included the Windward Islands of Barbados, St Lucia, St Vincent and Tobago, and the Leeward Islands of Antigua, Montserrat, St Kitts and Nevis. A few colonists also tried to settle on the South American mainland, particularly in Guiana. In 1663 Charles granted Willoughby the area known as Surinam: about four thousand people travelled here, collapsing with sickness as soon as they landed. Further north, the Bermudas, granted to the Earl of Southampton fifty years before, were run as a separate company.

Despite this exploitation, in the British imagination these tropical islands still retained the aura of a refuge, the haven from civil strife that Marvell had celebrated in 'Bermudas' in 1654 where the island, riding 'unespied' in the bosom of the ocean, provides a 'grassy stage/ Safe from the storms and prelates' rage'. The overwhelming natural profusion, the oranges like lamps in the green night, the melons falling at the sailors' feet, were a gift of Providence. God was their pilot, and he meant the British to exploit the riches of these islands, just as he had given them the forests of New England or the lush soil of Virginia.

5 This Wonderful Pacifick Year

Methinks I see how throngs of people stand,
Scarce patient till the vessel come to land,
Ready to leap in, and, if need require,
With tears of joy to make the waters higher.
    JOHN WILD, 'Iter Borealis', 1660

AS RULER OF ENGLAND AND WALES, Charles had been greeted
with ecstasy. Yet he faced fundamental problems with regard to the
constitution and administration, the army and royal finances, and
the vexed issue of religion.[1] One of the thorniest initial problems
concerned the land that had been confiscated or sold under pressure
since 1649 by royalists who now vociferously asked for it back. He
and his team tried to resolve most of these issues through parliament, thus diverting any blame from the crown.

To ensure stable government it was vital, first of all, to settle the
constitutional status, since no one was very clear, after the republic,
exactly what the relative powers of monarch and parliament were.
To the French ambassador, Britain did not seem a monarchy at all,
since the laws so limited the power both of the king and of his subjects 'that they seem to be joined by indissoluble ties, in such a
manner that if one of the two parties were wanting, the other would
go to ruin'.[2]

From the start, Charles dated his reign not from the Restoration
but from the death of his father, and firmly established that his
regime was legitimate, its acts valid in law. In July 1660 an act
confirmed that while the judgements of the courts under the
Commonwealth on all *private* transactions should stand (thus
embracing the courts' decisions and the continuity of common law),

no *public* acts – the statutes passed by parliament – were endorsed, because they had never had the consent of the king.[3] Cromwell's legislation was thus simply wiped off the record as illegal.[4] In terms of legislation, Charles and his parliament were transported back in time, to 1641.

This return to the status quo of nineteen years before meant that all the radical changes that Cromwell's parliaments had made in the way the kingdom was governed were swept away. In the English counties and boroughs, the old system of administration was restored, complete with Lords Lieutenant, sheriffs and justices of the peace, prompting, of course, a deluge of petitions for places. The old House of Lords was soon reconstituted, including the twenty-six bishops, who would soon be a bugbear in Charles's attempts to achieve religious toleration. The concessions that Charles I had made before 1641, in the first year of the Long Parliament, were, however, accepted. These included the abolition of the old peroga-tive courts like the Star Chamber, which had been hated by the gentry for their power to impose taxes without parliamentary agree-ment, and the acceptance of the Triennial Act, which decreed that a parliament must be called at least once in every three years. Despite these limitations Charles II still emerged at the start of his reign with, theoretically, an astonishing degree of power. Within the bounds of the Triennial Act he could call parliament when he saw fit, appoint ministers, direct the army and navy and control policy at home and overseas. In return, parliament was bound to vote him money for the running of the realm, and extra funds for emergen-cies, like a state of war.

There lay the rub. In practice Charles's power was illusory, cur-tailed throughout his reign by lack of funds. He was the first monarch who had to rely on being voted an annual sum by parlia-ment in peacetime, and this meant that unless he could find funds elsewhere his parliament had to meet at least once a year. In 1660 a House of Commons committee estimated that the running of a peacetime kingdom would cost around £1,200,000.[5] The crown's current income from estates and fees was a third below this, so there was already a large sum to find. And while the estimate of £1,200,000 sounded reasonable, Charles never received even three quarters of this amount. The MPs tried to raise money through excise duties on beer and cider, and new taxes like the hated Hearth Tax of 1662, whereby householders had to pay one shilling for each fireplace within their house, to be collected twice a year.[6] But the duties and taxes were misjudged, inefficiently collected and embezzled by agents – there was never enough.

Furthermore, the promise Charles had made at Breda to make up the army arrears of pay put him in hock from the start. The New Model Army was a huge force of 42,000 men. Its soldiers were still fierce in their puritan and republican convictions, and Charles knew that he would have no chance if they ever rose against him. His first parliaments, packed with royalists and moderate presbyterians who detested the soldiers' sects and factions, were equally keen to disband the troops. Unfortunately for the royal coffers, the Commons underestimated the cost of the back pay and Charles had to raise £40,000, much of it from his own income. But still, the breaking up of the army was managed surprisingly successfully. Instead of turning into bands of discontented ex-soldiers wandering the land, to everyone's astonishment Cromwell's forces melted back into their communities, becoming bakers, tailors and candlestick-makers rather than beggarmen or thieves: 'this Captain turned a shoemaker; the lieutenant, a baker; this a brewer; that a haberdasher; this common soldier, a porter; and every man in his apron & frock, &c., as if they had never done anything else.'[7] The presbyterian minister Richard Baxter marvelled: 'Thus did God do a more wonderful work in the dissolving of this army than any of their greatest victories.' It was all due to Monck, he thought, and it was an astounding tribute to the general's authority, 'that they should all stand still and let him come on and restore the parliament and bring in the king, and disband themselves, and all this without one bloody nose!'[8]

Charles cleverly persuaded parliament to let him keep some 'guards' and 'garrisons'. In effect, although the hated term was studiously avoided, this was a standing army. By sleight of hand he won back the power over the troops that the Commons had so fiercely wrested from his father. He kept Monck's streamlined republican regiment, 'the Coldstreamers', as his household troops. These were the men who had marched from Coldstream, Monck's last Scottish camp before the troops crossed the icy Tweed in December 1859 and headed for London. He also kept a troop of elite cavalry, the Royal Horse Guards, or 'the Blues', many of whose officers were former exiles, who had served under the King of France beside his brothers James and Henry. Soon he would also create the Royal Dragoons, officially to guard Tangier, their name coming from the 'dragon' muskets they carried. Then in 1665 he created 'the Buffs', the Royal East Kent Regiment, ostensibly to fight in Holland. Almost by stealth, Charles mustered forces of his own, highly trained and supremely loyal, whose ranks also gave him a useful way of rewarding petitioners and handing out places.

The constitutional issues and the fate of the army were dealt with quickly. But other problems took longer to solve, especially the question of religious toleration. Religious differences, after all, had been the first cause of revolt in his father's time. Their faith lay deep in the hearts of most men and women; many had made great sacrifices for it, some gladly, others with a lasting bitterness. During the Interregnum the Anglican bishops had faced sour humiliation: their archbishop, William Laud, had been executed; they had been expelled from the House of Lords, their dioceses had been removed, and the very office of bishop scratched from the rolls. They were determined on reinstatement and, in some cases, on revenge.

While many Church of England congregations wanted to return to the prayer book as amended by James I, with its annual round of holy days and feast days, the presbyterians wanted the plain form and more democratic organisation established under Cromwell.

Outside the church itself, a host of sects – often loosely bundled together under the name 'Anabaptists' – wanted to retain the freedom to pray and preach as the spirit moved them. Even the Quakers hoped for better days than they had experienced under hostile Interregnum regimes. (Their movement had sprung up like fire in the early 1650s, and they had seemed dangerous to Cromwell's state because they believed God spoke directly to each individual soul, and denied all worldly authority, abjuring oaths and sacraments as well as fine clothes and hat-doffing.) Meanwhile those people who had never bothered much about the Lord under any guise sauntered in new clothes of brilliant colours, rejoicing in the return of May Day festivals and Christmas feasts.

It was assumed that with the coming of a king there would be a return to a state church. Nonetheless, many hoped that their freedom to worship would continue. Charles, they thought, had promised this at Breda, in these words:

Because the passion and uncharitableness of the times have produced several opinions in religion, by which men are engaged in parties and animosities against each other (which, when they shall hereafter unite in a freedom of conversation, will be composed or better understood), we do declare a liberty to tender consciences, and that no man shall be disquieted or called in question for differences of opinion in matter of religion, which do not disturb the peace of the kingdom, and that we shall be ready to consent to such an Act of Parliament, as upon mature deliberation shall be offered to us, for the full granting that indulgence.[9]

This statement had appeased the sectaries of the army and smoothed the way to the Restoration. And now that Charles was back, the moderate puritans and presbyterians who had always stayed loyal to the Crown understandably assumed that their freedom to worship would be safe.

Charles was officially Supreme Governor of the Church of England. It was difficult, though, to determine exactly what sort of church the Church of England should be. Should it reinstate the bishops and return to the 1559 prayer book, creating a milder version of the church that Archbishop Laud had left in 1642? Or should it allow for the feelings of the presbyterians, with their Calvinist beliefs in the authority of scripture, in justification by faith, and their churches ruled not by appointed bishops but ministers working with Church committees and synods? Many presbyterians objected to the prayer book, feeling that the prescribed forms for communion, baptism, marriage and burial were too like Catholic rituals. They wanted each of their ministers to be free to pray according to the promptings of his own spirit, and their services to revolve around the pulpit, not the communion table. A minister, too, should be able to punish the sinners in their midst, and expel them from the congregation of the saved. And should all the sects be compelled into the Anglican fold, or should those that could not accept compromise be left to continue with their own forms of worship?

Immediately there were practical problems as well as matters of principle. Many petitions came from clergymen who had lost their livings during the Commonwealth and begged to be reinstated, while an equal number came from their rivals, presbyterian ministers anxious to keep their current places. Initially, Charles and Hyde took the side of the latter. Within three days of Charles's arrival in London, a royal proclamation decreed that no one would be ejected from his living except by a court of law or an act of parliament. In September the decree was modified to say that the ministers who had been ousted during the Commonwealth could regain their places if they compensated the existing holders: yet another round of buying and selling places was soon under way.

Charles and Hyde knew that they had to move fast to bring the two sides together. The bishops were reinstalled in their sees, some taking their place humbly, others, like Christopher Wren's ageing uncle Matthew at Ely, crowing in triumph. But Charles signalled that he might listen to the presbyterians too, by appointing ten presbyterian chaplains to his household (though limits were put on their long sermons). One was Richard Baxter, a self-educated preacher from Kidderminster, an influential writer and an earnest, anxious man. 'The King gave us not only a free audience,' he remembered, 'but as gracious an answer as we could get.' Charles said that he wanted them to reach an agreement, not 'by bringing one party over to the other, but by abating somewhat on both sides, and meeting in midway; and that if it were not accomplished, it should be long of ourselves and not of him'.[10] So relieved were the presbyterian band that one elderly preacher 'burst out into tears of joy'.

Charles planned a double policy. Comprehension, inclusion of low church puritans and presbyterians within the Church of England, would be matched by indulgence, toleration of the sects who preferred to worship separately. His hope for a healing compromise, a triumph of common sense, was bolstered by the model for union that had been developed by Archbishop Ussher, the Anglican Archbishop of Armagh in the 1640s, and promoted by Richard Baxter in 1655, a form of 'primitive episcopacy' that limited the power of bishops by linking them with the presbyterian synods. In the summer and autumn of 1660 Charles and Hyde arranged informal meetings between leading Anglicans and moderate presbyterians. Both sides then met at Clarendon's current base, Worcester House, in September. After the tired clerics worked tetchily through several drafts, the Worcester House Declaration was issued on 25 October, a solution, Baxter told Clarendon with relief, 'such as any sober honest Ministers might submit to'.[11] The bishops, the Declaration explained, were 'only to ordain and exercise jurisdiction with the advice of their presbyters'. Individual priests could avoid 'Popish' ceremonies like baptism, and rituals like the use of the crucifix and the wearing of surplices, while parish priests would have the right to expel members of their congregation as they did in the 'free' churches.[12] In addition – a pronouncement that upset the presbyterians as well as the Anglicans – those who did not wish to be brought into the Church should be free to worship as they liked.

When parliament returned after their long recess in November the Worcester House Declaration was presented as the basis for a bill. But already the mood in parliament had changed as the firm Anglicans sensed their power and became determined to fight presbyterian inroads. On 28 November the Commons rejected the bill. From now on it appeared that Charles's bid for a policy of conciliation that might, if adopted, have created a single, flexible, and inclusive church, was doomed to fail.

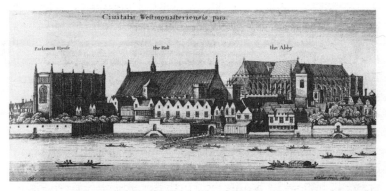

Wenceslaus Hollar, Westminster from the river, showing St Stephen's Chapel, where the Commons met, Westmister Hall and the Abbey, with skiffs crowding up to Westminster stairs

The glorious summer was rapidly turning into an autumn of disquiet. Religious issues aside, even the stoutest royalists were angered by the problem of the land that had changed hands in the wake of the civil wars. Many royalist gentry had been forced to sell estates when prices were falling, to pay the fines imposed on them. Now they wanted their land back, or at least some compensation.

The Convention Parliament made it clear from the start that they would distinguish between private sales and 'public acts' like confiscation. The former were regarded as legal transactions: the land had gone for ever. Confiscated lands, by contrast, had to be returned to their original owners. These included crown and church lands and some private estates which had been taken by the republic and then sold, often to army officers. The process of reclaiming them was difficult, as sale had followed sale, and sometimes the first owners were dead, so that it was by now very hard to untangle the deals and to assess the value, although Charles set up a commission to assess compensation. And while the crown and the Church usually got their land back, scores of private owners had to fight for their property, either by pressing forward with lawsuits or pushing private bills through parliament. The extraordinary thing is that they largely succeeded: most royalists – especially the great nobles – were back in their old houses within ten years. But many among them were crippled by the huge mortgages taken out to regain their land.

The gentry had thought that life would swing on its axis back to the old easy days. Baffled, they bombarded Charles with their requests. The crush of petitioners in Canterbury was repeated in London. John Evelyn, who was trying to present letters sent from Henrietta Maria, was shocked by the way people literally pressed about Charles:

It was indeed intollerable, as well as unexpressable, the greedinesse of all sorts, men, women & children, to see his Majesty & kisse his hands inso much that he had scarce leasure to Eate for some dayes, coming as they did from all parts of the Nation: And the King on the other side as willing to give them that satisfaction, would have none kept out but gave free accesse to all sorts of people.'[13]

In greeting people so courteously, Charles was following the advice proffered the year before by his old tutor, the elegant and worldly William Cavendish, Marquess of Newcastle. Good manners were always the best tactic, wrote Newcastle, 'and, believe it, the putting off of your hat and making a leg pleases more than reward or preservation, so much does it take all kind of people'.[14] But he simply could not doff his hat to all. Over the coming months 'loyal petitions' arrived in their hundreds, even thousands. Corporations sent proclamations of loyalty. Companies sent requests for new charters. Countless individuals asked for restitution of lands or repayment of debts. Others begged royal pardons for offices held under the Commonwealth or for arms taken against the king. Still more asked for posts in the royal household, as clerks, officers of customs, keepers of forests. Evelyn himself was one of these petitioners, trying to keep close to the king. Like many, he had been loyal for two decades and more. In 1641 he had travelled to Holland and Belgium with Charles's sister Mary, Princess Royal; he had come back briefly to fight, and had then spent four years travelling to France and Italy, before his marriage to the young Mary Browne, daughter of the English resident in Paris. On the eve of the Restoration he published three royalist tracts, countering rumour and scandal.[15] He now hoped for a post for himself (and later for Mary in the service of the queen) and also wanted to settle the disputed possession of his house, Sayes Court, and to get back the money owed to his father-in-law for his work in Paris. Everyone who clustered round the court had stories like this, their own needs, hopes and fears.

John Evelyn, painted by Kneller as a Fellow of the Royal Society, c. 1689

Those petitions that reached the state committees were only a smidgeon of the whole. The place-seeking – and the exchange of cash that went with it – filtered down the whole pyramid. New place-seekers offered cash to those who had held them in the previous regime and thrust their petitions and demands on anyone with influence, from aldermen to landowners, accompanying their requests with gifts of money and plate. Complicated deals were done, and many positions were bought from former holders. It was rumoured that officials and go-betweens were making a fortune. Petitioners chose their intermediaries carefully, former parliamentarians applying to the king through Morice or Lord Manchester or through Albemarle (whose wife became notorious for the fees she charged). Anxious letters were written, tiring journeys taken. It was as if half the nation were holding out their hands and many were on the road to besiege Charles in person. All through the summer of 1660 they descended on London, jolting in their carriages over the rutted roads, changing horses and crowding into inns on their way from Northumberland and Dorset, Lancashire and Norfolk.

The long wait for answers to their many requests left petitioners feeling let down and angry. A witticism soon circled that Charles was passing an Act of Indemnity for his Enemies and Oblivion for his Friends. The joke wounded him sharply.[16] As early as August 1660, 'The Complaint of the Royal and Loyal Party to the King' bitterly lamented that those who had helped the king were now ruined, that the 'greatest opposers' were preferred to the leading places in government and at court, and that their petitions were never fully read, but were dealt with by secretaries, a charge that rings true. In March 1662 Pepys thoroughly enjoyed a scorching sermon by Richard Creighton, 'the great Scotch man', delivered with great gusto and wit before the king and the Duke of York. Creighton's text was 'Roule yourself in dust' and his theme was that it would have been

... better for the poor cavalier never to have come in with the King into England again; for he that hath the impudence to deny obedience to the lawful magistrate and to swear to the oath of allegiance &c, were better treated nowadays in Newgate then a poor Royalist that hath suffered all his life for the King is at Whitehall among his friends.[17]

The Cavalier gentry and the churchmen were not the only groups making demands. The merchants too were flocking to Whitehall. Many companies had received charters from Cromwell and numbered keen parliamentarians among their leading men. Some, like John Bland in *Trade Revived*, feared a new era of competition, calling for the old guilds to be revived to control their trades and for the king to regulate commerce as his Tudor predecessors had done. On the eve of the Restoration the twelve leading guilds had held a dinner for General Monck, and when Charles rode triumphantly through London they had turned out in their livery to greet him. The East India Company gave a huge gift of plate (most of the royal plate having been melted down in the civil wars), and all the companies and guilds made sure that anyone with royal connections was promoted so that they could play a useful part in deputations to the king. Not surprisingly, Charles encouraged them, especially when they brought gifts. He granted new charters to the East India Company and the Levant Company, to the Eastland Company that traded with the Baltic and even to the Merchant Adventurers, who had ostentatiously supported Cromwell. In July he went to the great City feast, 'with as much pompe and splendour as any Earthly prince could do', admiring the pageants along the route, despite the pouring rain.[18] He established a Council of Trade, which usually met in the Mercers' Hall, so that 'every interest may be righted' and listened to the members' advice on measures 'as may tend to the rectifying those errors which the corruption of late times have introduced'.[19]

But if the merchants were appeased, the nobles and gentry were increasingly frustrated. They were missing out on government posts and on the restitution of their lands, and Charles even seemed to wish to deny them justice. What they wanted, to persuade them that the bad times were truly at an end and that their day had come again in this 'wonderful pacifick year', was vengeance – and blood.

6 Family Matters

Lucretius with a Stork-like fate
Born and translated in a State
Comes to proclaim in English Verse
No Monarch rules the Universe
But Chance and Atomes make this All
In Order Democratical,
Where Bodies freely run their course
Without Design, or Fate, or Force.

EDMUND WALLER, introductory poem to Evelyn's
translation of Lucretius' *De rerum natura*

THERE WAS A CLEAR political danger in drawing analogies between Lucretius' atomic philosophy, fashionable among intellectuals, and the freedom of 'bodies' in social structures, whether it be the state or the family. Charles had never been free to run his course 'without Design, or Fate, or Force'. And ever since childhood one of the constraints on his freedom, which appeared minor but was not, had always been his relationship with strong women. As a small boy he had to find ways to negotiate life with his temperamental mother. Tiny and upright, a foot shorter than her eldest son, who had to bend down to talk to her, Henrietta Maria was a creature of the court, with an iron will. Her father was murdered when she was a baby, and she grew up under the eye of her dominating Italian mother, Marie de' Medici. She showed far more affection to the court dwarf, Jeffrey Hudson, a 'gift' to her from the first Duke of Buckingham, than to the children who were later born to her. As queen, she loved to act, playing leading parts in the lavish court masques, and she manipulated her own children like puppets in a game of power, raging and storming when they defied her. As a counter to his mother, Charles was cared for by the flamboyant Christabella Wyndham, his nurse (a formal title rather than a real task). She later greeted him as an adolescent in the West Country so effusively that the whole company were sure she had seduced him.

He grew up enjoying the company of women of wit and intelligence, and they abounded in his close circle. In the bitter winter before the news of his father's trial arrived, he danced and flirted in the Hague with the good-looking, effervescent women of the House of Orange, and his talented cousins, daughters of Elizabeth of Bohemia. Charles, however, was already in love. On a brief visit to the Hague in July 1648 he had met Lucy Walter. They were both eighteen. Lucy's parents were Pembrokeshire gentry who had separated when she was young, and she and her mother had lived in London, mingling in the down-at-heel royalist circles during the Civil Wars. In her teens she became the mistress of Algernon Sidney, the youngest son of the Earl of Leicester. The Sidneys, like so many families, had divided allegiances, and when Algernon went to fight for Cromwell Lucy turned to his royalist brother, Robert. She moved with him to the Hague, changing her name to 'Mrs Barlow', 'a browne, beautiful, bold but insipid creature', according to Evelyn.

Lucy and Charles became lovers and their son James – later Duke of Monmouth – was born in Rotterdam on 9 April 1649. It was a genuine love affair, but when Charles left for Jersey and then Scotland in 1650 Lucy had no means of support and soon turned to other men. After Charles returned, and told her their affair was over, she made ceaseless demands for money and caused numerous public scandals. At one point she came to London where she was arrested as a spy and sent to the Tower – causing much mirth in the newssheets – before being despatched back to the Netherlands. Worried for his son, Charles tried various means of inveigling him away, and even tried to abduct him by force. Lucy fought hard but eventually, in 1658, one of Charles's spymasters, Ross, snatched the nine-year-old James while her back was turned. He was brought to Paris, to the household of Henrietta Maria, where he took the name

Lucy Walter, Mrs Barlow, in the late 1650s

of James Crofts after his guardian, one of Charles's Gentlemen of the Bedchamber, William Crofts.

Lucy followed her son to Paris, where she died a year later, supposedly from syphilis. She was twenty-eight. She made a deathbed confession to John Cosin, later Bishop of Durham, declaring that she was Charles's legal wife, a claim that was never proved but would cause much trouble in years to come.

*

During his exile various unsuccessful schemes were set in motion to marry Charles off profitably and form useful alliances. The boldest and most hopeless was Henrietta Maria's attempt to force him on her niece, Anne-Marie Louise d'Orléans, duchesse de Montpensier, known as 'La Grande Mademoiselle' and one of the wealthiest women in Europe. Charles, who was half-hearted anyway, had no chance of such a prize. Among the duchesses and princesses of his relations his own first choice was his cousin Sophie. She was curly-haired, clever and completely natural, but also wise enough to see that such a marriage would be foolish. When Charles told her, as they walked by the canals in the dusk, that she was more beautiful than Lucy Walter, she slowly withdrew and their evening walks ended. In her memoirs she admitted that 'he had shown a liking for me with which I was most gratified', but she had 'sense enough to know that marriages of great kings are not made up by such means'.[1]

Whispers of affairs followed Charles as he moved from place to place. In Paris he became briefly infatuated with Isabelle-Angelique, duchesse de Chatillon, whose young husband had died in the wars of the Fronde in 1649. The engaging 'Bablon' was a charming widow with many admirers. When Charles visited her in the country, this 'raised a confident rumour that he was married to that lady', sighed the exasperated Hyde, just as his liaison with Lucy had done.[2] But his suit was never serious. The Duchess became a close friend of Minette and Charles remained fond of her. Her name often appears in his letters to his sister: he helped her to get a licence to import alum into England, which was used in the chalky make-up of court beauties; he worried about her second marriage to a German prince (which did not last long); and he assured Minette that 'upon any occasion that lies within my power, I shall ever be ready to serve Bablon'.[3]

The names were beginning to form a longish list. One of Charles's mistresses in exile was Elizabeth Killigrew, sister of the Killigrew brothers and now the wife of Francis Boyle, another son of the Earl of Cork. They met in the Dutch Republic, where Elizabeth was in the household of Mary, Princess of Orange, but when Elizabeth became pregnant she was swiftly bustled back to Ireland. Their daughter was born there, named Charlotte Jemima Henrietta Maria Fitzcharles. After the Restoration Charles made Elizabeth's husband Viscount Shannon, and she spent the rest of her life on their country estate.[4] Another affair was with Eleanor, Lady Byron, whom Evelyn marked down, with grand exaggeration, as 'the king's seventeenth whore abroad'.[5] Yet another was with Catharine Pegge, daughter of a Derbyshire royalist, with whom he had two children, Charles Fitzcharles, nicknamed 'Don Carlos', later Earl of Plymouth, and a daughter, Catherine. After he returned to London he installed this small family in a house in Pall Mall.

Still, the hunt for a respectable wife went on. In the early years of his exile, the possibility was raised of his marriage to Princess Louise, a daughter of the Orange stadtholder Frederick, and sister to the future William II, his sister Mary's husband. Seeing no advantage, the House of Orange quickly declined the offer. But ten years later Charles's strongest, and last, love abroad was Louise's sister, the lively Henrietta Catherine. This was a genuine, reciprocal passion, squashed by her grandmother Amalia, the elderly Dowager Princess of Orange, who was convinced of the hopelessness of Charles's quest to be king and probably equally put off by his philandering.[6] (Henrietta then sensibly married the safe and solemn German prince.)

Charles was not really as wild as the Dowager Princess thought, preferring long, easy relationships to perpetual hunt and chase. He had strong feelings, and if not faithful, he was loyal. But he had great charm, and when women flung themselves at him, as they often did, or were steered into his path by ambitious courtiers, he certainly responded with great sensual pleasure. In Halifax's view, his 'inclinations to love were the effects of health and a good constitution, with as little mixture of the seraphic part as ever man had'.[7] A couple of months before his return he enclosed a note in a letter to Lord Taaffe – who had been his emissary in his exchanges with

Henrietta – asking Taaffe to give it to '*la petite souris*' and adding, 'there is here a very pritty sourie but the divell ont is the dame is so jealous that it must be a very good mouser that can take it.'[8]

The prize that he did take, and would cling to over the coming years, was Barbara Villiers, Mrs Palmer, whom he met in Flanders just before his return. Barbara was another ravishingly beautiful and spirited young woman with impeccable royalist credentials. Her grandfather came from the powerful Villiers clan, and was half-brother to the first Duke of Buckingham. Her father, Viscount Grandison, had died of wounds received at the siege of Bristol in 1643, when she was three, and her uncle Ned Villiers was a founder of the resistance group the Sealed Knot, and one of Hyde's most valued agents. The Grandisons lost everything in the service of the crown, while her mother's merchant family, the Baynings, squandered their wealth on grand drainage schemes in the fens. And although her widowed mother married the Earl of Anglesey (her late husband's cousin and yet another Villiers), his estates too were sequestered. Like Lucy Walter, who was only two years older, the near-penniless Barbara shifted as best she could in the royalist circles of Interregnum London.

Like Lucy, too, she took a rich lover: she was 'a little lecherous girl when she was young', Pepys heard. At sixteen she became the mistress of Philip Stanhope, Earl of Chesterfield, an affair that continued even after she married the worthy but rich Roger Palmer in 1659. Discovering the affair, Palmer threatened to remove his wife from town completely (always the worst fate for women in Restoration drama). He was resolved, she wailed to Chesterfield, 'that nobody shall see me when I am in the country'. Her letter was almost an invitation to an elopement: 'for I am ready and willing to go all over the world with you, and I will obey your commands, that am whilst I live – Yours'.[9]

Chesterfield did not rise to the bait, being immersed in the disastrous plans for royalist uprisings that summer, which saw him imprisoned six times. In January 1660 he fled England for Paris after killing a man in a duel. At the same time, Roger Palmer joined those royalists who gambled on getting a good post at the hoped-for restoration by making a donation to the cause, in his case a substantial £1,000. He also acted as an agent, supplying Hyde with information about debates in the Council of State. Barbara may therefore have gone to Brussels, not aiming to reach Chesterfield in Paris, as has been suggested, but as an inconspicuous messenger. Meanwhile Hyde worked to get Palmer elected to the Convention Parliament, and Charles himself took an interest in his case, prompted perhaps by mentions of Palmer's 'gay wife'. There is no definite mention of their meeting, but when they did meet, Charles fell fast.

It was rumoured that when Charles left Whitehall, exhausted, on the night of his triumphant return to London, he went to bed, not in his palace, but with the mesmerising Mrs Palmer. The report was typical of critics who saw her malign influence everywhere, right from the start of the reign. But certainly, they were lovers within a month of his return. Barbara had piles of dark hair – rich auburn in some lights – 'alabaster skin', blue, near-violet eyes, and conversation-stopping sexual allure. And from the start her relationship with Charles had a political edge. She was no tool, being too intelligent and fiery to be used lightly. But her relations, especially her Villiers uncles, and her uncle by marriage, James Howard, Earl of Suffolk, prepared her for her role. They knew Charles's weakness for women, and believed that one path to power was through his bed. Halifax would later write that the placing of a mistress was 'No small matter in a court and not unworthy the thoughts even of a party':

A mistress, either dextrous in herself or well instructed by those that are so, may be very useful to her friends, not only in the immediate hours of her ministry, but by her influences and insinuations at other times. It was resolved generally by others whom he should have in his arms, as well as whom he should have in his councils. Of a man who was so capable of choosing, he chose as seldom as any man that ever lived.[10]

But Charles did choose. He ignored some offerings, took others casually and a few so seriously that his very government was affected.

In the summer of 1660 Roger Palmer moved into King Street, across the Privy Garden from Charles's apartments in Whitehall. Like a conjuring trick, a house had suddenly become available when Cromwell's cousin, Edmund Whalley, fleeing vengeance, sailed as fast as he could for New England. On 13 July the Palmers invited the king and the Dukes of York and Gloucester to a musical evening. Pepys was working late next door with Sandwich, when they heard music through the wall and stood listening at the old connecting door between the lodgings. They gathered that the king and his two brothers were there, 'with Madam Palmer, a pretty woman that they have a fancy to, to make her husband a cuckold'.[11]

For several months the affair was kept quiet and any gossip was quickly hushed up by Hyde. But by the autumn everyone in court circles knew the truth. Charles took Barbara with him to the races, and showed her off in the park. Courtiers ingratiated themselves with her in the hope she would say a word in their favour. Her family, above all, kept as close as they could, particularly Buckingham. Hyde's dislike of Barbara was partly due to her alliance with this cousin, whom he had blamed so often for distracting Charles in exile. He was also anxious, even in these early months, that the court's reputation for wildness would undo all his diplomacy. He forbade his own wife to call on her and refused to mention her name, referring to her from now on as 'the Lady'.

The summer was festive, but in the dog days, the mood at court darkened. In late August Charles's brother Henry, Duke of Gloucester, caught the smallpox that had spread through London in the heat. His doctors thought it mild, and his family were horrified when he died suddenly, on 13 September. At the age of nine Henry, with his sister Elizabeth, had been the last of the family to see their father, Charles I, on the eve of his execution. When he arrived in Paris five years later, he was incorrigible and wild after his long imprisonment, but he grew into a youth of great sweetness. Charles was badly shaken by the loss of this favourite brother, aged only twenty. As was the custom, his body was carried by barge after sunset from Somerset House to Westminster stairs, with torches flaring on the dark, lapping waters. He was buried at midnight in the Henry VII Chapel in the Abbey, the flaming torches being extinguished at his grave.

The court wore deep mourning for six weeks, and the opening of the new theatres was delayed until November. The family, however, still planned to spend Christmas together, the first time for twenty years. In late September Mary, Princess of Orange, arrived from Holland, barely escaping shipwreck off the Kent coast. Charles sailed down from London in his yacht to meet her at Margate, and escorted her regally up the Thames.[12] Although they had sometimes quarrelled, he was devoted to his brisk, strong-minded elder sister. But this was an awkward meeting since Charles had failed to persuade the Dutch States General to have her young son William made stadtholder, captain-general of the republic. She felt angry and betrayed.

More family troubles lay ahead. The court spread outwards from Whitehall, into the streets nearby, to the great mansions with their gardens running down to the Thames. One of these, Hyde's current home, Worcester House in the Strand, was the site of the first great court scandal of Charles II's reign. At twenty-six, James, Duke of York had never been thought serious in his affairs, but it now transpired that on 3 September 1660 he had secretly married the twenty-three-year-old Anne Hyde, the Chancellor's daughter. Anne had been a maid of honour to Mary, Princess of Orange, since 1655 and had met James during a visit to Paris the following year. When the exiled court was based in Brussels he visited her often, fell in love and in late 1659 agreed a marriage contract. To his alarm – since the sudden hope of a restoration made his chances of a noble marriage brighter – in the spring of 1660 she became pregnant. A few months later, the marriage contract was solemnised.

At first Charles refused them permission to marry, but he finally gave in. The ceremony took place at dead of night in Worcester House. In place of her father, Ormond's eldest son, the Earl of Ossory, gave the bride away. James's own chaplain Dr Joseph Crowther conducted the service, and the only other witness was Anne's maid, Ellen Stroud. The secret marriage did not surface into public knowledge for a while, but it was another source of anxiety while Charles was preoccupied with his Privy Council and parliament, with the settlement of affairs in Scotland and Ireland, the failure of his hopes for agreement about the Church and the imminent trials of the men who had signed his father's death warrant. James himself kept silent, denying all rumours, but when Anne gave birth to a son, on 22 October, and claimed repeatedly during her labour that they were married, he finally admitted the truth.

By then the news had been buzzing around the court for weeks. The marriage was a blow to the royal family. It threw away the diplomatic advantages to be gained by dangling the possibility of marriage to the duke before foreign nobility. Moreover Anne was a commoner, and the Stuart family stock fell with an alliance to the daughter of a Wiltshire lawyer. People joked that Anne smelt of her father's green lawyer's bag. Worse still, her baby son would now be second in line to the throne. Yet Charles's immediate reaction was one of loyalty to his old adviser. He knew that people would think Hyde was implicated, but he also recognised that the Chancellor adored his daughter and that her pregnancy and furtive marriage would outrage his stiff principles and pride.

As Hyde himself said later, in this crisis Charles acted with generosity and understanding. Realising that he knew nothing, he sent for Hyde's old friends, Ormond and Southampton, and told them to arrange a meeting for him with the Chancellor, but to break the news first, before he came in. Hyde was, as Charles expected, upset to the point of frenzy, threatening to turn his daughter out of his house as a whore, shouting that she should be sent to the Tower, impeached and executed and that he himself would sign her

Edward Hyde, Earl of Clarendon, engraving

arraignment. He was full of fear that people would think (as many did) that this was a plot on his part, to get closer to the royal family and the succession. When Charles entered, Southampton told him there was no point talking to his raging Chancellor, 'Whereupon his majesty', wrote Hyde, looking upon him with a wonderful benignity, said, 'Chancellor, I knew this business would trouble you, and therefore I appointed your two friends to confer first with you upon it, before I would speak with you myself: but you must now lay aside all passion that disturbs you, and consider that this business will not do itself; that it will quickly take air; and therefore it is fit that I first resolve what to do before other men presume to give their counsel: tell me therefore what you would have me do and I will follow your advice.'[13]

It was clever of Charles, alert to the quick spread of gossip and shrewd in his understanding of Hyde's nature, to appeal to him in the role of counsellor, jerking him back to responsibility, forcing him to think of action.

Charles stood by him again when five of James's friends, in a misguided display of loyalty, claimed to have had sex with Anne. They included Ormond's second son Richard, Earl of Arran; Harry Jermyn, nephew of Henrietta Maria's chamberlain and rumoured lover, the Earl of St Albans; Richard Talbot, another of James's Irish friends, later Earl of Tyrconnell; Charles Berkeley; and young Harry Killigrew. All of them loathed Hyde for different reasons. Their stories were scurrilous and clearly invented, although they have been repeated by court gossips ever since. Arran claimed Anne had pretended to be sick and lured him to a side chamber at the end of the gallery while his sister and Harry Jermyn were playing ninepins; Talbot said she had made an appointment with him in the Chancellor's own study 'and, not paying so much attention to what was upon the table as what they were engaged in, they had spilled a bottle full of ink upon a despatch of four pages, and that the King's monkey, which was blamed for this accident, had been a long time in disgrace'. Killigrew topped it all by describing them making love in a water closet overhanging the river, with three or four swans as witnesses.[14] The suggestion was that since Anne had so many lovers she had no proof that James had fathered her child: she had tricked him into an 'unlawful' marriage which could now be declared invalid.[15] The cruel stories were a heightened form of the malicious jokes the court loved. Charles was brisk, amused, and realistic: he had given his permission and since he was sure that the marriage was legal, it must stand. There was no question of it being annulled by an act of parliament, as parliament must never interfere with the succession. James must drink as he had brewed. (When he heard, Sandwich was more brutal, quoting his father's saying, 'He that doth get a woman with child and marries her afterward it is as if a man should shit in his hat and then clap it upon his head.'[16])

Charles showed greater calm than the rest of his family. Mary was indignant, and Henrietta Maria was outraged. With amazing aplomb Anne herself sailed through it all. In time she proved clever, witty and energetic and made herself a striking presence at court. As the courtier and writer Anthony Hamilton remembered, she had 'a majestic air, a pretty good shape, not much beauty, a great deal of wit' and an ability to pick out intelligent, promising figures at court. Furthermore, 'an air of grandeur in all her actions made her be considered as if born to support her rank which placed her so near the throne.'[17] James did not give up his womanising – in October, only a few weeks after his marriage, Pepys saw him talking 'very wantonly' to Barbara Palmer through the hangings which curtained off the royal pews in the Chapel Royal – but eight years later he would remark that 'in all things but his codpiece', the duke was 'led by the nose by his wife'.[18]

Barely a fortnight after Anne's son was born, on 2 November, Henrietta Maria arrived at Whitehall with her younger daughter Minette. The old queen came partly as the unofficial representative of Cardinal Mazarin, sent to smooth relations between the two countries, but she still had hopes of suppressing this marriage. Furious with James, she refused to recognise Anne as her daughter-in-law, to see their baby son, or to grant Hyde an audience.

Then came the next blow. While the quarrels about James and Anne raged, Charles's sister Mary, the Princess of Orange, fell ill. Her fever turned out, once again, to be smallpox. Charles sent his mother and Minette away from Whitehall to St James's Palace to escape infection but he himself stayed behind, visiting Mary constantly, regardless of risk. She died on Christmas Eve, aged twenty-nine, asking Charles to be the guardian to her son. This was not to be, but Charles kept William's picture in his bedchamber for the rest of his life.

Christmas was marked by grief for the deaths of Henry and Mary, and by lasting embarrassment at the awkwardness of James's marriage. Henrietta Maria's chilliness almost created a diplomatic incident, prevented only by Mazarin's firm messages and Charles's threat to stop the income from her English estates. Finally she and Hyde met – with deep reluctance on both sides – and on New Year's Day 1661, when Charles attended the baby's christening in Worcester House, she deigned to receive her daughter-in-law 'with much respect and love'.[19] In a further defiance of gossip, and to ward off questions in the House of Commons, Charles created Hyde Earl of Clarendon – having offered him the higher honour of a dukedom, which Hyde wisely refused for fear of provoking more jealousy.

Having lost this battle, Henrietta Maria decided to return to France. To the British public she was an ominous reminder of past wars, a foreign, Catholic beauty, heir to the Bourbons and Medicis, now shrunken and plain. Ever since her husband's execution she had dressed in black, offset by white lace, and she looked much older than her forty-nine years. Her slight, elegant daughter, however, won the people's hearts by her charm and tact. Like Charles, Minette had a natural graciousness, an instinctive, easy attentiveness to those around her. Although she was, in almost every respect, a French princess, Charles liked to remind her of her English heritage as an 'Exeter woman'. She had been born there in 1644, amid the flurry of war, and had been smuggled out of England at the age of two by her governess, Lady Dalkeith, who had walked a hundred miles to Dover, carrying the baby. In Paris she joined her mother, who brought her up as a Catholic.

Charles had known Minette when she was a small girl in Paris, but there was a gap of several years before he met her again in late

1659, on his way back to Brussels from Fuentarrabia. She was then fifteen, chestnut-haired, petite, coquettish. In the ten days they spent together, they became extremely close, with the intensity that sometimes defines the relationships of long-separated siblings, a sense of recognition, almost as if they shared a part of the same self. From then on, they wrote to each other more openly than to anyone else, and Charles showed all the protective affection of an elder brother, giving her presents and fighting her corner in the intense quarrels of the French court. In 1660 Minette became engaged to Louis XIV's brother, the temperamental, bisexual Philippe, duc d'Orléans, and the marriage was due to take place on her return from England. As Louis's brother the duke was given the courtesy title 'Monsieur'; after her marriage Minette would be 'Madame'.

In January 1661, she and Henrietta Maria sailed from Portsmouth, making a calm, slow start with 'little wind, very smooth water'. But Minette then fell ill and her ship returned to port. The great fear was that this was yet another onslaught of smallpox, but it turned out to be measles. Although that was serious enough in those times, after a few days she and her mother set sail again. This time their crossing was untroubled. 'The Princess was weak,' wrote Sir John Lawson in his journal when they arrived in France, 'yet had been very cheery all the way in her passage over.'[20]

Yet despite the relief of Minette's recovery, the New Year was darkened for Charles. The glitter of his return had dulled. Although he was still sure that the major political problems could be resolved, and was caught up in the passionate throes of his own affair with Barbara, everywhere, even in his family and his household, he felt the threat of trouble and death.

7 Blood and Banners

You are now to enquire of blood, of Royal blood, of sacred blood,
blood like that of the saints . . . this blood cries for vengeance and it
will never be appeased without a bloody sacrifice.
ORLANDO BRIDGEMAN's instruction to the jury at the trial of the
regicides

THE DEATHS IN CHARLES'S OWN FAMILY coincided with the
violent ends of some of the men who had condemned his father.
Charles had not wanted a bloody revenge. As soon as he landed, he
tried to cajole his parliament into passing an Act of Oblivion and
Indemnity as quickly as possible. This would offer a general pardon
for those who had opposed the crown, with the exception of the
regicides, the men who had signed his father's death warrant.
Fifteen of these were safely in the American colonies, or lying low in
Switzerland and Holland. But nineteen had surrendered immediately after the Declaration of Breda, having read the Declaration to
mean they would be pardoned if they gave themselves up within a
fortnight. Now they faced trial for treason. While they waited in
prison their fellows were rounded up and arrested.

The reactions differed greatly. Colonel Thomas Harrison awaited his arrest with calm, accepting that death would bring him face to
face with God. By contrast, Edmund Ludlow, who had hidden in
the alleys of London all summer, turned himself in and arranged
bail, but when he realised he faced execution, he escaped and fled,
eventually slipping away to exile in Geneva. The arrested men were
brought to London, paraded through the streets in irons and then
held in the Tower. Their families stayed in the capital all summer,
begging to see them and pleading their cause.

Many men connected with Cromwell's administration went into hiding. Among them was John Milton. In June parliament had ordered his arrest, and in August a royal proclamation called for two of his books to be burnt, the *Defence of the English People against Salmasius* and the *Eikonoklastes*. On the 30th of that month the public hangman flung these on the fire at the Old Bailey. Many influential intermediaries begged for clemency for the poet, including his old colleague Andrew Marvell, as well as the Secretary of State William Morice, Arthur Annesley, the Calvinist Earl of Anglesey, and Lady Ranelagh, sister to the Earl of Orrery and to Robert Boyle. In November, when Milton thought himself safe, he was imprisoned for a month, but released on payment of a fine of £150. But he wrote on despite his blindness and his political despair, working on *Paradise Lost*, his 'heavenly muse' still singing,

> . . . with mortal voice unchanged
> To hoarse or mute, though fallen on evil days,
> On evil days though fallen, and evil tongues;
> In darkness, and with dangers compassed round,
> And solitude.[1]

The two poets who had marched beside him behind Cromwell's bier took different courses under the new regime. Marvell became a dutiful, hard-working MP for Hull, an envoy to Russia, and later one of the government's most stinging critics, while Dryden turned into a court propagandist. Right at the start he tried to undo his blunder of writing 'Heroic Stanzas' to Cromwell by publishing his euphoric poem *Astraea Redux*. This welcomed the returning Charles as a second Augustus, celebrating a new Golden Age after the rule of the 'Rabble' in such reverent tones that a shocked Samuel Johnson found it positively sacrilegious:

> How shall I speak of that triumphant Day
> When you renewed th' expiring Pomp of May? . . .
> That star that at your birth shone out so bright
> It stained the duller sun's meridian light,

Did once again its potent fires renew,
Guiding our eyes to find and worship you.[2]

In *Astraea Redux* Dryden showed a belief in a guiding Providence, and a respect for monarchy that he would retain all his life. But he also noted the human frailty of the king, trusting – in slightly warning tones – that he had learned from his exile:

Inured to suffer ere he came to raigne
No rash procedure will his actions stain.

Dryden's swerve was far from unusual and his shift in allegiance illustrates very clearly how the mixed traditions of the Interregnum and Restoration could blend together. Short and squat (his friends called him 'Squab') with a piercing intellect and self-assured manner, Dryden was the eldest of fourteen children from a land-owning puritan family in Northamptonshire. His cousin, Sir Gilbert Pickering, was one of the judges at the trial of Charles I (although he did not sign the death warrant) and he later became Cromwell's Lord Chamberlain. As a counter to this, Dryden absorbed the classics at Westminster under the brilliant, firmly royalist headmaster John Busby. The clashes continued.[3] After Trinity College, Cambridge, he worked for the Commonwealth civil service, yet one of his closest friends was Sir Robert Howard, a son of the Earl of Berkshire. After the Restoration they shared a house, and in 1663 Dryden would marry Howard's sister Elizabeth. Setting his mind on court favour, Dryden would write a 'Panegyrick' on the Coronation, and New Year verses to Hyde, who helped to wring a dowry for Elizabeth from the king, late in payment but still an important court link.

Dryden's cousin Gilbert Pickering was one of the men excepted from pardon in the Act of Oblivion, although he escaped execution. But while Cromwellians shuddered, the royalist-packed Commons and Lords attacked the Act as a sign of weakness on the part of the crown. The net of exceptions should be spread wider, they argued. All who had dealt with public money must be brought to account and all who held public office should take oaths of allegiance and supremacy. As they fought against the too-lenient act, MPs constantly tried to add names to the list of exceptions. The debates were loud and heated and in addition, the two houses disagreed: more than once a man pardoned by the Commons was rejected by the Lords and vice versa. And even when a man's name was removed from the dread list, the Commons could still decide if he should keep his lands or lose everything.

Charles's speeches to the Lords and Commons became increasingly impatient, stressing the need for the speedy passing of the act as an essential foundation to domestic security. He begged his supporters to put aside personal grudges and animosities. Once or twice, through Clarendon, he intervened specifically in rows between the two houses. He promised, for eample, that the republican general John Lambert and the politician Sir Henry Vane, both sentenced to death by the Lords, should be reprieved, as the Commons wished, because they had not been present at his father's trial. Vane, however, conducted such a brilliant defence that Charles allegedly thought it was too dangerous to let him live: he was eventually executed on Tower Hill in June 1662. Lambert's fate was almost worse, incarcerated for a quarter of a century in island gaols, until his sanity collapsed.

Charles's speeches were doubtless drafted by Clarendon, but they reflected his own desire. He knew he could leave it to parliament to obtain a bloody revenge, leaving his own hands relatively clean. But he disliked bloodshed and politically, in purely pragmatic terms, he was wary of creating martyrs. Mercy and indulgence, he insisted, would make his opponents 'good subjects to me, and good friends and neighbours to you and we have then all our end, and you shall find this the securest expedient to prevent future mischief'.[4] It took three months to get the Act of Free and General Pardon, Indemnity and Oblivion through. When it was passed, on 29 August 1660, the

Speaker of the House presented the list of exceptions with this warning: 'We deal not with men, but monsters, guilty of blood, precious blood, royal blood, never to be remembered without tears.'[5]

In October the first defendants appeared at the Old Bailey. The procedure at their trials was fair, but the odds were stacked. The judges and prosecutors had already met in secret sessions, allegedly to decide on procedure but actually to prepare the indictments so that they could not be questioned by the defence: the accused were not charged with murdering the king but with 'compassing and imagining' his death.[6] The jury were vetted for their loyalty and the judges were royal appointments. Among them was the newly ennobled Earl of Sandwich, sitting in silence as men who had been his fellow soldiers in the field were brought into the court, to face almost certain death.

Within a week several of those on trial were convicted, and sentenced to be hanged, drawn and quartered: the sleds carrying the condemned men to Tyburn passed near to Milton's house in Holborn. The first to die was Colonel Harrison, trusting in the God who had protected him so often in battle: 'By God I have leapt over a wall, by God I have run through a troop, and by God I will go through this death and he will make it easy for me.'[7] As he came to the scaffold the crowd booed and jeered, 'Where is your Good Old Cause now?' Harrison replied calmly: 'Here in my bosom, and I shall seal it with my blood.' The spectacle did not end with Harrison's hanging. Cut down semi-conscious, he lay on the scaffold, and the executioner ripped out his bowels with hot tongs, cut out his heart and displayed it to the crowd before he threw it into a bucket. Then he hacked Harrison's head off and showed this too to the mob. Finally his body was quartered with a cleaver, and the parts carried off to be displayed on the gatehouses of the city.

Each of the eight men executed over the next few days received the same treatment. Royalists exulted. 'I saw not their execution,' wrote the sober scholar John Evelyn, 'but met their quarters, mangld & cutt & reaking as they were brought from the Gallows in baskets on the hurdle: o miraculous Providence of God.'[8] But after a fortnight of such scenes, many in the crowd around the scaffold were expressing admiration for the brave speeches of the condemned rather than cheering for the king, and the sober citizens of London were retching at the stench of their burning bowels. This was enough.

The execution of the regicides, October 1660

The remaining regicides were held in prison over the winter, still officially under sentence of death. Others would soon join them. In December the Marquess of Argyll appeared suddenly in Whitehall, gaunt and ruined. Charles refused to see him. He was taken to the Tower and in the spring of 1661 he was sent to Edinburgh to face trial and although it was hard to prove his involvement in the regicide, or to justify the accusation that his activities in the 1650s amounted to treason, Argyll was found guilty, and beheaded in May 1661. His head was placed on the same spike on which he had impaled the skull of Montrose.

Over the next two years Clarendon's men hunted down others, pursuing them across Europe and America, either dragging them back to trial or employing men to murder them abroad. Charles, however, was against such dirty tricks. Clarendon told Sir George Downing, the ex-Cromwellian now hounding his old colleagues in Holland, that he did not think the king would ever give instructions to have the regicides assassinated, such a measure being against his dignity as a king and a gentleman.

Not all who were captured were charged and tried: in defiance of Magna Carta, some were sent to Jersey or the Isle of Man, technically outside the jurisdiction, where Habeas Corpus did not apply. But the cry for vengeance still rang out. One refugee to the continent was old Sir Archibald Johnston of Wariston, one of the original signatories of the Scottish covenant. In January 1663 he was arrested in Rouen, brought to England (kidnapped, said his supporters) and imprisoned in the Tower. That June he was sent up to Edinburgh, so broken in body and mind that he could not recognise his own children: it seemed unnecessary and cruel to execute him. With his customary ferocity, Lauderdale described how the Scots Commissioners heard 'a petition from that wretches children showing that he has lost his memorie & almost his sence & praying for delay till he may be in a fitter condition to dye'.[9] Charles refused to show mercy and Wariston was executed in Edinburgh on a gallows of 'extraordinary height'. His young nephew, the writer Gilbert Burnet, later Bishop of Salisbury, walked with his uncle to the scaffold.

In the winter after the first executions angry mutterings were heard. On 16 December, secretary Nicholas wrote to the Sheriff of Wiltshire, at Charles's command, saying that they had intelligence that 'several Persons of looss Principles and of known disaffection to Us and Our government have furnished themselves with such quantities of Arms and Munitions as may justly give suspicion that it is designed to disturb the peace and tranquillity of this Our Kingdom'.[10] The Sheriff should raise searches and take action to safeguard the

peace, and 'use all possible diligence to prevent any tumults, insurrections or mutinous and unlawful meetings'. This was a false alarm,
but the government were jittery. They reacted sharply when another
crisis seemed to threaten in London itself. On the feast of Epiphany,
6 January 1661, a small group of 'enthusiasts' of the Fifth
Monarchist sect, led by the wine cooper Thomas Venner, marched
through London crying 'No King but Christ', vowing to keep their
swords unsheathed until Christ's kingdom should triumph and
worldly powers be reduced to a 'hissing and a curse'. They spread
alarm through the streets for three days, fighting off the City's
trained bands, until they were finally beaten at Cripplegate and fled
into hiding at Kenwood, near Highgate. When Charles heard the
news, as he was saying goodbye to his mother and sister at
Portsmouth, he dashed back to Whitehall. Gradually the would-be
rebels were rounded up and fifteen ringleaders hanged.

Even as they hung in the wind the royalists bayed for still more
blood. Charles, they said, had been too soft on his enemies. Calls
for the deaths of more of the regicides grew louder, accompanied by
a symbolic vengeance as ghoulish and theatrical as the trials and
executions. One article of the Act of Oblivion had made the Act
retrospective so that the list of 'exceptions' could include four dead
men: Oliver Cromwell, Colonel Henry Ireton, John Bradshawe
(chief judge at the trial of Charles I) and Thomas Pride, purger of
the Long Parliament. In late January their graves were dug up. On
the anniversary of Charles I's death, 30 January 1661, while the
clergy offered prayers for the king in churches across the land, the
coffins were taken to the Red Lion inn in Holborn. Carters then carried the rotting bodies in their shrouds to the Old Bailey and
propped them up limply against the bar, so that the judge could pronounce the death sentence for traitors. Then they were dragged on
sledges through the streets, and hanged unceremoniously at
Tyburn. At sunset the dangling corpses were taken down, their
heads cut off and their bodies flung into a pit beneath the gallows.
The crowd was vast. The heads of Cromwell, Ireton, and Bradshawe

were stuck on poles above Westminster Hall, alongside the crow-pecked skulls of Thomas Harrison and John Cooke. (A fortnight later, it was rumoured, wrongly, that 'Cromwell's head is stolen away since it was set up'.[11])

In the weeks that followed, this lynching of the dead continued. Parliamentary leaders, colonels, admirals, preachers, teachers, even Cromwell's mother and daughter were disinterred. Once the mob had hooted at the bodies, gravediggers threw the remains into a large pit in St Margaret's Westminster.

These deaths, real and symbolic, were part of the spectacle of London. The Dutch painter William Schellinks, being shown around the town by Huguenot merchant friends established in London, went to see the lions in the Tower and the minting of the new money there, attended the playhouse and watched the king dine in public. But he also watched a woman burned alive for stabbing her husband with a tobacco pipe, and on 6 February 1662, he made careful notes of the punishment of three men who had attended the trial of Charles I, but were spared execution because they did not sign the death warrant. 'We walked with thousands of people to Tyburn,' Schellinks wrote,

and saw there Lord Monson, Sir Henry Mildmay and Mr Wallop lying in their tabards on a little straw on a hurdle being dragged through under the gallows, where some articles were read to them and then torn up. After that they were again dragged through the town back to the Tower. Their sentence is that they are to be dragged through under the gallows on this day every year.[12]

The executions and ritual punishments confirmed the king's power as arbiter of vengeance and dispenser of mercy. But he also had to re-establish the royal glamour. The year before, the Marquess of Newcastle had written at extreme length, advising Charles on how this should be done. Newcastle looked back to tradition and Tudor power: a king must control the militia, win over the City, be a firm head of the Church, restrict the press, curb the universities and squash the lawyers. He should sweeten the pill with royal grandeur, fairs and feast-days: bread and circuses. 'Ceremony though it is nothing in itself', wrote Newcastle, 'yet it doth everything – for what is a king, more than a subject, but for ceremony and order. When that fails him, he's ruined.'[13] What preserves kings more than ceremony? he asked:

The cloth of estates, the distance people are with you, great officers, heralds, drums, trumpeters, rich coaches, rich furniture for horses, guards, martialls men making room, disorders to be labored by their staff of office and cry 'now the king comes' . . . even the wisest though he knew it and was accustomed to it, shall shake off his wisdome and shake for fear of it . . . you cannot put upon you too much king.[14]

Charles took heed. In early April 1661, while elections were being held for the new parliament, in a glorious three-day ceremony at Windsor Castle he formally installed all the Knights of the Garter created in the past twenty years. The records of the knights had been held and updated, in his father's day, by Matthew Wren, as Dean of Windsor, and then, when he became Bishop of Ely, by his younger brother Dean Christopher Wren. But the dean's house was ransacked by parliamentary forces and the Garter papers stolen and he worked painstakingly to recover the records until his death in 1658. They were returned to Charles II by his son, the future architect of St Paul's, Christopher Wren, on 11 August 1660. Their return was a key moment of restoration, in all senses, and the beginning of a lifelong association between Charles and Wren.[15]

A week after the Garter ceremony, Charles created new Knights of the Bath in Westminster Hall.[16] His nobles, many already impoverished, had to buy expensive new robes, like the Duke of Hamilton's carefully listed outfit:

1 pair of silk trousers, 1 pair of trunk breeches and doublet of silver tabby with silver lace, silver and white satin ribbon and three of knots of the same ribbon and a pair of shoes: a surtout of crimson velvet lined with white taffeta with hood, sword, scabbard and belt of the same.[17]

Having cemented relations with the nobility, Charles played to the masses. At Easter, he had performed the humble Maundy Thursday task of washing the feet of paupers at Whitehall. And on the day before his coronation, which was planned for 23 April – St George's Day – he revived the old tradition of the Coronation Eve cavalcade, carrying the monarch from the Tower to Westminster. He was acutely aware of the importance of playing to English monarchical traditions, tying him to earlier glories like the magnificent processions of Elizabeth I, and the route was designed by John Ogilby as a virtual parade of propaganda.

When the day came, Charles travelled by royal barge from Whitehall to the Tower, where he was greeted at eight in the morning by the Knights of the Bath. It was a full day, from dawn to dusk, for the king and for many Londoners. 'Up early,' wrote Pepys, 'and made myself as fine as I could, and put on my velvet coat, the first day that I put it on, though made half a year ago.'[18] With his colleagues from the Navy Office, Pepys and his wife Elizabeth went to a flag-maker's in Cornhill where they took over a room 'with wine and good cake, and saw the show very well'. And a fine show it was: knights and squires, barons and bishops, soldiers all in white, and even a company dressed as Turks. The streets were railed and gravelled, keeping the crowds at a respectful distance as the king rode by. He wore his plumed hat, while the Duke of York in front and Monck behind both rode bareheaded. Charles thrilled the people by singling out individuals in the throng, mingling state with the common touch. The houses along the route were hung with banners and rich carpets, and the ladies leaned out of their windows. 'So glorious was the show with gold and silver, that we were not able to look at it, our eyes at last being so much overcome.'

The heavy dose of gold and glory came at a cost. 'The City, upon this occasion,' wrote one pamphleteer, 'was at a very *great Expence*, to which, as it was understood, they were obliged by their *Charter*.'[19] The dirty streets of the city were transformed into a grand stage set and the aldermen and companies paid £10,000 for four triumphal arches a hundred feet high – imitating the Romans, said Ogilby. The themes were appropriate: 'The King's Happy Arrival' in Leadenhall

Street, a naval display at the Royal Exchange, a Temple of Concord in Cheapside and and an optimistic Garden of Plenty in Fleet Street.²⁰ The slogans used, however, also reminded the king that this great Restoration was dependent on the will of the people. *Unitas*, they declared, *Pater Patriae* and *Mens Omnibus Una*. Players performed long pageants at each arch. At St Paul's the pupils of Christ's Hospital stood on a scaffold while a boy delivered a speech. At one impromptu stop, like a good opportunist politician, Charles allegedly stopped at a tavern to kiss a newborn infant.

Next morning, the foreign ambassadors and British nobles and the lucky civil servants with a place in Westminster Abbey rose early, putting on their finery at dawn. Once in their seats, they settled

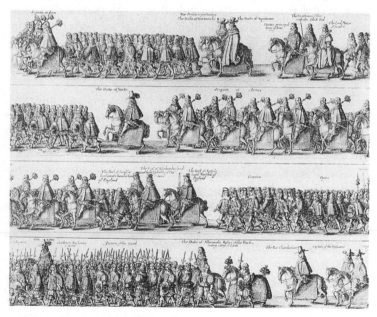

Hollar's frieze ran across the pages of John Ogilby's *Entertainment of Charles II, in his Passage Through the City of London to his Coronation*, 1662. It shows Sergeants at Arms preceding the dukes of Normandy and Aquitaine, followed by Black Rod and the Lord Mayor. The next group includes the Lord Chamberlain and Lord Marshal and finally, after a phalanx of footmen and pages, comes the king (bottom left), with Monck riding behind as Master of Horse.

down to wait, admiring the rich blue carpet that stretched from end to end of the abbey. The details of the ceremony had been planned for months, by the Garter King of Arms, Sir Edward Walker. At eleven Charles entered, his head bare but his garments a mass of crimson and gold and ermine. One problem that had faced the organisers was that the coronation regalia had been melted down during the Commonwealth, including the royal crown of St Edward. The goldsmith Sir Robert Vyner replaced everything exactly as it had been, at a cost of £30,000.[21] From the abbey door the new regalia was carried before the king, Ormond bearing the crown, Albemarle the sceptre, Buckingham the orb and Lord Shrewsbury the sword. These were laid on the altar and then the barons of the Cinque Ports – Buckingham and Albemarle again, with Lord Berkshire and Lord Sandwich – held a cloth of gold over Charles for his anointing. When the Archbishop of Canterbury placed the crown on Charles's head a great shout swelled through the abbey. The nobles filed up to swear their loyalty, 'and a Generall Pardon was read out by the Lord Chancellor, and medals flung up and down by my Lord Cornwallis, of silver'. Those medals looked back to the miraculous escape from Worcester. They showed an oak in full leaf, with the motto *Iam Florescit*, 'Now it flourishes'.

More ceremonies followed, but by now Pepys, who had got to the abbey soon after four, desperately needed to piss, so he sneaked out and across to Westminster Hall. There, in the great space where Charles I had faced his accusers at his trial, he saw the women (including his wife Elizabeth) waiting on specially built scaffolds. When the king arrived he sat at the high table, and lords carried the opening course up to him on horseback. Between courses, Sir Edward Dymock, 'the King's Champion', rode in 'on a goodly white Courser', fully armed, with a plume of blue feathers in his helmet. To the blast of trumpets he vowed to 'adventure his life against any who denies the king'. Then, riding slowly on, he threw down his gauntlet and paused, reining in his horse. Three times he repeated his challenge, but no one came forward.

This engraving of the coronation shows two moments. In the middle distance the Archbishop places the crown on the king's head, as the great cry echoes round the Abbey from the nobles seated in their ranks. In the foreground, Charles is enthroned on the dais.

There was music, feasting and drinking, and a satisfying scuffle over a canopy between the royal footmen and the barons of the Cinque Ports. After a month of downpours, prompting prophecies of mud, sodden cloaks and ermine trailing in puddles, the sun had shone all day: 'not one drop of raine, falling in all this time,' wrote one loyal chronicler, 'as very much had done at least ten days before'.[22] Then around six in the evening, thunder rattled, lightning flashed and the rain came down – the omens for the new reign could be read both ways. Edmund Ludlow was one who felt sure the storm signalled the wrath of the Lord at the destruction of his work. Before the meal was half ended, he wrote, 'this mock king was enforced to rise and run away'. While his supporters read this as an expression of heavenly joy, Ludlow thought that 'others, more understanding in the dispensations of the Lord':

supposed it rather a testimony from heaven against the wickedness of those that would not only that he should rule over them, but were willing to make them a captaine to leade them into Egiptian bondage; from which the Lord by his providence plainly spake his desire to have delivered them.[23]

Although the fireworks were cancelled Pepys noted that the city still 'had a light like a glory round it, with bonefyres'. He and Elizabeth went to Axe-yard, where there were three great fires 'and a great many great gallants, men and women' who made them kneel and drink the king's health, 'Which we thought a strange Frolique. But these gallants continued thus a great while, and I wondered to see how the ladies did tipple.'[24] At last Pepys sent the women home and went on to another friend, who held the post of Yeoman of the King's Wine-cellar. They drank the king's health 'till one of the gentlemen fell down stark drunk and lay there spewing'. Pepys staggered to sleep at Sandwich's house, waking to find that he was spewing too. 'Thus did the day end with joy everywhere.'

The coronation that began with prayers in the abbey ended with drunks in the gutter. But Charles was safely crowned. He had established his power in relation to parliament, disbanded a hostile army, wreaked vengeance on his father's killers and established a public image of mystery and glamour. The awe he inspired was offset by his affability, and – so far – only slightly undermined by the wildness of his court. The celebrations continued, with smaller tributes, like the presentation of Evelyn's 'Panegyric to Charles the Second'. According to Lord Mordaunt Charles asked warily if this was in Latin and 'hoped it would not be very long'.[25]

When the new Cavalier Parliament opened in May, Charles took his seat in Westminster Hall in full regalia, wearing his heavy crown, surrounded by his officers of state, with the lords and bishops in their places. Then he summoned the members of the Commons, who rushed into the Upper House, standing behind their Speaker at the bar, to hear the royal address. The MPs Charles faced were even more fiercely royalist than the Convention Parliament that had greeted his return. They were largely the sons of country gentry, and many were also staggeringly young. When this was pointed out to Charles he allegedly declared, 'What matter, I will keep them till they grow beards' – which he did, for the parliament was not formally dissolved until eighteen years later, in 1679. The arguments about the Act of Indemnity still rumbled on, and Andrew Marvell reported to the Hull Corporation that he feared the debates would never end. 'But his Majesty is most fixedly honorable & true to that business as in all things else so that by Gods blessing I hope we shall arrive at an happy period in it. Otherwise we shall be broken against that rock.'[26]

A month after the coronation, the date of 29 May, Charles's birthday and the day he had entered London in 1660, was set aside as a perpetual holiday: 'The anniversary of His Majesty's most Joyful Restitution of the Crown of England'. The chaplain Peter Heylyn preached to a packed chapel in Westminster, reminding them how Charles had been pursued for years across the continent 'like a partridge by a falcon', and had returned to his country 'not with an Army to besiege it, to smite it with the edge of a sword, but as a Prince of Peace, or the Son of David'.[27]

Two months later, the youthful parliament put forward a bill for the execution of nineteen more regicides. Charles could not be seen to pardon them, but he wanted no more bloodshed. Clarendon, as so often, thought of the solution: the Bill 'should sleep in the houses' and not be brought to the king for his consent. Charles agreed. 'I must confess,' he scrawled, 'that I am weary of hanging except upon new offences.'

'After this business is settled,' suggested Clarendon, 'shall I mooue it heare? That wee may take care that it comes not to you?'

'By all meanes,' Charles replied, 'for you know that I cannot pardon them.'[28]

8 Whitehall

WHEN CHARLES ARRIVED, he planned to transform the dilapidated
palace at Whitehall into a royal residence that would rival the
Louvre and the Escorial. But Whitehall defeated him. This palace
with its shadowy corridors and hidden stairs was almost a character
in his story, shaping his life.

Driving from the City, down the Strand, past the new square of
Covent Garden and the streets stretching up to Holborn and St
Giles, coaches swooped around the corner at Charing Cross,
straight into the long paved space that led to the jumble of
Whitehall. On the northern side a long wall, built by Cromwell, hid
the trees of the park and the sheds the Protector had built for his
troops, which now housed the Royal Horse Guards. On the river
side, behind a row of Elizabethan buildings, the spaces of Scotland
Yard rambled down to the wharves, a clutter of timber yards and
cider-press houses, heaps of coal and timber, bricks and tiles. Here
lay the offices of the Lord Steward's department and the busy Office
of Works.

Next came the Great Gate, giving a glimpse into the courtyard
behind, and then the Banqueting House where Charles I had met
his fate. Past this, the road squeezed beneath the Holbein Gateway.
Designed by Hans Holbein for Henry VIII, the gate arched over
passers-by like a misplaced Tudor castle, crowned with red-brick
turrets. Then the paved way narrowed until it ducked through a
second gate. This short stretch was King Street, or 'The Street', the

main highway through the maze of Whitehall. Carts clattered over the cobbles, and the gables of inns hung over the way. A web of alleys led off into small courts and gardens – Gardiner's Court, Cherry Tree Court, Bowman's Lane – and the grander lodgings of courtiers squeezed next to ordinary houses.

Whitehall was less a palace than a sprawl of separate buildings, a royal village, with tiled roofs and thatched roofs, paving and cobbles, and as many rats as the tenements nearby. A narrow public right of way snaked behind the Banqueting House, across the Great Court and between the palace buildings to the river, where boatmen waited for their fares at the wooden landing stage of Whitehall Stairs. Just upstream a long jetty with a gallery above, called a 'bridge', ran out into the Thames so that the royal family and their courtiers could enter their barges, whatever the tide. Standing on the bridge, gazing downriver, Charles could see the heavy, greenish waters of the Thames curving round the bend, sucking at the walls and watergates of the old mansions – Arundel House, Worcester House, Somerset House – flowing on until it rushed under the arches of London Bridge, hidden from view.

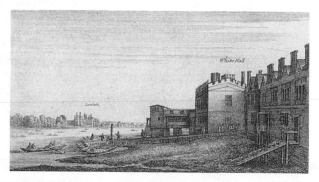

Whitehall stairs, looking upriver to Lambeth on the opposite bank, with the sloping public landing-stage and the covered royal 'bridge' beyond.

The place was a mess, a mix of styles, from the elegant Renaissance Banqueting Hall to old timbered gables and Dutch-style hipped roofs. Over the years courtiers had built rooms and apartments, higgledy-piggledy, clustering like barnacles along the side of the long Privy Gallery that ran from the road to the river and filling up the corners of the squares. One of Charles's first acts was to divide the buildings around the Cockpit, across King Street on the western side of Whitehall, known as 'the Parkside', into yet more lodgings. Albemarle was given the Cockpit itself and the buildings next to it, and Ormond the Tiltyard Gallery and neighbouring houses. When Wren commissioned the mathematician Ralph Greatorex to do a survey in 1670, he found that fifteen hundred rooms were available for courtiers, rented out to around a hundred different people.[1]

The royal apartments were a warren in themselves. Facing the river, they were traditionally reached by crossing the courtyard from the Great Gate and then progressing through rooms that marked increasing stages of intimacy, from Great Chamber to Presence Chamber, to Privy Chamber, and then to smaller rooms like the 'Lords' Chamber and Vane room (where James I had installed a weather vane on the roof, linked to a system that showed the wind direction from inside). Then the route turned right into the King's Bedchamber – this was the most private space, but even so it was often crowded. The habit had grown up, however, of reaching the Bedchamber by taking a shortcut from the stairs into St James's Park, and walking down the long, covered Privy Gallery that stretched across from the Holbein Gate. So the Bedchamber was under attack, as it were, from both sides.

In France, the royal bedchamber was a key space in court life, even a place to receive ambassadors, and in 1660 Charles raised the Whitehall Bedchamber to similar status. He had the room decorated to resemble that in the Louvre, with the bed with its crimson damask covers set in a special alcove, separated from the rest of the room by a gilded railing with two gates for access and framed with 'two great draperyes with two flying boyes in them'.[2] The panelling above the chimney had moulded columns, the floor

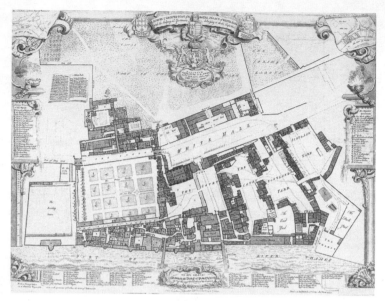

George Vertue's engraving of the 1670 plan of Whitehall

copied French marquetry, the walls were draped with hangings. The artist John Michael Wright painted a grand allegorical scene for the ceiling, showing Astraea, daughter of Zeus and embodiment of justice, returning to earth to bring a new Golden Age – with Charles himself floating in the clouds, and cherubs supporting a flying oak tree.

Next to the Bedchamber were four smaller rooms, including a dressing room and a cabinet or closet, the inner sanctum that no one could enter without permission, where Charles kept his favourite paintings. (John Evelyn took some of his relations to court in October 1660 to see these rarities, which included miniatures by Peter Oliver, copying Raphael, Titian and other masters, fine cameos and intaglios, tapestries and books.) But the official Bedchamber was clearly no comfortable place for actual sleep, or for any privacy at all, with diplomats and petitioners arriving while you were dressing, so in 1662 Charles created a new, private bed-

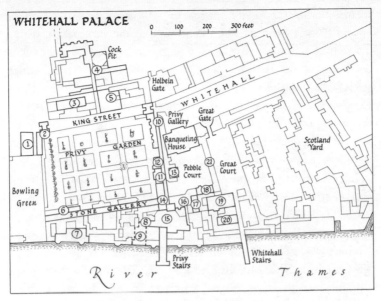

WHITEHALL PALACE, apartments and state rooms: 1 Castlemaine 1660–3,
2 Sandwich, 3 Tennis Court, 4 Albemarle, 5 Monmouth, 6 Prince Rupert,
7 Duke of York, 8 King's Bedchamber, 1663, 9 Volary Buildings, 1667,
10 Castlemaine, 1663–8, 11 King's Bedchamber 1660–3, 12 Bathroom and
Laboratory (below), 13 Council Chamber (above) 14 Vane Room, 15 Queen's
apartments, 16 Privy Chamber, 17 Presence Chamber, 18 Guard Chamber,
19 Great Hall, 20 Chapel, 21 New Gallery, 1669.

room in the 'Turk's Gallery' overlooking the river. This was a long,
draughty walk from his other great luxury, his bathroom beneath
the Privy Gallery, with its tiled floor and sunken bath, filled with
water heated in a copper in a small room next door. He had this
thoroughly overhauled in 1663, with new panelling, carving and
curtains and a painting over the chimney, as well as a little palisade
in the Privy Garden to stop people peering in. It even had hangings
of crimson Genoa damask, and a small feather bed.[3]

From the cluster of royal rooms the Stone Gallery stretched
towards Westminster, with another above, known as the 'matted
gallery'. At the far end of this, overlooking the river, lay the apart-

ments of James, Duke of York, and opposite were those of Charles's cousin Rupert, who had been honoured at the Restoration with a pension of £6,000 a year and lodgings in the palace. Rupert's windows looked out onto the great space of the Privy Garden, which stretched up to the street. (The one person Charles did not find a London home for was Rupert's mother, Elizabeth of Bohemia, who arrived in 1661. Instead she moved into the house belonging to Sir William Craven, who had been her loyal companion in the Hague for many years, and was secretly rumoured to be her husband.)

In every courtyard and gallery, in corners and up staircases, were smaller rooms, perfect for secret meetings. The architecture, as the historian Ronald Hutton has put it, 'was admirably suited to Charles's style of kingship, at once very open and very devious'.[4] Nothing could be more different from Versailles.

Everything was shabby, having been neglected during the Commonwealth even though Cromwell had used the palace for his base. A hasty, but expensive, redecoration began before Charles set sail: by June the royal apartments had already soaked up £1,200 worth of refurbishments. But to begin with – even though he planned to sweep it away – Charles loved its chaotic informality, and rarely spent a night away. It took him back to the world of his childhood and youth, although it was not the place of his birth – that had taken place a few minutes away at St James's Palace, a quieter spot altogether, set among the green, leafy surroundings of the park. But as a boy, Charles had watched the players gathering for the masques under the painted ceiling of the Banqueting House. He had played in the Privy Garden and on the Bowling Green with his brothers and sisters, Mary, James, Elizabeth and Henry. Only Minette had not known Whitehall. Before the war these royal childhoods had been happy, with winters at St James's and summers moving from one royal palace to another: Greenwich, Oatlands, Hampton Court. And when Van Dyck painted the children in 1637, Charles I had taken the great canvas to Whitehall and hung it above the table in his breakfast chamber.

In the dignified, ceremonial days of Charles I, access to Whitehall was carefully controlled. But his son opened the palace to all. Anyone could wander through the Great Gate, although porters stopped 'those who pressed with rudeness or disorder, carried unfit weapons, divines not wearing their robes and those of inferior quality who came muffled, masqued or otherwise disguised'.[5] And because people now often approached the palace from the park, Charles also built a grand outside staircase on that side.

In the early years he handed out keys like sweets: 150 double keys, for entry to the ordinary rooms, were cut by the royal locksmith in 1661, and at least ten treble keys, opening the state rooms and the King's Bedchamber.[6] Outside these inner sanctums, it was easy to stage casual meetings in the crowded corridors: well-connected members of London's great companies hovered here, listening for news and cornering those who might forward their aims. Charles hoped that such easy access would make people of all views feel they might reach him, preventing conspiracies and hardening of discontent. By the end of 1661 however, it was clear that this was not the case, and he gradually grew more circumspect, rearranging the rooms and making it more difficult to reach him.

When he thought of redesigning Whitehall, Charles remembered the great buildings he had seen abroad, particularly the Louvre, a model of an urban riverside palace, regular in plan and formal in style. Almost straight away the architect John Webb, the nephew and former assistant of Inigo Jones, presented him with plans that involved demolishing all the old buildings except the Banqueting House. As his surveyor, Charles appointed Sir John Denham, well known as poet, playwright and gambler, and a busy courier for the exiled court in Paris, but hitherto no architect. Beneath him worked ranks of officials, from the comptroller to the master carpenter, down to mason, glazier and wood carver.

Every morning the officers met in Scotland Yard to decide on work for the day. The labourers had to turn up when the bell rang, and set to work, with half an hour for breakfast. Much of Whitehall was a perpetual building site, with ropes and bricks, scaffolding and tubs and half-built walls. Like all Charles's offices the 'King's Works' was always strapped for cash, and every year they ran over their budgets, both the 'ordinary' allowance, set at £10,000 in 1663 for regular maintenance, and the 'extraordinary' allowance for new building projects.[7] Loans were raised against various tallies and taxes, but the cash arrived in 'driblets' and craftsmen and workmen were owed large sums, sometimes for years. Within a year, partly because of lack of money and partly because of the difficulty of moving all the courtiers from their various apartments, Charles abandoned his plans and set Webb to work instead on ideas for a new palace in Greenwich.[8] The rambling corridors and galleries of Whitehall remained unredeemed. The walls were covered with tapestries and hangings but still the wind whistled round corners and made the candles splutter. When it rained, the yards were full of mud and puddles, and in stormy weather, when the tide was high, the Thames lapped into the cellars and flooded the kitchens.

When people spoke of 'Whitehall', they could mean the place or its inhabitants, 'the court': high-ranking servants of the crown, families of dukes and earls, whose rank entitled them to a place within royal circles, or the King's own cronies, his companions in drinking and womanising, at the races and the theatre. But the court was also a great unwieldy structure of officials and servants, so elaborate that no one was very sure how it worked. Technically, it was divided between the 'Chamber' (the household 'above stairs') and the 'Household'. The Chamber was under the sway of the Lord Chamberlain, Edward Montagu, Lord Manchester, assisted by the vice-chamberlain, Sir George Carteret, who had played host to Charles in the early years of exile in the Channel Islands. Their staff was huge, almost nine hundred people, and they were responsible for ceremonial and security, and for all the state rooms – the Banqueting Hall, Great Hall, Presence Chamber and Privy Chamber, and the Chapel Royal.

The Household, meanwhile, dealt with the supply of services under Ormond, as Lord Steward. (Within it, there was also the separate department of the Bedchamber, the intimate servants of the king, which operated independently.) The Household was a profitable place for sharp financial spirits like Stephen Fox, who had looked after Charles's money in exile and was appointed clerk comptroller in 1660, in charge of the daily household expenses. Fox had joined the court twenty years ago when he was thirteen, and though he was only a servant, he had often played with Charles and James who were about the same age. In exile he had risen from page-boy to a Gentleman of Horse to Charles, taking over the accounts for the stables and organising the constant travel, (and lending money for his gambling debts). In 1661 he was given an additional role, as paymaster to the King's Guards, eventually solving the problem of their erratic pay by undertaking the loans himself so that they would be paid regularly, taking a shilling in the pound commission, which eventually made him very rich indeed.[9]

Beneath the high officials and organisers like Fox, whom Charles valued because he was easy-going and sweet-natured as well as efficient, the Household as a working institution encompassed about five hundred people. It was essential, Charles thought at first, to keep up the lavishly appointed life suitable to a king, as grand as his cousin, Louis XIV. And while he ridiculed the elaborate formality of the Spanish court, where, as he put it, the king 'doth nothing but under some ridiculous form or other; and will not piss but another must hold the chamber-pot',[10] he always travelled with an elaborate entourage. When Henrietta Maria and Minette visited England at the end of 1660, Charles dashed off a note asking Clarendon if he had time to visit Minette at Tunbridge Wells before parliament adjourned. The Chancellor reckoned he could: 'I suppose you will goe with a light Trayne?'

'I intend to take nothing but my night bag.'

'Yes,' scoffed Hyde, 'you will not go without 40 or 50 horse!'

'I counte that part of my night bag,' replied Charles.[11]

Many Household posts were sought for status, and paid for with hard cash. This was quite accepted and indeed it was rare not to pay. Fox pocketed a hefty sum from selling posts, and the lists of places sold by Ormond as Lord Steward show that he raked in well over £15,000.[12] Among the petitions which piled high, crinkling at the edges as the secretaries shuffled demands, were requests for positions with titles like something out of Arthurian romance: Yeoman of the Wood-yard, Elder Yeoman of the Slaughterhouse; Yeoman of the Confectionery, Brusher of the Robes, Comptroller of Tents and Revels. Sons and grandsons followed their forebears in the royal service as messengers, trumpeters, librarians, picture dealers, barge masters and watermen. Daughters and granddaughters also claimed their place on the grounds of loyalty to the royal cause. Joan Collins applied 'for the place of Turn-Broach in the Royal Kitchen, having lost a leg at the battle of Edgehill', while Bridget Rumney asked to be restored 'to the office of providing Flowers and Sweet Herbs for the Court, granted by the late King to herself and her late mother, who, with her own two sons, was slain at the battle of Naseby'.[13] A certificate notes that she was appointed 'Garnisher & Trimmer of the chapel, presence & privy lodgings'.

The cost of paying, feeding and housing such a staff was huge. Traditionally the whole court ate at about eighty communal 'tables' at the crown's expense. These were looked after by the Board of Greencloth who supervised about twenty departments, like the Kitchen Larder, Buttery and Pantry, and also oversaw 'Purveyance', the royal right to buy supplies at cost.[14] From time to time the amount of tables had been labelled an anachronistic magnificence, but Charles I had cast aside all attempts to restrict it. In 1660 all the court tables were fully revived, although the practice of purveyance was stopped, with the results that costs soared. Not that the food was good – courtiers familiar with the cuisine of France and the banquets of Italy lamented that English cooking was very dull, but it would be another century before sauces and ragouts transformed the much-vaunted 'English plain fare'. The royal chef Robert May, now in his early seventies, published his own cook-book praising national cookery, looking back nostalgically to the grand feasts of Henry VIII and Elizabeth I, with sides of beef and elaborate tarts and custards.[15] The only real changes were outside the court proper: the exotic fruits grown in the new Dutch glasshouses; the private suppers and French taverns where the meal was presented *à la française* with a whole array of dishes arriving at once; the coffee and chocolate in the coffee-houses and soon the arrival of tea.

Tradespeople also lined up for posts or presented ancient bills from the previous reign: clock- and watchmakers, printers, fishmongers, saddlers, tailors, upholsterers. Thomas Hooper applied to be 'combmaker to his majesty, as he has been to the last two late Kings', while Dr Robert Morison became botanical physician and chief herbalist, caring for the Privy Garden and the physic garden at St James's. His herbal medicines shared space with the pots and leeches of four other physicians, and a royal chirurgeon, or surgeon, as well as two apothecaries.

There were also posts for musicians, artists and the 'sculptor to his majesty'. Charles I had been a passionate art collector, sending emissaries around Europe and making great acquisitions, like the collection of the Gonzaga dukes of Mantua, a host of Raphaels, Titians, Caravaggios and Mantegnas at one swoop. After his execution, a series of sales had scattered these treasures but Charles II was determined to regain what he could. The process began before he set foot in Dover. On 9 May 1660, the day after the proclamation of the Restoration, the House of Lords set up a committee to collect information as to where the king's goods, jewels and pictures might be, and to advise on getting them back. The Commons was granted special powers of seizure, and an order was published that anyone possessing such goods should hand them to the Commons, on pain of forfeiture. By the time Charles arrived in Whitehall the walls were no longer bare.

The remaining empty niches and faded patches where large

canvases had hung were partly filled by the works he brought with him from Europe. He had bought some paintings of his own while he was in exile but these were trebled by the 'Dutch Gift', organised by the Anglophile connoisseur Constantijn Huygens at the Restoration. Together with a rich bed of state, this was a present from the Dutch Republic, anxious to atone for earlier rudeness. The works of art, largely acquired from the collection of the Reynst brothers in Amsterdam, included twelve antique sculptures, twenty-four Italian paintings – one of them a superb Titian – and several modern Dutch scenes. When the collection arrived it was exhibited in the Banqueting House and when Charles paid a formal visit to view it, he was clearly delighted.

Charles needed someone he could trust to take charge of the staggering trove of pictures and he turned, without hesitation, to Thomas Chiffinch. Old enough to be his father, Chiffinch had been attached to his service since Charles was fourteen, and had taken his young family abroad during the exile. On his return, he was made Keeper of the King's Jewels, while his wife became laundress and seamstress to the king. Charles and Chiffinch puzzled hard, consulting John Evelyn, as to exactly where all these priceless works of art should be placed to provide a suitably awe-inspiring and magnificent display, to impress foreign princes. Chiffinch was well rewarded, and by 1663 shared the post of receiver-general of all the plantations in Africa and America.

But the hunting for the lost artworks still went on. Emanuel de Critz, the former Serjeant-Painter, reckoned he had spent £900 in rescuing from Parliament 'the incomparable statue of the late King by Bernino and £300 more to buy in statues, pictures etc now in his majesty's possession'.[16] As 'Master of Our Great Wardrobe', Sandwich was responsible for collecting the goods when Charles issued a proclamation to try and recover royal property. This claimed that:

during the manifold Disorders of the late time – much Plate, Jewels, household-stuff, Cabinets, Statues, Inscriptions, pictures, Drawings, Sculptures,

Rugs, Stones, ancient Coyns, Medals, books, Manuscripts, Pieces of Art and the goods and chattels which did belong unto our late dear father, our Mother the Queen or to Our Self have been purloined and embezilled, dispersed, detained and conceald.[17]

In his 'Princely Clemency and care to prevent suits and prosecutions', the notice declared, the king was now placing a public advertisement: if the goods were restored no prosecutions would follow. Slowly, piece by piece, throughout Whitehall, he was restoring his kingly state.

9 Courtiers and Envoys

But if in Court so just a man there be
(In Court a just man, yet unknown to me)
Who does his needful flattery direct,
Not to oppress and ruin, but protect . . .
Who does his arts and policies apply
To raise his country, not his family . . .
If such there be, yet grant me this at least:
Man differs more from man, than man from beast.

ROCHESTER, 'A Satyr against Reason and Mankind'

CHARLES HAD AN IDEAL of the courtier, but it was one from which he
often slipped. The model of the perfect courtier had been set early in
his life by the Marquess of Newcastle, who was, in Clarendon's words:

A very fine gentleman, active and full of courage, and most accomplished
in those qualities of horsemanship, dancing and fencing, which accompany
good breeding; in which his delight was. Besides that, he was amorous in
poetry and music, to which he indulged the greatest part of his time; and
nothing could have tempted him out of those paths of pleasure which he
enjoyed in a full and ample fortune, but honour, and ambition to serve the
king.[1]

Charles absorbed some of Newcastle's advice, like the virtue of a
calm indifference to study and to religion, both of which, his tutor
felt, could preoccupy a nobleman to the detriment of his exercise of
power. Equally, he admired Ormond's wit and easy elegance, and,
like him, he believed in making life look effortless. But he had
another model, his cousin Louis XIV, now free of the control of his
mother and Mazarin and firmly installed on his throne. Like
Charles, Louis loved his pleasures yet remained always elegant and
polite with 'a flood of wavy hair around his beautiful face'.[2]

Although Charles never aspired to the numbing protocol of the French court, there was a visible hierarchy at Whitehall, despite the more informal mood. In cold winter evenings in the large drawing room, the king and the inner circle of nobles stood around the fire, while lesser courtiers, talking among themselves, had to hover in chillier corners. Yet Charles had the gift of making everyone feel important. He took careful note of the minor, yet useful presences around the court, beckoning them forward, letting their relatives come and view the curiosities, including a fabled 'unicorn's horn', talking easily about every subject under the sun. In January 1662, for example, he called in John Evelyn to pass the time while Samuel Cooper was sketching his profile for the new milled coinage, which would come into circulation in March the following year. Evelyn held the candle, since Cooper preferred sketching at night '& by candlelight for the better finding out the shadows; during which his Majestie was pleasd to discourse with me about severall things relating to Painting & Graving &c.'[3]

Samuel Cooper's profile sketch of Charles II, for the new milled coinage

Yet however easy he made life look, Charles ordered his court according to his own wishes. At the heart of court life was the royal Bedchamber, and at the heart of court circles were the twelve Gentlemen of the Bedchamber appointed by the king. In manipulating court politics Charles granted and withdrew this position of honour with a certain steeliness, a quick way of indicating who was in and out of favour. The department of the Bedchamber had been invented by James I as a kind of personal cabinet, a forum to discuss policy away from the Privy Council. The Gentlemen were peers, often holding other high offices, and most of Charles's appointees were his intimate friends and old supporters. The Gentlemen were responsible for the private rooms, where the king paced and argued and made his own political choices, free of his council. To be part of this group, so close to the king, was to warm yourself at his fire – a position that gave much influence, and patronage. The Gentleman on duty spent the night in the Bedchamber with the king, sleeping on a trestle bed put up every evening, a closeness that allowed him to ask favours – a commission for a poor relation, a boon for a friend – and gave Charles a space to discuss life freely. At their head, as 'First Gentleman and Groom of the Stool', Charles placed Sir John Grenville, who had been with him since he was a boy and whose closeness to Monck had done so much to bring about his smooth restoration. But Grenville also held important positions in his native West Country – he was Lord Steward of the Duchy of Cornwall and Governor of Plymouth – and was often absent. The real 'First Gentleman' was Charles himself.

The next level of courtiers were the twelve Grooms of the Bedchamber, men like Ned Progers, who provided the king's linen and attended him constantly in his rooms and at meals, and undertook delicate and sensitive commissions. Almost all the Grooms had been with Charles in exile, some even sharing his humiliations in Scotland. Below them came the six Pages, who really ran the royal apartments, taking care of the clocks and pictures, building the fires, making sure the rooms were clean and running innumerable secret errands. The intimacy was extraordinary. At the very end of Charles's life, Thomas Bruce, Lord Ailesbury, remembered him retiring to bed, and how 'according to his usual custom, he went to ease himself, and he stayed long generally, he being there free of company, and loved to discourse, nobody having entrance but the lord and groom of the bedchamber in waiting'.[4] In this most private space, 'he laughed and was most merry and diverting: I holding the candle and the groom of the bedchamber, Mr Henry Killigrew, who always had some amusing buffoonery in his head, held the paper.'

The frontispiece to *The Courtier's Calling*, 1675,
showing the deference due to the King

This was a public life to an extreme degree. As Charles moved through the days, his existence seemed encrusted, as if he were wearing a heavy robe, with layer upon layer of tasks, row upon row of people. But among the flocking crowds that scuttled down the galleries of Whitehall, some characters stood out. As well as the quartet of grandees – Clarendon, Ormond, Nicholas and Southampton, who pursed their lips disapprovingly at the antics of the young – there were a few older courtiers in their late forties, like Tom Killigrew, now officially the Master of the Revels, and the volatile George Digby, Earl of Bristol.

Bristol's father had been Charles I's ambassador to the Spanish court. He had grown up there, becoming fluent in the language, until his father was recalled when he was twelve. In the political upheavals before the Civil War, as MP for Dorset, he had challenged royal misgovernment, but had shifted sides to oppose the attainder and execution of Strafford, the king's minister and friend. From then on he became one of the monarch's most passionate defenders and outspoken advisers, often not with the best results. Despite his recklessness, Charles II valued Bristol's loyalty in the past, and his knowledge of Spanish in the present. In exile he had been one of the inner circle, although he lost all his offices when he converted to Roman Catholicism in 1658 – an ill-timed piece of opportunism aimed at winning him more influence in Spain. At the Restoration he was restored to his old lands and titles, and as Earl of Bristol, he became a striking figure at court. Talented and extravagant (he bought Henrietta Maria's former palace at Wimbledon in 1661), he was full of tempestuously self-destructive schemes, famous for his flamboyant entertainments and heavy gambling.

Although they did not always take him seriously, Bristol stood out amid the younger courtiers. Both Charles and James had their own confidants, particularly James, who had a separate court of his own, like a grand French duke. Among their closest friends were Ormond's two sons, the twenty-six-year-old Thomas, Earl of

Ossory, and Richard, Earl of Arran, now twenty-one. They were among the leaders of the several Irish families at court. One of the richest courtiers, Charles's Groom of the Bedchamber Daniel O'Neill, came from a proud native family from County Down, but most of the Irish, like the Ormonds, the Hamiltons and the Talbots (five brothers who were constant thorns in Charles's side), belonged to Anglo-Norman or English families who had owned lands in Ireland since the fourteenth century or before. James Hamilton, another Groom of the Bedchamber, was the eldest of nine children of Irish Catholic aristocrats, although he himself became a protestant. His mother was Ormond's sister, and the Hamiltons, like the Ormonds, had joined the exiled court and were granted lands at the Restoration. James's brother George became an officer of the Horse Guards, and their younger brother Anthony later poured a mass of carefully collected court gossip into the quasi-fictional *Memoirs* of his brother-in-law, the comte de Gramont. (The *Memoirs* give him another 'm', as 'Grammont'.) Hamilton also wrote acclaimed French fairy tales, and indeed the French class the 'memoirs' as one of the popular *romans prétendus historiques* of the time.[5]

In contrast to the Irish, very few Scottish peers, with the exception of Sir Robert Moray, made the English court their base. They preferred to look after their interests in Scotland, coming south only when they had business. The bulk of courtiers, unsurprisingly, came from the English nobility, headed by the old ducal families: Grafton, St Albans, Newcastle, Richmond, Beaufort, Devonshire, Norfolk. But the lesser gentry were represented here too. One man who won the hearts of both the royal brothers was the Somerset-born Sir Charles Berkeley. In exile he had been a cavalry officer under the command of James, whose influence won him a knighthood, the post of lieutenant-governor of Portsmouth, and the receipts from mooring fees on the Thames below London Bridge. All this made him rich enough to buy a house beside the Whitehall bowling green.[6] Now he commanded James's regiment of guards and was one of his closest friends. In 1661 he was elected MP for New Romney, one of several court placemen in the Cavalier Parliament.

Charles came to love Berkeley. Not especially clever, witty or handsome, he was a good listener and a perfect confidant, who would happily dash between the king and Barbara. He had no pomposity, and the more Charles showered honours on him, the more easy-going he seemed; 'and so sincere in all his proceedings', records Gramont's *Memoirs* drily, 'that he would never have been taken for a courtier'.[7] Swimming through court intrigues as if everything was easy, in 1664 he married one of the prettiest and nicest of the Queen's ladies-in-waiting, the dark-haired Mary Bagot. Berkeley's sincerity had added charm since it was hard, sometimes, for Charles to distinguish between true friendship and self-interest. He found it difficult to deny requests, showering favourites with honours, posts and gifts. This had been a weakness, in Clarendon's view, from the early days of exile, when it was understandable for a boy of great 'sweetness of disposition', floundering in insecurities, to think he could buy love and lasting loyalty: 'If I did not hope he would outgrow that infirmity it would break my heart.'[8]

Already there were cliques. One formed around the Duke of York, another around the charismatic Duke of Buckingham, with his pale, long face and elegant, fluttering hands. 'When he came into the presence chamber,' remembered Dean Lockier, ''twas impossible for you not to follow him with your eye as he went along – he moved so gracefully.'[9] Buckingham, like Charles, was a natural actor, yet unlike Charles, he had found no role. He was restless and volatile. During that first summer he was busily pushing through his petition for the return of his estates. In exile he had gradually sold off the treasures from his father's York House – books, statues and paintings including nineteen Titians, seventeen Tintorettos, two Giorgiones, thirteen Veroneses, three Leonardos, thirteen Rubenses and three Raphaels. Now his fortune had returned. His lands in Yorkshire, his rivers and forests, mines and rents, and new, lucrative posts brought him a fabulous income of £20,000 a year. But all of this was swallowed up in mortgages and loans, taken out at exorbitant rates. All the time, his debts were spiralling.

Charles was still suspicious of Buckingham after his switches of allegiance in the 1650s. He kept him out of the Privy Council and did not admit him as a Gentleman of the Bedchamber until August 1661. But however doubtfully he eyed him, their shared history bound them, and Buckingham made him laugh. Buckingham's wit was a political tool. His party piece was his mimickry of Clarendon, when he hung a pair of bellows from his belt to imitate the Great Seal and limped goutily across the room, thrusting out his belly, pursing his lips and grimacing at the company as he bemoaned the antics of the dissolute young. A friend followed, slinging the fire-tongs over his shoulder like a mace. The act was ludicrous, but uncomfortably close, an act of demolition through ridicule. Buckingham could mimic anyone: no one was safe, even the king.

Charles was always eager for entertainment. He was notably indulgent, for example, to the young 'men of mirth' as Clarendon called them, several still in their teens, like Charles Sedley, Charles Sackville (Lord Buckhurst), Henry Savile and Tom Killigrew's son Harry. In 1661 Ormond reported gloomily that 'the king spent most of his time with confident young men, who abhorred all discourse that was serious, and, in the liberty they assumed in drollery and raillery, preserved no reverence towards God or man, but laughed at all sober men, and even at religion itself'.[10] This group, with Buckingham and, later, Rochester (who was only thirteen in 1660), would soon form the core of the libertine wits, challenging decorum and questioning the nature of rule, and self-rule.

The court was swept by crazes, for yachting, for dancing, for new forms of music. One of the first things Charles wanted to do was to re-establish a full body of musicians and singers to provide songs and dances and fine music for the Chapel Royal. Before he even arrived, when Henry Lawes and the English composers were writing celebratory compositions, six French musicians turned up, explaining that they had been commissioned to write the 'festive music'.[11] In November 1660, Sandwich reported an evening at Whitehall when John Singleton, a member of the royal orchestra, was royally snubbed: 'after supper, a play – where the King did put great affront upon Singleton's Musique, he bidding them stop and bade the French Musique play, which my lord says doth much out-do all ours'.[12]

Charles admired the violins of the string band of Louis XIV, and he liked strong melodies and dance forms like the new gavotte, minuet and bourrée, 'something he could tap his feet to'.[13] One of the Italians at court was a gifted guitarist. With his fingers flying over the strings, he made it look so easy that a delighted Charles sent guitar lessons to Minette in Paris. But as Anthony Hamilton noted caustically, 'The truth is, nothing was so difficult as to play like this foreigner':

The king's relish for his compositions had brought the instrument so much into vogue, that every person played upon it, well or ill; and you were as sure to see a guitar on a lady's toilet as rouge or patches. The Duke of York played upon it tolerably well, and the earl of Arran like Francisco himself. This Francisco had composed a saraband, which either charmed or infatuated every person; for the whole *guitarery* at court were trying at it; and God knows what an universal strumming there was.[14]

While the evenings were spent in dancing, at plays or at cards and dice, many of the courtiers' days – in between hard sessions of the Privy Council – were spent in hunting, riding, sailing, tennis. Pepys made constant, laconic notes of the times when the Navy Board were due to meet their admiral, the Duke of York, and found him out hunting. Charles was less keen, but went out often and paid regular sums to his Serjeant of Buckhounds, his huntsmen and his grooms. In fine weather the court walked in the Park, or drove out in their carriages, and on summer evenings they took to the Thames in their decorated barges, with supper and music.

In the early years Charles often dined at the houses of his nobles,

Francis Barlow's frontispiece to John Playford, *Musick's Delight on the Cithern*.
A young man in courtier's dress is studying his book to learn new tunes for the
cithern, a guitar with wire strings, while older instruments like the mandolin, bass
viol and kit hang unused on the wall.

or went with James to supper and music at the houses of the French
and Spanish ambassadors, being reluctant to miss a good evening's
wine and music among the court beauties and 'the most illustrious
libertines of his kingdom'.[15] When Charles dined out, the procedure, as described later by the Italian Magalotti, was a typical mix of
the ceremonious and the casual. The table was set for one, but
many more covers waited on the sideboard and were brought forward as Charles called the people to dine with him, usually all the
courtiers standing round. 'There the King relaxes, he is wholly
intent on eating; above all he no more remembers that he has a kingdom than would the most private gentleman who might sit at that
table.'[16] Sometimes, too, a large royal party set off to dine at
courtiers' houses in the nearby countryside.[17]

Wherever they were, men drank deep. Albemarle's iron reputation was reinforced by his capacity to hold his drink when all
around him collapsed, rising in the morning and going to parliament as if nothing had happened. Some drank to forget – one

common feature of the courtiers was that their confidence and glamour disguised staggering debts. They spent money like water, to appear richer than they were, like the Earl of St Albans, who made a point of losing thousands at the gaming table.[18] In fact even some of the greatest grandees were as poor as church mice. Ormond had debts of £130,000; the Duke of Norfolk borrowed £200,000; Buckingham was in hock to the tune of £135,000. Nearly all of them were caught in elaborate webs of mortgages and re-financing of loans.[19] They had responsibilities as well as grand positions. The older ones were married: Buckingham to the long-suffering Mary Fairfax, Bristol to Lady Anne Russell, daughter of the Earl of Bedford, and Ossory to the well-connected Aemilia van Nassau, whom he had met in the Netherlands in 1659. But although they were no longer single men filling empty hours, they behaved as though they were. They lived for the moment, strutting and playing.

Drunken evenings ended in quarrels and scuffles and the drawing of swords. Courtiers brawled at taverns and fought at the cockpit. Violence was in the air. Abroad, these young men had fought duels over trifles – in 1659 Richard Talbot had wounded a man over seven sovereigns won at tennis, while Clarendon defined his younger brother Gilbert Talbot as the most useless type of courtier, 'a half-witted fellow who did not meddle with any thing nor angered any body, but found a way to get good clothes and to play, and was looked upon as a man of courage, having fought a duel or two with stout men'.[20] They brought the habit back, following the dangerous French pattern whereby the seconds also fought, with swords and short knives. In August 1660, when Bristol taunted Buckingham that he had done little during the years of exile to deserve his wealth, Buckingham immediately challenged him. A full-scale duel was only stopped by Charles treating his two courtiers like children and confining them to their lodgings until their tempers cooled. At the end of the month he issued a proclamation forbidding duelling altogether, but it had little effect. Two years later, on 18 August

1662, when Harry Jermyn fought and killed Colonel Giles Rawlins. Pepys spoke for many when he wrote that 'The Court is much concerned in this fray; and I am glad of it, hoping that it will cause some good laws against it.'[21] He hoped in vain. Only five months later the House of Lords issued a formal 'reprehension', demanding an apology to the house from Lord Middlesex, who had challenged the Earl of Bridgewater in a furious letter, full of 'many expressions most unfitting and most unworthy of a Person of Honour'. Middlesex's rage stemmed from his belief that Bridgewater had conspired in the absconding of his Turkish servant, being 'partial and privie unto the going away of my Moore'.[22] This spat, like many, was food for gossip. Through letters, newssheets, lampoons and satirical ballads, the doings of the court spread like idle chatter. The gilded honour that courtiers defended in their duels seemed already tarnished.

The corridors of Whitehall resounded to quarrels as well as mirth. Sometimes, too, cries of angry despair. The main cause of this grinding of teeth was gambling. Gaming was only officially sanctioned during the Christmas feast and Charles himself, it was said, disapproved. Yet on Twelfth Night in January 1662, Evelyn was horrified to see the king open the revels by throwing the dice in the Privy Chamber. 'He lost £100, the yeare before he won 150 pounds: The Ladyes also plaied very deepe: I came away when the Duke of Ormond had won about 1000 pounds.' When Evelyn left the courtiers were still playing cards and dice. He shook his head at 'the wicked folly vanity & monstrous excesse of Passion amongst some loosers, & sorry I am that such a wretched Custome as play to that excess should be countenanc'd in a Court , which ought to be an example of Virtue to the rest of the kingdome'.[23] In this complaint, he was not alone.

Even the starchiest of court events could turn into a rout. 'All the Chancellor has put forward is nothing for me as compared to a *point d'honneur*, connected, were it ever so slightly, with the fame of my crown.' Thus, in Jusserand's translation, with its 1890s flavour, wrote the young Louis XIV to his ambassador in London, Godefroy comte d'Estrades, in January 1662.[24] It is hard for us today to make sense of the ludicrous lengths to which monarchs went to protect their honour through formal gestures, whether it be in saluting ships at sea (Charles was obsessively concerned that all other nations should salute the English men of war) or in being placed at a royal reception on the right hand of the monarch rather than the left. Yet as with the crowds coming to Charles to be touched for the King's Evil, the symbolic gesture embodied genuine belief. An ambassador – however pot-bellied and pompous – *was* the king, his incarnation on foreign soil. Any slight was felt as keenly as a physical assault or an act of war, and honour was defended, sometimes to the death.

Foreign ambassadors tripped over themselves in their rush to greet Charles now that he was back on the throne. There were 'ordinary' and 'extraordinary' ambassadors, the latter being nobles sent for special celebrations or to add weight to a diplomatic move. Charles greeted them all with great dignity, employing his warmest charm on representatives of countries that had helped him during the exile, and presenting a chilly face to those that had not. The custom was for an ambassador to settle in the capital, sometimes for several weeks, setting up his households, complete with livery, foot soldiers, coaches and assorted finery, so that he had a stylish entourage before making his formal entrance. This entrée, as it was called, was a finely staged fiction. The ambassador had to go back downriver to Greenwich and 'arrive' as if he had just sailed from his home port. From there he was rowed up the Thames in a state barge to the Tower, where tumultuous crowds watched his welcome to the City. Then he was driven to Old Palace Yard in Westminster, at the head of a grand parade, in which the ambassadors of all the other countries also rode in their carriages.

One of the first emissaries to go through this elaborate charade was the Prince de Ligne, Ambassador Extraordinary of Philip IV of

Spain. The Prince arrived at Tower Wharf on 13 September 1660 with, as the traveller Peter Mundy recorded, three hundred followers and 280 horses. He had sixteen gilded coaches, drawn by black horses, escorted by trumpeters and pages whose capes were so laden with gold and silver lace that 'the ground was hardly to be discerned'.²⁵ A day or so later, as was the custom, the Prince was received in great splendour in the Banqueting House. The walls were lined with tapestries, musicians played in the balcony, and courtiers and officials crowded in on all sides, thrusting themselves forward between the Yeomen of the Guard to get a good view.

The reception of the Prince de Ligne in the Banqueting Hall,
with the crowded gallery above

The Prince's entry set a standard for grandeur and ceremony which the French ambassador was determined to meet. D'Estrades was a sinuous, courtly figure renowned for his cold-blooded duels. In July 1661 Louis XIV sent him to London with instructions to forward a treaty with England and to protect the dignity of the French crown, 'allowing no ambassador to go before him', except that of the Holy Roman Emperor, keeping the Spanish on his left (rather than the distinguished right), and the Venetians firmly behind.[26] Unfortunately Londoners always took against the French. In addition, the Spanish ambassador of the day, Baron de Watteville, lived in great style and spent money freely, a sure route to popularity. The tension was serious because both France and Spain, perpetual rivals, wanted an alliance with England. Charles had ended Cromwell's war with Spain, which was already petering out, by a formal treaty two months after he reached London, but his family links to France, reinforced by Minette's marriage to Monsieur and his own admiration for all things French, tilted the balance towards Louis.

The inevitable conflict between the ambassadors was sparked, to no one's surprise – although the scale did genuinely shock – by competition over their position in a procession. The French insisted on preceding the Spanish, and vice versa. Guessing that there would be trouble, when the Venetian ambassadors arrived Charles persuaded both the French and Spanish to stay away. Louis, however, was mortally offended and insisted that d'Estrades be present when the Swedish delegation made their entrée in October. While his ambassador was making preparations, Louis heard from a spy in Albemarle's household that the General (as Albemarle was known) had offered to send Scottish and Irish soldiers to guard the Spanish coach. They would be waiting in the streets near Tower Hill. D'Estrades, he said, must make sure his coach took prime position and must keep his guards close 'for fear that at the crossing of some street these Scotch and Irish rush in with might and main and stop you and let Watteville go'.

Londoners looked forward to a good brawl. Early on the morning of 10 October 1662, the streets were full of soldiers and echoed with the noise of people running. When the procession gathered, the French shouted and jeered. The Spanish stayed silent. Seeing this, Pepys was sure they would lose. Quickly he had breakfast and ran from the Tower to Cheapside, only to find he had already missed the fight. Contrary to his expectations, the Spanish had won. De Watteville had taken the precaution of putting iron chains beneath the horses' harness, so that the French could not cut their carriage loose; the French had not. Having marooned their coach, the Spanish fell on the French with their swords, and then charged on in their coach, all the way to the Royal Mews at Charing Cross. 'I ran after them', wrote Pepys, 'through all the dirt and the streets full of people, till at last, at the Mewes, I saw the Spanish coach go, with fifty drawn swords at least to guard it, and our soldiers shouting for joy.'[27] When he had seen it turn in 'with great state' at York House, where the Spanish Ambassador had his rooms, he ran to the French headquarters, full of glee 'for they all look like dead men, and not a word among them but shake their heads'. The Spanish victory was all the greater, people said, because the French had outnumbered them four to one and were armed with a hundred pistols as well as swords. 'We had a great battle here upon the *intrado* made by the Swedish ambassador,' wrote the Bishop of Elphin, adding more details of the ungodly fray with considerable relish.[28] 'The King's guard of horse and foot were spectators, but let them fight on without parting them.'

This was no trivial affray. D'Estrades told his boss, the French Foreign Minister Lionne, that five of his fifty guards had been killed and thirty-three wounded. In addition he had been attacked personally twice, a musket ball had whizzed through his hat, and a mob had surrounded his house.[29] Charles was aghast, particularly at rumours that his own courtiers and soldiers had aided the Spaniards.[30] Quickly, he sent John Evelyn on a fact-finding mission, with detailed instructions as to whom he should interrogate. Evelyn scurried around town, questioning officers at the Tower and others, and wrote 'a narrative in vindication of his Majestie & carriage of his officers and standersby &c'.[31] As soon as the ink was dry, Charles wanted to send the papers to his ambassador in Paris. Next day he had second thoughts, spotting Evelyn at Whitehall and asking him to soften a passage or two in his report. It was late before Evelyn gave it in, 'and slip'd home, being my self much indispos'd & harrass'd, with going about, & sitting up to write, &c.'

Although men had died, no one could be arrested or tried for murder because all involved claimed diplomatic immunity. His pride hurt, d'Estrades refused to attend the English court. Louis supported him and protested furiously, both to Charles and to the King of Spain. He won this round outright, as Philip IV of Spain – nervous that this might even be a pretext for war – recalled de Watteville and conceded French precedence on all state occasions. In London, Charles issued a decree forbidding ambassadors to send their coaches to follow any entrée at all. Yet this in itself provoked more upsets and the word 'decree' had to be changed to 'resolution'. No one could decree anything to the King of France.

The life of the envoys and ambassadors could be wearing on the soul. Like a man waving frantically from a quagmire, in June 1662 the diligent Venetian envoy Francesco Giavarini burst out in one of his despatches. 'Hard necessity forces me to break silence,' he wrote. 'This is my seventh year at this Court after six in Zurich and in France. I hoped I should be removed from a country always agitated by strange events, always subject to serious peril, never free from expense and unbearable discomfort.'[32] He longed to go home.

10 The Coming of the Queen

She has as much agreeableness in her looks altogether, as ever I saw:
and if I have any skill in physiognomy, which I think I have, she must
be as good a woman as ever was born.

CHARLES II to Clarendon, 21 May 1662

BARBARA PALMER, by then obviously pregnant, had stayed quiet
through the sombre autumn and winter of 1660, when Whitehall
was mourning the deaths of the Duke of Gloucester and the
Princess of Orange. Her baby, Anne, was born in February 1661.
Roger Palmer accepted her as his child, but she was also later publicly acknowledged by Charles. By April Barbara herself was back
in the public eye. Three days before the coronation, where her
Villiers relations were conspicuous in the ceremony, Pepys spotted
her at a play in the Cockpit. He eyed all the beauties there, but
'above all Mrs Palmer with whom the King doth discover a good
deal of familiarity'. Pepys fell for her badly. He lusted after her – she
appeared in his dreams – partly because she was the king's. His
desire made him one with the king, and at the same time it made the
king like other men, just as the sight of the little dog shitting in the
boat had done. Pepys 'filled his eyes' with Barbara, he said, watching her again in July and August and September, when, he sighed, 'I
can never enough admire her beauty.'[1]

Charles clearly felt the same. But he was also realistic. Since the
autumn of the previous year, he and Clarendon had been hunting
for a suitable wife, who would bring a substantial dowry and provide healthy heirs. The European powers who had shunned him in
exile were now keen to cement an alliance. The French ambassador
allegedly offered the Chancellor £10,000 to push their interest,

which Clarendon declined with public proclamations of horror. Instead he proposed protestant princesses from Germany, whom Charles roundly turned down, saying that German women were 'all foggy and I cannot like any one of them for a wife'.[2] Tensions between the House of Orange and the Dutch government ruled out princesses from the Dutch Republic, and Charles also refused to consider any woman who had rejected him during his exile. In the end, since all protestant candidates were eliminated, and there were no possibilities in France or Spain, the choice fell on the Portuguese Infanta, Catherine of Braganza.

Portugal was keen to claim an ally against Spain, from whom Catherine's father King John had wrested his country's independence twenty years before. Such a match had been proposed years earlier and now Portugal offered an unheard-of dowry of £360,000 – two million crowns – and threw in the trading posts of Bombay and Tangier (which Charles had to look up on the map). Mesmerised by such potential wealth, and intrigued by a flattering miniature proffered by the Portuguese ambassador, Dom Francisco de Mello de Torres, in return Charles promised ten thousand troops as support in the struggle with Spain.

The marriage contract took many months to bring to fruition. The Spanish were set against it, spreading rumours that Catherine was deformed and could never bear children. The pro-Spanish Earl of Bristol even travelled to Parma to look at two Habsburg princesses – abandoning the idea when he saw that one was very fat and the other very ugly. (Charles banished Bristol from court for his impertinent interference, not for the last time.) The French, by contrast, favoured the match, and Henrietta Maria, who had been so horrified by James's marriage to Anne Hyde, for once sided with her old enemy Clarendon, seeing in Catherine a safe Catholic soul.

By the spring of 1661 all was decided. Charles informed Parliament of his decision, and wrote charmingly to his proposed bride. He had already written to her mother the queen. 'I send you here my Letter that is for the Queene of Portugal', he scribbled in a note to Clarendon, "tis the worse Spanish that euer was writt . . . looke it ouer and see if I have written it right, and send it me back againe.'[3] In late July, when William Schellinks took a ferry down the Thames, he noted the convoys of merchant ships but also several warships, waiting to join the fleet that would go and collect Catherine.[4]

Fearing they would lose influence after this marriage, the Villiers and Howard families worked to ensure Barbara's position as Charles's mistress. In mid-October 1661, Charles requested his Secretary of State William Morice to make out a grant for Roger Palmer to be made an Irish earl. His title would be Earl of Castlemaine, and his estates in Limerick would descend to 'his heirs of his body, gotten on Barbara Palmer, his now wife'. Leave the date blank, he asked, adding a P.S.: 'Let me have it as soon as you can.'[5] But there were obstacles. The humiliated Palmer initially refused to accept the offer, while Clarendon would not let the patent pass the Great Seal. (It was noted, too, that it was only Barbara's children who would be heirs to the title, not those of any future wife, if she should die.) Palmer's anger was partially assuaged by granting him the marshalship of the King's Bench, and the patent was transferred to Dublin, out of Clarendon's jurisdiction. Charles waited almost a month and then on 8 November peremptorily demanded a warrant making Palmer Baron of Limerick and Earl of Castlemaine, 'and let me have it before dinner'.[6] Roger Palmer was still far from pleased, refusing for some time to use his title. It was in reaction to his woes, some said, that he now converted to Catholicism.

In late January 1662, Pepys wrote, 'There are factions (private ones at Court) about Madam Palmer. What it is about I know not, but it is something about the King's favour to her, now that the Queen is coming.'[7] Anticipating the arrival of the queen, and also of Henrietta Maria who was due to move back to England in the summer, Barbara had been angling for an official position at court and had won agreement from Charles that she would be appointed as a Lady of the Bedchamber to Catherine. Such a post would give her security, and enable her to offer patronage to her friends, so that she could build her own camp of supporters. She was nervous. Although Charles's devotion was obvious, many courtiers who had curried favour with Barbara had now dropped her, including the Duchess of York and Buckingham. Mary Villiers, Buckingham's sister and now Duchess of Richmond, notoriously said she hoped that Barbara met the same end as Jane Shore, Edward IV's mistress, who had died in poverty and squalor, her body, according to story, flung on a dunghill.

Their change of tack was a miscalculation. Barbara was pregnant again, and in May she announced she would give birth at Hampton Court, the place where Charles was due to spend his royal honeymoon. Murmurs of disapproval volleyed around the court. In early April Dr Jasper Mayne preached what Pepys considered 'a very honest' sermon at Whitehall to the prospective royal bridegroom, in which he 'did much insist upon the sin of adultery – which methought might touch the King and the more because he forced it into his sermon, methought beside his text'.[8]

Meanwhile Charles's bride was on her way. Sandwich was despatched on the *Royal Charles* to lead his fleet to the Mediterranean, first to fight the Barbary pirates of Algiers, which he did with great success, then to take over Tangier. This proved less troublesome than expected but it was clear that Tangier was very vulnerable to attack, and a great project was started – which would continue all through Charles's reign, swallowing time and money – to build a mole, a long breakwater that would create a defensible harbour. Having installed a garrison, Sandwich finally set out to fetch Catherine from Lisbon. At the last minute there were problems about the dowry. This had still not been collected, partly because the Portuguese had spent it on their continuing war with Spain, and to Charles's distress it was largely paid in sugar and spices rather than cash. But at last, to the sound of cannon, Catherine boarded the *Royal Charles*, and settled down in her cabin, newly decorated and gilded, with velvet hangings and costly carpets.

From the Tagus the fleet sailed north up the Atlantic coast and then across the Bay of Biscay. Catherine stayed below deck, afflicted by both shyness and seasickness. In the terrible gales, even the crew were sick, as some jolly doggerel describes:

> Here laught a sailor, while another cry'd
> He'd change this great Fish-market for Cheapside.
> The deck with sick men covered; so that
> It look'd like the valley of Jehosaphat.
> Alive, or dead they knew not, like men shot
> With dreadful Thunder, live, and know it not.[9]

The Duke of York was sent to meet the fleet as it sailed into Portsmouth on 13 May. By the time Catherine tottered on deck after the troubled voyage half of Whitehall had descended on the port. Teams of carpenters and upholsterers had worked for weeks turning the Governor of Portsmouth's house into a makeshift palace, with suites for the king and the queen. In London Charles ordered a crimson velvet bed for the Queen's Bedchamber in Whitehall, lined with cloth of gold, and commissioned a painting of St Catherine by John Michael Wright to set over her mantelpiece.[10] And while James entertained Catherine in Portsmouth, Charles rushed through official business in Westminster. On 18 May the Privy Council sat until eleven at night while all the bills that were due to be passed in parliament were read aloud to them, including the key religious legislation, which would have such grave consequences.

It was characteristic of Charles to pack so many things into a day. His official work done, he walked over to dine with the new Lady Castlemaine, as he had done every night that week. On the eve of Catherine's arrival, when guns were fired in salvo from the Tower and bonfires flared outside all doors, Barbara's house alone was in darkness. Within, the scene was curiously domestic: Sandwich's housekeeper, Sarah, prying from next door in King Street, reported that 'the King and she did send for a pair of scales and weighed one another; and she, being with child was said to be heaviest'.[11] The little charade proved, to Barbara's eyes at least, that she outweighed the queen, not least in her ability to produce heirs.

Next day Charles stayed in town until all the parliamentary business was finished, leaving for Portsmouth around nine o'clock at night. A crowd waited for him at Westminster, as he jumped into his royal barge for the short trip to Whitehall stairs. Trumpeters blew their fanfares as he landed. Then 'with all the company wishing him good luck', he took his seat in his coach, 'which was ornamented with very magnificent carvings, with six most beautiful stallions belonging to the Duke of Northumberland harnessed to it. He and many other noblemen accompanied his Majesty in carriages and on horseback, besides a brigade of horsemen and his runners.'[12]

Charles and Catherine looking happy on a Staffordshire slipware charger.

The fine coach carried Charles to Guildford, where he had two hours' sleep before taking to the road again, arriving exhausted in Portsmouth in the evening. Catherine was weak after her seasickness, cold and fever. She was twenty-three, and despite her slight buck teeth, Charles thought her charming, slim and small with a pale, oval face and large dark eyes. As he reported to Clarendon, in a tangle of defensive negatives, 'her face was not so exact as to be called a beauty, though her eyes were excellent good, and there was nothing in her face that in the least degree can disgust one'.[13] He was determinedly hopeful, and, as it turned out, strikingly accurate in his judgement, when he added that she looked like a good woman. But Catherine was not as malleable as he had hoped. Her first act on landing was to refuse English ale and ask for a cup of tea, an exotic drink that she would do much to popularise. She would not accept her English attendants and she soon changed back from the English dress in which she landed, into her more decorous national clothes.

The immediate difficulty the couple faced concerned language, since Catherine spoke neither French nor English. Much bowing and gesturing went on. The next problem was religion. To satisfy Catherine's devout faith, a priest performed a secret Catholic ceremony in the queen's private chamber. Then Bishop Sheldon officiated at an Anglican ceremony in the improvised Presence Chamber in the Governor's house. Catherine and Charles sat side by side on small thrones, railed off from the audience: she wore a veil of English lace and a rose-coloured robe, decorated with lovers' knots in blue ribbons, which were later handed out to the guests as mementos. But the ceremony was a penance to Catherine. According to Burnet, writing after Sheldon had been made Archbishop of Canterbury, Catherine 'was bigoted to such a degree, that she would not say the words of matrimony, nor bear the sight of the archbishop. The king said the words hastily: and the archbishop pronounced them married persons.'[14] The wedding night was non-eventful, the marriage unconsummated. Charles told

Clarendon that he was so tired after his ride from London 'as I was afraid that matters would have gone very sleepily'. He told Minette, more baldly, that it was because Catherine had her period – as Minette too had on her wedding day, making the duc d'Orléans shudder with horror. 'Monsieur le Cardinal m'a fermé la porte au nez', Charles wrote, 'but I am content to let those pass over before I go to bed to my wife, yet I hope I shall entertain her at least better the first night than he did you.'[15]

Perhaps he did. At any rate he wrote effusively to Clarendon, approving Catherine's looks and her conversation, and even more warmly to the Portuguese queen, praising her daughter's 'simplicity, gentleness and prudence'.[16] The next week was packed with balls and dinners and receptions. Everyone watched the royal couple. Sir John Reresby, in town with the Duke of Buckingham, thought it

very decernable that the King was not much enamoured of his bride. She was very little, not hansome (though her face was indifferent), and her education soe different from his, being most of the time brought up in a monastery, that she had nothing visible about her to make the King forget his inclinations to the Countess of Castlemaine.[17]

Anthony Wood put it more tersely, and prophetically: 'a little woman, no breeder'.[18]

On 29 May, Charles's birthday, they returned to London. It was a sweltering day, the kind of weather when Londoners and their wives took a boat over to Lambeth, to the gardens at Fox Hall (later Vauxhall), to eat cakes and drink ale and wander down the shady avenues. Charles and Catherine were denied such pleasures. They arrived at Hampton Court at nine in the evening, their coaches bowling past in a cloud of dust. It was so hot in the state dining room that the sweat dripped off the courtiers' faces, the ladies' make-up ran, and Charles had to whisk Catherine away before she collapsed.[19]

The old palace was in a poor state, with countless leaks from the roof dripping into buckets in the corridors. Charles had his own

Carolo ii D.G. Mag. Brit. Fr. et Hib. Regi &c. Hanc Sereniss Reginæ Catharinæ Effigiem humillime consecrat
Cum Privilegio Reg:
G. Faithorne

Faithorne's engraving of the portrait of Catherine of Braganza, painted in Lisbon by Dirck Stoop a year before her marriage. Her wide farthingale was very old-fashioned in England, and her hairstyle, looped across her forehead in the Spanish and Portuguese fashion, was thought extremely odd.

priorities – in the first couple of years he had the tennis court refitted and stables repaired – but nothing had been done to the building itself. There had therefore been a great rush to get it ready for the royal honeymoon, 'a great deal of whitewashing and matting, putting up ledges for hangings, painting and gilding a balcony'.[20] The suite of rooms prepared for Catherine was decorated, and furnished with a looking-glass sent by Henrietta Maria and with the fine bed given by the Dutch States General, which, by a twist of fate, had originally been ordered by William II of Orange for Princess Mary. Before Catherine's arrival the park was planted with avenues of lime-trees and a new canal glittered serenely in the sun.

Charles was patient and attentive, teaching Catherine English, taking her for rides, finding her presents, and asking Minette to hunt in Paris for the papier-maché saints she liked to have in her chapel and could not find in protestant London. The two gondolas that the Venetian senate had given Charles the year before were brought down on 6 June, and the king and queen floated blithely on the canal. Catherine had now adopted English dress and was wearing silk dresses in sweet-pea colours, but her retinue kept their black farthingales, with their tight bodices and skirts jutting out like shelves at each side. They looked strikingly old-fashioned and foreign, as Evelyn described them, 'the traine of Portugueze Ladys in their monstrous fadingals or Guard-Infantas, their complexions *olivaster* and sufficiently unagreable'.[21] Later, Catherine came to really like the light English dresses with their revealing bodices, and enjoyed dressing in breeches which showed off her legs. She turned out to be good at archery, and enjoyed fishing. But for now, rather lost and eager to please, she was a formal little figure at odds with the noisy court.

Barbara, meanwhile, had sulked ever since Charles left for Portsmouth. When Pepys saw her at the theatre, it spoiled his evening, he wrote, 'to see her look dejectedly and slighted by people already'.²² There was no doubt which camp he belonged to. Towards the end of May, walking across the Privy Garden, where nearby householders hung out their washing, he was stopped in his tracks by 'the finest smocks and linen petticoats of my Lady Castlemaine laced with rich lace at the bottomes, that mine eyes ever beheld; and did me good to look upon them'.²³ With the king away Whitehall seemed a desert, as Barbara waited for the birth of her child in the June heat. When the baby arrived, it was a boy. Roger Palmer immediately reappeared and had him christened as a Catholic. Furious, within a week Charles was back in London, arranging for a Church of England priest to perform a counter christening. This took place in St Margaret's, Westminster, on 18 June. Charles himself, and Barbara's aunt, the Countess of Suffolk, now an attendant to the queen, stood as sponsors to the tiny Charles Palmer, Lord Limerick.

Charles, meanwhile, had been manoeuvring to have his mistress even closer, as a Lady of the Bedchamber. He had promised her this before Catherine arrived, and Barbara was skilled at making him feel guilty at her alleged ruin. Quiet though she was, Catherine knew what was going on. When she saw the name 'Castlemaine' on the proposed list of her attendants, she struck it off sharply. But when Barbara was presented, at first Catherine did not catch her name. She received the unknown woman calmly and let her kiss her hand: and then, on learning who she was, she collapsed to the floor, suffered a nose-bleed and wept furious tears. Charles apparently saw this as play-acting and defiance. In the aftermath, both husband and wife railed at the Portuguese ambassador, Charles complaining that Catherine should have been kept informed of his earlier life, Catherine attacking him for lying in the character he had given the king. She was distraught, lonely, confused by the new language and customs, hating the food and finding the London water 'like poison' compared to the clear streams of Lisbon.

Charles would not give up his battle on Barbara's behalf and despite Clarendon's obvious hostility to her, he now asked him to plead her cause with the queen. With profound reluctance, later commenting that it was 'too delicate a province for so plain-dealing a man as he to undertake', Clarendon agreed.[24] His tactic was not to excuse, but to ask the queen to be realistic. Catherine, 'with some blushing and confusion and some tears', said that 'she did not think that she should have found the king engaged in his affection to another lady'.[25] Surely, he countered, she had not expected this active thirty-year-old to be 'ignorant of the opposite sex'.

Far from accepting the situation with humour, as Clarendon suggested, Catherine stood firm. Meanwhile Clarendon lectured Charles, to equally little effect. He brushed off Clarendon's reminders that he had himself censured Louis XIV for forcing his queen to receive his mistress at court as 'such a piece of ill-nature, that he could never be guilty of'.[26] His honour was involved, Charles declared, rather unconvincingly: 'he had undone this lady and ruined her reputation, which had been fair and untainted till her friendship with him'.[27] In July he wrote to Clarendon, warning him not to try to divert him from his resolution.

You know how true a friend I have been to you. If you will oblige me eternally make this business as easy as you can, of what opinion soever you are of, for I am resolved to go through with this matter, let what will come on it; which again I solemnly swear before Almighty God. Therefore, if you desire to have the continuance of my friendship, meddle no more with this business, except it be to beat down all false and scandalous reports, and to facilitate what I am sure my honour is so much concerned in. And whosoever I find to be my Lady Castlemaine's enemy in this matter, I do promise upon my word to be his enemy as long as I live.[28]

Clarendon could show the letter to Ormond if he liked, but his mind was made up.

Struggling with parliament, fighting off petitioners, lectured by Clarendon over policy, Charles felt that his private life was one area where he must be able to exert his will. Egged on by his young courtiers, who reminded him that his grandfather Henri IV had openly kept a mistress at the French court, he remained stubborn. Fulfilling his earlier threat, he packed Catherine's retinue off home to Portugal: only a few priests, maids and the ageing Countess of Pendalva remained. Barbara seized the moment. On 15 July she ordered everything in King Street to be packed – plate, clothes, jewels, furnishings – and decamped to her uncle's house at Richmond, conveniently close to Hampton Court. She also took all the servants, leaving Roger with empty rooms and one decrepit porter. Her uncles George and Ned Villiers then signed a bond guaranteeing her debts up to £10,000. Her marriage, in all but name, was almost over.

The summer honeymoon was almost over too. There was a furious row, during which Catherine raged, wept, and declared she would go home, an empty threat as her mother, and her country, would view her return as a disgrace. The frustrated Chancellor's account was vivid:

The passion and noise of the night reached too many ears to be a secret the next day: the whole court was full of that, which ought to have been known to nobody. And the mutual carriage and behaviour between their majesties confirmed all that they had heard or could imagine: they spake not, hardly looked on one another. Every body was glad that they were so far from the town, (for they were still at Hampton Court,) and that there were so few witnesses of all that passed. The queen sate melancholic in her chamber in tears, except when she drove them away by a more violent passion in choleric discourse: and the king sought his divertisements in that company that said and did all things to please him; and there he spent all the nights.[29]

Catherine kept to her room, while Charles went out with his court, kissing 'that company', Barbara, in public. When the royal couple met, they still did not speak.

As if in accordance with their mood, the weather changed and floods swamped the land. In late July, in pouring rain, Charles was ferried in his barge downriver to join the Duke of York as both brothers were preparing to sail in their yachts with the flotilla collecting Henrietta Maria from France. Storms caught the little fleet off the Goodwin Sands. James lost his mast and Charles's yacht went aground and was in danger of breaking up, but was rescued by Prince Rupert and other experienced seamen. The fleet was driven back to Kent, denuded of cables, sails and spars.[30]

Finally James and Charles brought their mother back. She set herself up at Greenwich, in the hunting lodge built for her long ago by Inigo Jones, until quarters were fitted out for her at Somerset House. For months now, builders had been enlarging and refitting the Queen's House at Greenwich, smartening it up with 'Egipt marble' chimneypieces and new plaster ceilings.[31] The windows were reglazed and the rooms were swept. But when she stepped ashore from the royal barge, Greenwich was still scurrying with builders. It was Charles's most ambitious building work, a visible embodiment of his drive to become a monarch in the continental style. The previous year he had sent Denham and Evelyn to discuss the site.[32] Plans were drawn for a new palace and models made. Within months, much of the Tudor palace was pulled down, rooms and towers, roofs and galleries. Everything was carefully stored to be used again: between February and October 1662 nearly half a million bricks were cleaned and stacked.[33]

The queen mother thus walked into dust and mud and timber. But nothing daunted, she summoned her supporters and paid gracious calls on them at home, although her conversation may have made some demands on their patience. 'Went to see the Q: Mother', wrote Evelyn in his diary, 'who was pleased to give me thanks for the Entertainment she receiv'd at my house, after which she recounted to me many observable stories of the Sagacity of some Dogs that she formerly had.'[34]

A month after Henrietta Maria arrived, on 23 August, Charles and Catherine were rowed back on the royal barge from Hampton Court to Whitehall. Every boat that could be hired was taken and the water around Westminster was thick with wherries and sculls, decorated in celebration. Cheering crowds lined the banks and wharves and the slippery water stairs. It was, thought Evelyn, 'the most magnificent Triumph that certainly ever floted on the Thames', greater even than the Venetian pageant on Ascension Day when the Doge embraced the ocean: 'His Majestie & the Queene, came in an antique-shaped open Vessell, covered with a State or Canopy of Cloth of Gold, made in the forme of a Cupola, support-ed with high Corinthian Pillars, wreathed with flowers, festoones and Gyrlands.'[35]

The progress from Hampton Court to Whitehall, 23 August 1662, with the canopied barges of the livery companies accompanying the King and Queen.

Pepys was watching from a roof at Whitehall. 'There were 10,000 barges, I think,' he wrote later, 'for we could see no water for them, nor discern the King nor Queen.' When they landed the great guns on the other side of the Thames fired a salute. But there was a warning note, a figure in the crowd. 'That which pleased me best', wrote the adoring Pepys, 'was that my Lady Castlemayne stood over against us upon a piece of White-hall – where I glutted myself with looking on her.'[36] Roger Palmer was with her. They nodded, but did not talk, and every now and then one of them would take their child from the nurse and dandle it in their arms. When a scaf-fold collapsed, Barbara alone among the grand ladies rushed to help an injured child. It was windy, and she borrowed a hat from a man she was talking to, a very ordinary hat, 'But methought it became her mightily, as everything else do.'

It was obvious to everyone at Whitehall that Charles thought so too. Barbara had returned to King Street and Charles was up at six, ready before seven and by eight or nine was in her room, spending most of the day with her. The crowds in the Presence Chamber ignored the queen and clustered around the mistress. And while Catherine tried to ignore the situation, her bravery and apparent good humour outraged her supporters, like her chaplain Peter Talbot, who urged her to fight, describing Barbara as an 'enchantress'. To Catherine, Talbot's language implied actual witchcraft, a force that she – like most people in Europe, and in Britain – took extremely seriously. Alarmed, she told Charles. He in turn told Barbara, who stormed and wept and demanded Talbot's immediate dismissal.

As it seemed as though Catherine could not win, she adopted a new approach. That November, one observer, Edward Weston, wrote home to his wife in the country, 'I have sene the young Quene who is the very picture of modesty.'[37] Indeed, he thought (perhaps with an agenda of his own), she offered a pattern to all wives in her unworldliness, since she hated patches and paint so much and avoided looking in the mirror. Her great virtue in Weston's eyes was her obedience, and, he added, 'It is generally believ'd the King loves her very passionatly.' This was hardly so, although Charles did value Catherine's new manner. He had gambled that he could have both queen and mistress at court and his game plan, shabby as it sometimes seemed, appeared to have worked. Increasingly isolated, Catherine had pulled herself up and decided on tactics of conciliation, rather than confrontation. At last she accepted Barbara as a Lady of the Bedchamber.

11 Land

And now I'm here set down again in peace,
After my troubles, business, voyages,
The same dull Northern clod I was before . . .
Just the same sot I was e'er I remov'd,
Nor by my travel, nor the Court improv'd;
The same old-fashion'd Squire, no whit refin'd.

CHARLES COTTON

THERE WAS A BACKGROUND to Charles's hectic court and political life that he did not really see. How well did he know the countryside and the towns of the nations that he was so proud to rule?
On his sole visit to Scotland in 1650, Charles had seen the east-
coast towns and Edinburgh with its lawyers in their chambers and
ministers in their kirks. He did not like what he saw. He had never
been to Ireland, or crossed the border into Wales. As for England,
in 1651 he had ridden with his army from north to south, across the
northern counties and down to the Severn, stopping in Midland
towns like Stafford before the defeat at Worcester. He knew the
West Country from his youth during the Civil Wars and from his
perilous ride after Worcester. So far, that was the only time that he
met people closely enough to gain a sense of their lives.

Many of his MPs and peers, by contrast, went to the country as
soon as the parliamentary sessions were finished. Each time they
moved back and forth, the landed grandees took their favourite
chairs, desks, carpets and hangings. Setting out in their up-to-the-
minute coaches, with glass windows and improved, though far from
perfect, suspension, they were sometimes followed by a dozen or
more carts. All the landowners were intent on building up their

estates after the ravages of past years, or making a start on new lands the king had granted them. Clarendon, immersed in Privy Council business, wrote in February 1662 to his son at Cornbury. He was sorry about the dearth of trees, but understood that more were ready to plant and advised digging holes in readiness. He reminded him to plant the lime trees, to pay the workmen on time, and to tell the gardener to set seeds in 'a round or square place' which might be a fine thicket in three or four years' time.[1] The dreamed-of future lay in the cherished land.

William Cavendish, Marquess of Newcastle, retreated to the country altogether. Although he concealed it well, he was hurt at being left out of the circle of high-ranking appointments, and asked to exchange his regular duties at court for occasional attendance, so that he 'might retire into the country and settle, if possible, his confused, entangled and almost ruined estate'.[2] After a week on the road the Cavendishes arrived in Nottingham, a fine town with a good market. From there it took them another day, travelling through Sherwood Forest, to reach Welbeck Abbey, a gloomy enough house at the best of times but now, after their long absence, denuded of furniture, paintings, and all comforts. One of Newcastle's first acts was to restock his farm, ordering 'sixty bullocks, twelve cows, six teams of oxen, six horses and hundreds of sheep and pigs'.[3] This was only one of many projects he had to undertake. He also owned estates in Nothumberland, and smaller ones in Yorkshire, and in Somerset, Devon and Kent. Meanwhile his cousins, the Devonshire Cavendishes, owned Chatsworth, most of the Peak District and thousands of scattered acres elsewhere.

Charles's nobles were repossessing the land as fast as they could. In the early 1660s Henry Somerset, Lord Herbert, Marquess of Worcester and Lord Lieutenant of Wiltshire, settled down at Badminton. To begin with his income was small, as he was paying off his father's debts through a trust, but by the end of the decade his fortunes had mended. His wife Mary could buy damask linens and wax candles, tapestries and paintings, and exotic plants, and he could buy more land. He added nine hundred acres to his deer park, dissected by avenues that radiated from Badminton like the signs of the zodiac from the sun. Further away, he bought land in Monmouthshire and Gloucestershire, and took over his father's manors in Bedfordshire, Dorset, Glamorganshire, Hampshire, Herefordshire, Hertfordshire, Westmorland. The map was dotted with the Somersets' land.[4] Such landowners returning from exile, inspired by the grand estates of Holland and France, introduced new plants, shrubs and trees and laid out formal gardens with canals and statues and vistas, orangeries and hot-houses.

There were many large landowners like the Cavendishes and Somersets, and no one quite worked out the complexity of all their landholdings, even for the purpose of taxes. And no one, including Charles, was absolutely sure how many people lived in England, although again, several people tried to calculate this. It seems that the population dipped slightly at the end of the 1650s to around five and a half million – and most of them lived in the country.[5] In distant areas the change from crown to Commonwealth and back made little difference to the lives of those who worked the fields or toiled in the mines. Their relationships with their landlords and employers, whether they be puritan squires or royalists returning to their manor houses, were based on custom and deference as they had been for two hundred years.

The roads that the Romans laid down were still the main routes, converging on London like a spider's web. The rivers, too, were highways, carrying barges full of goods: the Thames and its many tributaries; the Trent, curving through the Midland counties before flowing north to meet the Humber; the Severn, snaking along the borders of Wales and flowing down to the estuary and the port of Bristol, with boats carrying fruit and corn and hops, timber and iron, wool and woven goods. Bristol was now England's second city, with thirty thousand souls, thriving on the import of sugar and tobacco from America and the West Indies, pulling in local people to work in the new sugar-houses and tobacco factories. The greatest

Francis Barlow's frontispiece to John Ogilby, *Britannia*, 1675

trade, however, as Charles well knew, was still in wool and cloth. English wool came in many varieties, from coarse to fine, short to long, and each region produced a different kind of cloth, their manufacture regulated by a mass of statutes. The price was lower than in Tudor times, largely due to over-production, but Charles protected the cloth industry by banning the export of raw wool, thus denying it to foreign weavers (although the quality was so high that many bales were smuggled out to continental markets).[6]

Charles heard from his committees and from his own land-owning courtiers how some counties relied largely on agriculture alone, like Leicestershire with its sheep farms and Northamptonshire with its good grazing land. But he heard less about the day-labourers who worked that land, who might earn only three and a half pence a day in winter and four and a half pence in summer.[7] (The accepted cost of living for a week for the poor was four or five shillings.) When Barbara Castlemaine gambled £500 in a single evening at cards, she was throwing away years of earnings for a hedger or ditcher in the English countryside.

For the larger tenant farmers and big landowners, however, life was improving. The harvests were good, and the growing towns needed feeding. Farmers began to look for 'improvement', a newly fashionable word, particularly attractive to royalists who had regained their land and needed to pay off large debts. The rush to enclose the land was less obvious than in the days of Elizabeth, but there was still a sudden surge in private bills, passed by a parliament that closed its eyes to infringements of the old laws.[8] On their enclosed land, farmers were keen to adopt new techniques. In the beef-fattening lands of the southern counties they planted clover and lucerne, introduced in the 1650s, to enrich the pasture and provide winter fodder. The turnip was tentatively cultivated in Norfolk and Suffolk. Elsewhere, brave spirits made a start with the unpopular potato, as recommended by John Forster in the aptly named *England's Happiness Increased* (1664). Experts published tracts on fertilisers, lime and ash, on irrigation and the flooding of water meadows, on clover, crop rotation and the germination of seeds.[9]

In many counties industry and agriculture went hand in hand: weaving, hosiery, shoe-making and silk-weaving in Nottinghamshire, furniture-making in Buckinghamshire; cloth-making in Somerset, iron-smelting, ship-building and rope-making in Sussex, tin-mining in Cornwall. In Essex, whose farmers produced cheese and corn and calves for the London markets, Dutch and Huguenot settlers had encouraged a growing textile industry, and Colchester was now the centre of the 'New Draperies', woven in the villages around, dealing in lighter weaves than the old broadcloth and kerseys. Further east, the East Anglian counties were slowly rising in prosperity as the fens were drained. Pumps turned by windmills sucked the water from the marsh. Corn grew where the reeds had waved.

Far to the north, in Buckingham's fiefdom of Yorkshire, the townsfolk were prospering: the clothiers of Leeds, Wakefield and Halifax; the cutlery-makers of Sheffield. Further north still, the great landowners and industrialists of Northumberland and Durham coined money from coal and iron, sending thousands of tons of coal each year to London, Holland and France, and as far as the Mediterranean. Horses drew cartloads of 'black gold' along primitive wooden railways down to the docks. And along the coast, glinting over the sandbanks at the mouth of the Tyne, fires burned night and day, evaporating brine in the salt pans. On the other side of the Pennines, Manchester, Bolton and Rochdale were beginning to work cotton imported from the Middle East. In the mountains of Cumberland and Westmorland, the people depended on sheep and salmon-fishing, but even here there were copper and silver mines in the hills and gunpowder mills in the deep valleys. Sir John Lowther, MP for Cumberland, rarely visited his estate on the northern fringes of the county, staying in London and directing work through his estate and colliery agents. But he expanded his collieries as fast as he could, selling coal to Dublin, and built the port and town of Whitehaven to invest in voyages to Virginia and the Baltic.[10]

For most people local trade was more important than such grand designs. Every county had its weekly markets and seasonal fairs and chapmen's rounds. The chapmen, with their heavy baskets – some so large that it was like carrying a table – were licensed by local corporations. They walked the roads carrying ribbons and muffs, ballads and books, to the remotest farmhouses. The lace and pins and stockings in their packs were made by people in the towns, and as such trades flourished so the markets prospered and new shops opened, selling small goods like cutlery and clocks. The country gentry, however, were wary of the growing towns since many tradesmen and artisans were nonconformists and former supporters of Cromwell. So the towns developed their own identity on a more informal, but powerful, level. The irony was that when local merchants prospered and sought a better way of life they started hankering for a title, forsaking their town roots and their dissenting faith – and moved to the country.

One aspect of the countryside gripped everyone's attention. While there were relatively few protests about enclosure of commons, people did resent encroachment on woodland, cherishing their rights to collect timber for building houses and fences, or brushwood for fires. Once a wood was enclosed, to get the timber they had to trespass. Once caught, they were prosecuted. How could old rights be reclassified as crimes?

The forest was an emblem of national freedom and the plight of the woodland came to be seen as a symbol of the devastation of the country as a whole. During the Commonwealth, merchants had exploited the timber from confiscated lands and the trees had been felled, brushwood taken and saplings uprooted.[11] Newcastle estimated that around £45,000 worth of timber had disappeared from his Midland estates. His wife, Margaret Cavendish, wrote that she 'had never perceived him sad or discontented for his own Losses and Misfortunes', yet when he saw his ruined park at Clipstone, where the trees had been felled for charcoal, she saw that he was troubled, 'only saying, he had been in hopes it would not have been so much defaced as he found it, there being not one timber-tree in it left for shelter'.[12]

The use of wood for local industries was one thing that could not stop: between 1660 and 1667 over thirty thousand trees went to feed the iron furnaces in the Forest of Dean.[13] But the woods also had particular meaning to Charles, since they provided timber for his navy. It was partly as a result of a plea from the Navy Board that in 1662 John Evelyn took on the task of surveying the scarred woodland. His book *Sylva, or a Discourse of Forest Trees, and the Propagation of Timber* (1664) was a plea for a complete regeneration of the countryside and above all for the planting of trees. It was dedicated to Charles, the monarch whose very life had been preserved by the sheltering branches of the oak. And although it was full of practical advice on everything from producing mature timber to pollarding coppices and growing nut trees, it was equally full of classical allusions and rhetorical flights, a hymn to the forest as the heart of England.

For some Restoration writers the countryside and rural life were still hallowed by the notion, however false, of a Georgic idyll, remote from the bustle and corruption of city and court. Poets and writers developed a dream of rural England as a retreat, and the country as a fragile realm, easily lost. Charles Cotton, the 'old-fashion'd Squire, no whit refin'd', was in fact a highly cultured poet. In the 1660s he was living in Staffordshire with his first wife, his cousin Isabella, and their many children, acting as a magistrate and local revenue commissioner. A passionate fisherman, he contributed to his friend Isaac Walton's *Compleat Angler* and when he could, he retreated to his library, writing a popular burlesque of Virgil, *Scarronides*, and later achieving fame as the translator of Montaigne. Yet still, he was happy to style himself a 'countrey bumpkin'.[14] And despite all the work there was to do at Welbeck, Margaret Cavendish declared roundly – and often – that she would not leave its peace 'to live in a metropolitan city, spread broad with vanity, and almost smothered with crowds of creditors for debts'.[15] Her tenants might have disagreed, but when she compared country to town her conclusion was clear: 'In short, there is so much difference in each sort of life as the one is like Heaven, full of peace and blessedness, the other full of trouble and vice.'

As king, Charles existed in that world of trouble and vice. He enjoyed being in open parkland or on the downs, hunting and hawking, riding and racing, but he was no farmer George, with an interest in turnips and pigs. When he left his capital, he travelled with his courtiers, taking his own small world with him, whether to Newmarket in the east or to Oxford or Bath in the west. Like most Londoners, he rarely ventured north. When he travelled, he carried the breath of Whitehall on his clothes, and the dust of London on his boots.

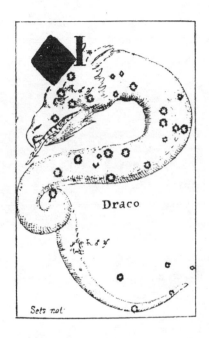

Draco

Sets not:

The Ace of Diamonds showing the constellation 'Draco', 'The dragon',
in astrological playing cards of the time of Charles II

12 Tender Consciences

I am no Quaker, not at all to swear,
Nor Papist, to swear east and mean the west;
But am a Protestant and shall declare
What I cannot, and what I can, protest.
         ROBERT WILD, 'The Loyal Nonconformist'[1]

ALL OVER THE LAND, in cities and market towns and country villages, nonconformist subjects were anxious about their future. As a
matter of principle, Charles wanted to set aside the strict, persecut-
ing ways of the church in his father's day under Archbishop Laud,
and as a pragmatist he recognised the strength of the presbyterians
and wanted to satisfy them. Yet in practice, before a single law was
passed, the old forms of Anglican worship were already being used,
and high church trimmings like surplices and choirs had begun to
be fashionable again.

From the start, Charles himself used the old Book of Common
Prayer at Whitehall. He attended services in the Chapel Royal in his
own private gallery, looking down through a window on his
courtiers in the main body of the chapel. On the feast days, dressed
in formal robes, he came down to join the congregation. William
Schellinks was there at Candlemas in February 1662, when the
music was 'extraordinarily beautiful', and a sword was carried
before the king, who knelt at the altar and placed his alms, gold
pieces, in a fine silver dish.[2] The small panelled chapel had been
vandalised during the Interregnum, its stained glass broken, its
cross pulled down and wall paintings plastered over, before it was
repaired for Cromwell's use, with a huge central pulpit. Now it
had carpets and wall hangings and galleries for court and musicians.

A new style of court music flourished. Soon after the Restoration Pepys heard 'very good Musique, the first time I remember ever to have heard the Organs and singing-men in Surplices in my life'. A few months later he heard an anthem, 'ill sung, which made the king laugh'.[3] The new master of music, Henry Cooke, assembled a choir (including the father of Henry Purcell, who was then a toddler growing up near Westminster Abbey across the square). Pepys admired their rendering of Psalm 51, arranged for five voices, 'And here I first perceived that the King is a little musicall, and kept good time with his hand all along the anthem.'[4] In 1662 the royal strings were ordered to play in the chapel, disconcerting traditionalists like Evelyn, who lamented that instead of the 'antient grave and solemn wind musique accompanying the Organ' he had to listen to violins 'betweene every pause, after the French fantastical light way, better suiting a Tavern or a Play-house than a Church'.[5]

The king liked a good anthem, and he liked a good sermon. He appreciated the preaching of scholars like Isaac Barrow, and the sermons of clever, articulate men with genuine faith like Thomas Ken and Robert Frampton, even though they might rebuke him for his way of life. (Ken refused to put Nell Gwyn up for the night in Winchester, but Charles still made him Bishop of Bath and Wells.[6]) But while he enjoyed the ceremony, he was almost too clever, and too sardonic, to understand the depths of feeling and bitter animosities that religion could arouse. He confessed that the logic of the factions and splits defeated him: why did Anglicans condemn dissenters from cutting loose from the mother church, when the Church of England itself had split from Rome?[7] He disliked the fuss over ritual, the 'wrangling about forms and gestures'.

Clarendon agreed, although in contrast to Charles, he had a deep, almost fatalistic faith, holding that history was the working out of providence and it was a ruler's duty to fulfil the laws of God as well as the crown. But to begin with, he too wanted inclusion. It was safer, he thought, to bring dissenters *into* the state church, rather than forcing them out and fuelling future conflicts.[8]

In some ways, it was already too late. As soon as the Restoration was secure, the old forces had made their move. Around seven hundred of England's nine thousand ministers had left their parishes by the end of the first year, either because the original incumbents paid them to get their livings back, or because they were forced out by local Anglican landlords. As far as the sects outside the church were concerned, magistrates saw that there was no need to wait for any new religious legislation: plenty of useful statutes remained from Tudor days. The thirty-two-year-old John Bunyan was one of many convicted under such an act. A tinker's son, briefly a member of the New Model Army, and now attached to the Bedford brotherhood of Baptists, on 12 November 1660 Bunyan was arrested while preaching in the village of Samsell. He was taken before the magistrate Francis Wingate, a zealous Anglican, and a landowner whose estate had suffered badly during the Interregnum. Citing the Elizabethan Act against Conventicles, Wingate committed Bunyan to Bedford gaol.

The act decreed that the penalty for preaching to such gatherings was three months' imprisonment, to be followed by transportation if the offender would not give up preaching and conform to the established church.[9] In January 1661, when Bunyan appeared at the quarter sessions, the odds again seemed stacked against him, since the chief magistrate was Sir John Kelyng, a loyal Cavalier, counsel for the crown in the trial of the regicides and a future judge. Kelyng (whom Bunyan dubbed 'Lord Hategood') took the case seriously, exchanging detailed scriptural arguments before lapsing into frustrated bluster when he saw that Bunyan would never promise to stop preaching – a simple move that would have won his freedom. Despite many petitions, Bunyan lingered in gaol for twelve years. Yet he was no belligerent protester. He wrote from prison that he did not plan to disturb the peace of the nation. He looked upon it as his duty, he said, 'to behave myself under the King's government, both as becomes a man and a Christian; and if occasion was offered me, I should willingly manifest my loyalty to my Prince, both by word and deed'.[10]

*

Most dissenters were prepared to abide by the law as long as they could worship in peace. Their situation, however, was imperilled in January 1661, when Venner's uprising roused all the old fears of puritans and 'fanatics'. Dissenting meetings, whispered government spies, were held only on pretence of religion; their real aim was revolution. Rattled, Charles issued a proclamation against 'Fanaticks and Sectaries' (acknowledging that it infringed some part of the Breda promise), by which meetings of 'Anabaptists, Quakers and Fifth Monarchy men, or some such like appellation' were forbidden.[11] The Privy Council ordered the Lords Lieutenant to raise the

The frontispiece to *The Dippers Dipt*, a satirical account of the Baptists and other sects by Daniel Featley, chaplain to Charles I, published in 1645 and reissued in 1660.

militia and hunt down anyone suspected of disaffection to the king or his government. Over four thousand Baptists and Quakers were imprisoned.

Charles was less rigid and vindictive than the bishops and the partisan gentry in parliament. The fear of uprisings cast its shadow over the Savoy Conference, the next meeting of the church leaders and presbyterian divines, which opened on 15 April 1661 at Savoy Palace, the seat of the Bishop of London, Gilbert Sheldon. Dark-haired, beetle-browed, intense and intellectual, Sheldon had been a leading figure in Oxford life since the 1630s. He had been a chaplain to Charles I and had stayed in touch with royalist hopes during the Interregnum. As soon as Charles II returned, he was appointed Dean of the Chapel Royal and then Bishop of London. Sheldon had been a reformer, in opposition to Laud in the 1630s, but he took a far harder line than the king and Chancellor in his designs for the restored church. The Florentine Lorenzo Magalotti, visiting London a few years later, had no doubt of his ambition or his duplicity, dismissing him as of 'very ordinary birth . . . a man of great refinement, of much talent and brains; externally all mildness and internally all malice'.[12] This was unfair, but Sheldon was certainly shrewd and determined. He only attended the opening days of the conference, and then left the delegates alone, but everyone present accepted that he was the 'doer and disposer' behind the scenes.

The conference was supposed to work out the fine print of an Act of Uniformity broad enough to bring in the dissenting factions, but the presbyterians were wary and Baxter and his fellow campaigner Edmund Calamy – who had both turned down offers of bishoprics – scrupulously debated every point. The way was set for months of wrangling. Baxter, for one, was convinced that they were speaking to the deaf and that the bishops would accept none of their demands, but would wilfully misinterpret every utterance as a signal of lingering republicanism. His despair is clear in his notes, where raised eyebrows count as much as formal speeches:

Among all the Bishops there was none who had so promising a Face as Dr Sterne, the Bishop of Carlisle: he look'd so honestly, and gravely, and soberly, that I scarce thought such a Face could have deceived me; and when I was intreating them not to cast out so many of their brethren through the *Nation* as scrupled a ceremony which they considered indifferent, he turn'd to the rest of the Reverend Bishops, and noted me for saying 'in the Nation': 'He will not say "in the Kingdom", saith he, 'lest he own a King.' This was all that ever I heard that worthy Prelate say.[13]

The Savoy Conference broke up in the summer, leaving the detailed working out of the church agreement to the new parliament. Sheldon manipulated this passionately loyal parliament with great skill, chivvying the reinstated bishops in the Lords, and organising pet MPs to steer through votes for the legislation he wanted, rather than for a broader settlement. In mid-May, within two weeks of its

Archbishop Sheldon, by Samuel Cooper

opening, the Commons passed an order decreeing that all MPs should take the sacrament according to Church of England rites, and commanding the Solemn League and Covenant to be burned.

Charles did not help his own cause. Later in the year it was widely noted that he and Barbara and the Duke of York – and Sheldon – all enjoyed the new production of Ben Jonson's *Bartholomew Fair*. The performances included the original puppet show, mocking the puritans, which had not been acted for forty years. As a rather shocked Pepys noted, 'it being so satyricall against puritanisme, they durst not till now; which is strange they dare to do it, and the King to countenance it'.[14] Two puppets were even made up to look like Baxter and Calamy. Charles found it hard not to be irreverent. A little later he joked to the Bishop of Derry, who had been deep in discussions with the nonconformists, 'telling me he heard I had been fighting with the beasts at Ephesus'.[15] If this was the attitude of the court the response of parliament was no surprise. Repressive laws against dissenters were inevitable.

The first legislation was the Corporation Act in December 1661, which decreed that all magistrates, and anyone holding municipal office, had to take the oaths of allegiance and supremacy, swear that taking up arms against the king was illegal (thus damning all those who had fought on parliament's side in the Civil Wars), and abjure the Solemn League and Covenant. This effectively wrested power in the corporations and the countryside from the hands of nonconformists and returned it to the Church of England gentry, nostalgic for the restoration of an 'old order' that had never really existed.

The Corporation Act was Charles's first real defeat. He had gambled on the force of reasonable argument and had been defeated by the entrenched interests of the church, the vehemence of Sheldon and the deep-held suspicions of his parliament. His defeat did not, however, affect the Christmas revels. And at Whitehall at least, he could demonstrate that different modes of worship could be brought together peaceably. On 12 January 1662, the whole court trooped over to St James's, where the famous Huguenot preacher Alexander Morus, who had taught in the Netherlands and in Geneva, 'preached or rather harangued' the court on the theme of '*all things operate for the best to those who love God, &c*' in French, in front of the King and the Duke of York, the French ambassador '& a world of Roman Catholics'.[16]

But still, at the start of the year Charles's ministers were becoming anxious about the nonconformists' response. In January, rumours of plots prompted Clarendon to suggest supplementing the local militia with special troops, to be led by the Duke of York. The very suggestion horrified the Commons, raising as it did the old spectre of a standing army which would give its commander power to rule without parliament.[17] The idea was dropped, but there was a hum of fear about what might happen next, among both dissenters and Anglicans. The mood was superstitious, ready for omens. On 13 February Charles's aunt, the redoubtable Winter Queen, Elizabeth of Bohemia, died at Leicester House. Next day, St Valentine's Day, saw gales and pouring rain, which swelled into a tempest to match the storms before Cromwell's death. Because she and her husband had been swept from their throne by Catholic forces at the very start of the religious wars in Europe, Elizabeth had become almost a protestant martyr, the subject of many myths and stories. To the superstitious the gales that swept across all Europe, like the religious wars of the past, were linked to the passing of this Winter Queen. In Britain, several people were killed as roofs were ripped off, chimneys collapsed. Three thousand oak trees were toppled in the Forest of Dean, the vital nursery for the navy's timber.[18] The London streets, wrote the merchant Thomas Rugg, were full of 'brickbats, tileshards, spouts, sheets of lead . . . hats and feathers and periwigs'.[19] When Pepys set off the next day to join his wife and Sir William Penn at the opera he found his way blocked by broken bricks and tiles.

Holding their beaver hats and tugging at their wigs as they dashed to Westminster, the frightened MPs tried to push through a bill which would expel presbyterian ministers even before a full Act of Uniformity was passed. Knowing that the king and Clarendon would try to have this thrown out by the Lords – as eventually happened – on the eve of the Lords' debate a Commons deputation went directly to Charles in a threatening mood. He reminded them that on his return he had promised these ministers that they could stay in their livings.

Whereupon they said the Commons might possibly, many of them, be tempted not to pass the bill intended for the enlarging of his revenue . . . to whom the king answered that if he had not wherewith to subsist two days, he would trust God Almighty's providence, rather than break his word.[20]

Brave words, but Charles's promises were already proving fragile. He told his presbyterian chaplains, for example, that the rituals in the old Book of Common Prayer would be adjusted to their liking, yet the previous autumn he had given the task of revision to the Canterbury Convocation, which, with the York Convocation, was one of the two elected assemblies of the Church of England. Within weeks they made six hundred changes. The new prayer book was sent for approval to the Lords in December, and was passed by the Commons in March 1662.[21]

That month, Charles addressed the Commons in the Banqueting House. His position was difficult since, as the MPs' deputation had implied, he needed their goodwill to get his money. In his address, after a heartfelt plea that they finally settle finances, he turned to religion. 'Gentlemen,' he began, 'I hear you are very zealous for the Church, and very solicitous and even jealous that there is not expedition enough used in that affair.'[22] He thanked them, drily, presuming this sprang from 'a good root of piety and devotion', and then tried to steer them away from rumours that his concern for nonconformists meant that he did not support the church: 'I must tell you I have the worst luck in the world, if, after all the reproaches of being a Papist, whilst I was abroad, I am suspected of being a Presbyterian now I am come home.' The new prayer book, he said, proved his good intentions, but, he warned them, 'the well settling of that affair will require great prudence and discretion and the absence of all passion and precipitation.'

The warning went unheeded. On 19 May 1662, the very day that Charles was due to dash to Portsmouth to greet his Catholic queen, the *Act for the Uniformity of Publique Prayers and Administration of Sacraments* was finally passed. The act decreed that all ministers must be ordained by a bishop and must subscribe to the new prayer book and the Thirty-nine Articles, or quit their livings by St Bartholomew's Day, 24 August (the gap of time was to allow the prayer book to be printed and distributed).

There were already intimations of protests. In June the execution of Sir Henry Vane at the Tower drew vast crowds. However hard the officials tried to suppress Vane's long speech – snatching his papers from his hands, and bringing trumpeters up under the scaffold to drown his voice – his brave words, justifying the cause he died for and praying for the good of the country, impressed all the witnesses. Soon a biography of Vane was published, with a laudatory sonnet by John Milton, which had been written ten years before, in 1652, when Vane was fighting in parliament for the separation of church and state. Nervous of uprisings, and unhappy at betraying his promises, Charles suggested to the Privy Council that the new act might be suspended for three months. Sheldon wrote angrily to Clarendon and told the Privy Council, in a blasting speech, that to suspend the act 'would not only render the parliament cheap, and have influence upon all other laws, but in truth let in a visible confusion upon Church and State'.[23] Sheldon made sure, too, that his views were widely aired: a virtual copy of his letter appeared in the government press, *Mercurius Publicus* (whose reach Charles underestimated, and rarely read). In late August, when Clarendon suggested that presbyterians should petition the king again, Sheldon leapt into action once more, ensuring that the Privy Council rejected their plea.

That August, too, the Commons passed the 'Quaker Act', which laid down that anyone who refused to swear an oath or who joined in a religious meeting with five or more others was liable to a fine of £5 or three months in prison. On a second offence this would rise to a £10 fine and six months' gaol with hard labour, and on a third, to transportation. Because of their rejection of worldly oaths, no true Quaker could swear the oath demanded, and so unless they were prepared to pay fine after fine, they faced years of imprisonment. One estimate suggests that fifteen thousand Quakers were incarcerated and 450 died in prison.[24] Many rotted in small country gaols, while others were packed into insanitary London prisons like Newgate, where the gaolers made money by granting privileges to those who could pay – meagre bedding, food, perhaps a window to let in some air – and crammed the others into the foul-smelling rooms of the 'Common side' where many died from disease. When Charles tried to soften the impact of this Act by issuing a proclamation for the release of Quakers awaiting trial in London, the Commons turned on him fiercely.

In his bid to deal with these issues sanely, Charles misjudged the strength of the bishops and the mood of his parliament, but not the mood of the dissenters themselves. He could see that although the Quakers defied the law, few threatened the state. Like Bunyan, and many nonconformists in this troubled time, the Quakers tried to turn their back on public quarrels. In 1660, quoting the words of Christ, '*My Kingdom is not of this World*,' the Quaker leader George Fox had written, 'my Weapons are *Spiritual, and not Carnal,* and with Carnal Weapons I do not fight . . . and I witnesse against all *Murtherous plots,* and such as would *imbrew the Nation in Blood*'.[25] Such protestations did no good. In the view of the parliament and Privy Council, the dissenting sects posed a threat. Church and state were once more bonded together. The underlying drive of much of the legislation that would follow had little to do with doctrine, but everything to do with the premise, succinctly phrased later by Halifax, that 'it is impossible for a Dissenter not to be a REBEL'.[26]

13 All People Discontented

Kind Friends I am resolved to discover a thing
Which of late was invented by Foes to our King
A Phanaticall Pamphlet was printed of late
To fill honest-hearted Affection with Hate.
But here lies the thing, God hath sent us a King
That hath Wisdom enough to extinguish that Sting.
The Phanatick's Plot Discovered [1]

The legislation of 1662 and the acts that followed were backed up by assaults on freedom of expression. As soon as the Act of Uniformity was passed, Convocation sent out a letter to all parishes. Pastors, they suggested, should teach the doctrine of the Church of England with 'modesty, gravity and candour', concentrating on morality and avoiding controversial tenets of faith like predestination.[2] A royal proclamation also warned against extravagant preaching, 'which has much heightened the disorders and continues to do so by the diligence of factious spirits who dispose them to jealousy of the government'. Preachers must not use sermons 'to bound the authority of sovereigns or determine the difference between them and the people, nor to argue the deep points of election, reprobation, free will etc.'[3]

The Licensing Act of 1662 tried to shut down the nonconformists' ability to spread their message in print, as well as from the pulpit. From now on, too, attempts were also made to control, or at least spy on, all kinds of meeting places, including taverns and coffee-houses. The Act's full title made its political nature clear. It was the *Act for Preventing the Frequent Abuses in Printing Seditious, Treasonable and Unlicensed Books and Pamphlets, and for Regulating of Printing and Printing Presses*, and it prohibited 'the printing or importing of any books or pamphlets containing doctrines contrary to the principles of the Christian faith or to the doctrine of government or of governors in Church and State'.[4] To ensure this, the Act reduced the number of presses. The roll of master printers was cut back from sixty to twenty, each master being allowed only two presses and two apprentices. In England, these were in London, Oxford and Cambridge, nowhere else.[5]

The licensing of books, before they could be registered with the Stationers' Company, was overseen by Roger L'Estrange, a veteran royalist journalist, notorious for his loathing of dissenters. After 1660, having overcome some suspicion from his accommodation with Cromwell, he became spokesman for the most rabid section of the Cavalier Parliament. In pamphlets like *Toleration Discuss'd* (1663), he refused to accept that presbyterians had played a role in the Restoration, blamed the nonconformists for the Civil War and argued for their suppression. Their printers, he claimed, corresponded in code and were in touch with exiles abroad. L'Estrange also set out to be the government's voice. In 1663 he launched the *Intelligencer*, which appeared each Monday, and the *News*, on Thursdays. He was also appointed surveyor of the press, with authority to hunt out unlicensed books and illegal presses. (Bunyan, in *The Holy War*, portrayed him as 'Mr Filth'.)

Though energetic, L'Estrange's efforts were largely unsuccessful. Many unofficial printers continued to publish unlicensed books, and in 1668 L'Estrange himself counted thirty-three such presses in London alone.[6] But his campaign was potentially dangerous because he could use the common law, as well as the Licensing Act, to catch his prey. Any slight on the monarch, the government or the church, in manuscripts as well as published works, could be labelled as sedition, and authors and printers thus risked being tried under the Treason Act, which classified as an offence 'all printing, writing, preaching, or malicious and advised speaking, calculated to compass or devise the death, destruction, injury or restraint of the sovereign, or to deprive him of his style, honor, or kingly name'.[7] The penalty on conviction was death.

In 1662 Elizabeth Calvert was living with her husband Giles and their four children in a tenement at the sign of the Black-Spread-Eagle, among the booksellers around Ludgate Hill and St Paul's. They had a shop on the street, a cellar below, four rooms above, and a little yard with an outside staircase and a privy. The shop had been a meeting place for radicals since the 1640s, and at the Restoration, when many printers fled into exile, the Calverts worked on. When Calvert and his former apprentice Thomas Brewster published a blatantly seditious book in support of the regicides, *The Speeches and Prayers of Some of the Late King's Judges*, and joined other booksellers in issuing *The Phoenix*, prophesying the return of the Solemn League and Covenant, L'Estrange leapt into action.

Giles Calvert and Brewster were arrested, tried, and sentenced to the pillory and a spell in prison. (The presiding judge at their trial was Sir Robert Hyde, Clarendon's cousin.) But Elizabeth carried on, printing the even more libellous *Annus Mirabilis, or The Year of Prodigies*, 'prognosticating mischievous events to the King'. Such pamphlets had long been a staple of cheap literature, linked to a strain of Calvinism that deciphered the hand of God in wonders and calamities in the natural world and saw God's providence in protecting England as a 'godly nation'. In royalist sermons, the Restoration itself was often described as an example of providence, but the *Annus Mirabilis* collections implied the opposite. The freakish events, storms and omens were seen as judgements on the nation for restoring a corrupt monarchy and licentious court, and a message to the bishops and all who suppressed freedom of religion.[8] God disapproved, and was warning his people of disaster. As publisher of the latest pamphlet, Elizabeth Calvert was briefly imprisoned. But the *Annus Mirabilis* and *Prodigies* broadsheets continued to spawn copies however hard L'Estrange tried to stop them.[9]

While Charles quarrelled with Catherine on their honeymoon and dealt with Barbara's tantrums and tears, the tension surrounding religion began to weaken his grasp on the nation's goodwill. At the end of June 1662 Pepys wrote anxiously in his diary:

This I take to be as bad a Juncture as ever I observed. The King and his new Queene minding their pleasures at Hampton Court. All people discontented; some that the King doth not gratify them enough; and the others, Fanatiques of all sorts, that the King doth take away their liberty of conscience; and the heighth of the Bishops, who I fear will ruin all again. They do much cry up the manner of Sir H. Vanes death, and he deserves it.[10]

People also protested against the new Hearth Tax and said they would not pay it unless forced to. Anthony Wood summed up the mood: 'This year a saying come up in London, "The Bishops get all, the Courtiers spend all, the Citizens pay for all, the King neglects all, and the Divills take all."'[11]

As the summer wore on towards St Bartholomew's Day, and the Corporation Act, Quaker Act and Licensing Acts were put into force, news of protests streamed into Whitehall, with reports of 'riding in the night' and secret hoards of gunpowder and arms. The royal guards were put on alert and with every rumour the troops pounced on the sects. Like any demonised minority, dissenters were always the favoured suspects: 'almost anything was believed that was said against a Nonconformist,' sighed Baxter.[12] More sermons poured forth on obedience to the civil law, and on the dangers of 'Phanatiques' and papists.

In late August, the time for the implementation of the Act of Uniformity drew near. On the last Sunday that ministers could preach unless they used the new prayer book and renounced the covenant, Evelyn went to church. His vicar obediently read the prescribed prayer book and preached on 'the necessity of obedience to *Christian Magistrates*, & especially *Kings*'. Platoons of guards were out in the City, noted Evelyn, expecting trouble.[13] On the road to Launceston during a tour of the West Country, Schellinks and his friends 'met so many black-coats or parsons that we did not know what to make of it. Some smoked a little pipe on their horses, some hung their heads, some were cheerful, others looked very melancholic . . . all the preachers had come there to swear the Act.'[14] In the town, the inns were full. 'The newly printed revised Book of Common Prayer had been sent the day before to our host and distributed, and he told us that there had been such a throng for it that they had almost torn his clothes off his back.' Next morning, with the book in their hands, all the clergymen came out of their chambers like bees from a hive, to ride to their parishes.

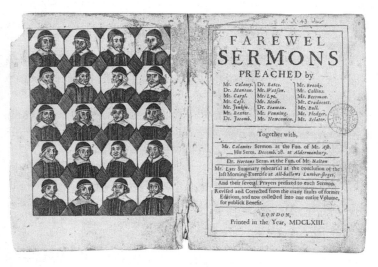

A published collection of the Farewell Sermons of leading churchmen who lost their livings in August 1662, including Edmund Calamy and Richard Baxter.

That Sunday, 24 August 1662, 936 parish ministers, including leading presbyterians and a third of the London clergy, left their parishes in the 'Great Ejection'. With this exodus, roughly two thousand ministers had now left the Church of England since May 1660.[15] They could not even teach, since schoolmasters were also obliged to conform with this Act, and hundreds turned instead to farming or labouring, scraping by on near-starvation rations. Many of their pulpits remained silent, as Sheldon had promised to fill the empty livings with better ministers than those who left, but had grossly underestimated the numbers needed.

At the same time, a nervous Privy Council and parliament over-estimated the numbers of dissenters, and the threat to order. In the provinces, county authorities kept the local militia under arms. Not surprisingly, in October, when government agents cajoled a tiny group of religious separatists among the London artisans into plan-ning an 'uprising', the whole force of the law crashed down on them. According to the informant William Hill, the plot's leader, a Smithfield knife-grinder who had once been a member of Cromwell's Life Guards, had vowed that the 'Rogues' at Whitehall would all be slaughtered and he himself would kill the king, to save England from 'the Tyranny of an Outlandish Dog'.[16] The Dutch would help the rebels with ammunition and shipping, and a force of five hundred men would seize Windsor castle. The intermediary between the Windsor troops and the Londoners was Thomas Tong, a distiller and tobacco merchant. The unrealistic 'Tong plot' was whipped up from low mutterings to a full-blown storm by over-zealous agents, while confusion grew among the conspirators them-selves. In the end five men were executed. The repression increased, and the spies intensified their searches.

The religious settlement was even harder on the people of Scotland and Ireland.[17] In Scotland, Middleton pushed the Scottish council and parliament to reinstate the bishops, a policy to which the former Covenanter Lauderdale, the Secretary of State for Scotland, was utterly opposed. About a third of the clergy remained loyal to the covenant and refused to join the newly established church. Over the winter of 1662–3 tension escalated between Middleton and Lauderdale, and in May Charles replaced Middleton as commis-sioner with the young Earl of Rothes, who was firmly under Lauderdale's thumb. But nothing could save the kirk – the bishops were in place and Scottish dissenters were harried, fined and imprisoned.

In Ireland too the episcopacy was restored: two archbishops and ten bishops were consecrated on a single day in January 1661 in St Patrick's Cathedral in Dublin. But outside the church the majority of people were still Catholic, apart from a minority of Scots nonconformists in Ulster, and in 1649, when he made his agreement with the Catholic lords, Ormond had promised that they could follow their religion. The Irish parliament was stoutly against any such toleration, but Ormond tried to find a way by asking leading Catholics to draw up a statement, a 'Remonstrance', in 1661, which declared that all rulers were 'God's lieutenants', whom all subjects were bound to obey, and no foreign power (in other words the Pope) could overrule a king in his own country. Twenty-one peers and many leading laymen signed, but only seventy out of the country's two thousand priests. Five years later it was formally rejected at a meeting of the Catholic clergy. If they had signed, this could have been a step to legal toleration. As it was, Catholic worship was still technically outside the law, although the Remonstrance did succeed, in Ormond's words, in separating the 'quiet and unquiet spirits', driving a wedge between moderates and militants.[18] And while the Irish parliament prohibited meetings by all separatist religious groups, in practice the authorities found it easier to accept the status quo, and tolerate the Catholics. This inevitably outraged the protestants, and the mood remained uneasy and fearful.

In England and Wales, Sheldon's bishops and their allies held that the legislation restored the true church. To those cast out, however – to Baxter, Bunyan and thousands more – the church and the legislators were forwarding a reign of Antichrist, a time of lewdness, luxury and godlessness. They were enemies of the good, the poor and the pious. 'Nebuchadnezzar will have his *Fiery-Furnace* and Daniel his *Lyon's Den* for Nonconformists,' wrote Bunyan.[19]

That autumn, Pepys's friend Robert Blackborne, a former Commonwealth naval official and convinced puritan, spoke bitterly of how thousands of 'pious Ministers of God' had to beg for bread, while the reinstated clergy behaved so arrogantly 'that they are hated and laughed at by everybody'.²⁰ The King should honour his promises of toleration as a matter of prudence:

He tells me that the King by name, with all his dignities, is prayed for by them that they call Fanatiques, as heartily and powerfully as in any of the other churches that are thought better: and that, let the King think what he will, it is them that must help him in the day of war. For so generally they are the most substantiall sort of people, and the soberest.

Of all the old soldiers of the New Model Army, how many could you see begging on the streets? asked Blackborne. None. All had taken up trades. By contrast to the rowdy young royalists, with their daggers in their belts and swords by their side, these old soldiers were so peaceable that 'the King is safer from any evil meant by them a thousand times more than from his own discontented cavaliers'.²¹ His Privy Council and parliament disagreed.

As the year ended Charles's wish to honour the 'tender consciences of his people' seemed crushed. In addition, many critics surmised that his hidden game was not to protect protestant dissenters but to benefit Catholics. It did not help that only a month after the non-conformist ministers were ejected, the queen's Catholic chapel at St James's, built for Henrietta Maria by Inigo Jones, was declared ready for Catherine, staffed by Benedictine friars and Portuguese Franciscans. The queen attended, conspicuous in her devotion. So did noted protestants at court, not least Barbara Castlemaine. Was Charles perhaps, already a Catholic himself?

Charles's relaxed attitude towards Catholic dissent was not solely a matter of his own leanings, or concern for his friends. Roman Catholics accepted authority without question, even if it be the authority of pope rather than sovereign, whereas puritans taught people to obey God and their consciences rather than man – an easy route to defiance. The freedom to debate that had been claimed since the Reformation, he came to think, had led people to argue matters of state as well as religion. Gradually, with the constant talk of plots, Charles's initial tolerance gave way to frustration with the mass of sects 'each interpreting according to their vile notions and to accomplish their horrid wickednesses'.[22] His irritation was increased by the flood of sermons attacking the pernicious influence of Rome or the sins of lewdness in high places. These were directed straight at him, his mistresses and his friends, and he resented them.

Charles rather encouraged the view that he took his faith lightly: that he slept for the sermon, but woke for the music. He declared several times that a man's religion was personal and private and should never be the subject of persecution. His own beliefs are hard to pin down, suggesting an uneasy fit between public pronouncements and private feelings. As king, he held to his father's strict injunction that he should uphold the doctrines of the Church of England. In exile he had been horrified when his mother tried to bully his younger brother Henry into Catholicism, yet at the same time he was astounded when he discovered the number of penal laws against English Catholics, and declared himself determined to abolish them. All his life he was surrounded by Catholics, including his mother, his wife, at least two of his mistresses and, from 1669, his brother James. There is no evidence that he became a Catholic convert in his years abroad (the Pope would hardly have kept this coup a secret), although his later minister, Halifax, vowed that 'when he came into England he was as certainly a Roman Catholick, as that he was a Man of Pleasure; both very consistent by visible Experience'.[23]

It was part of Charles's mask, his innate duplicity, thought Halifax, to joke and tease and make the world think he cared nothing for religion. Ormond, who had stuck strongly to his own protestant beliefs in the midst of a large Catholic family, also believed that Charles was a convert, having seen him at mass in Brussels, but he did not think this necessarily made him a devout believer. It was not, Ormond thought, that Charles was a total sceptic, or an atheist: he showed little concern for religion, yet 'he did not want a sense of it'. He set aside time for private devotions and professed his belief in the Deity, the Messiah and the afterlife, 'but had very large notions of God's mercy, that he would not make his creatures for ever miserable on account of their personal failing. Upon this notion he indulged himself in his pleasures.'²⁴ Ormond noticed too that he laid little stress on the different systems of religion 'and would frequently take delight to tease his brother, who was very serious and zealous in his way, with reflecting on the scandalous lives of some popes, and laughing at some particular tenets of the Roman Catholics'.²⁵

For Charles, religious attitudes were inseparable from politics. In domestic matters he must appear a stout protestant, but in his international dealings it was in his interest to make it appear to his cousin Louis XIV that he was a Catholic at heart. One catches something of Charles's own dry wit in the French ambassador's report, 'He will do nothing against our religion, except under the pressure of Parliament. I find he is well aware that no other creed matches so well with the absolute authority of kings.'²⁶ His flippancy and scepticism may also have been a mode of self-defence, a way of warding off the over-earnest. The keen-eyed Magalotti noted this horror of anything deep: 'Serious men terrify him, merry and amusing ones fill him with delight.' But, he thought, 'He is very light hearted about religion, but if he were obliged to reflect upon it I do not think he would find salvation outside the Catholic faith.'²⁷

14 The King Street Gang

You sit above and see vain men below
Contend for what you only can bestow;
But those great actions others do by chance,
Are, like your beauty, your inheritance.
        DRYDEN, 'To the Lady Castlemaine'

RELIGIOUS POLICY was one area where Charles's private life col-lided with his actions as the crown. In the summer of 1662, the Bedchamber Crisis, as it became known, when Barbara Castlemaine fought to become part of Catherine's retinue, was a matter of high politics as well as sex.

Clarendon doggedly maintained his hostility to Barbara and to her friends, forbidding his wife to receive her, or speak to her at court. He could not accept that the king was no longer the adoles-cent he had chivvied long ago and still lectured him at length. But by now Charles was shaking off his long habit of deference to his adviser. Clarendon seemed old and priggish and his refusal to accept his mistress was exasperating. For her part, Barbara's rage made her long, she said, to see the Chancellor's head set on a spike, like the regicides at Westminster Hall. The spirited courtier Daniel O'Neill wrote to his old friend Ormond in Ireland, 'I dare say she says no less to the King for there is no limit to her power nor his fondness.'[1] Then he joked, linking Barbara's 'parts' – her intelli-gence – to her private parts, 'It's happy her parts does not answer else she would make mad work.'

Barbara's parts, her cleverness and shrewd assessment of political realities, were far from lacking. She was aiming at a new role in British court life, that of an official '*maîtresse en titre*', like the powerful mistresses of French monarchs. Recognising the power of image-making, she was one of the first to patronise Lely when he was made court painter in 1661. Lely adored her, declaring that her 'sweetness and incomparable beauty' were 'beyond the power of art'. He painted her in many guises: as a pensive, penitent Magdalen with hair streaming over her shoulder; as a powerful-looking Amazon, or an Arcadian shepherdess. He even painted her as St Catherine, an ironic tribute to the queen, and as quasi-Madonna with her infant son, a deliberately provocative pose, since, unlike the queen, she appeared to be pregnant again.[2] These portraits, copied in paint and engraved as prints, established a template for court beauty: sloe-eyed sexiness, full lips, sloping shoulders and snowy bosoms.

Lely's portrait of Barbara Castlemaine in her blue robe, holding her son Charles Fitzroy, has ironic echoes of the Madonna and Child: the baby is not her husband's child but the son of the most powerful being in the land.

Barbara was continuing her campaign to control the Queen's household by manoeuvring to have the Countess of Pendalva sent back to Portugal, thus depriving Catherine of her chief link with home. Not only was Barbara's aunt, the Countess of Suffolk, her Mistress of the Robes, but her supporters among the loyal Killigrew family were in key positions, Sir William as Catherine's vice-chamberlain, his sister-in-law Charlotte as Keeper of the Sweet Coffers (looking after gloves and feathers, fans and hats and perfumes) and soon his wife Mary as one of her dressers.[3]

The Castlemaine house in King Street operated as a kind of alternative court salon. Many returning courtiers decorated their apartments in the French style, with lighter furniture, candlelight reflected off mirrors, and Turkey carpets and polished plate shining against the old panelling. Barbara's cook was good, and after dinner her guests could drift into another room for cards or for music. Friends gathered for the witty conversation and excellent food, but also because the king was often to be found there in an off-duty mood so that it was easy to get him on one side. Barbara virtually ran her own royal 'withdrawing room', like the circle that gathered around the queen or the queen mother in the early evenings, where both sexes were welcome and the talk was informal. But here the mood was far livelier, and flirtation and politics mixed. King Street became a base for a particular group of courtiers, united chiefly by their hostility to the Chancellor. Clarendon had alienated many individual courtiers for different reasons, and both the Catholics and presbyterians at court blamed him, as much as the bishops, for the Act of Uniformity. The King Street clique contained partisans for both the Catholic and nonconformist cause, as well as young politicians on the make.

Among the Catholics, the most vehement was George Digby, Earl of Bristol, who was now, in Clarendon's view, doing all he could to please the king, arranging 'meetings and jollities' and inviting Charles and Barbara to his country house in Wimbledon.[4] Also in Barbara's salon was the rising star Sir Henry Bennet, who was not a Catholic but whose history and pro-Spanish views linked him firmly to Bristol, although at this point he also carefully kept in with Clarendon. Like Clarendon, Bennet came from a modest family, but with connections at court: one of his aunts was married to Thomas Killigrew and his cousin Will Crofts had long been a key figure in Charles's household. As a young man, Bennet had entered Bristol's service in 1643 as his secretary and had then followed his relation, Sir Kenelm Digby, on his journeys to seek help for Charles I in Rome and Paris. He then became a secret messenger between Henrietta Maria and Ormond in Ireland before joining the exiled court, and acting as secretary to James, Duke of York, whom he heartily detested.

Bennet was one of the wild group of courtiers who provided some diversion after the disaster of Worcester and Charles became very fond of him: his letters to his 'dear Harry' are some of the liveliest and most intimate of the exile, jumping easily from politics to gossip and the latest style in cloaks. In 1657 he was knighted and sent as an ambassador to Spain and he had remained in Madrid at the Restoration, returning to London in April 1661. This was rather late to stake a claim to the best posts, and Bennet was now looking for a way to lever himself up, if not through Clarendon then through Barbara Castlemaine and her allies.

In his early forties, Bennet was a striking figure, stalking the Whitehall corridors wearing a black velvet suit and swirling cape. He was extremely tall, with pale eyes set in a long, dark face made sinister by a black plaster worn to cover a Civil War scar on the bridge of his nose. A tireless worker, able to read five languages, he appeared cold and secretive yet curiously exhibitionist at the same time. While people laughed at him for his fastidious 'Castilian' air, even his enemies admitted that when he was at ease he could be charming, and 'had the best turns of wit in a particular conversation'.[5] Furthermore, 'he had the art', wrote Burnet, 'of observing the King's temper, and managing it beyond all the men of that time'.[6] Charles knew his talents and gave him his head – it is hard to tell quite who was 'managing' who. In August 1661, partly through Barbara's influence, Bennet was made Keeper of the King's Privy Purse, an extremely useful position that allowed him to dole out large sums of money on request, without going through official channels.

The protestant partisans in this circle included Barbara's cousin Buckingham, who despite his erratic ways stoutly espoused the presbyterian cause until his death. There were also several members of the distinguished Montagu family, headed by the Lord Chamberlain, the Earl of Manchester. His ambitious sons, Edward and Ralph, were now Masters of Horse to the King and the Duke of York respectively, and their cousin, Sandwich, was also a prominent guest when Barbara gave a ball that autumn. Barbara herself – to the surprise of those who thought she had no serious aims, – fought fiercely for the cause of the nonconformists. 'You will hardly believe it,' hissed O'Neill, 'but it's very true, that the powerful Lady is . . . the fiercest solicitor these ejected Ministers have. She has falne out with the king.'[7] But although they had fallen out that autumn, Charles's passion had not abated and he showered her with favours 'all which the virtuous Quene bears with a masculine courage and patience'. A fortnight later, O'Neill confessed he could not see how the tranquillity of the court could continue: how could Catherine endure 'the neglect of the king and the insolency of the dame'.[8]

Barbara's support for the nonconformists may have stemmed less from principle than from a desire to unseat Clarendon, whose arrogance had by now also upset Bennet. In exile, Clarendon had been Bennet's mentor, but he was wary of the younger man's ambition and blocked him from two posts, first as ambassador to France in January 1662 and then as Postmaster General, a position that Charles, urged by Barbara, had openly promised him. In mid-September O'Neill drily surmised that Clarendon's stubbornness was an error, enraging Charles, and that 'this puts the King upon an other designe that Bennet will find more his advantage in and that will less please the chancellor'.[9]

He was right. The next month, October, the King Street faction took two steps nearer to power. First Charles persuaded one of his two Secretaries of State, Sir Edward Nicholas, who was now nearly seventy, to take a golden handshake of £10,000 and retire to the country. Nicholas went, believing that his son would succeed him. Instead Charles gave the post to Bennet, who immediately moved into rooms at Whitehall, knocking out a doorway that led onto the king's private stairs so that they could meet without people knowing. Next, he gave Bennet's old place as Keeper of the Privy Purse to Charles Berkeley. 'The young men get uppermost,' wrote Pepys on 17 October, 'and the old serious lords are out of favour.'[10] Mopping up the gossip, Pepys labelled Berkeley 'a most vicious person', having been told by the King's surgeon, Mr Pierce '(at which I did laugh to myself)', that Berkeley had offered Pierce's beautiful wife £300 a year to be his mistress. Pierce added that no one had the king's ear more than Bennet and Berkeley and Lady Castlemaine.

Bennet's new position was one of real influence. In consultation with the inner 'foreign committee' of the Privy Council, the two Secretaries of State were responsible for all diplomatic negotiations, dividing the territories between them. Bennet's brief included France, Spain, Portugal, the Dutch States, Flanders, Italy, Turkey, 'Barbary' and the Indies, while Morice looked after Denmark, Sweden, Russia, Poland, Switzerland, the Holy Roman Empire and the German states. But Morice was seldom at court and in reality Bennet ruled all. At Ormond's request, he also took over Irish affairs. In addition, he supervised security at home, managing the Post Office and the secret service.

So far Clarendon had dealt with all these matters, even though they were not strictly his province. Now he found, to his alarm, that Bennet was acting alone, without asking his advice. Clarendon's popularity sank still further, if that were possible, when news broke in late October of the sale of Dunkirk to the French for five million livres. This was a ploy to bring in money, and also get rid of a port that was a permanent drain on the exchequer, but the symbolic impact of sell-ing Britain's one continental possession to her old enemy the French was incalculable, and damaging. At once there was outcry. London merchants sent a deputation to Whitehall protesting that the loss of Dunkirk would make shipping vulnerable to privateers, who would use it as a base, and Charles had to beg Louis XIV to issue an edict against them using the harbour. But the cash reward was great. The goldsmith Edward Backwell and others crossed the Channel in the fast royal yachts to collect the money from Calais. Backwell brought back two million livres at once and Charles and James dashed to the Tower to see the silver ecus glinting in their coffers at the Mint.[11] The rest of the money flowed through in quarterly payments.

At the same time, another, overlapping clique was forming in oppo-sition to the Chancellor, with the same determination to overturn the new religious laws. After spending some months at Greenwich, Henrietta Maria had moved into Somerset House in the Strand. Charles's sporadic account books, which noted oil-cloths for his barge, sums for Killigrew's revels, black velvet caps for watermen, summer liveries for choirboys and presents for the ambassadors, often listed gifts for his mother, including satin, silver lace and silver twists for a new dress.[12] At Somerset House, as at Greenwich, Henrietta Maria established her evening 'circle', which had been a key part of the court day when she was queen. Catherine dutifully attended, and so did many other courtiers, and often Charles and James dropped in. Secure of her place, Henrietta Maria set about winning friends – including Lady Castlemaine – and used all her influence to combat the new religious laws.

In the autumn of 1662 Clarendon lamented to Ormond, 'That which breakes my hearte is that the same affections continew still, the same lazynesse and unconcernednesse in business, and a pro-portionable abatement of reputation.'[13] These were the accusations he had levelled at Charles all through his youth, and in a way he was right. But habit had blinded him; far from being lazy, this autumn Charles was feverishly concerned with 'businesse'. Over the summer various members of the King Street set, including Bristol and Bennet, had met regularly at Manchester's house to lay plans against the religious legislation, and had drafted a declaration for the king to propose. In this they were helped by the presbyterian Lord Robartes, and by Anthony Ashley Cooper, Lord Ashley, a brilliant orator and a latitudinarian in spirit, who was rapidly becoming the patron of nonconformism in the Lords.

On 26 December, taking advantage of the fact that Clarendon was laid low by gout and confined to his house in the bitter winter weather, and thus unable to argue against him, Charles issued the 'Declaration to Tender Consciences' that Manchester and his allies had concocted. This proposed that until a proper bill could be put before parliament, the king should use his royal prerogative and position as Supreme Governor of the Church of England to suspend the penalties on dissenters. For a fee, protestant nonconformists could apply for licences to worship publicly, and Catholics to conduct private services.

It was a bold move, ruined by a fatal lack of nerve. Charles added a proviso saying that he would issue no formal declaration without parliament's consent. In February 1663, when the declaration was to be put forward as the basis for a bill, he put his case at Westminster. First, he objected personally to the severity of the laws. 'The truth is', he argued, 'I am in my nature an enemy to all severity for Religion and Conscience, how mistaken soever it be, when it extend to capital and sanguinary punishments.'[14] Secondly, he suggested, rightly, that current policy was shortsighted and was provoking the very unrest the Commons feared, adding with regard to dissenters that he wished he had 'such a power of indulgence, as might not needlessly force them out of the kingdom, or staying here, give them cause to conspire against the peace of it'.

This note of practical politics persuaded the Lords but stood no chance with the Commons. They refused to ratify the declaration, citing their fears that it would lead to Popery and increase the number of sectaries. The MPs were particularly outraged at the declaration's openness to Catholics, although Charles explained that they were included because so many Catholic families had served his father and himself during the wars.[15] In May, when it was clear the bill would make no progress, Charles withdrew his declaration. The defeat was stinging, and discouraged him for a long time from attempting to modify and tone down the religious settlement.

He had played too high, laying down a card that many felt he had no right to hold. As well as opposing his stance of toleration, most MPs felt that he had exercised a royal prerogative in matters of religion that he could no longer claim. Even those who favoured greater tolerance had been worried by the implication that such a prerogative could sweep away statutes already on the books. It seemed that a king was once more claiming to be above parliament and the law. Clarendon, who had not openly opposed the declaration, was horrified. The power it granted to the crown was not specific, he said in a moment of frankness that he would afterwards bitterly regret, but so open and far-reaching that it recalled the actions of Charles I, when he tried to obtain ship-money without having parliament's consent. This was a fatal slip, since it not only attacked Charles, but raised the spectre of the royal arrogance and parliamentary anger that had destroyed his father.

Knowing how much Clarendon's remarks would gall Charles, Bennet and many others waited for the Chancellor's dismissal. But annoyed though he was, Charles realised that his views were widely shared. This was not the time to make a move against him. Despite this, Clarendon felt the chill in Whitehall. By June he was almost in despair, confessing to Ormond that he was exhausted by his task: 'the truth is, I am so broken with it that were it not for the hope of once more seeing you, & consulting together, and trying like good men what we can, I would Passyonately contrive the getting into some corner, and to be forgotten.'[16]

One problem was, in Clarendon's view, that in the three years since the parliament was elected, every time a seat fell vacant great pains were taken to ensure that it was filled with one of the courtiers or royal servants. The new MPs therefore felt they should take directions from the king himself, rather than from Clarendon. He had got used to 'quietly managing' parliament to vote the way he wanted it to, and was alarmed in the spring of 1663 to see that Bennet and Bristol, working with the MP Sir Richard Temple, were now trying to direct parliament themselves, with far less subtlety. When news of Bristol's manoeuvrings got out, the House of Commons was furious at such interference from a member of the House of Lords, and Bristol was forced to make a public apology. Stung to the quick, he rounded on Clarendon.

Bristol was always likely to do something extreme, and the whole town ran with rumours. When Charles summoned him to explain

George Digby, Earl of Bristol, painted by Van Dyck in romantic pose.

himself, he was full of bluster and threats against the Chancellor. 'The king stood all this time in confusion,' as Clarendon described it, 'that though he gave him more sharp words than were natural to him, he had not that presentness of mind (as he afterwards accused himself) as he ought to have had.' In Clarendon's view, which he put into Charles's mouth, he ought to have called for the guard and sent him to the Tower.[17]

Batting Charles's angry objections aside, in July Bristol marched into the House of Lords and accused Clarendon of high treason. His grounds, absurdly, were that the Chancellor was furthering Popery, and that he had received bribes from the French for the sale of Dunkirk. Charles demanded to see Bristol's speech and told him that it was seditious. But Bristol carried on, even though Clarendon's son-in-law James told the Lords that the king disapproved and knew the charges were false. The matter was referred to the judges (all Clarendon appointees), who found the accusations absurd and threw them out. Bristol was banished from court and Charles ordered a warrant for his arrest. He fled, to spend the next three years in hiding. It was a blow for the faction around Barbara Castlemaine. Yet the public dislike of Clarendon was so great that three months after Bristol's hysterical speech, the French ambassador the comte de Cominges reported that London crowds were seen drinking his health as '*le champion de la patrie*'.[18]

Although Charles was angry with Bristol, Bennet and the others in the King Street set seemed exempt from his rage. In July, when Bristol was storming into the Lords, Charles granted new titles to Berkeley, creating him Baron Berkeley of Rathdowne and Viscount Fitzhardinge of Berehaven. (These were Irish titles like the Castlemaines', by-passing the Privy Seal and the criticism of the Commons.) In parliament Bennet was building up support, helped by the Devon MP Thomas Clifford and William Coventry, the bluff, independent-minded secretary to the Duke of York and commissioner for the navy. Both these newcomers were roughly the same age as Charles – new, rising men.[19]

15 'Governed as Beasts'

. . . For on Earth
Who against Faith and Conscience can be heard
Infallible? Yet many will presume:
Whence heavie persecution shall arise
On all who in the worship persevere
Of Spirit and Truth; the rest, farr greater part,
Will deem in outward Rites and specious formes
Religion satisfied.

JOHN MILTON, *Paradise Lost*, Book XII

CHARLES WAS RIGHT to fear that unrest would flow from the new religious statutes. Sectarian pamphlets and republican broadsheets and almanacs multiplied, and in the summer of 1663 the Privy Council ordered the militia to ride into the countryside to break up conventicles, nonconformist meetings. One Wiltshire officer, William Levett, reported with pride to his colonel that his troop had ridden into Marlborough and 'assaulted the burial place of the Quakers at Wanton and laid it waste'.[1] In retaliation the outraged townsfolk stoned the Lord Lieutenant, Lord Herbert, as he rode through the town and he and his friends were forced to draw their swords and fire their pistols to disperse the crowd.

Everyone was on edge. Because the sects had been so active in the New Model Army, people muttered that former soldiers would rise up, as they had done recently in Ireland, and would join in a rebellion led by the regicides in hiding in Holland or by former parliamentarian generals. A well-organised plan to seize Dublin Castle was uncovered in June. This involved several members of the Irish parliament and army officers, including the self-proclaimed 'Captain' Thomas Blood, who later promoted himself to colonel and became famous for trying to steal the crown jewels. About fifty soldiers in the castle were ready to join them, having got arms and gunpowder out of the store, 'by the folly of the storekeeper's boy'.[2] The Dublin plot unnerved the authorities on the mainland. There were early hints too of a planned rebellion in the north, to be led by republican exiles, and the name of Edmund Ludlow, now living in Geneva, was mentioned as a leader (as it would be in every such scare until 1667).[3] Letters flew between Clarendon and Charles's ambassador in the Hague, Sir George Downing, who had been Cromwell's ambassador before, and knew the country well. Orangist supporters, gathering information with enthusiasm, plied him with details of religious and political exiles, including skilled artisans, merchants and former soldiers.

Charles and the Privy Council were used to rumours and to begin with they took them lightly. Bennet told Ormond that he was sure that rumour of the northern uprising was a false alarm, and Charles himself agreed. According to Clarendon, 'the continual discourse of plots and insurrections had so wearied the king, that he even resolved to give no more countenance to any such informations, nor to trouble himself with enquiry into them'.[4] Instead, he said, he would leave the peace of the kingdom to the vigilance of the civil magistrates. But the intelligence from the north (much of it supplied by Bishop Cosin of Durham) was so persistent and persuasive that the militia was raised. According to government spies, a group of presbyterians and Anabaptists were planning to capture Whitehall and seize Clarendon, Monck and the Duke of York, in order to force Charles to carry out his Breda promises, and to abolish the hated Excise and the Hearth Tax.

In early August Buckingham, as Lieutenant of the West Riding, was sent to Yorkshire with a troop of horse, to round up the rebels. Most of the leaders were former republicans and army officers who had been part of the administration of the north during the Interregnum. Several fled to Holland and others turned informer, but in October the Deputy Lieutenant of the North Riding made eighty-eight arrests. A couple of nights later, small clusters of armed men gathered in Yorkshire and Westmorland, but dispersed when they realised they were not, as had been promised, part of a nation-wide revolt. Buckingham helped to conduct their examination in York, 'diverting himself at nights with his deputy lieutenants and officers, or dancing with the ladys, where hapnd many adventures'.[5]

As Buckingham danced, delighted at the chance to get back into Charles's good graces, the rebels, with supporters who had not taken up arms but had only talked of an uprising, lingered in gaol. In the end, after a series of trials, twenty-two were executed. After his fierce, though failed, efforts on behalf of the dissenters, Charles felt personally wounded by the rebellion, and urged the judges sent up from London to be severe. 'It would very much conduce to the settlement of the public peace', he told Sir Godfrey Copley in February 1664, 'if more of those heinous offenders were made examples to deter others from the like mischievous practices.'[6] Roger L'Estrange magnified the revolt in the press, finding eager readers among hysterical Anglican royalists like the East India merchant Humphrey Gyfford. 'Gag, crush and geld them', Gyfford fumed, so 'that in our generation they shall not be suffered to foment, scratch or bite and in good time that there may be no more of their breed, which God of his mercy grant.'[7]

The Privy Council took fright, sending out arrest warrants for the remaining Commonwealth leaders who were still at large. The government also turned furiously against the unlicensed press. In October 1663 one of L'Estrange's dawn raids found the printer John Twyn turning out copies of *A Treatise of the Execution of Justice*, a call to rebellion, citing biblical precedents and asserting the 'godly duty' to remove the 'Bloody and Oppressing' house of Stuart.[8] For this, and for an earlier tract against hereditary monarchy, Twyn was hanged, drawn and quartered, a horrendous punishment out of all proportion to his so-called crime. Two fellow printers were on the jury that convicted him. He argued, unsuccessfully, that he was merely the printer. He did not know the book's content, and had simply agreed to print one thousand copies for the bookseller Giles Calvert because he needed the money. Calvert had died in August 1663 and Twyn had, he said, just sent the printed sheets to Calvert's widow Elizabeth.

The 'Confederate' printers Thomas Brewster and Simon Dover and the bookbinder Nathan Brooks were also rounded up. Their trial was set for February 1664, at the same time as Twyn's, but they were tried only for libel and not for treason. They were put in the pillory, charged heavy fines and sent to prison, where both printers later died of illness. Great crowds followed their funeral processions. Like Elizabeth Calvert, their widows worked on, loyal to the cause. (L'Estrange called Ann Brewster and another woman printer, Joan Darby, 'a couple of the craftiest and most obstinate in the trade'.[9]) The Commonwealth sects had given women the freedom to speak out, and in the conspiracies of these years they were as active as the men, at least according to the informer John Ironmonger:

Designs are often carried on chiefly through women, some the wives of prisoners, who have access to their husbands' fortune, have access to them, and to others on pretence of soliciting for them, and write in covert terms of trade or meet each other to convey intelligence &c. Secret meetings are often held at Channell's, a milliner in Tower Street, also at Hackney, and at schools kept by matrons for young women.[10]

The printers continued to supply the booksellers and all the country fairs. The Quakers, in particular, did not recognise the state's right to suppress the written word, any more than they recognised its right to stop Quaker men – and women – from preaching. They organised the distribution of their publications centrally, and their printed works, letters and records created a sense of community that stretched across the land. They were not cowed by authority. The Quaker Charles Bayley, imprisoned in the Tower in the Plague Year, wrote directly to Charles, *The Causes of Gods Wrath Against England . . . in a Letter to the King.*

One effect of the suppression of the sects was to make people look inward, to use 'spiritual weapons' not carnal ones, as Fox had said,

Growing up in grandeur. In Van Dyck's great painting of 1632, which hung in the Long Gallery at Whitehall, the three-year-old Charles stands at the knee of his father, Charles I, while his mother, Henrietta Maria, holds the baby Mary, later Princess of Orange. Behind the crown, clouds gather over the distant Parliament House and Westminster Hall.

Charles II, in extravagant, quasi-Roman dress, as founder and patron of
the Royal Society in 1662.

James, Duke of York in 1661: blonde, handsome and stubborn.
The solemn Mary, Princess of Orange, in the early 1650s.
Henriette-Anne, 'Minette', aged sixteen, when she paid her first visit to England.
Their dashing cousin, Prince Rupert, cavalier and scientist, son of Charles I's sister,
Elizabeth of Bohemia.

Charles II's colourful cavalcade through the City on 22 April 1661, the eve of
his coronation, winds beneath the triumphal arches. The king dominates in his
plumed hat, while the Duke of York in front, and General Monck behind,
both ride bareheaded.

Ceremony and crowds. The Prince de Ligne, ambassador extraordinary of Spain,
arrives at Tower Wharf before making his formal entrée at court.

'The General', George Monck, whose march south cleared the way for the Restoration.
Edward Hyde, Earl of Clarendon, weighed down by his Chancellor's robes.
The brilliant but volatile George Villiers, Duke of Buckingham, wearing his enormous, fashionable periwig.
James Butler, Duke of Ormond, the model of a stylish courtier, with his long fair hair curling over robes of state.

Charles II's stormy mistress, the sloe-eyed beauty Barbara Villiers, Countess of
Castlemaine, painted by Sir Peter Lely around 1662 as a mythological figure of
Justice, a force to be reckoned with.

The lonely young queen, Catherine of Braganza, having abandoned her
Portuguese hairstyle and clumsy farthingale. But although Lely transforms her into
an acceptable court beauty her face is still puffy and sad.

Two views of Whitehall from St James's Park. In both, Charles walks in a gaggle of courtiers, with his spaniels scampering in front and guards parading in the background. The first suggests the informal, rural park, with deer and cows, and the second leads the eye to the Banqueting House across the road and the new staircase to the Privy Gallery and to Barbara Castlemaine's apartments above the Holbein Gate.

to raise consciousness not to raise arms. Bunyan wrote, in his *Prison Meditations*, in 1665:

> For though men keep my outward man
> Within these Locks and Bars
> Yet by the faith of Christ I can
> Mount higher than the Stars.[11]

His spiritual autobiography, *Grace Abounding to the Chief of Sinners*, appeared in 1666, and he worked on *Pilgrim's Progress* in his Bedford gaol. *Paradise Lost* too is a work of this kind, offering to the fallen Adam, and to the poem's reader, the prospect of 'a paradise within thee, happier far' than the lost Eden, to be attained through personal spiritual renewal.[12] This too could be a refuge for the soul in times of 'heavie persecution'.

Boosted by their successes, the church establishment planned even harsher legislation. When the frail William Juxon, Archbishop of Canterbury, died in June 1663, his successor, inevitably, was Sheldon. Once in place, Sheldon set about gathering information by conducting a survey of all the dissenters in his diocese and issuing virulent propaganda against them. It was his view, often quoted, that only a resolute application of the law could cure the 'disease' of nonconformity. It was necessary, he declared, 'that those who will not be governed as men by reason and persuasions should be governed as beasts by power and force, all other courses will be ineffectual, ever have been so, ever will be so'.[13]

Sheldon had firmly opposed all Charles's attempts to suspend or modify the laws. He now began drafting the Conventicles Act of 1664, which made it illegal for anyone over sixteen to attend a meeting of more than five people 'under colour or pretence of any exercise of religion' without using the Book of Common Prayer.[14] This time, remembering Yorkshire, Charles supported the Act and ensured it was fiercely implemented. By now the law against meetings was so strict that one man was imprisoned simply for reading printed sermons to friends at his own house: he begged to be released, 'his family being numerous and his means small'.[15] Sheldon then took a further step, requiring his bishops to find out where ejected ministers lived, what they were doing, and how active they were in terms of a threat to church peace. This was in preparation for the Five Mile Act of 1665, which forbade the ejected ministers and schoolteachers to come within five miles of corporate towns, or the parish where they had formerly preached or taught.[16] This time, while a third of any fines collected went to the crown, and a third to the local corporation, a third was set aside for informers who had furthered the conviction, a new and insidious form of oppression.

The Five Mile Act was the last of the cluster of penal religious laws known as the Clarendon Code – unfairly, since Clarendon had many reservations about them. But the Lord Chancellor was the head of the legal system. And Clarendon was Sheldon's old friend. Both had been members of the philosophical and literary circle who had met at Lord Falkland's home, Great Tew, in the 1630s. Then they had been reformers, criticising the harshness of Laud, but now they were oppressors in their turn.

The application of the laws varied greatly from town to town, county to county. Not every Church of England priest followed the prayer book and puritan pastors often conformed on paper but not in practice, like Ralph Josselin in Essex, who managed to go without putting on a surplice or using the prayer book for many years. In some places, where a dissenter or former minister was charged with offences against the acts, the magistrates simply refused to prosecute, especially in corporations with a solid core of puritans: Bristol, Gloucester and Taunton in the west, Newcastle upon Tyne in the north, Canterbury and Dover in the south, and Norwich and Great Yarmouth in the east. In Great Yarmouth, the laws were strictly applied for the first four years, but after new bailiffs were elected dissenters began to meet again. In other towns, however, penalties were imposed harshly. In Bunyan's small Bedford community, dissenting preachers went into hiding, or were resigned to going in and out of prison.

The Anglican establishment was not altogether repressive. An influential group of clergy, including several future bishops like John Wilkins, Edward Stillingfleet and John Tillotson, had supported comprehension and were sympathetic to moderate presbyterians. Wilkins, for example, advocated a religious life based not on dogma but on piety, works and tolerance. Known as the 'Latitude-men' in the 1650s and later dubbed Latitudinarians, they worked hard towards greater toleration later in the decade. Yet by then it was too late. Sheldon and his allies had created a schism between the established church and dissent that would never be healed, like the old rift between the church and the Catholics. The effects would be immense, not only in the assault on nonconformity but on the whole political, commercial and cultural life of the country for a century to come.

16 The Spring of the Air

Since that this thing we call the world
By chance on atoms is begot,
Which though in daily motions hurled
    Yet weary not,
    How doth it prove
Thou art so fair, and I in love?
    JOHN HALL, 'An Epicurean Ode'

CHARLES WAS FAR MORE AWARE than Clarendon and his other older advisers that ways of thinking were changing. This was most obviously the case with religion, where so many sects appealed to individual judgement rather than the guidance of a minister in their relationship with their God. But it was also true in the wider realm of philosophy, especially natural philosophy. Here too, there were competing systems explaining the ways of nature. The ancient Aristotelian thinking and the medieval hermetic tradition of the alchemists clashed and overlapped with newer Paracelsian chemical theories and the mechanical theories of Descartes. There were arguments, in particular, about the nature of space. Was the empty space between objects a vacuum, or was the universe full of invisible but touching and intermingling bodies, a 'subtle aetherial fluid'?

This might seem to have little to do with kingship, but Thomas Hobbes, Charles's teacher in Paris, had made natural philosophy overtly political – and anti-clerical – in *Leviathan* in 1651. Hobbes had given a fair copy of the manuscript to the young King on his return to France after the defeat at Worcester, and his views and anti-Catholic stance were found so dangerous by Henrietta Maria that within a couple of months he was hounded from court. But although Charles was briefly upset by *Leviathan*, 'his majestie had a good Opinion of him, and sayd openly that he thought Mr Hobbes never meant him hurt'.[1]

Hobbes was a 'plenist', belonging to the camp that believed the universe was full of matter. There could be no such thing therefore as 'incorporeal bodies', the very term was a contradiction. So when priests referred to souls, to spirits, to angels and divinities in these terms they were talking nonsense. But it was useful non-sense, as it allowed them to set up an invisible authority in oppos-ition to the civil power, the sovereign. For Catholics, this invisible power was embodied in the Pope but the protestant sects, even more dangerously, appealed directly to the Bible. Hobbes saw this as one of the causes of civil war, a point he repeated in his condem-nation of clerics in *Behemoth* in 1668, alluding to 'Ministers, as they called themselves, of Christ; and sometimes, in their sermons to the people, God's ambassadors; pretending to have a right from God to govern every one in their parish, and their assembly the whole nation'.[2]

The material world was also the great concern of Robert Boyle, the seventh son of the Earl of Cork and younger brother of Lords Burlington and Orrery. 'I could be very well content', he wrote, 'to have scarce looked upon any other book than that of nature.'[3] But Boyle – like Newton – found no conflict between nature, subject-ed to the enquiries of reason, and his religious faith. Reason itself was a divine light, granted to mankind. The main aim of his enquiries, Boyle said, was to raise in himself and others 'vaster thoughts of the greatness and glory, and of the wisdom and good-ness of God'.[4] In terms of natural philosophy, he rejected all gov-erning philosophical theories like plenism, in favour of a new experimental science that would gather information through observation and experiment and then make deductions as to cause and effect. Telescopes and microscopes had shown that things long taken for granted were other than what they seemed. In 1660 Boyle was making claims about the nature of the prime element, the air, and using his new, expensive air-pump. Nothing could be certain: everything had moved into the realm of probability.

Robert Boyle, engraved with his air-pump below left, and furnace, crucibles and instruments to the right.

Was this also a dangerous challenge to ideas of authority? This approach did not only question established systems but the pre-eminence of reason itself. Simply in terms of the way these philosophers thought, an attack on the hierarchy of understanding could

also have political undertones, as shown by Robert Hooke's sugges-
tive language: 'The Understanding is to order all the inferiour services of the lower faculties; but yet it is to do this only as a *lawful
Master*, and not as a *Tyrant* . . . It must *watch* the irregularities of the
Senses, but it must not go before them, or *prevent* their information.'[5]
Boyle's *New Experiments Physico-Mechanical* was published in June
1660, the honeymoon month of the Restoration. In it Boyle
explained what his air-pump could do, its failures as well as successes, establishing himself as a modest man of good faith who had
no wish to hoodwink his readers – just as Charles initially presented himself as a 'sober man' who wished not to impose rigid systems
but to heal rifts that were not of his making. Charles was intrigued
by the new knowledge. He wanted to accommodate different views,
to be open and accessible to all his subjects while still claiming the
authority that Hobbes saw as vital to stability.

Like Boyle, Charles was convinced that the way to create a con-
sensus, a platform for agreement and inclusion, was to create a
forum where men of all persuasions could come to discuss new
ideas without rancour. The church, for example, had been split by
profound animosities, 'which, when they shall hereafter unite in a
freedom of conversation, will be composed, or better understood'.[6]
In this case the 'free air' of discussion was supposed to be the
Worcester Conference, while in natural philosophy it was the club
at Gresham College which quickly developed into the Royal
Society. Boyle and his allies – who included clerics like John Wilkins
– used a language similar to that of the moderate churchmen, being
wary of 'enthusiasts' and sectaries, 'dogma' and doctrine. Like
Charles at Breda, Boyle wanted to embrace dissidents within the
group, rather than creating enemies outside. And, he insisted, they
could only be persuaded by a positive use of language: showing the
alchemists, for example, how close their practice was to experimental chemistry, while being careful not to attack their underlying
ideas. 'Quarrelsome and injurious' words must be abjured; courtesy
was vital:

For if I civilly endeavour to reason a man out of his opinions, I make myself but one work to do, namely, to convince his understanding; but, if in a bitter or exasperating way I oppose his errors, I increase the difficulties I would surmount, and have as well his affections against me as his judgment.

This was also Charles's preferred approach: affability and courtesy were important weapons in his arsenal, whereas Clarendon made enemies by his quick temper and disdain for opponents. At the Savoy Conference in 1661 the calm air of discussion had quickly broken down into 'bitter or exasperating' argument: once they felt openly slighted, the presbyterian ministers threw up their defences.

Charles was therefore intrigued by the approach of the experimental philosophers, especially their call to lay aside factions and unite in a common search for knowledge. The novelty of their work also attracted him. Like many young aristocrats of the time, he liked the oddity of their findings and the mechanical ingenuity of their inventions. He had first become interested at the age of sixteen, when he and Buckingham were spending bored months in St Germain. In the view of his first governor Newcastle, and his earlier gentle tutor Brian Duppa, later Bishop of Winchester, physics and chemistry and mechanics were not part of a gentleman's education, let alone a future king's, but Charles was inquisitive by nature, entertained by the new and the strange. In Paris his current tutor, John Earle – author of *Microcosmographie, or, A Peece of the World Discovered in Essayes and Characters* – read with him daily, and Charles also studied mathematics with Hobbes, who was an extremely influential natural philosopher as well as a political thinker. Suddenly inspired, for once Charles worked hard, grappling with the 'mechanics of physics' of Descartes, making himself into a competent chemist and poring over the mathematics of navigation, which fascinated him already because of his love of the sea.

When Charles moved into Whitehall at the Restoration, he set up a sundial in the Privy Garden, and his private cabinet contained a huge portfolio of maps of Britain by Dutch engravers as well as a curious model ship. His love of clocks was famous, and he was said to have seven clocks in his bedroom, all chiming at different times, as well as one in the antechamber which told the direction of the wind as well as the time. The grandfather clocks of the day were great old monsters, eight foot high, with a huge swinging pendulum and a tendency to bong, bong every quarter of an hour. But in 1660, among the clocks in Charles's cabinet at Whitehall, there was one 'that shewed the rising & setting of the son in the Zodiaque; the Sunn represented in a face & raies of Gold, upon an azure skie, observing the diurnal & annual motion, rising & setting behind a landscape of hills, very divertisant'.[7]

This clock was up-to-date as well as beautiful, having been made by Ahasuerus Fromontal, a Dutch-born clockmaker who was the first to make pendulum clocks in England, following the system that Christiaan Huygens had published as recently as 1658. During the latter days of the exile courtiers like Alexander Bruce (later Earl of Kincardine) and Robert Moray had filled their empty days with their experimental interests: Moray had a chemistry laboratory and both worked on pharmacology and medicine. They were also intrigued by clocks, and in 1658 began corresponding not only about pendulum clocks but about new watches that might keep time well without varying. They worked on improved clocks with great enthusiasm, both before and after the Restoration. Later, in the Hague, Bruce worked with Huygens on marine clocks, 'pendulum-regulated timekeepers', an attempt to solve the problem of measuring longitude.[8] In days to come Charles would always have the latest technological wonders, like the spring-driven pocket watches designed by Huygens and Hooke – and a servant to wind up all his clocks. Charles also had his own laboratory beneath the Privy Gallery at Whitehall, where doctors undertook occasional anatomical dissections and demonstrators mounted experiments. After his death John Evelyn dismissed him airily as 'a lover of the sea, and skilful in shipping, not affecting other studies, yet he had a laboratory and knew of many empirical medicines and the easier mechanical mathematics'. But he was more serious than that. On his restoration he was keen to promote the new knowledge, and Sir Paul Neile and Robert Moray kept him abreast of the experiments and arguments among the philosophical clubs of Oxford and London.

He also welcomed his old tutor Hobbes, whom he had spotted in the Strand two or three days after his first arrival in London and quickly invited to court. He enjoyed the irascible Hobbes's 'witt and smart repartees', delivered in his mild West Country tones. Hobbes was good company, and sang bawdy songs, very badly. The wits at court liked to provoke him, remembered his friend Aubrey, but he feared none of them and replied in kind; 'The King would call him the beare; Here comes the Beare to be bayted.'[9] Charles treasured Samuel Cooper's miniature of the old man and granted him a pension, and Hobbes in turn dedicated his *Problema Physica* of 1662 to the king.

Thomas Hobbes, by Samuel Cooper

The new natural philosophy and the old overlapped. Chemistry and alchemy were a diversion of the princes of Europe and had been taken up by many courtiers during the exile. Among them was Bristol's uncle, Sir Kenelm Digby – an ardent Catholic, Chancellor to Henrietta Maria in exile, whose life as a soldier, lover, rake, pirate and scholar reads like a romance. He was a friend of Hobbes and a disciple of Descartes, but also a student of the old Aristotelian systems, and of Paracelsian chemistry and alchemy. For several years, he had set up a laboratory at his house, which became a salon for philosophers and writers, mathematicians and alchemists. Charles was particularly interested in alchemy and in 1660 Elias Ashmole, eager to gain favour at court, presented him with three of his alchemical works, published during the Interregnum: a translation of the works of the astrologer John Dee, adviser to Elizabeth I; an anthology of alchemical verse, *Theatrum chemicum Britannicum*, and his treatise, *The Way to Bliss*. (Perhaps overdoing things, his gifts to Charles also included a pickled foetus in a bottle.)[10] Charles responded generously, making Ashmole Comptroller of the Excise, appointing him Windsor Herald, and, almost more significantly, giving him full powers to collect and transcribe any documents he found useful.

Not all the savants were men. Boyle's older sister Lady Ranelagh was a great patron of intellectuals and virtuosi in her house in Pall Mall. Margaret Cavendish, now settled back at Welbeck, had already caused a stir during her exile in Antwerp by outlining her materialist views in her *Philosophical and Physical Opinions* in 1655. At Ragley Hall in Warwickshire, Anne, Viscountess Conway – a year younger than Charles – had her own alchemical laboratory and was deep in the study of abstruse texts on theosophy and mysticism. She conducted a long correspondence with the Cambridge Platonist philosopher Henry More and her house became a centre of scientific discussion. Her own book, *Principles of the Most Ancient and Modern Philosophy*, published in 1690, after her death, was much admired by Leibniz.[11]

Country houses, London mansions and coffee-houses were thus

full of talk of chemistry, physics and mechanics. During the Commonwealth different groups of theorists and experimenters had continued their research in groups that mingled royalists and parliamentarians, Anglicans and puritans, holding that these interests transcended all religious and political allegiances. 'It is strange', Boyle wrote in 1647, 'that men should rather be quarrelling for a few trifling opinions, wherein they dissent, than to embrace one another for those many fundamental truths, wherein they agree.'[12] During the 1650s, the circles that formed around John Wilkins in Oxford and Samuel Hartlib in London, and the neo-Platonists in Cambridge, had all argued for toleration and reason.

Their curiosity encompassed the universe, from the stars in the heavens to the veins in a human body and the microbes in the plaque on their teeth; from the telescopes and astronomical discoveries of Galileo and Kepler to Harvey's work on the circulation of the blood and Leeuwenhoek's development of the microscope. England's hero was Francis Bacon, who had set out a system for a new, systematic hunt for knowledge, based on observation and experiment. In *The New Atlantis*, written in 1626, he had put forward the idea of a public repository of knowledge and base for research. Called 'Solomon's House', this would be dedicated to 'knowledge of Causes, and secret motions of things, and the enlarging of the bounds of Human Empire, to the effecting of all things possible'.[13]

Mathematics and geometry now seemed to many the key to explaining the motions of the world, exemplified by the mechanical philosophy of Descartes, which sought to define all natural phenomena in terms of the impact, and repulsion, of bodies on each other. Different groups worked together in an atmosphere of passionate discussion: in London at the College of Physicians; at the so-called 'Invisible College', the circle surrounding the Prussian exile Samuel Hartlib, which was particularly interested in medical, agricultural and educational reform; and at the loose-knit club known as the 'Philosophical College', whose interests ranged across astronomy, mathematics, anatomy and mechanics.

One of the most dynamic members of this last group was the young cleric John Wilkins, a populariser of Copernicus, Galileo and Kepler and a writer on ideas of the universe and on mechanical powers. Applying theory to practical matters, he wrote vividly on the planets and on cryptography and language, and in his *Mathematical Magick, or, The Wonders that may be Performed by Mechanical Geometry* he moved from simple machines like levers and pulleys to prophetic visions of flying machines, submarines and automata. Politically and theologically, Wilkins straddled the rift between parliamentarians and royalists. In his youth he had been a chaplain at court, but in the Commonwealth he became a supporter of parliament, marrying Cromwell's sister Robina in 1656. When he became Warden of Wadham College, Oxford, he was famously open-minded, 'with nothing of the Bigotry, Unmannerliness, or Censoriousness' found elsewhere in Oxford.[14] Men from London and Cambridge flocked to his discussion groups, including John Wallis, later Professor of Geometry, the mathematician and astronomer Seth Ward, whom Charles appointed Bishop of Exeter, and students like Robert Boyle and the young Christopher Wren.

Many were also members of the 'Great Clubbe' founded by another extraordinary figure, William Petty. As Cromwell's doctor in Ireland he undertook a huge survey of the country and developed an interest in quantifying facts that brought him the name of England's first political statistician. When Petty left Oxford, his club moved to Wilkins's lodgings at Wadham. In 1654 Evelyn visited Wilkins and was delighted by his transparent apiaries, built like castles and palaces, and by the 'many other artificial, mathematical, Magical curiosities' including a thermometer and a 'monstrous' magnet.[15] (On the same trip he met 'that miracle of a Youth, Mr Christopher Wren'.) When Wilkins left in 1659, to become Master of Trinity College, Cambridge, the group dispersed, some staying on in Oxford, others moving to London.

So much had happened in intellectual life during the Interregnum that the prevailing mood by 1660 was buoyant and optimistic. The

Restoration itself seemed like an energising transfusion, filling most natural philosophers with hope. It brought back to the capital men who had been in exile, or in the provinces, alert for new opportunities. Many of the aristocrats, merchants and gentry who now filled London, especially during the parliamentary season, were avid collectors and 'virtuosi', eager for the novel and strange. In particular, the royalist exiles who had been together in Paris brought new ideas from their contacts with Descartes, Marin Mersenne and Pierre Gassendi. London was also becoming the centre of the scientific instrument trade: in Long Acre and Chancery Lane you could buy microscopes, thermometers and telescopes of the finest quality. With the talk of experiments went an entrepreneurial vigour, a desire to apply the findings of the scholars to boost industry and create wealth, a matter of perpetual interest to Charles. But with it too went an anxiety that the new explanations of matter and energy might lead to unbelief, however much the leading figures justified their searches in terms of understanding the mysteries of Creation and the ways of God.

17 The Royal Society

Where dreamy *Chymicks* is your pain and cost?
How is your oyl, how is your labour lost?
Our *Charles*, blest *Alchymist* (though strange
Believe it future times) did change
The Iron age of old,
Into an age of Gold.

ABRAHAM COWLEY, 'In Commendation of the Time . . .'

SOME OF THE NATURAL PHILOSOPHERS who gathered at Oxford were among the crowds hurrying back to London at the Restoration. Wren was there already, having been recommended by Wilkins to Cromwell, at the age of twenty-five, as the new Professor of Astronomy at Gresham College. The college, on the edge of the City of London, between Bishopsgate and Broad Street, had been founded in the 1590s by the City merchant Thomas Gresham and was very different from the traditional universities of Oxford and Cambridge. Its professors lectured in English as well as Latin, to anyone who chose to come, and it had strong links to the City, with its interest in navigation and mathematics. Petty was also now at Gresham and in 1660 the London and Oxford groups began to merge.

Wilkins, who lost his Cambridge post but was soon given a London parish, was still a central figure. On 28 November 1660, after an astronomy lecture by Wren, ten of these men met and determined to form a society, with Wilkins in the chair; twelve more, including Sir Kenelm Digby, were elected a fortnight later. The initial club included a smattering of courtiers, notably Viscount Brouncker, a mathematician and translator of Descartes, and Sir Robert Moray, who would be Charles's chief link to the group. Moray was one of those interesting characters whom Charles always enjoyed talking to. Born and educated in Scotland, he had a lifelong interest in mathematics, chemistry and engineering: as a soldier in the French army in the 1640s, he had spent fifteen months in prison in Bavaria, studying the works on magnetism of Athanasius Kirchner. After Worcester, he worked with the royalist resistance before joining the court in exile. He was fifty at the Restoration, a man of strong presbyterian principles and a firm, though more moderate, ally of Lauderdale. Moray was one of the first courtiers to be given rooms in Whitehall. A laboratory was next to his rooms, and he and Charles would work there together. When Samuel Sorbière visited three years later, he found it 'very edifying', he said, 'to find a Person imploy'd in Matters of State, and of such Excellent merit, and one who had been engaged a great Part of his Life in Warlike Commands, and the Affairs of the Cabinet, apply himself in making machines in St James's Park and adjusting Telescopes'.[1]

After the royalists' exile in Paris and the Low Countries, especially Leiden, it was fashionable for aristocrats to be interested in instruments, clocks, and experiments. Prince Rupert, who had been acclaimed as a genius at mathematics in his youth, was fascinated by mechanics, and his library was full of works on anatomy, chemistry and physics. As well as Moray and Brouncker, early courtier members of the society included Pepys's boss, Lord Sandwich, Sir Alexander Bruce and Sir Paul Neile. In October 1660 Charles himself spent an evening at Gresham, 'where he was entertained with the admirable long Tube, with which he viewed the heavens, to his very great satisfaction, insomuch that he commanded Sr P Neile to cause the like to be made'.[2] The thirty-five-foot telescope was set up in the Privy Garden. On the day after Charles's coronation, Christiaan Huygens (who had skipped the Coronation to watch the transit of Mercury) spent the day with the Duke of York and others, observing 'the conjunction of Saturn with the moon, in the garden at Whitehall, with Mr Neile's long telescopes'.[3]

At the new club the courtiers were joined by old experimenters like Kenelm Digby and Ashmole, by London lawyers, doctors and intellectuals, by writers like Dryden, and Oxford and Cambridge scholars like Wallis and Ward. Several were brilliant amateurs, like John Evelyn, who had been working for years on his great, unpublished book on gardening, *Elysium Britannicum*, and whose voluminous manuscripts show an interest in art, poetry and theology as well as alchemy, medicine, mathematics, physics, mechanics, natural history and chemistry.[4] The new society was really an extension of the kind of clubs that met in the coffee-houses or in private houses: over the next fifteen years, the membership was top-heavy with noblemen, politicians and country gentlemen, with a solid body of clergymen, lawyers, doctors and civil servants and a small sprinkling of City merchants.

Their aim, said the first historian of the Royal Society, Thomas Sprat, was to enjoy 'the satisfaction of breathing a freer air, and of conversing in quiet one with another, without being engaged in the passions, and madness of that dismal Age'.[5] The group now established hoped, they announced, to begin 'a more regular way of debating things; and that, according to the manner in other countries, where there were voluntary associations of men into academies for advancement of the various parts of learning, they might do something answerable here for the promoting of experimental philosophy'.[6] In its stated aims and its hope to match the private academies of Paris and Florence, the new club was a step towards answering the calls for a permanent college that had been made by Bacon, Hartlib, Wilkins and others. (Evelyn was one of many who had dreamed of some form of college – in his case an idealistic, even monastic centre somewhere in the country.) The new era, with its promise of stability, seemed the right time to set up the society on a firm basis. Moreover the country now had, William Petty declared with comic inaccuracy, 'a Philosophicall and Mathematico-Mechanical King, one that cared not for the vulgar exercise of the body'.[7]

To succeed, they knew they had to win the goodwill of the king. Moray told him straight away about their first gathering and brought back a warm message of approval. Immediately they set to work, drawing up a list of contributions and experiments. Dr Merret was to talk on the history of refining, Dr Goddard to show his experiments 'on producing colours by mixing chemicals', and Mr Boyle was asked to bring in his cylinder and 'to shew at his best convenience the experiment of the air' – his air-pump was the great attraction, wheeled out to entertain the Danish ambassador a few weeks later.[8] The group embarked on experiments with pendulums as well as papers on shipping. On 16 January 1661, at the 'Philosophic Club', Evelyn saw a demonstration of the Torricellian experiment, using a mercury tube to show that the atmosphere had weight (the basis of the barometer). The Society set up a committee to plan a 'quicksilver experiment', an investigation into air pressure, testing how a mercury barometer would work on the summit of the 12,000ft Pica de Tenerife. In early January, over a pot of ale, Ralph Greatorex impressed Pepys with the plans for this expedition and next day Pepys went with him to Gresham College '(where I never was before) and saw the manner of the house, and find great company of persons of Honour there'.[9] Everyone involved felt exhilarated.

There were also more practical initiatives, like drawing up a 'history of Mechanical trades'. Evelyn provided a list of headings, and the detailed work was done later, sporadically, by others. Evelyn also found support for publishing his own work, *Sculptura: or the History and Art of Calcography and Engraving on Copper*, for which Prince Rupert, a man with a passion for experiment, promised to teach him the secret of mezzotint which he had practised himself in 1658; this had been developed in the early years of the century but never publicly explained.[10] Every week there were new experiments, particularly with the air-pump. 'We put in a Snake but could not kill it, by exhausting the aire,' wrote Evelyn cheerfully, 'onely made it extreamly sick, but the Chick died of Convulsions out right, in a short space'. The other great diarist, Pepys, also suggests how wide-spread the interest was, dining with acquaintances who describe the habits of snakes or tarantulas, or who show off after dinner with 'Chymical glasses, which break all to dust by breaking off the little small end – which is a great mystery to me'.[11] These small blown-glass bubbles, which exploded when punctured and crumbled to dust, had been demonstrated at the Royal Society the year before, and had also been studied by Margaret Cavendish while in exile in Antwerp in 1657.[12] They became known as 'Prince Rupert's drops', and the London ones were probably by-products from the glass-houses that Rupert had set up in Chelsea and Windsor, where he supervised the furnaces himself in a sooty old apron. In March 1661 Charles himself sent one of these drops for the society to investigate: 'the reasons were considered, but so many objections made, as was hard to solve'.[13]

The society's concerns ranged wide. They undertook tests at the Minories – the furnaces of the Mint, in the Tower of London – to see if materials became heavier when burnt. They discussed bar-nacles and snowflakes, the reproduction of vipers and the nature of gravity. In the summer they tried out a diving bell in the dock at Deptford, letting down by cable a heavy contraption of cast lead, in which a brave pioneer spent nearly half an hour under water. They puzzled over poisons, watched plants flash like gunpowder in a fire, and tried to capture a spider within a circle of 'ground unicorn's horn'. The forward-looking Dr Clarke described the 'manner of injecting into the veins' while the alchemists talked of 'sympathetical cures'. A matter of great debate was a letter received from Huygens concerning the rings of Saturn. When Wren read of his discovery of Saturn's first moon he dashed off a long reply, claiming that he and others had observed this two years before.

Collaboration was often spiced with competition and argument. As the minutes show, the society's varied interests and haphazard exploration often led them into curious cul-de-sacs, as much as solid achievement, but they always maintained their belief that knowledge gained from observation and experiment had to be preferable to the dubious conclusions derived from preconceived theories. In 1661 Boyle published *The Sceptical Chymist*, a dialogue between an old-style hermetic philosopher and a modern sceptic who wants to question the Aristotelians, Paracelsians, alchemists and other theorists, in an effort to drag 'the chymists' doctrine out of their dark and smoakie laboratories' and bring it 'into the open light, and shew the weaknesses of their proofs'.[14]

In March 1661, Sir Robert Moray was elected president of the society, an ideal link between Gresham and the court. Very cannily, knowing of Charles's old link with the family, and also of his love of intricate inventions, Moray intrigued Charles by describing the work of their talented young star, Christopher Wren, who had now left Gresham to become Professor of Astronomy in Oxford. Wren had already sent the king some drawings of a flea and a louse, as seen through a microscope. Charles was entranced and in May, Moray and Neile instructed Wren that 'The King hath commanded us to lay a double Charge upon you, in his Name'.[15] He had asked him to make:

a Globe representing accurately the figure of the Moon, as the Best Tubes represent it: and to delineate by the Help of the Microscope the Figures of all the Insects, and small living Creatures you can light upon . . . If it were needful to add any further Excitement to your industry, we should tell you how much our whole Society is rejoiced, that his Majesty has a just Esteem of your Parts, and honours you with his Commands.

Wren declined to make the microscopic drawings, but he did set about his lunar globe. In earlier Oxford days Wilkins and Wren had built an eighty-foot telescope to observe the entire face of the moon and to map this, Wren had developed a special eye-piece. Now he put these beautiful maps onto a globe of painted cardboard, and had it mounted and presented it to Charles (without showing it to the society), inscribed with the dedication, 'To Charles II, King of Great Britain, France and Scotland, for the expansion of whose

Dominions since no one Globe can suffice, Christopher Wren dedicates another in the Lunar Sphere'. Charles placed this elegant, evocative lunar globe, showing all the hills and valleys, gleaming surfaces and shadows, on its stand in his cabinet, and showed it to all who came.

Hanc Tabulam invenit & incepit Anton: Verrio,Perfecerunt Godhofredu.Kneller & Jac:Thornhill Equites.

Wren's portrait, in the Sheldonian Theatre at Oxford, shows him pointing to the new skyline of London. He holds his plan of St Paul's, and his mathematical instruments, celestial globe and telescope are by his side.

The society became another of Charles's diversions. In January 1661 he sent Moray down to a meeting, with two magnets and a message 'that he expected an account from the society of some of the most considerable experiments upon them'. In March he sent Sir Paul Neile with his 'five little glass bubbles', two filled with liquid and two solid; in July he sent Sir Samuel Tuke, with a paper of seeds that had been sent to him from Warwickshire, where it had 'rained wheat'.[16] He chatted to Evelyn, as he sat at supper at Whitehall, about the recent viewing of Saturn through Neile's large telescope, and kept Petty in conversation for half an hour in front of forty lords, 'upon the philosophy of Shipping, loadstone, skreen'd guns, the feathering of arrows, the vegetation of plants, the history of trades, etc.'[17]

Charles was quick to notice any work that might have a practical use like Evelyn's book *Fumifugium*, about smoke pollution in London. This touched on his own dreams of rebuilding London as a city to rival Paris, free from the smoke that belched from lime kilns and breweries, tanneries and soap boilers, coating everything with soot, indoors as well as out, making tapestries yellow and oil-paintings brown and choking the flowers and fruit. One solution might be to move the trades downriver, creating a new river frontage with fine houses instead of warehouses; another would be to surround the city with a belt of greenery, with flowering shrubs and herbs. This was an attractive idea that caught Charles's attention. He discussed it with the author as they sailed upriver on the way back from his yacht race to Greenwich in October 1661 and asked Evelyn to prepare a bill for the next session of parliament, saying he was determined to have something done about it, but in the end this was yet another plan too ambitious and costly to realise.

There is a faint feeling of a tease about some of his requests to the society, a suspicion that Charles rather enjoyed making the learned men scurry. Sometimes his questions were good ones. On 17 July 1661 Neile mentioned that 'the king had, within four days past, desired to have a reason assigned, why the sensitive plants stir and contract themselves upon being touched'. Immediately Wilkins, Clarke, Evelyn and Goddard were appointed as a sub-committee to examine the nature of this little plant that shrinks back when touched, *mimosa pudica*, and a group including Brouncker and Moray spent an afternoon bent over the specimens in Thomas Chiffinch's garden near St James's Park.

This was not a waste of time, either botanically or in terms of pleasing Charles. In October the society petitioned the king for a charter, which was granted on 15 July 1662, for a Royal Society 'for the Improvement of naturall knowledge by Experiment'. A second, more precise charter replaced this nine months later.[18] The charter meant that the society now had a constitution, and certain rights and privileges, the most important being that it could license books under the 1662 Licensing Act – a way of freeing the Fellows' work from potential censorship by the church. The king also donated a mace, which was placed before the president at all meetings.

The society was now put on a formal footing. Members paid a subscription of ten shillings when elected, and a shilling a week for meetings, 'whether present or absent'. To begin with they planned to do all the work themselves, providing papers and lectures as well as demonstrating experiments. This soon turned out to be too much and too chaotic, and in November 1662 Robert Hooke, cross-tempered, thorough to a degree and at times inspired, who had been working as Boyle's assistant, was appointed as Curator of Experiments. This was the one salaried post, from which Hooke earned £80 a year, plus £50 for a lectureship. Hooke organised the demonstration of experiments, helped by a laboratory assistant, and was also supposed to look after the society's collections, for which he cared very little. In the side-rooms and attics of the old half-timbered house, built by Gresham a century before, equipment and material piled up and collected dust: birds' nests and honeycombs and wasps' nests, jars and pots with human foetuses and lizards' lungs; lodestones of all shapes and sizes, 'Sympathetic Powder' to heal wounds, rhino-horns and hair-balls.

Charles heard of Hooke's demonstrations. In July 1663 he threw the society into a flurry when he threatened to descend on a meeting at Gresham in person. What should they show him, what experiments should they put on? A committee was formed and resolutions made: Colonel Long promised 'to bring in his apparatus of insects, some snakes eggs, his collection of curious stones . . . some ermines and lizards, natives of England; as also some exotic beasts skins'.[19] Dr Clarke 'promised to shew that a frog will live above twenty minutes after his heart hath been taken out, and ceased to move'. Another Fellow was asked to 'prepare the dissection of an oyster and a lobster'. The greatest burden, as usual, fell on Hooke:

MR HOOKE was charged to shew his microscopical observations in a handsome book to be provided by him for that purpose: to weigh the air, both in the engine and abroad; to break empty glass balls; as also to let the water ascend into them after they have been emptied; to provide the instrument for finding the different pressure of the atmosphere in the same place, as likewise the hygroscope made of the beard of a wild oat.[20]

But was this what was needed? Wren thought the whole project of a royal display too difficult: chemical experiments would be too dirty and slow, anatomical demonstrations too gruesome, mathematical proofs and astronomical measurements too bewildering, while a display of agricultural and industrial machinery would take too long to organise. Knowing Charles's love of theatre, Wren suggested that his interest was in surface display rather than the laborious underlying research: 'the key that opens treasures is often plain and rusty: but unless it be gilt, the key alone will make no shew at court.'[21] He therefore suggested to the President, William, Viscount Brouncker, that they needed something surprising and spectacular but nothing resembling a fairground conjuror. How about a circular barometer, or an artificial eye? Or a compass in water, on springs, so that Charles could 'sail by land', navigating in his coach?

The promised visit, perhaps luckily, never happened. Nonetheless, the interest of the king and the Duke of York and Prince Rupert gave their work status and won eminent members for the society, aristocrats, bishops and statesmen who boosted its reputation abroad.

Soon they had foreign Fellows, the first being Samuel Sorbière, in June 1663, and Christiaan Huygens, who visited England several times after his first trip in 1661. Sorbière, a French protestant who had translated More's *Utopia* and Hobbes's *De Cive*, caused a storm on his return to France by writing an account of the society, which their spokesman, Thomas Sprat, considered insulting. His worst fault was that he revered Hobbes, and saw him as heir to the society's idol, Bacon. Supporting Hobbes, he also managed to insult Boyle, Wallis and Clarendon (whom he described as knowing the law, but understanding little else). He even implied that in conversation, Charles himself had shared his views: "'tis agreed on all sides that if Mr Hobbes were not so Dogmaticall, he would be very useful and necessary to the Royal Society, for there are few people that can see farther into things than he, or have applied themselves so long to the Study of Natural Philosophy.'[22] Uproar followed. Sprat replied vehemently, and the two kings – Charles and Louis – had to intervene to cool tempers on both sides of the channel.

The unfortunate Sorbière had, however, found the society's proceedings astonishingly orderly, describing their meetings in a large room at Gresham College, with a table by the fireplace and two rows of simple wooden benches, one higher than the other, as in an amphitheatre. The President sat in his elbow-chair behind the table:

They address their Discourse to him bare-headed, till he makes a sign for them to put on their Hats . . . He is never interrupted that speaks, and Differences of Opinion cause no manner of Resentment, nor as much as a disobliging Way of Speech. There is nothing seemed to me to be more civil, respectful and better managed.[23]

Many meetings focused on the 'strange' in terms of the bizarre or the freakish, like the objects collected by dilettanti for their cabinets:

an exotic new fruit, the pineapple from Barbados; a report of a woman who sweated so much that you could take a quart of ill-smelling water from the palms of her hands; a miraculous varnish that would defy rust.[24] But technical innovation was also of interest. One aspect of the society's work was a patriotic drive towards the 'improvement' of crafts, trades and agriculture, and at a meeting on 15 October 1662 Moray reported the king's wish that no patents for new inventions should pass, until the society had approved them. Of their eight committees, established in 1663, the greatest enthusiasm was roused by those for mechanics, the history of trades, and agriculture.

The mechanical committee was particularly concerned with inventions and carriage improvements, vital for transport, and in 1663 the agricultural committee were busy discussing a recent petition to the king 'for a patent to practise a secret of making all grain grow plentifully in any barren ground, without laying on any dung or compost'; and 'for spurring vines and orange trees into sudden growth'.[25] There were also explorations of technology, including the development of the silk industry, and whenever members of the society went abroad as envoys, they were asked to bring back reports about everything from mountain ranges to local diseases, from the design of palaces to the growth of plants.

The first complete volume actually published by the society was Evelyn's *Sylva*, which prompted a nationwide interest in landscaping and tree-planting. Its second publication revealed entirely new realms. This was Robert Hooke's *Micrographia*, published early in 1665, superbly illustrated in copper plates, showing the world hitherto unseen but now visible through a microscope, from the tip of a needle to the scales on a fish. The exchange and spread of such information was invaluable, although several of the most brilliant Fellows actually did their experiments elsewhere. The naturalist John Ray, whose pioneering work on the classification of plants was so vital to the history of botany, was hampered by painful leg trouble and could rarely come to meetings, but sent in

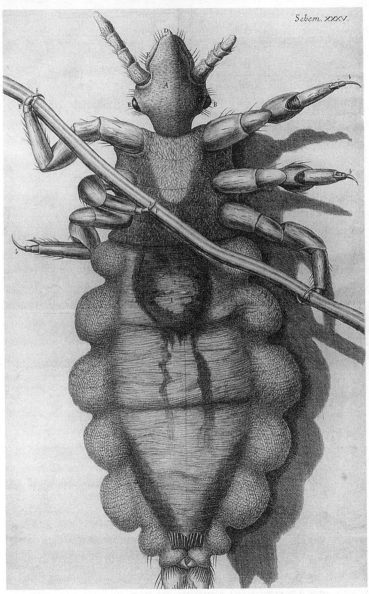

Hooke's drawing of a louse, made with the aid of a microscope
for *Micrographia* 1665

his reports by letter. Robert Boyle eventually set up his own laboratory in his sister Lady Ranelagh's house in Pall Mall, where he lived, and wrote directly for the public rather than for the Fellows, while Isaac Newton – still a skinny, lank-haired student in 1660 – wrote his works on optics and mechanics in isolation at Cambridge. The society pushed for their publication, but tension always remained between the fiercely materialist enquirers like Hooke and those like Newton who still sought truth in the old hermetic texts and the mysteries of alchemy. Arguments also often surfaced as to who had made key discoveries or inventions first.

At the start the Fellows had ambitious plans to collect knowledge in all spheres, involving elaborate questionnaires. The whole universe, their secretary Henry Oldenburg claimed, would be 'taken to taske'.[26] This great scheme proved impossible, but Oldenburg's own massive correspondence, backed up by the *Philosophical Transactions* which he founded in 1665, provided a web of scientific intelligence stretching across Europe. This desire to communicate was combined with a wish to clear aside the rhetoric and mystification of the scholastic tradition. A new interest in language led to deep, vexed questions of perception, expression and the relation of human consciousness to the world itself. The society also confronted the idea put so powerfully by Hobbes that as language was always the construction of a society, it could never approximate to the 'things' themselves. Two strands came together here. One was the desire of the scientists to describe their findings clearly, to avoid what Sprat (in a paradoxically rhetorical outburst) called 'this visious Abundance of *Phrase*, this Trick of *Metaphor*, this Volubility of *Tongue*, which makes so great a Noise in the World . . .' The other strand derived from the attempt of puritan preachers to speak directly and simply to their congregations – seen in the sermons of Wilkins, and his follower John Tillotson. In Wilkins's words, 'Obscurity in the discourse is an argument of ignorance in the minde. The greatest learning is to be seen in the greatest plainness. The more nearly we understand any thing our selves, the more easily we expound it to others.'[27]

As a remedy to linguistic extravagance, wrote Sprat, the society resolved:

> to reject all Amplifications, Digressions, and Swellings of Style; to return back to the primitive Purity and Shortness, when Men deliver'd so many Things, almost in an equal number of Words. They have exacted from all their Members, a close, naked, natural way of Speaking; positive Expressions, clear Senses; a native Easiness; bringing all Things as near the mathematical Plainness as they can; and preferring the Language of Artizans, Country-Men, and Merchants, before that of Wits, or Scholars.[28]

This, then, was another important route of access to mysteries, of which Charles would have approved. Yet it had an interesting political slant, looking to the plain speech of the people rather than the wit of the court, and a practical one, putting science at the service of trades and crafts. Wilkins went even further than this, attempting to find a universal language, comprehensible to all nations, almost with the precision of mathematics.

Although he was intrigued, Charles was not exactly forthcoming with funds. In October 1662 he sent orders for a small grant to be made out to Moray and Boyle, in trust for the society, from funds in Ireland, but it turned out that these funds had already been promised to other claimants. A few years later, in 1669, he granted the society Chelsea College, which had been founded by his grandfather to train protestant priests. The idea was that they should use this as a base, but the society never moved in and the property caused them nothing but headaches. Charles eventually bought it back in 1682, as a home for old soldiers, the Royal Chelsea Hospital, and the society then invested the proceeds in the East India Company. Beyond this was that there was simply no government money to be had. When Colbert and Louis XIV, who had instructed his ambassadors to find out about the Royal Society, established the state-funded Académie des Sciences in 1666 the Fellows made bitter comparisons. Charles's special interest in navigation, however, did prompt him to found the Mathematical School at Christ's Hospital in 1673, and the Royal Observatory at Greenwich two years later, two significant achievements.

After his initial burst of interest he sat back and let the Royal Society run its own affairs, while enjoying his own alchemical experiments at Whitehall, and sending his good wishes and a side of venison for their annual dinners. Although he was made a Fellow, he was never so involved as James and Prince Rupert. The latter deluged the society with papers, submitting ideas for testing 'a gunpowder eleven times stronger than normal; a novel water pump; an early machine gun; a perspective aid for artists; and improved sea charts and navigational instruments'.[29] By contrast Charles's enquiries grew ever more flippant. In July 1663 Sir Robert Moray 'mentioned that the King had made an experiment of keeping a sturgeon in fresh water in St James's Park for a whole year: it was moved to kill it and see how it would eat'.[30] Charles's interest was still largely in curiosities of the natural world, plants, bees, fish. Once he sent 'that wonderful horne of the fish, which struck a dangerous howle in the keele of a ship, in the India seas' (in fact off Barbados) 'which being broake off with the violence of the fish, & left in the timber, preserv'd it from foundring'. Some months later Moray turned up with 'a discourse on coffee written by Dr Goddard at the King's command' and in August 1666 mentioned 'that the King had been discussing of ant's eggs, and inquiring how they came to that bigness, which sometimes exceeded that of the insect itself'.[31]

The Royal Society suffered because their scientific researches seemed so abstruse, while their social schemes proved too ambitious and expensive, whether it was Evelyn's ambitious plan for London or Petty's desire to reform taxation. Petty was mocked at court as a conjuror or a fanatic. In February 1664 Pepys recorded that 'the King came and stayed an hour or two, laughing at Sir W Petty, who was there about his boat, and at Gresham College in general . . . for spending time only in weighing of ayre and doing nothing else since they sat'.[32] He once called the Fellows his 'fous', his court jesters, and

Hollar's frontispiece to Thomas Sprat's *The History of the Royal Society*, 1667, shows the bust of Charles II being crowned by Fame, with the Society's first President, Viscount Brouncker, in a classical robe on his left, and Francis Bacon on his right.

took substantial bets on the results of their experiments: Moray reported that 'the King has laid a wager of fifty pounds to five for the compression of air by water: and that it was acknowledged, that his Majesty had won the wager'.[33]

The society had shown that a forum could be created where debate was open yet contained, and posed no threat to the state, and although Charles had wanted more practical results and less pure research, he was pleased to be called 'Patronus et fundator'. In Hollar's frontispiece to Sprat's propagandist *History of the Royal Society* of 1667, the King's bust, crowned with a laurel wreath by Fame, stands on a plinth with Lord Brouncker on his left and Francis Bacon on his right, and the air-pump, quadrants, and other instruments in the background.[34] Quizzically, he raises an eyebrow at posterity.

In his own laboratory Charles dabbled with Moray and the 'King's Chymist', Nicaise Le Fèvre (often called Lefebure), whose interests were more alchemical. Charles was intrigued by the old secrets of alchemy, whose philosophy of transformation, regeneration and purification embraced both matter and spirit, finding a universe of hidden correspondences between microcosm and macrocosm. Like all alchemists he felt the lure of quicksilver, the mercury that flowed and collected and pooled and separated, and showed such dramatic and varied transformations, turning into red crystals when mixed with nitric acid, into poisonous white powder when heated, into amalgams with other metals. It seemed to transcend solid and liquid, heaven and earth. Anything that might change base metal into gold was bound to appeal, but Charles was also moved by the human and spiritual analogies, the transformation of man to a state of perfection, and of society from an iron to a golden age.

18 Card Houses

Thou sayst I swore I loved thee best
And that my heart lived in thy breast;
And now thou wonderst much that I
Should what I swore then now deny,
And upon this thou taxest me
With faithlessness, inconstancy;
Thou hast no reason so to do:
Who can't dissemble, ne'er must woo.

JOHN DANCER, *The Variety*

CATHERINE RELAXED as her English improved and she enjoyed herself more. She did, however, have to put up with constant small humiliations. When Henrietta Maria arrived in the autumn of 1662 she brought with her Charles's son by Lucy Walter, who was still being introduced – with no one fooled – as James Crofts, the nephew of William Crofts, his guardian in France. Fascinated observers noted the shifting alliances in the queen mother's evening circle. Here was the queen, wrote Pepys in September, 'not very charming, yet she hath a good, modest and innocent look . . . here I also saw Madam Castlemayne and, which pleased me most, Mr Crofts the King's bastard, a most pretty spark of about 15 year old' (he was thirteen), 'who I perceive doth hang much upon my Lady Castlemayne and is alway with her.'[1] The royal party stayed until dark and when they left, into the leading coach piled the king and queen, young James – and Barbara.

Although the autumn of 1662 was troubled by fear of plots after the ejection of the nonconformist ministers, for the court, there was always time for pleasure. Towards the end of November Londoners woke to find their rooftops covered with snow, the first for three years. It was the start of weeks of icy cold. Charles took Catherine to St James's Park to watch people skating on the new canal. This was a novel diversion, learnt in Holland by many exiles who had brought back their iron and steel skates. The watchers were entranced, among them John Evelyn who waxed lyrical about the 'strange and wonderful dexterity of the sliders', how fast they sped by, 'how sudainly they stop in full carriere upon the Ice, before their Majesties'.[2] Evelyn went home by water, 'but not without exceeding difficultie, the Thames being froze, greate flakes of yce incompassing our boate'.

Appropriately, the snow coincided with the arrival of three envoys from Tsar Alexis of Russia. Charles greeted them warmly, acknowledging the Tsar's kindness during his years of exile and his boycott of trade with Cromwell's Commonwealth. York House was fitted out for the Russians at considerable cost, the City's trained bands and the King's Guards turned out to escort them, and the people flocked to admire them, or to laugh and jeer. The tall Russians in their great fur hats were dashing figures as they rode in their coaches through the crowded streets, their attendants following with hawks on their wrists to present to the King. At their audience in the Banqueting House the gallery was so packed that people feared it might fall. They wore tunics embroidered with gold and pearls and bore gifts of furs – sable, black fox and ermine – Persian carpets, cloths of gold and velvet and even 'sea-horse teeth'.[3] Charles was given a gold glove, on which he held three hawks, while the chief envoy raised the letters from the Tsar ceremoniously on high and then prostrated himself full length at the king's feet. The envoys had come to bring congratulations and to ask for a loan. They did not get one, but Charles did repay the money that the Tsar had lent him twelve years before, when he was at his lowest ebb.

Rebellions forgotten, the mood at court was festive. Charles and Catherine watched plays in the Cockpit, and as Christmas approached the builders put up scaffolding for seats in the Great

Hall and made a stage for the King's Company. Not everyone approved. On Christmas Day old Bishop Morley preached in the Chapel Royal on 'goodwill towards men', distinguishing between true Christian joy and the 'mistaken jollity' of the court, particularly their 'excess in playes and gameing'. In Morley's view the groom porter, who supervised the court gambling in the twelve days of Christmas, was no better than a second in a duel. 'Upon which', noted Pepys, 'it was worth observing how far they are come from taking the reprehensions of a Bishop seriously, that they all laugh in the chapel when he reflected on their ill actions and courses.'[4]

Dancing was as much part of court life as gambling and plays, and on New Year's Eve Charles gave a great ball. For the first dance, the French *branle*, he led out Anne, Duchess of York, while James led the Duchess of Buckingham, and the young James Crofts took the hand of Barbara Castlemaine. This was followed by a stately courante, and then, impatient for livelier tunes, Charles ordered country dances, 'the King leading the first which he called for; which was – says he, *Cuckolds all a-row* the old dance of England'.[5] Between Christmas and Lent, every night saw a different kind of entertainment. In late January Ambassador Cominges reported rather primly to Louis XIV that there was a ball and a comedy every other day, and the rest of each day was spent in play, either in the queen's rooms or Lady Castlemaine's 'where the company does not fail to be treated to a good supper. In this way, Sire, is the time occupied in this country.'[6]

On 2 February Catherine gave a Candlemas masquerade, celebrating the ancient festival that marked the mid-point of winter between Christmas and Easter. 'The queen was a woman of sense,' declared Gramont's memoirs, 'and used all her endeavours to please the king, by that kind obliging behaviour which her affection made natural to her: she was particularly attentive in promoting every sort of pleasure and amusement especially such as she could be present at herself.'[7] This particular night was long remembered for Buckingham's complicated practical jokes, for the lavish and bizarre dresses, with yards of gauze, silver tissue and yellow rib-bons, and for the noisy, stamping country dances. Here, as so often, the plain short queen was surrounded by glamour. Yet Catherine's goodness won many hearts. Perhaps she took solace, too, in the fact that Charles slept with her often, no matter how many mistresses he had.

He did so, she knew, to beget an heir. And at court Catherine had to contend with his children as well as his women. The Castlemaine children were tucked up out of sight in their rooms across the Privy Garden, but Charles doted publicly on Jemmy, as James Crofts was called, who had his father's dark hair and dark eyes and a sweet, open temperament. No one pretended he was clever. When he arrived at Henrietta Maria's court at the age of nine after his trou-bled childhood he could hardly read or write, and although Charles had ordered intensive teaching, he was still far behind his peers. Almost as soon as he arrived the tale began to spread that he was in fact the lawful heir, Charles having married his mother in secret. This was reinforced when Charles made him wealthy, granting him an income of £8,000 a year, derived from a patent regulating the export of all new drapery. He also began negotiations for James's marriage.

The chosen bride was Anne Scott, the twelve-year-old Countess of Buccleugh, who shone as one of the best young dancers at the New Year ball. Since her father stipulated that she marry someone of the same name, James changed his name from Crofts to Scott, was knighted, and soon ennobled as Duke of Monmouth. After the wedding, which took place on 20 April, soon after his fourteenth birthday, he was given the additional title of Duke of Buccleugh. Although Anne would remain with her parents until she was eight-een, Charles ordered a new set of lodgings to be constructed for the young couple in the Cockpit. In a typical Whitehall improvisation, the old Great Tennis Court built for Henry VIII was divided into two floors, with new chimneys and staircases, sash windows and lavish plaster-work ceilings.[8]

The queen was kind to Monmouth and welcomed him to her rooms, where he played cards with her maids of honour. Eventually she won his deep affection. But his presence was a constant reminder that she had as yet borne no legitimate heir, whereas Barbara Castlemaine had produced a child each year and was pregnant again. Barbara's greed and ambition were flagrant. All the Christmas presents given to the king found their way to her, and at the king's ball her costume dripped with more jewels than those of the queen and the Duchess of York put together. Sarah, the cook at Sandwich's house, next door to Barbara's, told Pepys that the king supped there four or five times a week and 'most often stays till the morning with her and goes home through the garden all alone privately'.[9] Even the sentries, watching him stride across in the dawn, knew all about it. But this year such excursions would end, when Barbara was given fine new quarters within Whitehall itself, over the west end of the Privy Gallery and Holbein Gate, with the upper floor overlooking the park.

Even so, Charles appeared slightly less enamoured with Barbara than he had been, and sharp courtiers began to spy out another beauty who might help their cause if she became his mistress. Soon they thought they had found one. Before Catherine's arrival Henrietta Maria and Minette had recommended suitable attendants from France. At least two of her maids of honour were French, Mademoiselle de la Garde and Mademoiselle Bardou, but a third girl from Paris was Frances Stuart, whose father, a son of Lord Blantyre, had been a physician at the court of Henrietta Maria in exile. Frances's widowed mother had brought her to England in January 1662, with a glowing recommendation from Minette.

Dressed in Paris fashions and speaking fluent French, *la belle Stuart*, as she was known, was approaching her fifteenth birthday. She danced beautifully, was playfully childish and gossipy, and laughed at all Charles's jokes: here was no brilliant, independent, scheming mind à la Castlemaine. 'It was hardly possible for a woman to have less wit and more beauty,' decided Gramont. In fact Frances would grow into a far cleverer and more capable woman than such a judgement suggests, but in the early 1660s she was very young, and enjoyed being the new darling of the court. Her current passion was said to be building card castles, an abuse of good cards that baffled the men engaged in the high-bidding games in her apartments. Buckingham, always on the look-out for a route to Charles's favour, paid her lavish attention, building sky-high card castles, writing songs, making up stories and generally becoming indispensable. Barbara Castlemaine too saw the charm, and the danger, of the slender, fair-haired adolescent and enrolled her as a sexual accessory: 'The king, who seldom neglected to visit the countess before she rose, seldom failed likewise to find Miss Stewart in bed with her.'[10] In February 1663, the two apparently undertook a mock marriage, 'with ring and all other ceremonies of church service, and ribbands and a sack-posset in bed and flinging the stocking'. And then, 'my

Frances Stuart, by Samuel Cooper

Lady Castlemaine, who was the bridegroom, rose, and the King came and took her place with pretty Mrs Stuart.'¹¹ It was all public, all a 'frolique' – but not quite.

Charles's dalliance with Frances had begun before New Year. After the audience for the Russian envoys, Charles, the Duke of York and assorted nobles, including the Earl of Chesterfield, had rolled into Frances's apartments at Whitehall, talking of the extraordinary appearance of the ambassadors. When Will Crofts declared that the Russians, as if in a fairy story, all had handsome wives, and all their wives had handsome legs, Charles maintained that no woman had such fine legs as Miss Stuart. To prove the truth of his assertion, 'with the greatest imaginable ease', Frances immediately showed her legs, riffling her skirts up above her knee.¹² Colonel George Hamilton, one of her many would-be lovers, was later astounded by Frances's competitive desire to prove her beauty, and her total lack of concern at showing off her body. 'I really believe', he declared, 'that, with a little address, it would not be difficult to induce her to strip naked, without ever reflecting upon what she was doing.'¹³

Charles was amused by Frances, and by his courtiers' intrigues and rows, ribaldry and wit. But to outsiders the court had begun to seem scandalous, cut off from reality. MPs muttered about the court's extravagance, and about Charles's open adultery and bastard children, asserting that neglect of his wife was the reason why she had not conceived. Under such criticism Charles's attention swerved back to Catherine. In May 1663, in hope that the waters would aid conception, he took her to the spa at Tunbridge Wells, where Henrietta Maria had gone before his own birth. 'Every method of getting a successor to the English Thorne is to be tried', Cominges explained, 'and the King on his part contributes all that could be asked of true affection and regular assiduity.'¹⁴

Within easy reach of London, Tunbridge was a fashionable resort. Catherine's entourage stayed in the neat houses that straggled around the Wells, and in the mornings they drank the waters and promenaded down the tree-shaded walk. One side of this was lined with shops for lace and jewellery, gloves and stockings, with a new amusement, the 'raffle' copied from the fair at St Germain. On the other side lay the market, where country girls with straw hats sold their produce. In the long afternoons they watched the courtiers play bowls, a diversion that astonished Ambassador Cominges. In France this was the sport of labourers and servants, whereas here, he reported, it was 'the exercise of gentlemen . . . and the places where it is practised are charming, delicious little walks, called bowling-greens, which are little square grass plots, where the turf is almost as smooth and level as the cloth of a billiard table'.[15] The green was also a gaming-table, since every spectator was free to lay a bet, and in the evenings it became a ballroom where courtiers whirled on the smooth turf until the early hours. Catherine loved Tunbridge, inventing entertainments, and matching its natural ease and freedom by dispensing with ceremony. The town in its summer dress dripped with intrigue, as if the waters had gone to people's heads. 'Well may they be called *les eaux de scandale*,' wrote Cominges in July 1663, 'for they nearly ruined the good name of the maids and of the ladies (those I mean who were there without their husbands).'[16] It did not suit everyone. Two years later the young rake Henry Savile decided, 'that Tunbridge is the most miserable place in the world is very certain, and that the ladies do not look with very great advantage at three in the morning is as true'.[17]

Back in London, it was rumoured, untruly, that Charles had made Frances his mistress.[18] Certainly Barbara was suspicious, and anxious not to lose her hold on him. In early July, raised voices echoed across the Whitehall courtyard. Barbara vowed she would never receive Frances in her apartment again; Charles that he would not set foot in them unless she was there. Barbara turned on her heel and left for Richmond to take shelter with her uncle. Charles shrugged, but he still pursued her upriver on the pretence of going hunting. During these quarrels Catherine seemed to shine, and could even administer a sardonic put-down. In early July, when Barbara commented on how long the queen sat patiently while her dresser got her ready, Catherine replied, 'I have so much reason to use patience that I can very well bear with it.'[19] A fortnight later, seeing her in Hyde Park, Pepys noticed how pretty she looked in her short crimson petticoat and white laced waistcoat, 'and her hair dressed *a la negligence*'.[20] Charles was riding hand in hand with her and ostentatiously ignoring Barbara, who looked on unsmiling in her yellow plumed hat. No courtiers now rushed to help her down from her horse, and she had to rely on her servants. Afterwards, said Pepys, in Catherine's presence chamber at Whitehall, 'all the ladies walked, talking and fiddling with their hats and feathers and changing and trying one anothers'. With a twinge of disloyalty he decided that Frances Stuart, 'with her hat cocked and a red plume, with her sweet eye, little Roman nose, and excellent *Taille*, is now the greatest beauty I ever saw I think in my life, and if ever woman can, doth exceed my Lady Castlemayne; at least, in this dresse'.

There were new amusements at court, including the Lottery, which Charles allowed Sir Arthur Slingsby to set up for one day in the Banqueting House, with four hundred prizes, including a coach, but mostly of furniture.[21] The town swung into summer pleasures. People walked out to see the birds in St James's Park, or to play at Pall Mall on the great sandy court. They strolled further, gathering in Hyde Park to watch the quality ride around the ring in their smart carriages with coats of arms on the door, hoping to see the beauty of the hour – in this case Frances Stuart. They took trips to the countryside, carrying picnics to the quiet village of Islington, driving out to the coaching inns of Knightsbridge, or hiring boats to take them upriver, where they could wander through the orchards and meadows of Chelsea. Back in town, men took their wives to smart taverns, like the Bear at the Bridge Foot across the river, where French food was served. In the evenings they drifted to the pleasure grounds at Fox Hall and Spring Gardens or the new Mulberry Gardens. Despite rebellions in the north, for many it was a season of moonlight and song.

Nothing entertained this leisured, gossipy world so much as the continuing affairs of the court's leading ladies. By late July 1663 Charles was reconciled with Barbara, while Frances stuck to the advice of her mother and Henrietta Maria, and resisted his advances. She was safe: Charles was known to be a kindly man who would never force himself on her. This summer Lely painted her appropriately in a glorious pose against a stormy countryside, holding a bow that hinted at her as a chaste Diana. (She loved having her portrait painted and being admired: the following summer Pepys spotted her after a sitting, 'in a most lovely form, with her hair all about her eares, having her picture taking there. There was the King and twenty more, I think, standing by all the while.'[22]) The frustrated Buckingham camp, who had banked on her becoming Charles's mistress, staged a weekend in August where the Duchess of Richmond invited a party to the country, including Charles and Frances. The ruse was so obvious that two uninvited guests swiftly appeared, first the heavily pregnant Barbara and then the queen. This time Catherine came without her chief attendant, Barbara's ally the Countess of Suffolk, declaring that 'she would not always have a governess at her heels, especially in places where the King was'.[23]

Given the court's extravagance, it was not surprising that when the accounts were done, even Charles was horrified. In his speech to parliament, requesting more funds, on 27 July, he promised that he was about to embark on economies. The money they granted him, he admitted, 'will do me very little good, if I do not improve it by very good husbandry of my own, and by retrenching those very expenses which in many respects may be thought necessary enough. But you shall see, I will much rather impose upon myself than my subjects.'[24] Following this, the Exchequer asked to see the domestic accounts. The household had been using the thirty-year-old establishment books, following the number of servants, and the meals given to courtiers in his father's reign. The estimated budget had been vastly overspent and drastic cuts had to be made. Charles cut the traditional round of court ceremonies, apart from the Garter feast, and gave up the grand dining in public. Only the most senior courtiers, about 180 people, retained full 'diets', board and lodging at Whitehall. Effectively, this cut the income of many royal servants by two thirds. Below stairs, the stern restructuring reduced the number of servants from over five hundred to around 220. 'On a sudden', the Earl of Anglesey told Ormond, 'above three hundred below stairs, most of which have families, are deprived of a livelihood, the splendour and dignity of the Court is taken away, and general discontent and murmuring occasioned hereby.'[25] (Ormond, now in Ireland, was still technically Lord Steward.) The discontent was certainly loud, though assuaged by a hint that the diets for the wider circle were only suspended. In fact they were abolished for ever.

Household costs were no longer the largest item in the peacetime budget, but two years later, the Treasury accounts still showed large outstanding bills and arrears of pay stretching back two years or more. The royal rat catcher was owed £12 and the bowling-green keeper £91, but over £500 was due to the watchmaker while the apothecary bills (perhaps including material for Charles's laboratory experiments) were ten times as much.[26] Still, although payments lagged behind, the economies of 1663 led to a change of tone at court. It became less a source of free meals for hangers-on and more of a social hub, a fashionable meeting place for the political and commercial elite.

The main court story, through all the travails of the year, was still the rivalry of Charles's women. But he was good at manoeuvring his way through rivalries. In natural philosophy he forwarded the cause of Boyle while remaining close to Hobbes; in politics he kept the loyalty of Clarendon yet slipped Bennet into power; in his household he brought radical changes while soothing the old courtiers' feelings. When it came to the three principal women in his life – Catherine, Barbara Castlemaine and Frances Stuart – he

sometimes looked harassed by the rows but balanced his relationships adroitly. He seemed able to shut off compartments of feeling
to banish internal conflict, either psychological or moral. With
regard to Catherine, he was careful always to distinguish her position as queen, ensuring that she was waited on with due ceremony
– even if she was forced to have Lady Castlemaine among her
women. He made sure that her rooms were fine and despite the cuts
he now ordered a new canopy for her bedchamber, made from thirty-two yards of the inevitable crimson damask, with new bolsters
and hangings, chairs and stools. His cash books were dotted with
small payments for little presents, like satin and silk 'Sweet bags' or
a white taffeta pillow.[27] But his main preoccupation remained the
need for an heir. The Tunbridge magic had failed, so now they
looked to a different spa. In August 1663, while reports were flooding in of rebels in the north, and the Exchequer was struggling with
his household accounts, Charles set out with Catherine on a trip to
Bath.

This was supposed to be a modest private tour, without courtiers
or officers, yet it turned into a minor royal progress to Bath, Bristol
and Oxford. On the towns along their route the mayors and aldermen made speeches and handed over gifts – a purse of gold in
Reading, and another in Newbury. John Aubrey squired them
round the old hill fort of Silbury and the standing stones at Avebury,
which were beginning to attract the attention of antiquarians keen
to find an ancient glory in England's past. Lord Seymour entertained them at Marlborough, Sir James Thynne at Longleat and the
Herberts at Badminton, although the old manor house was too
small to ask the whole royal party to stay, a humiliation that Herbert
found hard to live down. But despite this warm hospitality, the journey across the Cotswolds, with its steep scarp slopes, deep wooded
valleys and rutted roads, was misery for the queen. The weather
was dreadful and they travelled on, with 'storms of wind and rain so
great . . . that her Majesty will hardly hazard herself again for a
dinner in this mountainous country'.[28]

In Bath both Charles and Catherine went to the baths, a highly ritualised yet intimate routine. It was the custom to go early in the morning, having undressed to your underclothes in your lodgings, the men in 'underpants' under their shirt, the girls and women in shifts. The bathers were carried, discreetly, in a sedan or enclosed chair but at the steps to the baths the men, including the king, stripped off their shirts and plunged into the water. Afterwards they lay on linen sheets in a warmed bed and drank mulled wine 'to regain their strength'.[29]

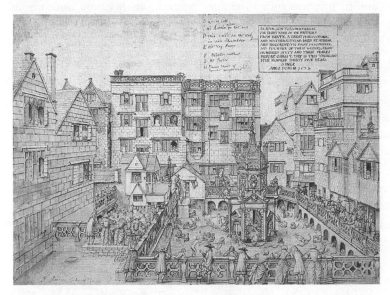

Spectators in fashionable clothes lean over the parapet to watch men and women floating and plunging in the elegantly designed King's and Queen's Baths.

Bath was still filled with meetings about political matters, formal and unofficial, and was merely a brief respite between journeys. On their way back in September Charles was due to visit Clarendon's country seat at Cornbury, but a few days before, he abruptly declared he would like to visit Oxford and see the university – of which Clarendon was an able and committed Chancellor. The colleges were empty in the vacation and there was no time to make grand plans, but the dons received Charles and Catherine in St Giles' meadow with rounds of speeches, before they entered the city by torchlight. Oxford, always a royalist stronghold, was profiting from the Restoration. This year Christopher Wren, who had just watched his first building rise, the chapel at Pembroke College, Cambridge, commissioned by his uncle Bishop Matthew Wren, was working on the ambitious plans for the theatre in Oxford. This had been approved by Charles in April and would be paid for by Gilbert Sheldon. It was called the Sheldonian in his honour, 'built for ye Oxonian Acts and for Playes also'.[30]

The Sheldonian Theatre, David Loggan, *Oxonia Illustrata*, 1675.

Oxford was golden and serene, but emotional pressures still dogged the court. Frances had travelled with Charles and Catherine among the maids of honour, while Barbara had stayed in London awaiting her confinement. Her baby was born on 20 September, a son named Henry (promoting rumours that the real father was Henry Jermyn, whom Charles had banished from court for a flirtation with her the previous year). Two days after the birth Barbara was on her way to Oxford. Two days later still, after Charles had inspected new buildings in Christ Church meadow, he spent the night at her lodgings. She was there, in the background, when he touched the crowd for the King's Evil and went to Convocation, liberally bestowing degrees of Masters of Arts on favoured members of the court not known for their brains, including Berkeley and Monmouth.

There was still no royal pregnancy. Catherine returned to Tunbridge Wells and while she was there Charles supped with Barbara, their quarrels forgotten. Yet in October, when Catherine fell seriously ill, Charles was suddenly consumed with worry. He stayed by her bedside every day, treating her with great tenderness. Catherine's condition worsened rapidly, not helped by the doctors' attentions, the bleeding, the blistering, the piling of dead pigeons at her feet. In mid-October, Bennet told Ormond that the doctors offered little hope and she was expected to die within days: 'tomorrow is a very critical day with her: God's will be done. The king coming to see her this morning, she told him she willingly left all the world but him; which hath very much afflicted his majesty, and all the court with him.'³¹ At the start of November she received the extreme unction. Angrily, Charles threw out the Portuguese doctors and the attendants who had made her stay up two nights without sleep, one night to write her will and the other to say farewell to her servants. He was seen on his knees, weeping by her bed. However, he still spent the nights with Barbara and also found time for 'his usual talk with Mlle. Stewart, of whom he is excessively fond'.³²

If Catherine died, Charles might marry again, and Frances's name was already being canvassed. But slowly Catherine's fever calmed, although she was left temporarily deaf and so weak that she could not walk for weeks. She too had her fragile dreams, her toppling card houses. In her delirium she harked back constantly to childbirth. At one point she thought she had three children, at another a little girl who resembled Charles. Once she told him sadly that her baby boy was 'very ugly'. 'No, it's a pretty boy,' he soothed her. 'If it be like you,' she said, 'it is a fine boy indeed.'[33] And even when she recovered, her first question was 'Where are the children?'

19 Beauties

Small is the worth
Of beauty from the light retired:
Bid her come forth,
Suffer herself to be desired,
And not blush so to be admired.
    EDMUND WALLER, 'Song – Go lovely rose'

WHEN THE NEW FRENCH AMBASSADOR Cominges reached
London in late 1662 his master in Paris, the foreign minister
Lionne, advised him to write an 'official' letter to Louis keeping him
informed of political developments and anything that might affect
French policy, and also to forward 'on a separate sheet the most
curious of the Court news'.[1] Cominges did his best, but he hardly
spoke a word of English and his spelling was interestingly phonetic:
the king went to 'Ouindsor', the queen to 'Bristau' or 'Qinzinton'
and court moved splendidly to 'Omptoncourt'. In official life this
mattered little since everyone spoke French except Clarendon, who
used Bennet as an interpreter, but it did hamper Cominges's gleaning of gossip. A better informed, though less reliable witness was the
comte de Gramont, to whom Cominges sometimes appealed for
explanations of odd English ways and words.

The traffic between the French and English courts was constant,
as Charles's letters to Minette make clear. After her marriage
Minette, now 'Madame', had become a popular figure, a keen
participant in ballets and masques. She was befriended by the brilliant women of court, like Mme de Sevigné and Mme de la Fayette,
and became a powerful patron of writers and artists. Racine dedicated a tragedy to her, and she stood sponsor to Molière's son and

protected him from slander in the arguments over *Tartuffe*. In his dedication to *L'Ecole des Femmes* Molière praised her charm and sweetness, and the characteristic '*affabilité genereuse*' that made people warm to her, as they did to her brother.

A string of courtiers went back and forth to Paris and even Charles's apothecary, Le Fèvre, acted as a messenger to Minette when he went to France to buy new potions. Whitehall had its own handful of resident Frenchmen, usually reluctant exiles from the Sun King's radiance. One was Charles de St Evremond, the influential critic, essayist and populariser of Montaigne in England, who had been banished for a satire on Cardinal Mazarin and was now living on a pension from Charles. He longed to return but would never set foot in France again, dying in London at a great old age, in 1703. Another was the comte de Gramont, who had been dismissed from court after pursuing one of Louis's mistresses. He arrived in late 1662, quickly working out the factions and attaching himself to Barbara Castlemaine. A high-spending gambler, within months he had trebled the money he brought with him from France, only to lose it all again.[2] The card sessions would last all day, ending with a select supper party at his own house, almost always including St Evremond. Gramont also chased the women, showering them with notes and presents, diamonds and brilliants from the London jewellers, and trinkets forwarded weekly from Paris: 'perfumed gloves, pocket looking-glasses, elegant boxes, apricot paste, essence and other small wares of love'.[3] He pestered them to give in and persecuted them still more when they said no.

Aiming for a rich marriage in Britain, he soon fell for Elizabeth Hamilton, Ormond's niece and one of three sisters of the courtier James Hamilton. Charles gave his consent and promised to find some sort of pension, but the constant ups and downs of their courtship caused great amusement. Eventually they married and returned to France in September 1664, shortly after the birth of their son. They would have left earlier except that Gramont had lost so much money on cards and sporting bets and was anxious to recoup some of it before he sailed. This vain desire continued to the very last day, prompting an amused note from Charles, given to the comte to carry to Minette:

This bearer has been so long resolving to leave this place, that I did not believe he would goe, till now I see his bootes are on, and he has taken his leave of me, and he gives me but a moment to write this letter, for tis not a quarter of an houer since he was looseing his mony at tennis, and he should have been gone two howers ago. I am affraide he comes very light to you, for though his wife has her loade, I feare his purse is very empty, having lost near five thousand pounds within these three months.[4]

Elizabeth Hamilton was beautiful as well as satisfyingly wealthy. The previous December, just before their wedding, Lely painted her, tall and big-bosomed, with brown ringlets and a dimple in her chin, in the pose of St Catherine. This was one of a small fleet of St Catherine portraits, homages to the queen, who had already been painted in this role by Jacob Huysmans. The court, however, was far from saintly. It was a hard place, particularly for women, if one reads between the lines of Gramont's memoirs, concocted by another of Elizabeth's brothers, Anthony Hamilton. These are often inaccurate as to date or place, but perfectly represent the kind of stories that courtiers found amusing, and the scandals they enjoyed. One feels that Hamilton did not much like the opposite sex; he died a bachelor in 1720, ensconced in St Germain with the exiled Stuart court. But the picture he paints of their treatment often calls on our sympathy.

Well-bred women vied to serve Catherine and Anne, Duchess of York. Their households offered the only place where women could hold official positions, swearing loyalty to their mistresses and undertaking particular duties and responsibilities, parallel to those of the high-ranking men: Mistress of the Robes, Groomess of the Stool, Keeper of the Queen's Privy Purse and so forth. The six or so Ladies of the Bedchamber (the ladies-in-waiting) were peeresses who provided company for the queen and duchess, positions that could give a woman access to power and benefit their families.[5]

Beneath them were up to ten or eleven Women of the Bedchamber or dressers, drawn from the upper gentry. And in the third rank, like the flounce of a final petticoat, were six to ten maids of honour. These were unmarried girls from gentry families, who were often given positions as a reward for their families' royalist loyalties. They were supposed to shine, and adorn the court. (Minette's recommendation of Frances Stuart, 'She is the most beautiful girl in the world, and the best fitted of any to adorn a court,' was a job reference as much as a private tribute.[6]) The maids attended the queen. They walked out with her in the park or to chapel, stepped out at the balls, took roles in the plays and sang, talked and played cards in her rooms. Their favourite game was ombre, not a name deriving from modest shades, but a version of the Spanish game 'L'hombre', a three-handed game, where nine cards are dealt and the rest is in 'stock', where the player on the dealer's right is 'the man', who decides trumps and starts the round. The games could last for hours. More practically, the maids were there to make good marriages, which Charles helped by granting a dowry of £2,000, although, as with most of his generous gestures, this did not always arrive as soon as expected, and sometimes not at all.

The maids were indispensable at Catherine's evening circle, which grew in popularity as her confidence increased. In 1664 she would move this from the formal Presence Chamber to her private 'withdrawing room', thus combining a certain grandeur with the informality of music and cards.[7] The evening gathering slowly became a central feature of court life, a place where the King seemed at ease, where the latest hot gossip was exchanged, and where the barometer of royal favour could be tapped and watched.

All the court women scrutinised each other minutely, criticising their fellows' style, their hair, their dress. It was lucky if one was witty and handsome, but misery if one was plain and quiet. And while the male courtiers fawned over their favourites, they sniped and cut them down at the same time. An early star and victim was Jane Needham, Lady Myddleton, a luscious beauty whom Anthony

Hamilton described cruelly as 'handsomely made, all white and golden' but pretentious and affected: 'The airs of indolent languor, which she had assumed, were not to everybody's taste; the sentiments of delicacy and refinement, which she tried to express without understanding what they meant, put her hearers to sleep; she was most tiresome when she wished to be most brilliant.'[8] Jane was pursued by both Charles and the Duke of York, but resisted becoming the mistress of either, falling instead for Ralph Montagu, the duke's Master of Horse.

Jane Myddleton

The women were on display, in a literal as well as figurative sense. In the mid-1660s the Duke and Duchess of York put together a collection of portraits of women of the court, later known as the 'Windsor Beauties', a set that also commemorated friends and political alliances. It became fashionable to collect such series, especially when mezzotint prints became available in the next decade. The ideal of pictorial beauty was lightness and grace, which Lely conjured with folds of billowing silks and satins, a type of fashionable undress whose expensive materials conveyed the sitter's status, while their looseness suggested the body beneath.[9] A century later Horace Walpole described these Lely costumes as 'a sort of fantastic nightgowns, fastened with a single pin'. Lely was in truth, Walpole felt, 'the ladies painter . . . He caught the reigning character, and

> – on the animated canvas stole
> The sleepy eye, that spoke the melting soul.[10]

Lord Capel's daughter Theodosia, who married Clarendon's second son, Henry Hyde, was a typical sleepy-eyed star, with, Gramont's memoirs recorded cattily, 'skin of a dazzling whiteness, fine hands, and a foot surprisingly beautiful, even in England: long custom had given such a languishing tenderness to her looks that she never opened her eyes but like a Chinese'.[11]

But all of Lely's portraits of court beauties were a version of his favourite, the almond-eyed Barbara Castlemaine. In December 1663, Barbara moved to the front of the court stage again when she announced, with no warning, that she had become a convert to Catholicism. The queen, devout Catholic that she was, remarked tartly that she did not think Barbara had done this 'for conscience sake'. Her horrified family asked Charles to make her retract, to which he is said to have replied that 'as for the souls of ladies, he never meddled with that'. There was much speculation as to her motive. Was it to appease her husband Roger Palmer, now serving in Venice? Or to situate herself even more snugly in the Catholic party at court? Or to be closer to the queen?

After her illness, Charles was still anxious about Catherine and full of good intentions, his concern running through his correspondence with Minette in late 1663. In these letters his writing ran straight, clear, untroubled across the page. The tone was open, straightforward about all physical matters like illness or sex, and childbirth, the mood occasionally marked by flashes of impatience, but usually buoyant and optimistic. Besides his evident affection ran an undercurrent of amusement and self-mockery, heard in ironic asides or deadpan juxtapositions:

My wife is now so well, as in a few dayes, she will thank you herself for the consernement you had for her, in her sicknesse. Yesterday we had a little ball in the privy chamber, where she lookd on, and, though we had many of our good faces absent, yet, I assure you, the assembly would not have been disliked for beauty, even at Paris it self, for we have a great many yong women come up, since you were here, who are very handsome. Pray send me some images, to put in prayer books. They are for my wife, who can get none here. I assure you it will be a greate present to her, and she will looke upon them often, for she is not only contente to say the great office in the breviere, every day, but likewise that of our Lady too, and this is besides going to chapel, where she makes use of none of these. I am just now going to see a new play, so I shall say no more, but that I am intierly yours. C.R.[12]

As she slowly recovered, Catherine often stayed in her own rooms, attending every office at chapel, while Charles cast his eye over the young beauties and went to the playhouse. Barbara tried hard to regain her place at his side. At a crowded performance of Dryden's *The Indian Emperor* on 1 February 1664, she ostentatiously left her box to go and sit between Charles and the Duke of York, disconcerting them both. Later that spring, Charles told Minette that he had been playing the good husband, going out with Catherine all afternoon: soon he would banish Edward Montagu from court for spending too long with the queen and even daring to squeeze her hand. But he celebrated the fourth anniversary of his entry into London by dancing at Barbara's lodgings, not with his wife.

Barbara was pregnant yet again, and when the baby, Charlotte, was born in September 1664 Charles acknowledged her at once. The French ambassador, taking his beautiful wife to dine with Lady Castlemaine, reported that Charles 'did the honours of the house in a way befitting more a host than a guest'.[13]

Inevitably, Barbara had her enemies. Shortly after Charlotte's birth she was attacked in the park by three masked noblemen, who hurled insults at her and compared her once again to Edward IV's notorious mistress Jane Shore. When she reached the safety of Whitehall, she fainted. As soon as he heard, Charles left everything and rushed to her side, ordering the park gates closed and all inside arrested. And he loved their four small children. Although he had taken time to acknowledge the previous baby, Henry, as his own, he still went up to his room and tucked him in at night.

These parallel families were accepted with little comment. His brother James, Duke of York, had two sons and a daughter in the 1660s with his mistress Arabella Churchill, the sister of John Churchill, Duke of Marlborough. He had other long-standing affairs, including Lady Southesk, Frances Jennings – sister of the Duchess of Marlborough – and Catherine Sedley. Yet he was also devoted to his strong, stout wife Anne. When Pepys saw the Yorks together in 1663 he winced at their 'impertinent and methought unnatural dalliances'. They were far too physical than was decent for man and wife, 'before the whole world, such as kissing of hands and leaning upon one another'.[14]

Even if openly accepted, a royal mistress had to be resilient. Barbara Castlemaine was a woman of courage and will, bold enough to adopt the libertine manners of the male courtiers and match her lover's infidelities. She had to endure constant stories about her sexual appetites and practices, being said to know all the variations in Aretino's *Postures*, the leading pornographic textbook ever since its first appearance in Renaissance Venice, and (perhaps truthfully) to have tried out Jacob Hall, the famous acrobat and rope-dancer, as a lover, to see if his tumbling limbs were as satisfying in private as in public performances. But if some court women like Barbara were clearly predators, most were prey, ogled as soon as they arrived by the gallants, who virtually laid bets as to who would bed them first. If they did give in, they faced acid satires on their prowess or anatomy. Winifred Wells, one of the maids of honour, was described as a tall girl who walked like a goddess but had a face like a sheep. She was one of several who succumbed to Charles, prompting a punning verse from Buckingham, imagining Charles exclaiming to his valet Progers:

> When the King felt the horrible depth of this Well,
> Tell me Progers, cried Charlie, where am I? Oh tell!
> Had I sought the world's centre to find, I had found it,
> But this Well! Ne'er a plummet was made that could sound it.

When one of the maids was said to 'drop a child' when dancing at a court ball, and it was picked up in a scarf, the mother was named as Winifred and the father as the king. This story sprang from one of Buckingham's practical jokes, in which an unnamed court lady stuck a cushion up her dress and pretended to be pregnant, before dropping the cushion on the floor. But it was then embroidered more darkly. It was said that the child was stillborn and the king took it to his closet and dissected it, joking that he had lost a subject.

A stream of young women arrived, fresh-faced, excited at the prospect of intimate court life: Miss Price, Miss Temple, Miss Hobart, Miss Jennings, Miss Boynton. Some made good marriages. Very few, with odd exceptions like Evelyn's platonic love Margaret Blagge, escaped with their reputation intact, and intense friendships were routinely suspected of being lesbian intrigues. The court was claustrophobically small – everyone seemed related to one another, by blood or marriage or old family connections. For example in September 1660 Ormond's daughter Elizabeth Butler, a striking figure with blue eyes and dark hair, married Philip Stanhope, Earl of Chesterfield, who was not only Barbara Castlemaine's first lover but the current Lord Chamberlain to the queen.

The countess's story illustrates the complexity of court relationships, and also the way that its members prized this hot-house life.
When she was pursued both by her cousin, James Hamilton, and,
more publicly, by the Duke of York, Chesterfield angrily whipped
her off to his country seat in Derbyshire. Once there, she took
vengeance on Hamilton, whom she blamed for this exile, by summoning him to rescue her and then leaving him to wait for hours
outside, in an icy winter night.[15] The nub of the joke, apart from the
discomfiture of the freezing lover, was the hideousness of being
exiled from the court and sent to live amid the 'precipices' of the
Peak District. The jibes in Restoration drama about the different
styles of life of the country, city and court were appreciated chiefly
because they were so profoundly felt.

Lady Denham

Despite the libertine culture, many husbands, like Chesterfield, suffered agonies of jealousy. After his first wife died, Sir John Denham married the young and flirtatious Margaret Brooke, one of two stepdaughters of the Earl of Bedford. When the Duke of York fell for her and she reputedly became his mistress in 1666, Denham had a breakdown. John Aubrey, whose gossip in this case is substantiated, reported that Denham was on his way from London to inspect the Portland Stone quarries, when he turned round and 'went to Hounslowe, and demanded rents of Lands he had sold many yeares before; went to the King, and told him he was the Holy Ghost'.[16] Denham recovered, but lost his position. Margaret herself came to a sad end, as Aubrey declares with satisfaction but without evidence: 'His 2nd lady had no child: was poysoned by the hands of the Countess of Rochester, with Chocolatte.' Another version blamed Denham himself, saying that he had poisoned her, while a different vein of gossip blamed the Duchess of York. And the beautiful Countess of Chesterfield also died, in the deserts of Derbyshire in July 1665, again rumoured to have been poisoned by her husband. The court could, indeed, be a deadly place.

20 Performance

No wit, no Sence, no Freedom, and a Box,
Is much like paying money for the Stocks.
Besides the Author dreads the strut and meen
Of new prais'd poets, having often seen
Some of his Fellows, who have writ before,
When *Nel* has danc'd her jig, steal to the Door,
Hear the Pit clap, and with conceit of that
Swell, and believe themselves the Lord knows what.
          BUCKINGHAM, Epilogue to *The Chances*

THE COURT was the supreme arena for showing off. The beauties
set out to allure, the men to impress. It was a constant performance,
with a feverish energy – too many young men, pent up, with too little to do. This was particularly true of the 'wits', like Charles
Sackville, Lord Buckhurst, who would later succeed his uncle as
Earl of Middlesex, and his father as Earl of Dorset. One of the
beardless boys in the new Cavalier Parliament, Buckhurst turned
twenty in 1663. His constant side-kick was the twenty-four-year-old
Sir Charles Sedley, 'Little Sid'. Both took easily to the hard-drinking
court, and both were known for their wit.

Wit could imply anything from a clever turn of phrase or a neatly applied epigram to venomous ridicule. It could also take the form
of burlesque performance, using parody and bawdy as aggressive
tools to ridicule authority and debunk deep-held beliefs. It was in
this sense that it formed part of what Anthony Wood called 'that
notorious business in the balcony in the Strand'.[1] In July 1663,
Buckhurst and Sedley, with the Lincolnshire squire Sir Thomas
Ogle, staggered into the Cock Inn in Bow Street, near Covent
Garden. 'Being all inflam'd with strong liquours', they went out on

to the balcony. Sedley then stripped naked, gave a jovial pantomime of lust and buggery, and preached a mock sermon which conflated priest, quack and pimp, 'saying that there he hath to sell such a pouder as should make all the cunts in town run after him'.[2] That done 'he took a glass of wine and washed his prick in it and then drank it off; and then took another and drank the king's health'. As an encore he pissed on the crowd in the street. A minor riot began as angry townsfolk battered the locked doors and hurled stones and empty wine-bottles through the windows. In court next day, Sedley was bound over to good behaviour on a bond of £500, which he tried hard to get reduced, declaring 'he thought he was the first man that paid for shitting'. In the end he borrowed the money for the fine from Charles himself – a gesture of royal amusement, instead of chastisement, which was quickly noted by hostile observers.

This impromptu farce attacked a host of targets at once, from the privacy of sex to respect for church and king. Shocked though the crowd were, there was little harm done except to the court's reputation. But earlier that year, Buckhurst, his brother and three friends had been arrested 'for killing and robbing a Tanner', on the road from Waltham. They were charged with manslaughter but acquitted, said Pepys drily, after creating 'a very good tale that they were in pursuit of thiefs, and that they took this man for one of them'.[3] Buckhurst pleaded the King's Pardon, which was granted. As his friend Rochester later remarked, 'my Lord Dorset might do anything, yet was never to blame'.[4] Yet this man of casual violence was also acclaimed for his culture and charm. Burnet, who knew him well, described him as a generous, good-natured man, charitable to a fault, quiet and solemn when sober but wild when drunk, in person a gentle soul but as a writer, ferocious: 'Never was so much ill nature in a pen as in his, joined with so much good nature as was in himself, even to excess; for he was against all punishing, even of malefactors.'[5] A poet and critic, Buckhurst was a generous patron of writers including Samuel Butler, Dryden, and Wycherley, and responded with awed admiration to Milton's *Paradise Lost.*

Charles Sackville, Lord Buckhurst, later Earl of Dorset; an older, sober image.
Horace Walpole thought him 'the finest gentleman in the voluptuous court of
Charles the second, and in the gloomy one of King William'.

The contradictions in Buckhurst were those of the court and the
King himself. Buckhurst and Sedley pushed the boundaries, with
Buckingham as their wild older statesman, and Rochester, who
arrived at court in 1664 aged seventeen, as their *enfant terrible*. They

shared their beautiful boys as well as girls, and mocked every sexual act and condition from masturbation to the pox. They could
never have got away with their transgressions if Charles had not
shared the same sense of humour. On one trip to Newmarket,
Buckingham invented a bawdy sermon just to amuse him.
Sometimes Charles himself joined in the parodic performances.
Many sermons, for example, had welcomed him as a returning King
David, but one day in 1665, after a riotous evening at the Spanish
ambassador's, a passer-by reported that towards daybreak 'the King
and the ambassador and a handful of others, having thrown away
their wigs, came along leaping and dancing in the moonlight, pre-
ceded by the whole band of violins, in imitation of King David
before the ark'.[6]

In a politer mode, the wits' attacks on authority found their way
onto the Restoration stage, which Charles patronised with passion.
In the new playhouses, the scrabble to find scripts led to many
revivals and adaptations of plays from before the wars, like Jonson's
The Alchemist and *Bartholomew Fair* or Beaumont and Fletcher's *The
Humorous Lieutenant*. But writers also drew on the tragedies of
Corneille, the early satires of Molière and the Spanish comedies of
Calderón. In the drama, as in the contrast between Buckhurst's
drunken performances and intellectual seriousness, there were
strange contrarieties. The comedies that mocked the follies of the
age had plots that touched the heart, while the tragi-comedies and
heroic dramas, echoing with the terms Honour, Duty, Love and
Hate, could make the crowd guffaw. 'I have observed', remarks
Dryden's character Lisideius (based on the cynical Sedley) in the
Essay on Dramatic Poesie, 'that, in all our Tragedies, the Audience cannot forbear laughing when the Actors are to die; ''tis the most
Comick part of the whole Play.'[7]

The conventions and contradictions were relished by a knowing
audience. The playhouses were part of the new polite world of the
Town, stretching between the City and Whitehall, but both theatres

were also on the hinterland of slums and underworld haunts. Bridges Street, just off Covent Garden, where the King's Company moved into their new Theatre Royal in May 1663, was cheek by jowl with the brothels of Drury Lane. The Duke's Company had been established in Lincoln's Inn Fields since 1662. It was surrounded by townhouses built in the last reign, inhabited by aristocrats, merchants and artists, but the Fields themselves and the alley of Whetstone Park behind were well-known haunts of prostitutes and thieves.

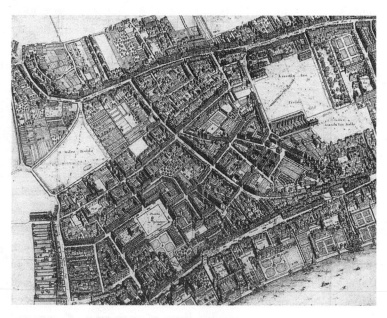

The only surviving plate from Hollar's planned 'Great Map' of London, c.1658, from the river to Holborn. The large riverside garden belongs to Somerset House, home of Henrietta Maria. The area north of the Strand is crowded, but there are still allotments and orchards, as well as the spaces of Covent Garden and Lincoln's Inn Fields.

Although the public theatres were more exclusive than they had been in Shakespeare's day, they were not a solely aristocratic purlieu. Merchants and professional men, artists and lawyers bought boxes and packed into the pit, 'cits' took the cheaper, second tier of boxes, and servants and shopkeepers crowded the gallery. The atmosphere of the Town, with its coffee-houses and shops, mingled with an older legacy from the court and the exile. Tom Killigrew, who ran the King's Company, had been a courtier of Charles I, while Davenant, manager of the Duke's Company, had been his court poet. Davenant had known the masques of Jonson and Inigo Jones, with their movable scenery, trap-doors allowing figures to rise from the abyss and ropes to fly in angels from above, and he brought these techniques into the theatre. The scenery had none of the symbolic reference of the masques, but was there simply to delight and 'astonish' (a favourite word), taking theatregoers from the 'tragic' scenery of Sicily or Madrid to the familiar comic territory of the Strand or Spring Gardens. The raked stage, behind the proscenium arch, allowed grand vistas 'upstage', but an apron still projected into the pit, with boxes on both sides, so that the actors could play intimately to the audience, swapping jokes and innuendoes.

The season lasted from September to June, the months when the law courts were active and parliament was in session. The playhouses were open six days a week, with actors rehearsing in the mornings, acting in the afternoons and sometimes trooping off in the evenings to play for the court. Over a season the companies might stage fifty plays, three different ones each week, old and new, ranging from broad farce to heroic verse drama. A new play rarely ran for more than six days at a time, with the playwright awarded the takings of the third night. The theatre was addictive – Pepys's diary is full of resolutions to give up going to plays, and equally full of his breaking them. Charles went to the theatre constantly, both for love of the plays, like Pepys, and because here he could play out his strategy of openness, sharing the entertainment, rubbing shoulders with the crowd, letting himself be seen. His presence there was part of the draw. The whole audience stood up as he entered, and waited until he took his seat in the royal box, in the centre of the first row of boxes. Everyone watched him, turning and gazing up from the pit, or leaning over the balconies of the boxes and galleries overhead. If he laughed, the play was a hit; if he stayed silent, yawned, or examined his nails, a chill fell on the production.

The auditorium could squeeze in seven hundred at a pinch. In the pit, where the green-baize-covered benches sloped gently back from the stage, the court gallants sat, shouting comments, ogling actresses and ribbing the orange sellers who stood in a row between the pit and the stage before the performance began. These were young girls carefully selected for their looks, their friendliness, their willingness to run messages for the rakes to women in the audience, and their sparky ability to talk back. In the Theatre Royal they were run by Mary Meggs, 'Orange Moll', who paid for 'full, free, & sole liberty, licence, power, & authority to vend, utter, & sell oranges, Lemons, fruit, sweetmeats, & all manner of fruiterers & Confectioners wares & Commodities'.[8]

Tickets – little round brass discs – were bought in a room next to the theatre, but seats were not reserved, allowing for much pushing and moving around. If you didn't like the play at one theatre you could go to the other, as described in George Etherege's *She Would if She Could*, where the fops run 'from one Play-house to the other Play-house, and if they like neither the Play or the Women, they seldom stay any longer than the combing of their Perriwigs, or a whisper or two with a friend; and then they cock their Caps, and out they strut again'.[9] If the crowd was too great, people pushed in without paying, provoking Charles to issue a stern proclamation against the 'diverse persons who doe rudely presse and with evill Language and Blows force their wayes into the two Theatres'.[10] Brawls and fights broke out, swords were drawn and on at least one occasion a man was killed. Sometimes soldiers were stationed outside the theatres until the play was over.

The packed theatres, suffocating on hot days, were ripe with the smell of sweat, powder and heady perfume. They buzzed with the chatter of fops, the heckling of the wits, the flutter of fans and the rustling of silk. In the crush, there was always a scent of sex, with assignations in the pit and the boxes, glances from audience to stage and back. The audience started flowing through the doors up to an hour before the play was due to start, which was usually around half-past three. The mood was like that of a club, where the latest gossip was exchanged. Cliques formed, rivalries brewed, political deals were made and information exchanged. The news heard here spread outwards, to dinner tables and coffee-houses, and through letters to friends and relations in the country.

The reopening of the theatres was followed by the arrival of two distinct groups of writers. One was composed of the courtiers them-selves, including Charles's old tutor William Cavendish, the Marquess of Newcastle. Cavendish had a taste for broad comedy, but the mood of the Restoration, so full of uncertainty, also lent itself to the mixed genre of tragi-comedy. This was usually a tragedy with a happy ending, or one where the tragic lead was a victim rather than a flawed hero. (The genre was popular with royalist audiences, it has been suggested, because there had been so much real tragedy in the recent past and the return of the monarchy demanded celebration, the triumphant overcoming of trials and obstacles.)[11] Like the romances of Mlle de Scudéry that Restoration readers so admired, tragi-comedies featured princes and princesses with exotic histories, and over-complicated love affairs. Dryden, as usual, pinpointed its peculiar character. 'There is no Theatre in the World', he wrote, in the mocking voice of Lisideius, 'has any thing so absurd as the *English* Tragi-comedie, ''tis a *Drama* of our own invention . . . here a course of mirth, there another of Sadness and Passion, and a third of Honour, and a Duel: Thus in two hours and a half we run through all the fits of Bedlam.'[12]

Charles himself prompted the first heroic play when he asked Roger Boyle, Earl of Orrery, if he thought it possible to produce an English form of French tragedy. Orrery later told Ormond that when he kissed the king's hand,

he Commanded me, to write a Play for Him . . . : And therefore, som
months [later] I presumed to lay at his majtys Feete, a Trage-Comedi, All
in Ten feet verse, & Rhyme. I had writt it, in that manner upon two
accounts; First because I thought it was not fit a Command soe extraordinary, shou'd have bin obeyd in a way that was Common; Secondly,
because I found his majty Relish'd rather, the French Fashion of Playes,
than the English.[13]

The hero of Orrery's *The General*, in 1661, was a soldier (like
Monck) who revolts against a usurper to restore the true king, amid
a welter of arguments on love and honour. (It roused Sedley to
spluttering sarcasm in the pit when he saw it in 1664.) Orrery's second play, *The History of Henry the Fifth*, was an even more vehement
exposition of the same themes, focusing on the 'restoration' of
English power in France, with lavish sets and costumes, including
the coronation robes lent by Charles and James. In heroic drama
everything was larger than life – armies fought to the sound of
drums and trumpets, heroes displayed staggering bravery and heartbreaking nobility, ghosts warned of sudden turns of fate. A favourite
subject, perhaps inevitably, was the triumph of the rightful king or
queen over wicked usurpers, but the plays also allowed dramatists
to explore serious themes like the clash between cultures, the meaning of sovereignty and hierarchy, and – a warning to Charles – the
disastrous effect of passion over reason.

The grand plots, often acted out in sweeping verse, were usually
balanced by comic sub-plots, bringing the plays nearer to the everyday world. Jonson and Beaumont and Fletcher were the great influences here, prompting a lasting argument between devotees of
Jonson's 'humour' and of Fletcher's 'wit'. Beaumont and Fletcher
were favourites because they caught the idiom of the court, while
their combative lovers, descended from Shakespeare's Benedict and
Beatrice, gave birth to the witty sparring couples of the later
Restoration stage. Compared to Shakespeare, Dryden decided,
'they understood and imitated the Conversation of Gentlemen
much better, whose wild debaucheries and quickness of wit in

Repartees no poet can ever paint as they have done'.[14]

Dryden himself was the leader in a new group, the professional writers. His first success, in 1663, was the *The Wild Gallant* at the Theatre Royal. Although it had a baffling plot (Pepys could never work out who the 'wild gallant' actually was), it had a witty script, and was staged at court a fortnight later. Dryden's friend Robert Howard (soon a powerful figure in opposition politics) also wrote for the stage. His farcical satire *The Committee*, which appeared to riotous applause in 1662, in the middle of the tension surrounding the Act of Uniformity, featured upstart, hypocritical puritans of Cromwell's London trying to stop two Cavalier couples retrieving their estates. The noble Cavaliers won, of course, with the help of their loyal but dim Irish servant Teague.

Charles influenced comedy personally, as he had tragi-comedy. This time he looked for inspiration not to France but to Spain. At his suggestion, in 1663, Sir Samuel Tuke adapted two comedies of Calderón to create the immensely successful *The Adventures of Five Hours*, which recast the grand issues of love and honour on a domestic scale, especially through the anti-heroic servants. The play started a trend, and for several years the stage swirled with Spanish 'cape and sword plays' (including three adaptations by the pro-Spanish George Digby, Lord Bristol). But although the Spanish dramas pleased the pit and the gallery with their exotic settings, action-packed plots and high moral sentiments, what audiences really wanted was more debauchery, frivolity and quick wit. And soon a new young dramatist appeared, George Etherege, who was eager to supply them in abundance.

Etherege was twenty-seven when his play *The Comical Revenge, or, Love in a Tub* was acted at the Duke's Theatre in March 1664. It was dedicated to Buckhurst: Etherege had written it, he said, as a calculated way to get to know him. The ploy worked. In 1663–4 Etherege and Buckhurst exchanged exaggerated verse poems celebrating prostitutes, wine, and pleasure in a rakishly self-conscious manner.[15] *The Comical Revenge* reflected all their wild living, with a romantic plot in rhymed verse and comic plots in prose. Its forth-right portrait of a rich, lusty widow jousting with the spendthrift hero who needs a rich wife made it an instant hit, running for near-ly a month. It was exuberant and vital, mixing realism and heroism, fantasy and ridicule. More significantly, it evoked the stifling social forms of Cromwell's England specifically to celebrate, by contrast, 'the freedoms of the present'. In its festive way it was a libertine manifesto.

A climactic scene from Etherege's *The Comical Revenge, or Love in a Tub,*
Act IV, scene vi

The Comical Revenge swept the actors along in constant motion. But while its energy was extreme, it was not unusual. In almost every production, the cast were stretched to their limit. They worked hard and were poorly paid, if touched by glamour and enriched by occasional gifts. The King's Company inherited stars from the generation before, like the comic Yorkshireman John Lacy, who made the crowd roar as the nonconformist Scruple in John Wilson's *The Cheats* in 1662, yet another bold performance in the middle of the debates about religious settlement. 'The new play called *The Cheats*', wrote Abraham Hill gleefully to his friend John Brooke, 'has been attempted on the stage, but it is so scandalous that it is forbidden.'[16] Charles loved Lacy and commissioned John Michael Wright to paint a triple portrait of him playing three different roles. But he was also impressed by the handsome Charles Hart, who excelled both as a man of honour and as a fine, witty gallant, and was said (without evidence) to be Shakespeare's great-nephew.

Davenant's company also had promising young leads, like Thomas Betterton, still only in his twenties, and Edward Kynaston, now playing male roles. But however fine the actors, the women were the real draw. New names appeared in court gossip, like Elizabeth Weaver, with whom Charles had a brief fling, Anne and Becky Marshall, Charlotte Butler and Elizabeth Davenport. Actresses and singers were sucked into the whirlpool of court sex, self-interest, and practical jokes. It was thought extremely funny when Aubrey de Vere, Earl of Oxford, who was a Privy Councillor, Gentleman of the Bedchamber, knight of the Garter and colonel of the Horse Guards – tricked the hapless Hester Davenport into a mock marriage that she believed was real. When she threw herself at Charles's feet demanding justice, laughter was all she got. When two maids of honour decided to play orange girls, they encountered the life of theatre women at first hand, being accosted at the playhouse – a normal fate for orange sellers – and then ambushed in their coach by the roué Henry Brouncker who had a house in the country 'always well stocked with girls'.[17]

The playwrights deliberately created opposing pairs of women to show them off: virtuous heroines and stormy villainesses in the tragedies, and smart-talking court ladies and innocent country girls in comedies. They also made sure that bodies were on show at every turn. The tragedies were full of rapes and rescues, and the comedies with breeches parts to show off the girls' legs. (Dryden's *The Rival Ladies* of 1664 gave double value, with *two* women disguised as pages pursuing the same man.) And when an actress spoke the prologue or epilogue she stepped out of her role, cracking sexual jokes and flashing innuendoes at the delighted audience. These moments, when the actors 'remove from Fiction into Life', greatly upset the critic Jeremy Collier: 'Here they converse with the Boxes and Pit, and address directly to the Audience . . . But here we have Lewdness without Shame or Example; Here the Poet exceeds himself . . . And to make it the more agreeable, Women are Commonly pick'd out for this Service.'[18] After the show, select playgoers went round the back to the dressing rooms, the 'tiring rooms', above the green room where the actors waited for their cues. To protect (and control) his actresses, Davenant lodged them in a house attached to the theatre, while Killigrew hired rooms in Drury Lane. Many were smart, clever girls from the streets, others – or this was their story – came from better-off families who had fallen on hard times.

The plays themselves were seductive, at once an escape and a mirror. In the theatre a man who had just come from practising new French dances could laugh at Paris fopperies, or a presbyterian could sneer at puritans without shame. Many topics were close to the audience's hidden concerns: the clash between generations, the forced, loveless marriages, the hypocrisy of piety, the greed of merchants. The lines of class were drawn constantly, allowing each part of the audience to laugh at the other. As the actors mimicked the court drawl and gestures, fashionable obsessions were mocked as affectation while also appearing an accomplishment. Indeed some plays were almost a handbook to polite manners, increasingly so in the comedies of the next decade, as when Bellair instructs Harriet in flirtation in Etherege's *The Man of Mode*:

YOUNG BELLAIR: At one motion play your fan, roll your eyes, and then settle a kind look upon me.
HARRIET: So.
BELLAIR: Now spread your fan, look down upon it, and tell the sticks with a finger.
HARRIET: Very modish.
BELLAIR: Clap your hand up to your bosom, hold down your gown. Shrug a little, draw up your breasts and let 'em fall again, gently, with a sigh or two, *etc.*[19]

And so it goes on, as Bellair says, 'Admirably well acted!'

The tone of voice and repartee were wickedly close to court speech.[20] Exactly the opposite was true of tragedy, where the actor followed strict rules of gesture and voice, pointing to his head to indicate reason, slapping his heart when evoking passion, raising his hands in suppliance to the Gods, shooting his arms forward with open palms to show horror. And there was magic in the theatre, as well as gossip and grand acting. When the King's Theatre closed for alterations, Pepys went backstage, 'to see the inside of the stage and all the tiring rooms and machines':

and indeed it was a sight worth seeing. But to see their clothes, and the various sorts, and what a mixture of things there was; here a wooden leg, there a ruff, here a hobby horse, there a crown, would make a man split himself to see with laughing, and particularly Lacy's wardrobe and Shotrell's. But then again, to think how fine they show on the Stage, by candlelight, and how poor things they are to look now too near hand, is not pleasant at all.[21]

Like Charles, looking at his court in a sober mood, he was almost bewildered to find that the glittering performance was an illusion.

The plays and poems and letters of the court show wit meaning many things, running up a sliding scale. At the bottom comes bawdy, the crude armoury of sexual, scatological and bodily jokes, graduating to buffoonery, slapstick and burlesque. The exaggerated imitation of burlesque – like Buckingham's mockery of Clarendon – was also a form of criticism and truth-finding, hunting the essence of a character. Ridicule of this kind was forensic, and much to be dreaded. At its finest, the wit of the court, and of the stage, was penetrating and questioning. To Dryden, fast repartee – 'a chace of wit kept on both sides, and swiftly managed' – was the chief grace of comedy and 'the greatest pleasure of the audience', one area where British writers utterly outdid the French. It flowered in a play of metaphor and phrase-making. It worked through opposition, antithesis and balance, slowly reaching agreement, or leaving an opponent silenced by a brilliantly closed barb, as in Charles's own punishing one-liners. Halifax found Charles's enjoyment of low comedy and broad humour demeaning, and his wit too fast, too prone to spy a weakness in people and turn it to jest: 'His wit consisted chiefly in the Quickness of his Apprehension. His Apprehension made him find Faults, and that led him to short sayings upon them, not always equal, but often very good.'[22] Charles's tartness was softened by his generosity, and his fellow-feeling, yet these, said Halifax (wittily), could also be a weakness, displaying a humanity and a delight in applause unsuitable to a king:

The Thing called Wit, a Prince may taste, but it is dangerous for him to take too much of it; it hath Allurements which by refining his Thoughts, take off from their dignity in applying them less to the governing part. There is a Charm in Wit, which a Prince must resist: and that to him was no easy matter; it was contesting with Nature upon Terms of Disadvantage.

But in his enjoyment of wit Charles was at one with his court and the polite culture of the Town. 'I do believe', one author would write, ten years hence, 'that never in any Age was there such a violent and universal thirst after the Fame of being Wits.'[23] To win, as Charles well knew, even in 'the governing part', in matters of state, you must keep your audience guessing.

IX

It's an Ill winde Blowes
Noe body Good

Proverbs, from a traditional pack of cards, reprinted in 1780

21 Money-men and Merchants

Nor can we doubt, but by the bounteous Source
Of Your Successful Right, not only We
But all the Merchants of Your Realm shall see
This Empory the Magazine of All
That's rich, from Phoebus rising to his Fall.
    JOHN OGILBY, *Entertainment*, a coronation appeal from
    the East India merchants

WHEN CHARLES RODE through London on the eve of his coronation, the triumphal arches proclaimed the City's hopes. As he approached the '*East-India* House', a youth dressed in Indian garb, accompanied by two black slaves, offered him tribute, while another rode up on a camel, with panniers full of jewels, spices and silks. The King, the Indian-robed speaker declared, was a phoenix, a treasure. He had the power to revive English trade, put paid to the Spanish and overcome the Dutch, and make London the emporium of 'All that's rich', from all nations under the sun. Further on, singers dressed as sailors hailed Charles as 'Great Neptune of the Main', claiming that the Royal Navy could whip the French, the Dutch, the Spanish and the Turk and 'seize on their Goods and Monies'.[1] England's greatness would spread across the seas and the world's wealth flood to her shores.

The view from the Custom House in the port of London, or the docks in Newcastle or the quays of Bristol, made the dream seem possible. Lone ships and convoys set out in the spring heading north for the Baltic or south to the Mediterranean, carrying tin from Cornwall, coal from Newcastle, pilchards from Plymouth, cloth and woollens from Devon and East Anglia. (Fine serges and light woollen 'stuffs' proved surprisingly popular in Italy.) In autumn the boats returned, unloading timber, pitch and tar from Norway, carpets from Turkey, currants from Spain, oil from Italy, wine from Bordeaux. Meanwhile larger and faster ships crossed the Atlantic to the West Indies and the American plantations, bringing back tobacco and sugar. And the beautiful Indiamen unfurled their great sails, setting off southwards, sailing round the Cape of Good Hope into the Indian Ocean, carrying bullion, cloth, lead and iron, and returning with holds fragrant with pepper and spices, heavy with calico and chintzes.

The Royal Exchange, London, engraved by Hollar in 1644,
with the crowd of merchants, including two Russians in fur hats on the left,
and a woman selling broadsides.

Luxuries filled the galleries of the Royal Exchange, the symbol of British mercantile glory. The fine Exchange had been built in Elizabeth's day by Sir Thomas Gresham, and his emblem, a golden grasshopper, topped its tall clock tower. Around the courtyard were four storeys of walkways, crammed with small shops. Beneath, in

the arched colonnade with its marble columns, the merchants made
their deals. The nonconformist clergyman Samuel Rolle remembered it with wondering nostalgia. 'How full of riches', he wrote,
'was that Royal Exchange':

Here, if anywhere, might a man have seen the glory of the world in a
moment. What artificial thing could entertain the senses, the fantasies of
men, that was not there to be had? Such was the delight that many gallants
took in that magazine of all curious varieties, that they could almost have
dwelt there (going from shop to shop like bee from flower to flower), if they
had but had a fountain of money that could not have been drawn dry. I
doubt not but a Mohamedan (who never expects other than sensual
delights) would gladly have availed himself of that place, and the treasures
of it, for his heaven, and have thought there was none like it.[2]

A host of languages and accents could be heard here and London's
own merchants included many of foreign origin. Several protestant
merchant families had come from northern France and from
Flanders, like the Rycauts, the Papillons, the Thierrys and the
Houblons. The Huguenot Thomas Papillon, an outspoken East
India director and Kentish landowner, had been brought to London
as a child. Sir John Houblon, who lived with his large family in his
mansion off Threadneedle Street, came originally from Lille.
Houblon was one of five merchant brothers, known for their religious devotion (two were later founding directors of the Bank of
England, of which Sir John was the first governor). They traded
chiefly with Portugal, Spain, Italy and the Mediterranean, but also
held directorships with the Levant and the East India companies.

Another group, the Jewish dealers, had arrived from Portugal,
Spain and Amsterdam in the mid-1650s. They were protected by an
agreement with Cromwell but although their synagogue in Cree
Lane was now one of the sights of the town they still had no written
permission to settle. In exile, Charles had promised Jewish bankers
in Amsterdam toleration in return for a loan, and he kept his promise. In 1664, when the Conventicle Act was passed, forbidding religious meetings, some hostile merchants and nobles saw this as a

way to eject the Jews, or at least to extract money for arguing on their behalf. But their leaders appealed directly to Charles, who, wrote Rabbi Jacob Sasportas, 'chuckled and spat at the business; and a written statement was issued from him, duly signed, affirming that no untoward measures had been or would be initiated against us'.[3] Charles remained generous towards the Jewish community throughout his reign, granting naturalisation to those who asked. Portuguese Jews helped Charles organise the payment of Catherine's dowry and the great speculators Duarte Da Silva and Gomes Rodrigues used London as a base to trade in bullion, jewels, wines and sugar across the world. The turnover of Jewish wholesale dealers was reckoned to be a twelfth of the total commerce of all the three kingdoms, paying thousands in customs dues each year.

Keen to foster London's trade, Charles had set up Privy Council committees soon after he arrived, including the Council of Foreign Plantations and the Council of Trade. The establishment of the latter in 1661 was a notable step, since it made public matters previously kept tight in royal hands, like the regulation of coinage, foreign trade and patents and monopolies.[4] The Council of Trade also promised to hear suggestions and complaints from all sides, thus reassuring the landed classes that their interests would not be swamped by those of the merchants. The letter patent made the King's enthusiasm clear. Charles had set up the council, it said, 'well weighing how considerable a part of our crown and government doth arise from foreign and domestic trade, in that they are the chief employment and maintenance of our people'.[5] He would be closely involved, open to suggestions, keen to 'bend our earnest affections & consultations of our own royal person'. And for the first few years he was closely involved, and the council was as open as he had promised. Thereafter, like many of Charles's offices, it became less accessible, moving to Whitehall and operating more as a royal advisory body.[6] Meanwhile ambassadors sallied out across Europe promoting trade agreements with Holland, France, Spain, Italy, the

German princedoms and the Scandinavian states. In 1662 Andrew
Marvell set out for Russia as secretary to Charles Howard, Earl of
Carlisle, trekking to Archangel in the Arctic north, on a long and
trouble-dogged embassy to regain the privileges which the Tsar had
cancelled after the execution of Charles I.

With the king committed to their interests, merchants could
dream of great fortunes. The conditions for creating individual
wealth were all there: the common law sanctioned property rights
and the making and enforcing of contracts; the networks of the companies and guilds ensured a good exchange of information; manu-
facturers were improving techniques, and boat-builders designing
better cargo ships – although in this they lagged behind the Dutch.
What they needed most, however, was cheap money to invest, and
here the English faced problems.

In the past, people had financed new ventures in a haphazard way
by borrowing from relatives or rich connections, setting loans
against the securities of bonds and mortgages. In the late middle
ages, London was home to foreign bankers who lent money on a
large scale to the crown, first the Italians (who gave their name to
Lombard Street) and then the Germans, and bankers from Genoa
and Venice and Amsterdam. But now the bankers were home-
grown. In these Restoration years, powerful money-men who had
risen under Cromwell strode down the Privy Gallery at Whitehall,
or received harassed Treasury officials and navy clerks in their panelled offices around Cheapside. This was yet another example, like
the work of the Royal Society and the boom in the book trade,
where Charles's regime built on the flurry of ideas and innovation
during the Interregnum.

Some of the new bankers were former scriveners, notaries who
negotiated loans and then began lending their own capital. But by
far the most influential were the London goldsmiths. For a century
or more, the goldsmiths had sold fine silver and gold plate to the
nobility and gentry, agreeing to take it back as security against loans
when times were hard. From pawn-broking they moved to full-scale

banking. People deposited cash with them, receiving a low rate of interest, and the goldsmiths lent it out again at a higher rate, set by law at six per cent. The rate had fallen sharply since the start of the century, but, to the chagrin of English investors, interest rates still remained higher than in Holland, where merchants or builders or farmers could borrow at four per cent. Risk also played its part then, as now, in establishing the rate: London's stayed high partly because financiers had lent to the crown, which often defaulted on its debts. The merchants now argued loudly that they needed cheap money, to invest at low cost in order to bring substantial profits home. In 1668, the ruthless entrepreneur Josiah Child firmly declared that 'all countries at this day are richer and poorer in exact proportion to what they pay, or have usually paid, for the Interest of Money'.[7]

Child and others complained that London had no financial quarter to rival Amsterdam, where the financiers clustered together, exchanging information and arranging spectacular deals in goods and currency. (Their journal, the *Price Courant*, even published exchange rates twice weekly.) But the London goldsmiths were catching up. They not only gave interest on deposits, but also discounted bills of exchange, accepted the new-fangled cheques, first issued in 1659, and issued 'goldsmiths notes', promissory notes that could change hands and circulate freely, creating a fluid movement of capital.[8] They also lent to each other, helping each other out when exceptionally large sums were needed or when the cash-flow failed, and they kept careful tallies so that they knew how exposed they were every week, every day and even, in some crises, every hour.

The goldsmiths had made overtures to Charles as soon as Monck reached London in January 1660, and at the Restoration he was extremely careful to bind them to his side. The most senior was the grey-haired Thomas Vyner, whose shop had provided the gold cup for Charles's own baptism in 1630. He did not look, however, like a natural ally. In 1649, as Sheriff of London, he had attended the execution of Charles I; later he carried the sword of state when

Cromwell rode through the city.[9] In the first Interregnum he made a fortune through East Indian investments, handled the money from confiscated Irish estates and became Lord Mayor. Yet in 1660 all his Cromwellian past was politely brushed aside. Almost as soon as he landed, Charles made Vyner a baronet, and he also smiled on his nephew Robert, who had just become a full member of the family firm at the Vine in Lombard Street.

Equally swiftly, Charles enlisted the help of Vyner's former apprentice Edward Backwell, who had been Cromwell's Treasurer of Dunkirk from 1658. Charles kept Backwell in this role and used him to handle the sale of Dunkirk in 1662, collecting and disbursing the great chests of silver shipped over from France. Backwell's heavy ledgers, the first run of banking accounts in Britain, with neat lists of incoming sums on the left-hand page and payments on the right, show the Dunkirk money flowing out in rivers and streams, the greatest sum to Carteret for the navy, the second largest to Stephen Fox for the king.[10] Backwell also handled the farming of the London Excise and the revenue from the Hearth Tax, as well as gifts to ambassadors and the distribution of prize money from captured ships. Every name one can think of in public life appears in his accounts, from Lord Mayors and ministers to courtiers and poets: Albemarle and Ashley, Bennet, Buckingham, Buckhurst, Dryden, Downing, Lauderdale, Pepys, Ormond and Orrery and on to the end of the alphabet.

The same names appear in the customer books of Sir Francis Child the elder, another goldsmith turned banker (no relation to Josiah Child). In his ledgers everything is recorded from the purchase of silver buckles and gold toothpicks, to huge loans to aristocratic estates.[11] The Vyners, Backwell, Child and others like them had all worked their way up through apprenticeships to become freemen of the Goldsmith's Company. Backwell's forebears were Bedfordshire yeomen; Child was the son of a West Country clothier; the Vyners came from a 'middling' Warwickshire family; Francis Meynell, whom Pepys called 'the great money-man', began as a fresh-faced apprentice from Derbyshire. Such men represented a new power in the land, one that would force the court more and more into partnership with the City. Decisions of state began to hang on the views expressed in the counting houses and coffee-houses of the Square Mile. The Vyners, for example, advanced over a million pounds to Ormond in his first years as Lord Lieutenant of Ireland, and he fumed over their high 'Irish rates' of ten per cent. Robert Vyner also lent a fortune to the king, beginning with £30,000 for the coronation regalia. In 1662, with Meynell and Backwell, he collected the same sum to repay the Russian loan that the Muscovy ambassadors came to collect. In 1665, he would stump up £330,000 for the navy, household and guards. He was not doing this out of a sense of national duty: his rates were a standard ten per cent on outstanding government debts, sometimes reaching fifteen or even twenty per cent. By the end of the decade the loans ran into millions and the interest payments were, theoretically, vast. He took risks, and there were unseen rapids ahead, but for now at least, the securities seemed safe.

When the French ambassador Cominges was insulted that the ministers did not leap to their feet to greet him on his arrival at the Lord Mayor's banquet, he did not realise that the aldermen and traders they were talking to were just as vital to the King of England as an envoy of the King of France. Although Charles kept them at a slight distance, the money-men and the merchants were as crucial to him as his great nobles, bishops and MPs. He needed their help, their influence in the city, their taxes and their loans. And beyond all this, for a king who loved ships, he was spellbound by the promise that his country would become – in a phrase used increasingly often as the decade passed – the undisputed 'master of the seas'.

The bankers' books also reflected this sea-going power. One set of figures related to loans to merchants, noted down as 'Adventures of the East India Company', 'Adventures of the Royal Africa Country' or, more vaguely, 'Adventures to Severall Places'. Cromwell had

John Michael Wright's painting of *The Family of Sir Robert Vyner*, 1673,
suggests the pride and status of the new bankers

boosted England's trade and Charles was determined to match him.
In 1661 parliament quickly confirmed and extended Cromwell's
Navigation Act of 1651, which excluded Dutch traders from the
English import trade. The new Navigation Act of 1660 was drawn
up by George Downing, who was a member of the Convention
Parliament as well as ambassador at the Hague, a difficult man, but
a moderniser with an acute grasp of the economic realities of British
life. Downing also cleverly tied the colonies into the act, by decreeing that all trade between Britain and the plantations, and between
the colonies themselves, must be in English vessels.[12] (The Irish
could be carriers, under specific conditions, but the Scottish ports, to
their fury, were omitted from the acts, although this did not stop the
flamboyant Glasgow 'tobacco kings' building up a trade of their
own.) A second act in 1663, the Staple Act, stipulated that the
colonies must buy all the goods they needed in England, closing a
loophole that had let them deal directly with European ports.

Downing also argued that British boatbuilders should concentrate on fast, large carriers, and suggested developing London as an *entrepôt* port to rival Amsterdam.

Under the new acts the western ports and the Atlantic trade in particular enjoyed a boom.[13] Ships set out from Bristol, Plymouth, Liverpool and Whitehaven in increasing numbers. For speculators, investing in ships and cargoes was attractive since an investment could be spread over several vessels and the cargoes were usually owned by a syndicate of four, eight or sixteen partners, sharing the danger of loss between them. And those dangers were certainly great. Storms and shipwreck, disease and pirates took a heavy toll. Sometimes a ship simply vanished, and no cause was ever found.

The two great British companies, the Levant and the East India Company, took different routes to offset risk. The Levant, like most companies at the times, was 'regulated', with each merchant trading independently on his own capital. The company was having a hard time in these years. Algerian pirates raided its ships, its agent in Constantinople struggled with demanding Grand Viziers, its deals were undercut by subsidised French rivals, and its price-fixing of imports and exports was attacked by independent merchants. Yet the company had a lasting allure and always attracted new apprentices, from the gentry as well as the city. Land and trade were not as antipathetic as Restoration comedies might make us believe. Many country gentry had been merchant adventurers under the Tudors, and trade, at least in the big city companies, attracted younger sons with no clear career. At the end of the decade Dudley North would write that the army, law and medicine were suitable but 'neither is merchandise to be condemned, whereunto in foreign lands persons of the most honourable condition do apply themselves'.[14]

Jack Verney was one young man who persuaded his reluctant father to buy him an apprenticeship.[15] In 1662, aged twenty-one, Jack set sail for 'Scanderoon', the English name for Iskenderun on the far eastern Mediterranean coast of Turkey, where English merchants landed bales of fine cloth, dyed in bright colours for the eastern market, and 'money goods' – pepper, cochineal, sugar and tin. These were carried inland and traded for silk and mohair and spices at Aleppo, the great trading post on the Turkish–Syrian border. At the other major depot at Smyrna, modern Izmir, seventy British factors and apprentices sweated in the Turkish heat, setting aside the local robes that their predecessors had adopted, in favour of black suits, silk stockings, white gloves and wigs.

Charles supported the Levant Company, appointing one of their men to check all lading bills, so that they could catch outsiders trading in their territory. But he knew well that the most crucial company, in terms of royal profit, was the East India Company. In contrast to the Levant, this was a joint-stock venture (copying the Dutch East India Company).[16] It raised money by issuing permanent dividend-paying shares, and each costly voyage was financed by selling up to five hundred shares at around £100 each. When the boats returned, the goods were stored and auctioned off gradually in a succession of sales, to avoid any sudden glut that might lower prices. As the cargo was sold, so the shareholders were paid. The risk, and the return, were thus widely spread.

In April 1661 Charles confirmed the East India Company's charter, an action sweetened by presents of plate worth £3,000 for himself and £1,500 for James. Both brothers were among the company's five hundred investors, and Charles was always careful to consider its interests. Forty years before, the Dutch had seized the East Indian island of Pulo Run, one of the Banda islands to the west of Papua New Guinea, which was the company's base in Indonesia, and burned its spice trees, thus depriving the company of a vital supply of cloves, cinnamon and nutmeg. Not only did Charles and his envoys press the Dutch hard to return the island, according to an agreement with Cromwell, but in 1662, when two of his most prominent courtiers, Henry Bennet and John Grenville, petitioned to import spices from Germany, Charles made sure that he consulted the company before granting their request.[17] As a compromise, he allowed free trade in the spices, but only until the company could set up a new base.

The East India Company had twenty-eight of the finest ships, sending half out each year. Instead of building their own vessels, the traders hired them, which cut their overheads (and led, incidentally, to the start of an insurance and shipping business in the City). Each long journey was arranged around the seasonal winds, with the ships stopping for provisions at the new South Atlantic settlement on St Helena. Some sailed as far as China, but the main destination was India, especially the great Mughal port of Surat, which traded in saltpetre, indigo and cotton from the interior. The presidency of the company was based here, protected by the local Mughal viceroy. Many English soldiers and company men now lived permanently in India, becoming part of an intricate two-way exchange of cultures. The exotic fusion is strangely illustrated in a Deccani painting where an Indian prince is entertained by a courtesan, gorgeously dressed in silk knickerbockers, with a cavalier's plumed hat on her head and a small King Charles spaniel at her feet.[18]

The fort and harbour of Surat in the seventeenth century

Charles had his own foothold in India, just down the coast from Surat, in Bombay, with its seven islands, which had been included in Catherine's dowry. But to begin with Bombay was a burden rather than a boon. Five ships sailed from England in March 1662, under the command of the Earl of Marlborough, expecting to take possession of all Bombay's dependencies. When they arrived, however, they found the Portuguese adamant that only the islands were included in the treaty. The deadlock took time to solve, and while Marlborough sailed home, the troops, already sick after weeks at sea, were left stranded on the small, uninhabited island of Anjediva near Goa. Hundreds died there of disease, and in 1665 only ninety-seven private soldiers marched into Bombay, out of the four hundred who had embarked. But when Surat was raided by a neighbouring Indian force, and the merchants needed to find a new deep-water port, Bombay, with its superb harbour, was the obvious choice. In 1668 Charles leased it to the company for a nominal annual rent of £10 in gold and Sir George Oxenden, president of the Surat factory, became its first governor.

The East India Company wooed Charles with presents, silks and jewels, rare birds and animals, and gave generous gifts to the favourite or mistress of the day.[19] The company showed off their treasures at East India House, which had a menagerie of exotic creatures from India and Virginia and a collection of rarities 'to gratify the curiosity of the public'.[20] Secure in the royal favour, the directors purred over their books, priding themselves on their meticulous record-keeping. They had reason to be pleased. In 1663 profits reached around £130,000, and the return on investment rose from twenty to forty per cent. The return for the crown was handsome too: between 1664 and 1667 the East India Company would lend the king almost a quarter of a million pounds.

Like the natural philosophers, the money-men were developing a new intellectual approach, questioning, observing, collecting data and building theories on how trade grew and money circulated.

They argued about money supply, interest rates and the best structure for trade to flourish, and pondered for the first time about the
'balance of trade'. Since the early years of the century one group of
thinkers had worried that the import of goods meant loss of physical
bullion – gold and silver – to overseas. In opposition, another group
asserted that 'value' lay not in intrinsic things like bullion but in the
act of exchange itself – in the great circulation of trade, money
returned amplified to its source. *England's Treasure by Fforaign Trade*,
by Thomas Mun, written in 1622 but published in 1664 (pointedly dedicated to the Lord Treasurer, Southampton), put it succinctly:
'Money begets trade and trade begets money'.[21] But while some
writers held that the market was infinitely flexible and elastic and
therefore backed freedom of trade and competition, as Samuel
Fortrey did in *England's Interest and Improvement* in 1663, others, like
John Bland in *Trade Revived* (1659) saw demand as finite, and therefore recommended monopolies and protection.

The language of trade, of contract, obligation and 'equity' provided a model of relationships, which, as Charles and others around
him slowly saw, could be applied to government as well as trade.
This way of thinking brought a new respect for mediation in disputes, social as well as mercantile, and the idea of 'coming to an
agreement', without invoking aristocratic codes of honour.[22] The
strength of the great companies also influenced the argument for
religious toleration since the directors of the Levant Company and
the East India Company included many nonconformists who could
not be dislodged, however hard Sheldon and his allies tried, and it
was important for the crown to keep them sweet.

As traditional sources of royal revenue from prerogative courts,
fees and fines halted or diminished, so the duties from customs and
excise, and loans from the companies, became vital to the
Exchequer. Charles himself was named as an investor in many ventures (though he rarely paid the sum marked against his name).
Hundreds of reports and letters relating to trade and the colonies
stacked up in the Treasury, and the offices of the Secretaries of State

and the Chancellor. In late 1663 and early 1664 these ranged from the East India Company's worries about negotiating with the King of Persia, to Governor Willoughby's problems with 'factious spirits' in Barbados and the recruitment of new settlers for the Carolinas and Jamaica.[23]

Trade also brought new ideas and broadened intellectual horizons. In the gallery of merchants, one of the most striking was Paul Rycaut, youngest son of a great Flemish shipowner and financier based in London. Rycaut became chancellor of the Levant Company's factory at Constantinople in the early 1660s. Soon he took on the role of ambassador, filling his notebooks with accounts of the sultan's empire, armies, people and culture.[24] In 1667 Charles received a copy of the beautifully bound, gold-tooled folio of his *Present State of the Ottoman Empire*, and ten years later came Rycaut's famous *History of the Ottoman Empire*, a source for writers ever since. Rycaut's orientalism had its inevitable bias, but his work was an exemplary example of the 'rational' belief – shared by his king – that men are, in essence, the same the world over and that the differences between communities stem not from the 'natural' inferiority or superiority of races but from external factors like climate, history or wealth.

These distant lands that the traders reached seemed exotic, strange, laden with treasure and sensual delights, and not all writers were as responsible as Rycaut when they came to describe them. In 1664 Thomas Head published a picaresque, pornographic novel, *The English Rogue*, that effectively turned India into a paradise of sexual fantasy. (It was banned as obscene, but swiftly republished.)[25] Travellers' tales of all kinds, serious or not, caught Charles's imagination, especially when linked to profit. In 1665, when the court was in Oxford, Prince Rupert introduced the French explorers Radisson and des Groseilliers, who had discovered an untapped wealth of fur in the wilds of North America. This wilderness could be reached, they said, by sea via Hudson Bay. The French would not back them, but with Rupert's urging Charles – who had loved the furs brought by the Muscovy embassy – took the risk. It seemed a good bet, with little to lose. Within five years, he granted a charter to the Hudson's Bay Company, with Rupert as its first governor. With sublime disregard for any local inhabitants the charter gave the company the right to trade in furs and exploit the mineral rights over all the land draining into the bay. The area named so vaguely was then unknown, but turned out to extend to a million square miles, from Labrador to the Rockies. The company were also obliged, decreed Charles, to hunt for the long-imagined North-West Passage. The Hudson's Bay charter completed his vision of Britain's trading empire, circling the globe and stretching from pole to pole.

22 One Must Down

Trade, which like blood should circularly flow,
Stop'd in their Channels, found its freedom lost:
Thither the wealth of all the world did go,
And seems but shipwreck'd on so base a coast.
DRYDEN, *Annus Mirabilis*

THERE WAS NO DOUBT that the most successful European traders, and England's greatest rivals, were the Dutch. There were grudges on both sides. The Dutch resented the English Navigation Acts, however impossible they proved to enforce, and complained that the new Fishery Company threatened their fishing in the North Sea. The British claimed compensation for captured vessels and still demanded that the Dutch honour their agreement to hand back the Indonesian island of Pulo Run. Each side accused the other of foul tactics. In particular the British were jealous of Dutch control of the Spanish routes to the East Indies and Spanish America, a licence granted after foreign vessels began to encroach on the trade routes of the declining Spanish empire.

At first, Charles was keen on obtaining a trade treaty with Holland. After the years of exile at the Hague, his household had many links by marriage with the Dutch.[1] But their fundamental political differences kept the countries apart. The republican States General were determinedly anti-monarchist, and Charles knew that Holland was sheltering Commonwealth rebels. From the Dutch viewpoint, Charles was a threat to their republic, since he clearly wished to restore the old powers of the House of Orange. This was an issue of intense personal importance to Charles, since it concerned his own family, notably his nephew William, his sister Mary's son.² William's great-grandfather, the first William of Orange, had led the United Provinces at the start of the war that followed their declaration of independence from Spain in 1581. His sons Maurice and Frederick, and then the latter's son, William II, later took over this role. The Princes were not, however, technically the heads of government. The 'states' or assemblies of each province, dominated by the Regents – rich city magistrates and merchants – sent representatives to the States General, which dealt with matters relating to the republic as a whole, under the leadership of their Grand Pensionary, currently the formidable Johann de Witt. But since the Princes of Orange were usually the elected stadtholder of all the provinces, a position which brought with it the post of captain-general of the armed forces, they wielded considerable power. With their control of the army and their personal wealth, William's forebears thus had an unofficial, but very real, semi-monarchical status.

When William II died in 1650, a week before the birth of his son, a long struggle began between the Regents of the States General and the House of Orange. The post of captain-general was abolished and some provinces agreed to leave the office of stadtholder vacant. Taking this a step further, in 1654, under pressure from Cromwell, the states of Holland agreed never to adopt a Prince of Orange as stadtholder. Matters improved slightly for the Orangists at the Restoration, when the Dutch were reluctant to offend the new King by slighting his sister and nephew, and a compromise was reached by which William was made a 'child of state', with a government allowance and the promise of an education that would fit him for some future major role. But when Mary died in December 1660, all this was thrown out. Since then, to Charles's fury, de Witt had turned his ferocious energy to demolishing the Orange cause. Beneath the surface, Charles's attitude towards the Dutch was always governed by his wish to restore to his nephew William the power that his father had held.

In mid-1662 ferocious Dutch lampoons and squibs circulated, blackening the name of the English King and the Prince of Orange.

Meanwhile Amsterdam was booming, having become the import–export hub and the money-lending centre for the whole of northern Europe. Its rich burghers built tall canal-side houses and had their portraits painted in imposing groups. Their 'brim-full vessels', as Dryden described them, brought balm and spices and gold and their decks were laden with exotic plants for hot-houses and gardens. The low interest rates meant that merchants could keep large inventories of stock and Amsterdam became the place where 'anything could be obtained, at any time'.[3] As William Petty exclaimed, the Dutch were the heirs of the great classical empires: 'Do they not work the sugars of the west, the timber and iron of the Baltic? The lead, tin and wool of Turkey?' 'To be short,' he added, and this was the key point, 'in all the ancient states and empires,

The approach to Amsterdam in 1665, crowded with merchant ships and yachts, with a city panorama behind.

those who had the shipping had the wealth.'[4] And those who had the wealth had the power.

One area in which the English tried to seize that wealth was Africa. In 1660 Charles granted a charter to 'The Royal Company of Adventurers Trading into Africa', to trade with the Gambia and Guinea. The company's first governor was the veteran voyager Prince Rupert, who had visited the Gambia in 1652, and the whole venture was not only 'Royal' but strongly royalist: more than half of the thirty-two named beneficiaries were courtiers, including Charles, Albemarle and Buckingham, and the Earls of Bath, Ossory, Pembroke, St Albans and Sandwich. When the company was reconstituted in 1663, with James, Duke of York at its head, the shareholders included twenty dukes, earls and peers, although many of these investors (including Charles) never bothered to pay the sum they had promised to subscribe, and the venture was hampered from the start, lacking almost a third of the promised capital of £120,000.[5] The court-controlled venture also upset the mercantile class by favouring the aristocrats at the expense of the seasoned companies. In 1662, for example, James snubbed an offer of a merger from the East India Company, which had been trading very successfully along the West African coast and had now lost its privileges. There was a hint that James and Rupert were challenging not only the Dutch but the class they disliked at home, the presbyterian merchants.

Initially the company was set up to trade in ivory and gold, from which 'Guineas' were first minted. But the main business soon became the lucrative supply of slaves to the sugar and tobacco plantations of the West Indies. No one spoke out against this traffic until the first Quaker complaints in 1671. Black servants were status symbols, appearing, beaming and dark, behind their pale, languid mistresses in Lely's portraits. Lord Sandwich happily brought back 'a little Turke and a negro' on his flagship from the Mediterranean in 1662 as pages for his daughters, an unremarked part of a cargo of exotics that included 'many birds and other pretty noveltys'.[6] But as far as slaves for the plantations were concerned, the vile trade was less lucrative than promised. Packed into the holds, many slaves died before they reached the plantations. Moreover, the planters were used to living on credit and rarely came up with ready cash, and complained of the company's high prices. (Their complaints reveal the extent of the trade: in 1664 one owner complained of the price of '3000 negroes bought by him of the Royal African Company at £20 a head'.[7])

An added difficulty was that West Africa was already a war zone. The English and Dutch had quarrelled over the gold reefs on the West African coast for many years, and the creeks and rivers and off-shore islands had long been a major site of Dutch trade. The Portuguese, the Danes, the Swedes and the French also sent ships, but were minor players in this early scramble for Africa. The first Africa Company ships found themselves under attack at sea, and unable to trade on land with a local population already linked to the Dutch. But the new company was aggressive, indeed so blatantly provocative that it has been seen less as a trading company than a kind of advance attacking force, organised by the court, to take on the Dutch.

Instead of promoting the settling of unoccupied land, the company made direct assaults on Dutch possessions. In 1661 it sent a convoy to seize Dutch holdings under Sir Robert Holmes, who had been a captain under Rupert, a man whom Pepys wrote off as a 'rash, rich coxcomb' and, on another occasion, as 'an idle, proud, conceited, though stout fellow'.[8] Holmes was a strong character, who could be seen either as a difficult-to-discipline, but well-intentioned naval man, or simply as an out-of-control, headstrong buccaneer, violent and hot-tempered and always lusting for action. His justification for attacking the Dutch factories on the coast was that these were in fact English colonies seized by the Dutch a decade before. One by one, he sacked the Dutch forts. In retaliation the Dutch seized company vessels and blockaded the Gold Coast, and their control of the whole coast became so fixed that within two years the

British company was almost bankrupt, and had to be given a new charter.[9] Once that was done, Holmes was sent south again, with the secret backing, indeed instructions, of the Privy Council.

In 1662, while the first African skirmishes were at their height, it seemed that a full-scale war was imminent. 'Great talk there is of a fear of a war with the Dutch,' wrote Pepys, worrying about demands on the navy office,

and we have order to pitch upon 20 ships to be forthwith set out; but I hope it is but a scarecrow to the world, to let them see that we can be ready for them; though God knows, the King is not able to set out five ships at this present without great difficulty, we having neither money, credit, nor stores.[10]

Yet war did not break out that year. In England, Charles was distracted by the religious controversies and the fear of rebellion and needed to concentrate his forces on possible unrest at home, rather than an enemy abroad. He also held back from war as long as he could, partly because he was trying to work out what the Dutch were really up to. De Witt was a powerful opponent, a 'professional calculator', a man who worked out the odds, as Charles himself did: 'in effect, the first probability theorist to govern a great power'.[11] It was hard to gauge his intentions, although Downing's intelligence network sent back copies of the States General's resolutions.[12] Downing made no secret of his contempt for the Dutch government, assuring Charles that after their experience against Cromwell's navy in the 1650s, when the crisis came they would not fight but would give in to English demands. He worked hard to resolve the problems of trade, and in September 1662 England and the United Provinces signed a treaty by which both sides agreed to drop compensation claims and the Dutch promised finally to hand over Pulo Run.

Meanwhile the hopes of English merchants were caught up in even more complicated tangles of European power-play and diplomacy.

The royal marriage treaty had committed Charles to helping Portugal against Spain, which retaliated by encouraging skirmishes at sea and in the West Indies. Charles soon tired of this obligation to Portugal: the Spanish attacks were costly, Bombay had still not been handed over and Tangier was proving impossible to defend. (In one ambush the Governor, Lord Teviot, with four hundred men, was killed in an ambush by the Moors.) After smoothing relations with Spain through Bennet and Bristol, Charles sent Sir Richard Fanshawe to Madrid to try to end the Spanish– Portuguese war, warning the Portuguese to co-operate and asking the Spanish for the same trading terms as the Dutch.

The overtures to Spain, in turn, caused problems with the French. Knowing that Philip IV of Spain was dying, and his weak-minded son Carlos was unlikely to father an heir, Louis XIV had revived the claim of his wife, Philip's daughter Maria-Teresa, to the Spanish Netherlands. As soon as Philip died, Louis intended to invade Flanders to claim her property. To prevent trouble on the northern borders of Flanders, in 1662, to the alarm of Charles and the British parliament, he signed a treaty with the Dutch. As part of this treaty, he agreed to support the Dutch if they were attacked.

On one level it would seem that the last thing Louis wanted was an Anglo-Dutch war, which would divert his troops from the campaigns he planned in Flanders. For that reason, watching the growing tension between England and Holland, he began long, delaying negotiations to mediate a peace. But on the other hand, he was trying himself to build up French trade and had just founded a French East India Company – a war might sap the wealth and strength of both these sea-going nations and allow French ships to capture their trade routes. Knowing this, many people in England suspected that he actually wanted, indeed actively prompted, an Anglo-Dutch conflict. But Louis was even cooler at this game than his English cousin, and gave nothing away. He could afford to play a long, slow game, while Charles was increasingly under pressure.

If war broke out, Charles wanted Louis on his side, if possible, and if not, then he wanted to be sure that he would not fulfil his obligations to support the Dutch. In July 1663 he put on a show of strength to impress Cominges, organising a general muster in St James's Park of four thousand soldiers drawn up in battalions, headed by Albemarle. But negotiations with the French foreign ministry once again became bogged down over protocol, as both Cominges in London and the English ambassador in Paris became obsessed with disputes over precedence and status.

There was, however, another route to the French king which could bypass the ambassadors. Minette, trapped in her marriage to the vain and spiteful Monsieur, was very close to Louis, and may even briefly have been his lover. Having proved her loyalty in tortuous court intrigues, she had his complete trust. From late 1663 Charles's letters to Minette often contained indirect messages to Louis.

After a lull, in the spring of 1664 English and Dutch hostilities accelerated again. The gossip in the playhouse and the coffee-houses was all of war. In February Pepys went to the coffee-house with his friend the hemp-merchant George Cocke,

Who discoursed well of the good effects in some kind of a Dutch war and conquest (which I did not consider before, but the contrary), that is, that 'the trade of the world is too little for us two, therefore one must down; 2ndly, that though our merchants will not be the better husbands by all this, yet our wool will bear a better price by vaunting of our cloths, and by that our tenants will be better able to pay rents, and our lands will be more worth, and all our owne manufactures, which now the Dutch outvie us in.'[13]

But was this really a merchant's war? Some people felt it was fomented by factions at court. Others thought Charles hoped to crush the Dutch republic in order to safeguard his own throne, or to aid the Orange cause.[14] But as far as trade was concerned, Captain Cocke was right to point first at the issue of cloth. In March 1664, a committee of the House of Commons was set up to look into complaints by clothiers about the state of their industry. The committee was then enlarged and its brief widened to include trading problems generally, and merchants were asked to bring their grievances to parliament, particularly those that related to Dutch traders. To some contemporaries, the hidden agenda was all too clear: the government wanted an excuse for war. Was Charles playing a devious game? Captain George Cocke told Pepys, 'The king's design is, by getting under-hand the merchants to bring in their complaints to the parliament, to make them in honor begin a war.'[15]

Some merchants were horrified at the threat of war, as a grave disruption. But there was no doubt that they feared the Dutch were gaining a monopoly of international trade, and that such a monopoly also implied a wider 'dominion' over the seas. Since 1662 the East India Company had submitted petition after petition couched in these terms, claiming, for example that the Dutch were aiming 'to perfect at once their long-designed work of ruining the whole trade of the English in India and dispossessing the Portuguese of the little that still remains in their hands'.[16] They also suspected them of planning to capture the Levant trade, and the navy provided convoys in the Mediterranean to protect shipping there. The Royal Africa Company in particular was adamant the Dutch must be stopped. On 21 April, Sir Thomas Clifford, now head of the Council for Trade, told the Commons that the Dutch were 'the greatest single obstruction to foreign trade'. The Commons agreed, passing a resolution to assist the king 'against all opposition whatsoever'.[17] From this point on, the war party – led by the Duke of York and Albemarle – urged full-scale conflict. Clarendon advised against it and so did William Coventry, both of them arguing cogently that trade was better served by peace and greater mercantile efficiency.

Everywhere the Dutch were roundly abused. A Dutchman, it was said, 'is a lusty, Fat, Two-legged Cheese Worm. A creature that is so addicted to eating Butter, Drinking Fat Drink and Sliding [skating] that all the world knows him for a Slippery Fellow.'[18] And because the Dutch themselves proudly proclaimed that they were 'masters' of the seas, of the Indies, of Africa – many British commentators saw their ambitions as imperial and global. Day by day the mood swung towards war.

News from West Africa travelled slowly. For weeks the ships tacked their way up the African coast, past the Straits of Gibraltar and the cliffs of Portugal, and across the Bay of Biscay. In the spring of 1664, the Privy Council finally heard that Holmes had captured the island of Goree off Cape Verde, one of the chief Dutch bases, and a string of other stations further south along the Gold Coast. To capitalise on this, Charles agreed to send the British warships south to Guinea under Rupert's command.

In May Charles showed off his warships, letting them parade in formation in the Channel, and two months later he took Catherine to see the fleet sail out of Chatham and down the Medway ('taking off his wig and *pourpoint* to be more at his ease, by reason of the extreme heat of the sun' and catching a bad, feverish cold as a result).[19] As he told Minette, he was still sure, or still hoping, that the Dutch would cave in. It was, however, increasingly difficult to calm the British public. 'Sir George Downing is come out of Holland,' he wrote in June, 'and I shall now be very busy upon that matter':

the States keep a great braging and noise, but I believe, when it comes to it, they will look twise before they leap. I never saw so great an appetite to a warre as is, in both thise towne and country, espetially in the parlament-men, who, I am confident, would pawne their estates to maintaine a warre, but all this shall not governe me, for I will looke merely at what is just and best for the honour and good of England, and will be very steady in what I resolve.[20]

If war did come he would be ready with good ships and men, and leave the rest to God.

Three weeks later he told her that he was providing a man-of-war to accompany eight East India vessels, stressing that this was only for fear of Dutch attacks. The Dutch ambassador had arrived, he said, and was begging him not to let the ships sail, lest hostilities might be sparked by the 'indiscretion of some of the captaines . . .

You may guesse, by such a simple proposition, whether these people are not affraide!'[21] To cap his show of strength he agreed that his forces should remove the 'nuisance' of New Amsterdam, the Dutch stronghold nestling in the heart of British colonies on America's eastern seaboard. In mid-May four vessels sailed from Portsmouth, commanded by Captain John Nicholls, arriving off New England in late July. Soon the British men-of-war appeared at the mouth of the Hudson river, having come, Nicholls told Governor Stuyvesant, to support the English title to the lands. The Dutch colony had no defences, and on 27 August Stuyvesant surrendered. New Amsterdam was handed without bloodshed to the English crown, having been granted in advance by a confident Charles to his brother James, Duke of York. As news trickled home, bells were rung in triumph. But Charles was very careful, in his correspondence with Minette, to convey to Louis – who was obliged by his treaty with Holland to act only if the Dutch were the victims, and not the initiators, of aggression – that this was simply a justified recapture of British property. ''Tis a place of great importance to trade, and a very good towne,' he wrote. 'It did belong to England heretofore, but the Duch by degrees drove our people out of it, and built a very good towne, but we have gott the better of it, and ''tis now called New Yorke'.[22]

Sending his letters to Minette through safe messengers, Charles tried to find a formula for a treaty of 'strict friendship' that might keep France out of the war. Meanwhile, despite the threat of conflict, trade went on. Ships sailed up the Thames to the Pool of London from the West Indies and the East, and from India itself. Some brought priceless gifts for Charles, including jewels in a purse of purple satin: a huge yellow diamond, a fine ruby, a blue-and-white sapphire, and a great pearl which he gave to Catherine.[23]

But the tension was rising. One of the Privy Council's fears was that the English republicans who had fled to Holland would use this as an opportunity to foment another uprising: they did in fact form an English regiment to fight with the Dutch. To find out about such plots, and about Dutch plans and naval manoeuvres, Henry Bennet set up a network of spies.[24] The system was profoundly inefficient, not only because the post was routinely opened and the coded letters were all too easy to decipher, but because many informers worked as double agents. William Scott, the son of the regicide Thomas Scott, former head of Cromwell's intelligence services, who had been executed in 1660, was now living in Flanders. He routinely fed Downing misleading information and as soon as the English agents were in place, Scott betrayed them to the Dutch.

In late summer, however – although this was not something the spies picked up – it seemed as if the Dutch were willing to enter talks. Through Downing, de Witt put forward a highly secret proposal, agreeing to many of the long-standing English demands.[25] Yet the Privy Council remained silent. Were they waiting for yet more concessions, or could it be, as some suspected, that they really wanted war after all?

In October the pretext came. Despite Holmes's successes, since early summer the Royal African Company had been complaining of 'insolent protests and threats from the Dutch' off the African coast.[26] The ships for Rupert's new expedition were almost ready to sail but the Dutch had pre-empted them. In October news reached the Privy Council that the admiral Michael de Ruyter had already sailed south with part of the Dutch Mediterranean fleet to West Africa. Charles at once ordered all naval vessels to join Rupert at Portsmouth, and appointed commissioners to supervise treatment of the wounded, and prisoners of war.

Waiting for action, the Duke of York was bored. Longing to deploy his fleet he spent all day and most of the night down at the wharves, seeing his ships armed and stores taken on board. Charles, too, visited the dockyards and boarded the ships, often dragging Catherine and her sea-sick ladies with him. In the November rain and hail he talked to the captains and watched the great new ships being launched. Swept up by such enthusiasm and by the simple longing for a fight, courtiers and aristocrats like the

A small Dutch warship, drawn by Hollar

Dukes of Richmond, Buckingham and Norfolk volunteered to serve on board ship, even if they could not tell one end of a hawser from another.

Both Charles and James were passionate about the navy, and knowledgeable about ships. The British navy had a range of warships, arranged in order of importance from the great first-rates, which could carry as many as a hundred guns, to the small sixth-rates.[27] The big three-masted first-rates, which were only brought out in wartime, were heavy, deep-hulled, powerful beasts, beautifully ornamented and carrying acres of sail. They needed enormous crews of up to eight hundred men, under the command of the captain and his lieutenants and the non-commissioned officers, and they also had to carry their own surgeons and doctors, cooks and carpenters, trumpeters and gunsmiths, and often a troop of soldiers, forerunners of the marines.

Discipline was harsh, space below decks was horribly cramped, sanitation non-existent. The crew survived the long periods of waiting largely through being permanently drunk – beer and spirits was one area the navy was liberal in. They were led by officers out for glory, often rash and violent, jealous of each other's victories and endlessly quarrelling among themselves. To add to the feuds, there was a clear division between the 'tarpaulins' – the commanders who had risen from the ranks during the Commonwealth, like Monck, Sandwich and Lawson – and the 'Cavaliers', who included veterans from Prince Rupert's civil-war fleet, like Holmes and Thomas Allin, and men whose command came through the patronage of the King or Duke.

This was the fleet now assembling. On 18 December, the Privy Council ordered attacks on Dutch shipping wherever possible. The next day, with only eight ships under his command, Allin attacked the Dutch Smyrna convoy coming out of the Straits of Gibraltar, thirty merchantmen and three men-of-war. He took three ships, bringing his prizes and his prisoners slowly back to port. At a meeting at Worcester House, Clarendon and Southampton, who were known to be against the war, finally admitted its reality, telling the company there was no longer time to debate if it should be 'war or no war: it was come upon us, and we were now only to contrive the best way of carrying it on with success; which could only be done by raising a great present sum of money'.[28] At the opening of the parliamentary session Charles appealed to the Commons in his speech, for a minimum of £800,000 upon which a back-bench MP, Sir Robert Paston, coached by Clarendon, that it should be no less than £2,500,000.[29] The silent house 'sat in amazement', until the motion was seconded, with all the court placemen carefully staying silent until the Speaker proposed the vote.[30] This massive grant, to be raised over three years, was the largest ever won by a monarch. But even this was too little, said the Navy Board, since there was so much pay in arrears and so many ships to be repaired before any real fitting out could be done.

Some MPs were suspicious that the funds were merely for court indulgences. Others, who had been urging war for some time, saw corruption in the Privy Council as the reason why it had not yet begun. Clarendon was currently building a huge house on land granted to him in Piccadilly, employing the best craftsmen and using the most expensive materials. Almost as soon as the scaffolding went up people had called it 'Dunkirk House', implying he had been bribed by the French. Now they called it 'Holland House', shouting that the bribes came from the Dutch. To get the money from parliament Charles had to promise that once he had the grant, he would not simply make a quick peace with the Dutch, and then spend it on himself.

The winter of 1664–5 was grim. In Paris, the Dutch ambassador Van Benningen proved alarmingly persuasive at keeping Louis to his word, and at blaming the English for all the hostilities, despite the good efforts of Charles Berkeley, sent as Charles's personal envoy. People seeking omens looked anxiously at the sky as a new comet flared across Europe. Out at sea, Sandwich charted its progress for several weeks in his log, seeing it as a broom sweeping the constellations, as if a creature of myth was interfering with his navigation: 'After sunset I saw the Blazing Star again in the Whale's Mouth . . . and observed his distance from Aldebaran . . . The stream of his light like a brush besome stretched out towards Orion's head.'[31] But Charles – unlike most of his subjects – chose to decide that the comet was a portent for good, and his court still celebrated the festivals of the New Year in their old style. And at Candlemas, 2 February 1665, there was a fine masque of ten dancers, 'surprizing his Majestie'.[32]

However relaxed he seemed, war was on his mind. In his letters, he teased Minette about her latest pregnancy, wishing her an easy labour: 'A boy will recompense two grunts more, and so good night, for feare I fall into naturale philosophy, before I think of it.'[33] The weather was so icy that he could hardly hold his pen, yet he wrote longer and longer letters, fearing that Van Benningen had used 'all possible artes and trickes' to make him seem the aggressor, and threatening that if no agreement with France was offered, he would look elsewhere, to Spain.[34] Meanwhile, backed by an eager parliament, he sent Sandwich, with eighteen ships, to hunt down the Dutch fleet in the North Sea.

In late February, disconcerting news arrived – the talk at the Exchange was all of de Ruyter's exploits and of the British being 'beaten to dirt at Guiny'.[35] Charles reassured the Commons that he had asked Downing 'to demand speedy justice and reparation'. He did not doubt, he said, that the States General, as good allies, would agree to his demands.[36] By now this rang hollow, but he still hoped that the Dutch would back down, and that if they did not, at least Louis would not feel bound to help them. Both hopes would prove false. The Dutch stood firm, while Louis called Charles's bluff about seeking a Spanish treaty, and blocked his attempts to find allies elsewhere. English envoys criss-crossed Europe seeking alliances. On their way back from Russia, the Earl of Carlisle and Marvell called in vain at the courts of Sweden and Denmark. No help at all was forthcoming, not from France or Scandinavia, Spain or Portugal. Britain was on its own. On 4 March 1665, Charles declared war on Holland.

23 The Itch of Honour

I looked and saw within the book of Fate,
Where many days did lour,
When lo one happy hour
Leaped up, and smiled to save thy sinking state;
A day shall come when in thy power
Thy cruel foes shall be;
Then shall thy land be free,
And thou in peace shall reign:
But take, O take that opportunity,
Which once refused will never come again.
          DRYDEN, Song from *The Indian Emperour*

THE NEWS THAT BRITAIN was at war with the Dutch was announced by heralds sent to the Exchange in London and to the major cities in the provinces. When she heard of it Minette wrote to her brother, clearly passing on a message from Louis. She wrote calmly that as it would 'not be desireable' for the French King to enter the war on the side of the Dutch, perhaps now was the time for Charles to come to a separate agreement that would keep the French neutral:

I beg of you to consider if some secret treaty could not be arranged, by which you could make sure of this, by giving a pledge that you would help in the business he will soon have in Flanders . . . Think this over well, I beg you, but never let anyone know that I was the first to mention it to you.'

Soon Louis sent two extra ambassadors to join Cominges, in what became known as '*la célèbre ambassade*'. As they drove from Dover to London, the new ambassadors reported, many people asked what their mission was, and 'being informed that we meant to secure peace between England and Holland, they without hesitation answered: "If they come for nothing else, they might as well go back"'.[2] One of the envoys was a lawyer, Honoré Courtin, a shrewd choice since Charles took to this short, rather absurd figure with his ironic smile, easy manner and clever mind. The other was the sixty-four-year-old Henri de Bourbon, duc de Verneuil, illegitimate brother of Henrietta Maria, and thus uncle to both kings, 'an handsome old man & a greate hunter' as Evelyn described him.[3] He had brought his dogs and two dozen horses with him. In all his months here the hunt seemed of far more importance than the war.

The old concept of honour that the duc de Verneuil represented, however lazily, underpinned Charles's attitude to the war as much as his mercantile interests. The two were strangely, dangerously, intertwined. And the conflicts between old and new values were often argued out in that mirror of the times, the theatre. Early the previous year, at the King's Theatre, Dryden and Howard had written and produced *The Indian Queen*. The play was set in Mexico and Peru, with a fictional 'restoration' plot, in which Montezuma, a noble savage who has to learn the restraints of so-called civilisation, is restored to the Mexican throne. The production was lavish and the play set a new style of heroic drama, dealing with the clashes of passion and duty, desire and honour. This was a self-consciously aristocratic mode, a resurrection of lost ideals of chivalry and the sun-like glory that surrounds a king, a glory that was fast disappearing from Charles himself. At one point, the fearsome queen Zempolla asks if honour itself is merely indulgent self-display:

> Honour is but an itch in youthful blood
> Of doing acts extravagantly good.

In the spring of 1665, Charles saw the King's Company perform the sequel, *The Indian Emperour, or The Conquest of Mexico*. Here – using the same sets and costumes for economy's sake – Dryden brought Europe face to face with the exotic New World, through the arrival of Pizarro and the supremely honourable Cortez. The idea of conquest itself was double-edged since Cortez is 'vanquished' by passion for Montezuma's daughter, Cydaria, while Montezuma is also enfeebled by love – a double warning to a womanising king. Cortez was played by Charles Hart and Cydaria (very badly) by the fourteen-year-old Nell Gwyn, in her first recorded role. The two stars, as everyone knew, were lovers. Love and war, distant as they seemed, echoed each other in fervour and despair.

In the real war, the young blades, and the not so young, were eager to prove their code of honour in the heat of battle. Their vaunted heroism would later inspire furious satire, and just as Marvell demolished the posturing of the war leaders, so Dryden's pretensions to grand heroic tragedy would be punctured by Buckingham and Rochester. This spring the words 'love' and

John Wilmot, Earl of Rochester

'honour' were also bandied about in the latest court scandal, starring Rochester himself. He was now eighteen and in need of a rich wife and for some time he had been pursuing the heiress Elizabeth Mallet without luck, although Charles himself urged her to accept him. In late May Rochester decided to abduct Elizabeth, and hired armed men to grab her on her way home from supper with Frances Stuart and bundle her into a coach. She was soon found, but Charles, enraged, sent Rochester to the Tower. A month later he sent the King a vehement petition, declaring,

That Inadvertency, Ignorance in the Law, and Passion were the occasions of his offence. That had hee reflected on the fatall consequence of incurring your Majesties displeasure, he would rather have chosen death ten thousand times then done it. That your Petitioner in all humility & sence of his fault casts himself at your Majesties feet, beseeching you to pardon his first error, & not suffer one offence to bee his Ruine.[4]

The comically self-abasing appeal would have fitted straight into a stage tragedy. Perhaps amused, Charles released him and bundled him off with a note to Sandwich, enlisting him as a 'volunteer' for the fleet.

While the court debated points of honour, both romantic and military, the Privy Council rushed to get ready for war. Urgently needing accurate information about the Dutch plans, they expanded the network of spies, both men and women. One person recruited was another future playwright, the first professional female English writer, the young Aphra Behn. In Surinam in 1663, Behn had met the dissident William Scott. He was clearly attracted to her, and Governor Willoughby alerted Bennet, who saw that such a connection might be useful. Tom Killigrew, who knew her well, also backed the idea of employing her. Behn was given vague instructions and set off to find Scott, who was now in Flanders, with the intention of gleaning information and persuading him to work for the British.[5] Her code name was Astraea, and Scott's Celadon. But this was no starry personal romance. Scott fed her false information,

Bennet failed to pay her and she had to pawn her rings to keep out of debtor's prison.[6] The whole intelligence system was a shambles. And while the information from abroad was scanty, the government were distracted by scare-mongering reports from informers at home, insisting that radical groups were colluding with the enemy and were waiting for the Dutch to invade so that they could rise up and topple the King.

By late spring, the hard-working Navy Board had managed to pull together a fleet of over a hundred ships, including converted merchantmen. But despite heroic efforts by civil servants like Pepys, vital supplies of tar and canvas and guns were still low, and unpaid suppliers refused to fill further orders. When the ships did sail, they were short of clothing and food, and indeed of sailors. Thirty thousand men were needed for a large wartime fleet and countless seamen were impressed against their will from country towns and fishing villages, and the back streets of Britain's cities. They deserted by the dozen when they reached port. Those who served could expect little reward. Instead of pay they received vouchers called 'tickets', which they often sold at lower value in the nearest seaport, made desperate by waiting for the cash.

Another problem, as Clarendon noted bitterly, was the need to make provision for the injured, and for the prisoners of war. In mid-April two Dutch vessels were captured and brought back to London. Technically any prisoners were now under the charge of the newly appointed commissioners for the prisoners of war, one of whom was John Evelyn. Since the other commissioners were either in the country or had volunteered to serve at sea, he rushed to Whitehall to take advice. Now came a moment, almost medieval, where courtesy and conflicting loyalties cut across hostilities, indicating again how Charles's court was poised between ancient and modern. Charles asked for one of the captains among the prisoners to be brought directly to him. This was twenty-three-year-old Cornelis Evertsen, the eldest son of the vice admiral of Zeeland, the

Dutch province most friendly to the House of Orange. When Evertsen arrived, Charles gave him his hand to kiss, granted him his freedom, questioned him about the battle and sent him off to the Dutch embassy with a gift of gold pieces, to await his passport home. His generosity was a gesture of honour. Orangists were not, he felt, and never would be his enemies, only republicans.

Samuel Pepys in 1666, by John Hayls

Meanwhile guards were sent to watch the prisoners at Chelsea, and Evelyn arranged for doctors to attend the wounded, 'both Enemies, & others of our owne . . . severall their leggs & armes off, miserable objects God knows'.[7] His experience brought home the suffering of the combatants and their families. Like many people, he sought someone to blame. Against a date at the start of this month, on the day set aside for public fasting, years later he added a note to his diary. This had been a day of humiliation and prayers, he remembered, 'for success of this terrible Warr, begun doubtless at secret instigation of the French &c to weaken the States, & Protestant interest'.[8] And this was only the prelude.

24 Lord Have Mercy upon Us

Ring o' ring of roses
A pocketful of posies
A'tishoo, a'tishoo
We all fall down.
ANON.

NOW ANOTHER DEADLY ENEMY ARRIVED. A wave of bubonic plague, carried by the fleas from infected rats, had been spreading slowly westwards across Europe. The plague was not unusual – in the last hundred years there had been at least four outbreaks, the most recent in 1626 – but its very familiarity filled people with dread. One or two cases appeared in Yarmouth in late 1664, and by early spring the outbreaks were sufficiently widespread to frighten wealthy Londoners.

The time seemed full of portents. The plague was linked to the war, and was said to have arrived on British shores in bales of silk from Holland, as if steered by Dutch malice. At the same time, at the end of February 1665 the great frigate the *London*, moored off the Nore, was destroyed by an explosion. More than three hundred men perished, with only a score surviving, horribly burnt. As a replacement, the City of London offered to give a 'great ship', to be built to a new design by Captain John Taylor, and a grateful Charles II decreed that its new name should be the *Loyal London*. Rumours arrived, untrue, of Dutch atrocities in Guinea, and others, sadly all too true, of British sailors capturing a French ship and torturing the sailors, burning their feet to make them confess their cargo was bound for Holland. Distressed and angry, Charles had the captain cashiered, the crew flogged in front of the fleet, and the goods sent back to the French owners. This did not bode well for his 'strict friendship' with France.

And all the time the plague spread. It took two forms. If the infected flea-bite was in the leg or arm, huge 'buboes' developed in the lymph glands, especially the groin: fever and vomiting followed, then delirium and coma and death within five days. Very occasionally people recovered, but with the second, less common form, where the infection went straight to the lungs, there was no hope. By March it had taken hold in the slums of St Giles, and the London rich began to pack up their goods. 'The ancient men', wrote Clarendon, 'who well remembered in what manner the last great plague (which had been near forty years before) first broke out, and the progress it afterwards made, foretold a terrible summer. And many of them removed their families out of the city to country habitations.'[1] In April Charles prorogued his parliament until September, telling them that he should be glad to meet them then, 'if it pleased God to extinguish or allay the fierceness of the plague'.[2]

In May Henrietta Maria left for France, and Catherine and her ladies, including Barbara, went down to Tunbridge. London was emptying. The savants of the Royal Society picked up their equipment and their notebooks and retreated to Durdans, Lord Berkeley's house at Epsom, with its beautiful gardens, fountains and sculptures, grottoes, bowers and summerhouses. Here Evelyn found Wilkins, Hooke and Petty in early August, 'contriving Charriots, new rigges for ships, a Wheele for one to run races in, & other mechanical inventions'.[3] When the plague closed Cambridge colleges, the twenty-two-year-old Newton went home to Woolsthorpe, where he tackled mathematical series, optics and theory of colours and, as he said, 'began to think of gravity . . . For in those days I was in the prime of my age for invention & minded Mathematicks & Philosophy more than at any time since.'[4] A generation older, a different kind of genius, John Milton, left his house in Bunhill Fields and retreated to Chalfont St Giles in Buckinghamshire, with his third wife Elizabeth and his angry, put-upon daughters. Here among the leafy lanes, with the city of death in the distance, the blind poet worked with his helpers on the final revisions of *Paradise Lost*. Dryden also left town. On the Wiltshire estate of his wife's family, the Howards, he worked on his long narrative poem *Annus Mirabilis*, celebrating the victories at sea, and on his *Essay on Dramatick Poesie*. The *Essay* took the form of a discussion between four characters, or rather an argument between Dryden himself and three courtiers and wits: Crites (Howard), Eugenius (Buckhurst) and Lisideius (Sedley). Its opening scene had the ring of a real event, as the four men drifted in a barge on the Thames on a summer evening, listening for the sound of cannon at sea, distracting themselves from fears for absent friends by arguing over the theory and practice of drama.

By early June 1665, when his scene from Dryden's *Essay* was supposed to take place, a heatwave was beginning. The sickness spread like fire. 'It stroke me very deep this afternoon', wrote Pepys on 17 June, who had taken to chewing tobacco as a preventative, 'going with a hackney coach from my Lord Treasurer's down Holborne – the coachman I found to drive easily and easily; at last stood still, and came down hardly able to stand; and told me that he was suddenly stroke very sick and almost blind.' Pepys got down, and found another cab, 'with a sad heart for the poor man and trouble for myself . . . But God have mercy upon us'.[5]

The full court did not leave London until the end of that month. On 29 June the courtyard at Whitehall was crammed with carts and coaches as people packed their bags. On 4 July Charles held his Privy Council at Sion House in Twickenham rather than Whitehall, and soon all his household were assembled at Hampton Court. Here and in nearby Kingston the houses of reluctant townsfolk were commandeered as lodgings, first for court and government officials and then for foreign ambassadors and their entourages. In the first fortnight of July it was estimated that thirty thousand people left the city. As they left, the *Newes* announced that by the Lord Mayor's orders, houses that were visited by the plague were to be shut up with all their inhabitants, and marked with a red cross in the middle of the door, with the words 'Lord have mercy upon us', until the danger passed. For many, this was a death sentence. Week by week the tally soared.

By mid-July the weekly toll was over a thousand lives, and rising. It was hard to find food, with the houses of so many brewers and bakers shut up. Many families camped in tent cities on the outskirts, but the plague found them there. For those who stayed, city life ground to a halt: 'no rattling coaches, no prancing horses, no calling in customers, no offering wares; no London cries sounding in their ears'.[6] People remained indoors, venturing out as little as possible. If they did, they might meet plague-infected people wandering the streets, or hear appeals from those shut up, calling through their

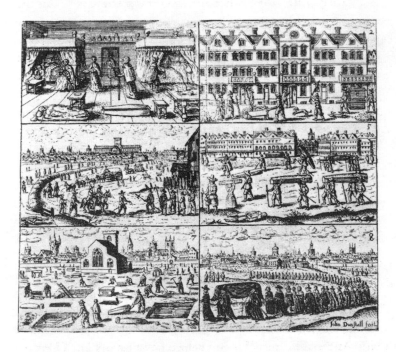

A Plague broadside, showing the plague nurses and the 'searchers' with their staffs, the carts carrying the dead, people fleeing from the city and families carrying coffins and bodies on trestles, while other victims lie unburied in the street.

windows for help. No one wanted the work of tending the sick and dying and removing their corpses, even at the rate of a shilling a day. Plague nurses came from the roughest class and many of them robbed those in their care and then abandoned them to their fate. Even worse were the 'searchers', old women – often understandably drunk – dressed in black and carrying white sticks. Their task was to go through the houses examining each corpse and reporting the cause of death. The pay was fourpence per body. Dogs and cats, who were thought to be carriers, were killed in their thousands, and the stench of dead animals and people filled the streets.

The infection was highest among the poor in their crowded tenements and to begin with the upper classes were sure that they would not suffer; 'the air has not been corrupted as yet'. But this changed. In early August, deaths rose to nearly three thousand a week, ten times the average, and by the end of the month the deaths reached four thousand, then five. Orders were read to the army and navy that anyone who fell sick must declare it at once: the ships stayed out at sea to avoid infection, and by this simple means most of the navy completely escaped. But on land, even on a country walk you could stumble across a dead body in the middle of a lane.

Most doctors fled London but the quacks that remained made a fortune, selling remedies such as Venice Treacle, Celestial Waters, Dragon Waters. The priests fled too, and some brave ejected ministers used their absence to return to their old parishes, earning the lasting gratitude of the stricken citizens. Wild preachers cried aloud in the streets that God's vengeance had come. As the plague worsened, government departments scattered to outlying districts, the Exchequer to the crumbling Nonsuch Palace in Surrey, the Navy Board to Greenwich. Charles arranged for Albemarle, who seemed undaunted by the threat, to stay in his Whitehall lodgings to supervise order in the capital. He was helped by William, Earl of Craven, Lord Lieutenant of Middlesex, who was himself the son of a London alderman. With furious energy, Craven organised the

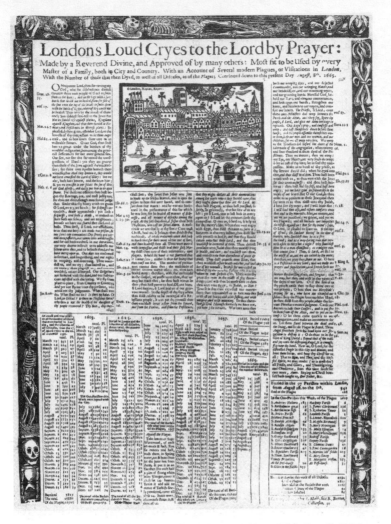

London's Loud Cryes to the Lord by Prayer. This broadside, published on 8 August 1665, contains texts appealing for mercy, repenting of sins, and begging God to hear the prayers of the people. Below are listed the numbers dying each week from plagues since 1591. In the woodcut, a skeletal Death with scythe and hour-glass salutes the fleeing people.

shutting up of houses and the mass burial of victims, handing out money from his own purse to feed the poor.

A guard at Hampton Court died, and Charles moved his court again, this time to Salisbury. The departure was a vast bustle (the queen's Portuguese attendants and priests alone took up eight coaches), and a vast expense, as coachmen and carters, exploiting the desperation of the people and fearing infection themselves, charged ever higher rates. But as the court moved, the disease moved faster. In Salisbury a royal groom fell ill and a man dropped dead in the street within a stone's throw of the king's house. Trying to overcome their fear the ladies of the court played bowls and developed a craze for telling each other their dreams.

Few things illustrated the gulf between classes more than the attitude to the plague in these months. To begin with there was fear but also a horrified curiosity as gentry, courtiers and diplomats noticed doors marked with crosses, or people with white rods walking in the street. Then came irritation: after all, the wealthy relied on the class most at risk, on tradesmen and grooms, on cooks and servants going to market. If one of their servants died they too might have to shut up their house. When a man died after spending a night with the servants of the Spanish ambassador Molina their house was shut up, and the ambassador's carriages were locked away. And when at last the eighteen-day quarantine was near its end, the woman who had washed the dead man's clothes fell ill, and the whole term of confinement began again. Molina's rage at the absence of those servants was incandescent.

The death toll in London reached its peak when the Bills of Mortality recorded 7,165 deaths from plague alone in the week ending 19 September. Increasingly too, as people travelled, the disease was reaching out into the countryside. In the famous case of Eyam, in Derbyshire, where the village shut itself off completely to prevent the infection spreading, the plague arrived in a parcel of cloth which was hung by the fire to dry, releasing the infected fleas. Slowly, across the country, the toll lessened as the cold weather came, killing the fleas. Those who had survived tended to have greater immunity, but the contagion lingered until spring the following year, and isolated cases occurred until November.

In London in the early autumn of 1665 coffins lay strewn in the streets, but they were too few for the mass of dead. Instead, the bodies were simply limed, piled onto carts and thrown in their hundreds into public burial pits. The shops were shut, the streets and alleys empty, and grass grew in the courtyards of Whitehall. The people of the great city shivered 'all in mourneful silence, as not knowing whose turne might be the next'.[7]

To all you ladies now at land
We men at sea indite;
But first would have you understand
How hard it is to write;
The Muses now, and Neptune too,
We must implore to write to you,
With a fa, la, la, la, la.

> CHARLES SACKVILLE, Lord Buckhurst, *Song
> Written at Sea, in the first Dutch War, 1665, the night
> before an Engagement*

AS IF TO BOOST his own spirits, in the spring of 1665 Charles bestowed honours on his favourites, raising their status as wartime leaders. Henry Bennet was created Baron Arlington, while Charles Berkeley was made Baron Botetourt of Langport and Earl of Falmouth. His trips to Paris as an unofficial diplomat were now at an end, and he was one of the first to volunteer to go to sea. At the same time Charles finally gave a dukedom to the Marquess of Newcastle.

In May the fleet gathered at Harwich under the Duke of York's command. The duchess too arrived in port with her throng of ladies. 'For the next fortnight,' wrote Sandwich's first biographer, 'the business of victualling was relieved by intervals of merry-making . . . Night and day were made merry by the sailors' wives and sweethearts. Countess, courtesan and country wench, jostled one another both in cabin and forecastle.'[1] The mood of these jollifi-cations was caught in Buckhurst's playful song of farewell:

> The King with wonder, and surprise,
> Will swear the seas grow bold;
> Because the tides will higher rise,

Than e're they us'd of old:
But let him know it is our tears
Bring floods of grief to Whitehall stairs
With a fa, la, la, la, la.

Finally they set sail. The three squadrons were commanded by the Duke of York, Prince Rupert, and Sandwich. With them went old hands like William Coventry, William Penn, William Batten, and the Cromwellian admiral Sir John Lawson. For a month, the British fleet waited, haunting the Dutch coast, hoping to meet de Ruyter's squadron or to catch returning Indian convoys. But the Dutch lay low and rations ran out, forcing the fleet back to the Norfolk coast. The long wait grated on men's nerves, and factions and feuds developed. Sent ashore with reports for the King, Berkeley groaned to Clarendon 'that they were all mad who had wished this war, and that himself had been made a fool to contribute to it, but that his eyes were open, and a month's experience at sea had enough informed him of the great hazards the king ran in it'.[2] Like many, he began to hope for peace. And so, wrote Clarendon, 'he returned to the fleet'.

On 3 June the Dutch were sighted off the Suffolk shore, a few miles out from Lowestoft. James, in his flagship the *Royal Charles*, led his fleet out to engage them. The great ships sailed in their favoured 'line-ahead' formation, stretched out in single file, 107 ships strung out for nearly seven miles.[3] The line was divided into three, the White squadron in the lead, under the Duke of York, the Red in the centre, under Sandwich, and the Blue in the rear, under Prince Rupert. Smaller vessels, the fifth- and sixth-rates, sailed alongside the warships ready to tow away damaged vessels, to relay signals and carry messages. The Dutch too had a hundred ships, including eighty-one warships and eleven large Indiamen. At first the two fleets passed on opposite tacks, quite far apart, and then they tacked again, the English in some disarray but still managing to keep roughly in line. When the White squadron came parallel to the enemy fleet, with about five hundred yards of water between them, the cannon were fired in great broadsides. The rumble of guns could be heard as far away as the

Hague, while in London people flocked to the open spaces, the banks of the river or the leafy park, to hear the cannons boom.

Sometimes, the ships came so close that the hulls crashed together, and the soldiers with their muskets rushed across onto the decks. The hand-to-hand fighting was fierce and bloody. When the Dutch ship *Oranje* attempted to board the *Royal Charles*, other ships came to James's aid. 'The vessels were grappled and locked together; the fighting at close quarters was furious; man after man was cut down, or his brains blown out by pistols held only a few feet away.'⁴ After an hour's desperate fighting, the *Oranje* surrendered, her men were taken prisoner and she was set on fire. The most terrifying weapons were the fireships, small boats filled with anything that could burn. Volunteers, with mad courage, sailed straight at their target then set the fireship ablaze and rushed to the stern, to escape, if they could, in a smaller boat. Once a fireship hit a larger vessel, its pitch and tar, sails and rigging went up like an inferno. At Lowestoft, the English used these to deadly effect. Their fleet had the wind, and fortune was with them. After the Dutch admiral Opdam was killed and his flagship blown up, the Dutch command fractured into a mess of conflicting commands. With many of their ships burned and sinking, they fled in confusion, in different directions.

London was alight with bonfires when the news arrived: cartloads of wood stood at the doors of the wealthy, ready to burn, and people ran inside to fetch their chairs and tables to hurl on the flames. The French ambassadors, who had decided it was not quite correct to light a bonfire to celebrate their ally's downfall, had their windows smashed by an angry mob.

For Charles, however, it was a bittersweet triumph. Thousands of sailors had died. He had lost many fine officers, including the old admiral Sir John Lawson. Worst of all, three of his closest courtiers and friends had been standing next to James on board the *Royal Charles*, when a single cannon ball struck them. All three were killed instantly and James was spattered with their blood and brains. They were Charles MacCarthy, Lord Muskerry, whose little dumpy wife

The Battle of Lowestoft, full of explosive drama.

had often been a butt of court jokes; Richard Boyle, second son of Lord Burlington; and his beloved Charles Berkeley, Earl of Falmouth. Heartbroken, Charles wrote to Minette,

I have had as great a losse as 'tis possible in a good frinde, poore C. Barckely. It troubles me so much, as I hope you will excuse the shortnesse of this letter, having received the newes of it but two hours ago . . . My head does so ake as I can only add that I am entierely Yours. C.R.[5]

Many who had seen Charles survive terrible blows of fate 'were amazed at the flood of tears he shed upon this occasion', noted Clarendon.[6] In the Chancellor's own view, Berkeley's death was good riddance, if not even 'a great ingredient and considerable part of the victory'. No one else had seen the qualities in him that Charles loved, and if he had lived, thought Clarendon with horror, who knows what heights he might have risen to. Pepys too had been suspicious of Berkeley, partly because of his animosity to the naval Commissioner William Coventry whom Pepys admired, and partly because he regarded him as little better than a royal pimp. He wrote on 9 June, 'The King, it seems, is much troubled at the fall of Lord Falmouth. But I do not meet with any man else that so much as wishes him alive again, the world conceiving him a man of too much pleasure to do the King any good or offer any good office to him.'[7] But, he added, he had heard on all sides that he was 'a man of great Honour', for volunteering and for his part in the battle. The satirical *Second Advice to a Painter* was cruellest of all:

> Such as his rise such was his fall, unprais'd;
> A chance shot sooner took than chance him rais'd;
> His shatter'd head the fearless Duke disdains,
> And gave the last-first proof that he had brains.[8]

On 22 June Falmouth was buried in Westminster Abbey, with a hero's funeral.

Despite the great loss of life, Lowestoft was a victory – but not a complete one. Alarmed by the bloody mess so near the Duke of York, and allegedly keeping a promise to the duchess to keep her husband out of danger, his second in command, Henry Brouncker, had called off the chase while James slept. The remnant of the powerful Dutch fleet ran free, to regroup and fight again.

After Lowestoft, Louis XIV urged Charles to stop the war now that he had proved his dominance at sea. Charles did not listen. He wrote angrily and at length to Louis, repeating his threat that he would seek an alliance with France's current enemy, Spain. And, he added, 'to your exception thereunto, lett me minde you that, according to the course of the World, those are better frinds who see they have neede of us, then whose prosperity makes them think we have neede of them'.[9] Both sides accused the other of stalling negotiations with regard to any sort of agreement, using the most feeble excuses. 'Since I have come back to my kingdom,' the French ambassadors charged Charles with saying, 'I have nearly forgotten the French language, and in truth the trouble I have in looking for my words allows the escape of my thoughts. I must need have delay in order to be able to reflect and meditate upon things proposed to me in that language.'[10] A frustrated Courtin offered to use Latin instead, a suggestion politely waved aside. Hunting for ways to catch his prey Courtin tried to enrol Frances Stuart, knowing her love of riding and suggesting to his masters in Paris that 'embroidered waistcoats sent her for the hunting' would be an appropriate present.[11]

The courtiers who were not at sea kept up their amusements, dinners and flirtations. Diplomatic tensions forgotten, they busied themselves finding a mistress for Courtin (although he was married with four children), obtaining new gun dogs for Verneuil, and drinking chocolate with the Spanish ambassador Molina. Alongside accounts of the plague and reports of the war, one French diplomatic bag contained the precise recipe for Molina's excellent brew. At a dinner given by Molina for Barbara Castlemaine and her friends the coachmen were so plied with drink that the guests had to use Spanish servants to drive them home, mortally offending those English servants who could still stand, and causing 'the greatest and most amusing disturbance imaginable'.[12] The bloody nature of the sea-battles was reduced to small talk: the Duke of York reported that his dog sought out the very safest place of all on board ship when they were fighting; the Spanish ambassador was received with pomp in the Banqueting House; the French foreign minister sent his young son to Charles's court to gain polish. Sometimes it was hard to remember that England was at war at all.

Shocked by Berkeley's death and James's narrow escape at Lowestoft, Charles had recalled his brother to Whitehall. As heir to the throne, his role as admiral posed too great a risk. That summer Charles, James and Rupert went down to Chatham. They sailed out to the fleet at anchor off the Nore, dined with the captains to rally morale, and, since Rupert refused at that point to contemplate a joint command, appointed Sandwich as the new admiral of the fleet, with Penn as his second in command. William Coventry, the most energetic commissioner for the navy, was knighted and made a member of the Privy Council. But beneath the brave display, the greatest anxiety, as always, was the lack of money to fit out and provision the ships.

Since the plague still raged, Parliament met at Oxford; for several months the townsfolk gaped at the sight of the courtiers in their brilliant silks and lace, and expressed their shock and annoyance at their drinking in the streets, their gambling and curses. Many of the courtiers were also MPs, and Charles relied on them now to push the Commons into granting more money. The initial huge grant for the Dutch war was already running out. Inspired by a speech from Clarendon, the Commons awarded another £1,250,000. But the accounts kept by the Treasury and the Navy Board made it hard to see where the first tranche of money had gone and this time the grant carried strict conditions. The whole sum must go to the war, and any loans raised on the security of the taxes, which would be slow in coming in, should be repaid in order.

This sensible proviso caused great arguments in the Privy Council, since Charles had talked over the conditions of the loans with Coventry and Downing (whose idea they were) but had not discussed them with Ashley, his Chancellor of the Exchequer. Ashley had then opposed the terms, thinking he was serving the King's interests, and was angry and embarrassed to find this was not so. When Charles sought to soothe matters by letting the whole Privy Council debate the case Ashley was appeased. But the splits between Clarendon and the new men became more and more apparent.

At sea, the main aim was to use the advantage gained at Lowestoft, and to try to capture Dutch trading ships, which were now avoiding the Channel and were thus forced to sail home around Scotland and down through the North Sea. Above all, the English captains wanted to capture well-laden East India convoys or to intercept de Ruyter, returning from Newfoundland with English prize ships taken off the American coast. But there were arguments now about strategy. If the whole fleet gathered in the North Sea, there was no protection for traders in the Mediterranean; yet if the fleet were divided, it would make it weak in any major engagement. The fleet was in fact weakened further by members of the Privy Council themselves, as Ashley, Albemarle and others fitted out privateers to hunt the Dutch, and many experienced sailors transferred from the navy to man them, lured by the hope of profits.

The long cruising off shore, waiting for the Dutch to appear, was expensive on rations and wearing on the spirit. The commanders yearned for action. In late July 1665 Sandwich's squadron was cruising near the Dogger Bank, hoping to catch the rich Indies fleet, when he heard that the Dutch Smyrna fleet, having been forced to come round the northern route, was sheltering at Bergen in Norway – 'that land of rocks which are terrible to seamen'.[13] He decided to head north and attack, urged on by the Duke of York, who stressed the profits to be gained: a single Indiaman could carry goods worth a quarter of a million pounds.[14] On board the flagship of Sandwich's commander, Captain Teddeman, was Rochester, keen for glory. He wrote to his mother from Bergen, heading his letter 'From the Coast of Norway, amongst the rocks aboard the Revenge'. They sailed to Bergen, he told her, 'full of hopes and expectation, having allready shared amongst us the rich lading of the Eastindia merchants some for diamonds some for spices others for rich silkes & I for shirts and gould which I had most neede of'.[15]

Norway was ruled by Denmark which had previously been friendly to the Dutch, and although the English envoy Gilbert Talbot was currently discussing an agreement with the Danish king, Frederick III, the news had not reached the port's governor. Sir Thomas Clifford was sent ashore to negotiate, but got nowhere. On 2 August the English ships entered the harbour, but the Dutch unloaded their priceless cargoes and stored them in the town's castle, placed ships across the harbour and mounted a battery on shore. When two English ships fired on the town, killing many inhabitants, they drew a rain of deadly musket fire in return. In a fog of smoke they withdrew, having captured only one ship and leaving dead and wounded citizens and burnt-out houses. Under the barrage of fire 118 men were killed, including Sandwich's cousin, Edward Montagu, and his friend John Windham. Near the end of the battle Windham trembled so fiercely that Montagu had to hold him up, and then a cannon ball hit them both. Rochester was standing beside them. Before the battle they had been discussing whether there might be life after death, and Windham and Rochester had made a pact that if there was, the first to die would come back and tell the other. But, said Rochester, he never did.[16]

Sandwich noted Rochester's courage. The following spring Charles made him a Gentleman of the Bedchamber and gave him rooms in Whitehall and £1,000 a year for life. A few months later Elizabeth Mallet forgave his abduction and married him.

After Bergen, inevitably, Denmark renewed its alliance with the Dutch. As the ill-thought-out attack showed, the itch for action was intensified by the hope of booty. At the end of August, in terrible gales, Sandwich's fleet did manage to capture twenty-three ships of a Dutch convoy scattered on the Dogger Bank. In theory, such prizes belonged to the crown: when sold, the money went to the Treasury, with some proportion to the capturing vessel's officers. In practice, since Tudor times the officers had doled out the rewards among themselves, sometimes making fortunes. Charles had already agreed to Ashley's suggestion that as Chancellor of the Exchequer and 'treasurer of prize money' he could account for prizes directly to Charles and dodge the Exchequer. This could bring riches, but also problems. Sandwich's captured ships included small trading vessels bringing salt from Bordeaux, oil from Gallipoli, sugar and cotton and gunpowder, but two were large Indiamen packed with valuable cargoes.[17] Thinking of his unpaid crew, and confident – or so he said – that the king would consent, he began doling out the Indiamen's goods immediately and selling shares in advance to friends and associates in the navy office, including Pepys. There was uproar at this open profiteering, and the unloading was stopped. For two months or more the great ships lay at anchor, bulging with riches.

Nervously, Pepys withdrew from the deal. When he visited the ships at Erith in November as the new surveyor-victualler to the navy, he bought silks and spices at knock down prices from 'dirty wretched seamen' in local pubs. And when he boarded the vessels he saw, to his astonishment, 'the greatest wealth lie in confusion that a man can see in the world. Pepper scattered through every chink, you trod upon it; and in cloves and nutmegs I walked above the knees, whole rooms full. And silks in bales, and boxes of copper-plate.'[18] Meanwhile Sandwich's opponents in the Commons, among them James, Albemarle and Coventry, demanded his dismissal. He lost his post and was only saved from impeachment by being despatched rapidly to Spain as ambassador. Two years later the whole business would be hotly debated in parliament as a case of embezzlement from the Exchequer.[19]

Hoping to balance flair with sense, Charles now divided command between the risk-taking Rupert and the solid Albemarle. Both had long experience of battle at sea as well as on land, though on opposite sides. Rupert had pursued and harried the Commonwealth fleet in the early years of the Interregnum, while Monck had commanded Cromwell's fleet in the first Dutch War of 1652–4. Meanwhile the Dutch proved that Lowestoft had not demolished their fleet, by staging a humiliating three-week blockade of the Thames. Faced with rioting by unpaid sailors, Charles begged loans, appealed to everyone from town corporations to bishops, peers to country magistrates, and raised £300,000 against the security of the promised parliamentary grant. He could not even pay the money he had promised to the Bishop of Munster, who had engaged the Dutch on land, and was sweeping unchecked across the inland provinces.

It was crucial, Charles thought, to show strength now, since Britain had a glimmer of an edge on the Dutch. They too were suffering from the war and popular feeling against the States General led to a new wave of enthusiasm for the Prince of Orange and his cause. People were heard shouting openly in the streets of Breda, 'Vivat the Prince of Orange and the Bishop of Munster'.[20] To keep this advantage, it was even more vital to keep France from openly supporting the Dutch. In France Henrietta Maria intervened, desperate to prevent a fatal breach between her two countries. Louis drove over to see her and St Albans at Colombes, and Minette joined them for long discussions, rousing intense curiosity in the English ambassador Lord Holles, who complained fiercely to Charles about being kept out. But the talks did not have the outcome Charles hoped for. In the autumn French troops marched openly to help their Dutch allies, driving back the Bishop of Munster's forces, and in November the *célèbre ambassade* finally went home, enduring a freezing quarantine before they could enter Paris.

The country waited anxiously, clamouring for news. A new newspaper, the *Oxford Gazette* (soon to be the *London Gazette*) appeared on 22 November 1665, edited by Arlington's right-hand man Joseph Williamson. It was 'very pretty', thought Pepys, 'full of news, and no folly in it' – a change from the rants of L'Estrange.[21] Christmas was tense. At the end of January 1666, Louis announced formally that he would enter the war, supporting the Dutch against the English. This prompted immediate fears of an invasion, especially when General Turenne went ostentatiously to review the troops at Calais. Ten days later Charles wrote briskly to Minette: 'we have had some kind of alarum, that the troopes which Monsieur de Turenne went to reviewe, were intended to make us a visite here, but we shall be very ready to bid them welcome, whether by sea or land.'[22] Messengers were sent post-haste to the coastal counties. In Norfolk, the MP Sir John Holland wrote to a neighbour that he had received the King's letter apprehending an invasion and calling out the militia, 'each musketeer to bring half a pound powder and half a pound bullet, each a matchlock, 3 yards of match, and every soldier a knapsack'.[23] With this impromptu home guard at the ready, on 10 February 1666, to loud cheering in the streets of London and across the nation, Charles declared war upon France.

26 The Long Hot Summer

. . . as when the sun new risen
Looks through the horizontal misty air
Shorn of his beams, or from behind the moon
In dim eclipse disastrous twilight sheds
On half the nations, and with fear of change
Perplexes monarchs.
MILTON, *Paradise Lost,* Book I

THE YEAR 1666 possessed magical numbers, '666' being the sign of the Beast in the Book of Revelation. For a long time almanacs had forecast doom. Some looked forward to the Second Coming, with titles like *Sagrir, or Domesday drawing Nigh.* Pamphlets were full of hints of apocalyptic omens, comets, eclipses and storms. In February Pepys bought an old work of prophecy, Francis Potter's *An Interpretation of the Number 666,* of 1642, dipping into it as the months went by. He finished it in November, intrigued by its elaborate numerical arguments and deciding that 'whether it be right or wrong', it was certainly 'mighty ingenious'.[1] The millenarian spirit even hit London's Jewish community, abuzz with Messianic fever. Reports arrived that 'a barque with silken sails and cordage, manned by a crew speaking only Hebrew, had been sighted off Scotland'.[2] The arrival of the prophet was believed so sincerely that Henry Oldenburg of the Royal Society wrote to Spinoza about it, and one man took a huge bet on the Exchange that the new arrival would be recognised by all the princes in the East.

Nine days before his declaration of war on France, on 1 February 1666, that very earthly prince, Charles II, returned to Whitehall, reassured that the plague was diminishing. A week later his court followed, including the pale queen who had, it was said, miscarried of a baby – a perfect boy – only a week before. Her grief was heightened by her rival's triumph: on 28 December, in her lodgings at Merton College, Barbara Castlemaine had given birth to a son, George Fitzroy, later Duke of Northumberland. Barbara, the 'witch', was the most hated target among all the garish, loud-mouthed courtiers who outraged Oxford's citizens. A note was pinned to her door in Latin, '*Hanc Caesare pressam a fluctu defendit onus*', translated by some wag: 'The reason why she is not ducked?/ Because by Caesar she is –'³ Charles offered £1,000 for information about the author. No one came forward.

The day after Charles's return the Lord Mayor, Sir Thomas Bludworth, arrived with speeches of welcome, and Charles knighted two sheriffs of the city. Tributes were paid to the officials, clergymen, doctors and others who had stayed through the plague. Charles employed all his charm on them, and on everyone who had endured the terrible months. The previous week, at Hampton Court, Albemarle had presented John Evelyn, who had stayed in London as a commissioner for prisoners of war. 'He ran towards me,' Evelyn said, '& in most gracious manner gave me his hand to kisse, with many thanks for my care, & faithfulness in his service, in a time of that greate danger, when every body fled their employments, & said he was severall times concern'd for me, & the peril I under-went.'⁴ Charles talked to him for an hour about his work, and the plague-stricken city.

The sickness did seem to be slackening. In his Essex parish Ralph Josselin wrote in his diary, 'March 4. Plague through mercy abates at London, 42 pl[ague] total 237, but a great increase at Colchester to 55. Yarmouth cleare. Lord heale our land, and open our trade, in mercy.'⁵ As the weeks passed Josselin noted the weather, cold and dry and windy, and jotted down the fast days and the bountiful catches of sprats, but his page was still dotted with the weekly plague figures, rising, falling, rising again like mercury in a barometer. Gradually the sickness decreased, flaring slightly in the summer heat and dying away the following autumn.

*

The French entry into the war spelled the end of Orangist hopes in Holland. Prince William's popularity had soared over the winter, and when he visited Rotterdam crowds carried him on their shoulders in triumph.[6] But de Witt now struck back, purging William's small court of key supporters. In England, the French declaration also had a dramatic effect. Arguments about Louis's motives surfaced again: he had incited the war in the first place, he wanted France to grab all the trade, in the Mediterranean, the East and West Indies, the cold coasts of Newfoundland; he already held sway on the continent, blocking all British efforts to make treaties. He wanted, in short, to be master of all. Louis, they cried, was an absolute monarch, fighting in the Catholic cause. There was more reason to fear papists working for the French, than dissenters in league with the Dutch. A new witch hunt began.

Charles's chief consolation at this point was the strength of his navy. Astoundingly, over the winter the boats had been repaired and made ready, despite a mutiny by workmen in Chatham dockyard, and angry complaints by skilled shipwrights about the money owed them. (In August Sir John Mennes estimated that £18,000 was owed to the men of the yard.[7]) Albemarle and Rupert left to take up their joint command on St George's Day, 23 April.[8] At the start of May the fleet gathered off the Nore, and Charles and James, sailing out from Chatham, visited it over three days, inspecting the ships and dining with the captains. Meanwhile the commissioners for the sick and for prisoners of war were commandeering every possible building in advance. Leeds Castle, in Kent, became a temporary prison, while Pepys and Evelyn pressed jointly for a new infirmary at Chatham. James, impressed, passed their plan on to Charles, and also recommended a second hospital be built at Harwich. But once again, there was no money. Before his trip to Chatham Charles wrote in weary tones to Minette, complaining of the terms of negotiation that Louis had offered:

however, I shall always be very ready to harken to peace, as a good Christian ought to do, which is all I can do to advance it, for I have long since had so ill lucke with the advances I made to that end, as I can now only wish for peace, and leave the rest to God.[9]

The ill luck continued. In mid-May faulty intelligence from Arlington's spies suggested that the French admiral, the duc de Beaufort, was bringing a fleet from the Mediterranean to join the Dutch off Brest. At the same time, Ormond reported rumours of uprisings in Ireland, to be backed by French troops. Believing that Beaufort's fleet was on its way from Gibraltar, and fearing that it was heading for landings in Ireland, the Privy Council decided to divide the British fleet in two, despite the weakening of its strength. Rupert was to lead a squadron of twenty ships to patrol off Plymouth, keeping an eye out for the French, and on 31 May, Albemarle sailed out with fifty-six ships to find the Dutch. Even as he sailed, news came that the intelligence about the French Mediterranean fleet was false. At once, James despatched an urgent message to Rupert, to sail north and join Albemarle. In another flurry of government incompetence, his message was fatally delayed in the sending.

About midday on Friday 1 June the Dutch fleet was sighted at anchor off Ostend, a great force of eighty-six ships, several carrying eighty or ninety guns. Albemarle ordered his fleet to strip for action, furling their extra topsails and keeping only their 'fighting sails' so that they could manoeuvre more easily. Instead of retreating into the mouth of the Thames to wait for reinforcements, he opened fire on the rear of the Dutch fleet. De Ruyter and Admiral Jan Evertsen, commanding the centre and van of the Dutch, turned their ships about to come to the aid of Cornelis Tromp in the rear, and fierce fighting began, 'the most terrible, obstinate and bloodiest battle that ever was fought on the seas', as one lieutenant remembered it.[10] The battle raged all day, driving the ships near to the Flanders coast, and many British vessels were badly mauled. The *Swiftsure*, the flagship of the Blue squadron which was leading the attack, sailed too far into the Dutch lines and was cut off from the rest of the fleet, overtaken and boarded. Her captain, vice admiral of the Blue, was the twenty-seven-year-old Sir William Berkeley, the younger brother of Charles

Berkeley. He had been accused of cowardice for leaving the fray at Lowestoft after his brother was killed, and was determined to prove himself. Although shot in the throat he refused to surrender. When they boarded, the Dutch found him dead in his cabin.

The Dutch also cut off the ship of the rear admiral, Sir John Harman, and attacked it with fireships, but Harman fought clear. At ten at night the English fleet sailed wearily westwards. Next day at seven, at the start of an unusually hot summer day, the guns boomed again. For many hours the ships tacked in their parallel lines, lurching and rolling as they trimmed their sails to turn and crash through the enemy line. Their billowing sails and fat-bellied hulls, rolling through the haze of smoke and fire, were brilliantly caught by the Dutch artist William van de Velde, who was with the Dutch fleet. Once again, as in the battles of the previous year, people on the outskirts of London could hear the guns, and Charles and James took their barge down to Greenwich and walked up into the park to listen. All they could hope was that Rupert's squadron would join the fleet, and that two hundred extra sailors now embarking in yachts from the Thames would also

William van de Velde the elder was with the Dutch fleet as an official war artist. Here he shows the start of the Four Days Battle, with the English bearing down on the Dutch. The *Swiftsure* is on the left, the *Royal Prince* in the centre, and Monck's *Royal Charles* in the middle distance on the right.

reach the battle in time. 'But Lord', wrote Pepys, 'to see how the poor fellows kissed their wifes and sweethearts in that simple manner at their going off, and shouted and let off their guns, was strange sport.'[11]

Many English ships had been so badly hit that next morning Albemarle placed sixteen heavy men-of-war between the Dutch and the damaged vessels.[12] But just as the enemy came within range, Rupert's squadron appeared on the horizon. His support stopped a rout, but could not halt the retreat completely, and as the English fled, the first-rate *Royal Prince*, with ninety guns, a veteran of many battles over fifty years, ran aground on the Galloper Sands. Although the tide floated her off, her rudder was broken and she was forced to surrender. De Ruyter ordered her crew of eight hundred men to be taken prisoner and then set her ablaze. 'She was like a castle in the sea,' wrote Clifford, 'and I believe the best ship that was ever built in the world to endure battering, but she is gone.'[13] On the final day the exhausted fleets clashed again. Low on gunpowder, the Dutch eventually turned for home, knowing that the English were too weak to pursue them. After Rupert's flagship lost its mast the English too limped back to port. Evelyn saw the proud fleet a week later, 'miserably shattered, hardly a vessel intire, but appearing rather so many wracks and hulls, so cruelly had the *Dutch* mangled us . . .. none knowing for what reason we first ingagd in this ungratefull warr'.[14]

Reports reached those on land fitfully, through different messengers, with different messages. 'Rumours of a great fight,' wrote Josselin on 3 June; 'wee prayd heartily for successe, & hope it, though some cry a losse.'[15] Two young sailors, Lieutenant John Daniel of the *Royal Charles* and a companion, who had both been sent ashore wounded, rode post to London, arriving with their faces still blackened and covered with pitch and tar and powder. Hearing of their arrival from Pepys, Charles took his hand, talked anxiously of the battle and asked to see them. When the sailors told him, in the Vane Room at Whitehall, that Rupert had reached the fleet, his relief was so great that he pulled out gold from his pocket and gave it to them. There were many stories of unlikely heroes, including Rochester, who had joined Sir Edward Spragge's flagship the *Dreadnought* on the eve of the battle, without telling anyone. At the fiercest point of the fighting, when Spragge could not find anyone willing to risk rowing through the fire to carry a message to his captains, Rochester volunteered, bobbing in his small boat while cannon balls and shot and burning spars whistled around him – no sober man, it was later said, would be brave enough to 'venture into a crazy Cock-boat out of a sound Ship, when 'tis but barely possible he may be saved'.[16]

When the final ambivalent news arrived, in the middle of the monthly fast day for the plague, Charles decided to celebrate the Four Days Battle, as it became known, as a victory. An order was given for bonfires and bells. People played music in the streets in the fine moonlit night, firing muskets in exhilaration. But the following day, like a hangover following a feast, a different story arrived, suggesting that the British had lost many ships and taken none. The expressions of merchants at the Exchange turned from delight to apprehension. 'The court gave out that it was a victory,' wrote Burnet years later, and public thanksgivings were ordered, 'which was a horrid mocking of God and a lying to the world.'[17]

For a few days the outcome was uncertain. Everyone rushed to find news: in the *Gazette* and the newsletters, in letters, in talk at the coffee-houses and taverns, at the Exchange or at the street corner. Newsletters, each with a different slant, were sold in markets and fairs. At court the gamblers judged the odds and laid bets on the *Swiftsure* and other ships being lost or saved. To outsiders, it seemed that the courtiers regarded the war as another game. And in fact, court life had continued much the same, if slightly subdued by plague, war and the death, in April, of Catherine's mother in Portugal, which plunged Whitehall into mourning. The famous beauties wore their hair plain, and applied no beauty spots or patches. The whole colour scheme of the court had turned to black and white, and Charles quipped that it looked as if it were inhabited by magpies. But in early summer the women of the court went again to Tunbridge, sending for players to entertain them.

Amid the tensions of the war, Charles's spats with Barbara were increasing, in number and ferocity, sparking from minor incidents into full-scale rows. A week after the Four Days Battle, Catherine provoked Barbara by saying slyly that she feared the King would catch cold by staying so late at her house. Oh no, Barbara replied before the whole court, he always left early, and if he did not appear before the small hours, he must be staying somewhere else. Charles, overhearing this public hint that he had other mistresses, took her aside, whispering furiously, and dismissed her from court. After three days with friends in Pall Mall, she asked if she should collect her things. She must first come and see them, said Charles, 'and so she came, and the King went to her and all friends again'.[18]

Charles was in no mood for such rows, or for his courtiers' bets on the battle. In the end the bleak figures spoke for themselves. In the Four Days Battle eight English ships had been sunk, compared to four Dutch, and nine had been captured. Five thousand English sailors and two thousand Dutch were dead or wounded. Three thousand more English sailors were prisoners. The loss of life was terrifying, the wounds appalling. The dead included admirals and officers, seamen, cooks and carpenters and cabin boys as young as twelve. Thousands of families the length and breadth of England lost men and boys they loved.

In the shipyards of both sides, another round of repairing and refitting began. The hospitals were full, and a hunt to find and impress new seamen was underway, rousing furious resentment. The sailors who had fought were still unpaid, and the families of prisoners were not compensated. On 10 July Pepys left for his office:

the yard being very full of women (I believe above three hundred) coming to get money for their husbands and friends that are prisoners in Holland; and they lay clamouring and swearing, and cursing us, that my wife and I were afeared to send a venison pasty that we have for supper tonight to the cook's to be baked, for fear of their offering violence to it – but it went, and no hurt done.[19]

The women got into the garden and crowded round his window, crying for money, lamenting the state of their families, shouting that their husbands had done so much for the king and were so badly treated, while the Dutch prisoners received allowances, and were also offering to take on the English seamen with good pay. 'I do most heartily pity them,' wrote the harassed Pepys, 'and was ready to cry to hear them – but cannot help them.' All he could do was give some of his own money to one woman, 'who blessed me and went away'.

The distress in the streets of London was matched by similar scenes in all the ports. The Privy Council discussed further censorship of the press and even closing down the coffee-houses. Meanwhile the ships of the Levant and East India Companies were stuck in port for fear of attacks: early in July the Dutch again sailed up boldly to the mouth of the Thames, to mount a blockade. Bad news also came from the colonies. On 18 July the West Indies Governor Willoughby sent a report to Clarendon saying that he was sailing to Barbados with his best ships, having heard that the Dutch had taken Surinam, and that the French were heading for Nevis. He set out with five ships and a thousand men but his fleet was caught in a hurricane off Guadeloupe: nothing was heard of his fate. It was rumoured, too, that twelve Dutch ships were on their way from Amsterdam to retake New York.[20]

Then came a sudden leap in fortune. On 25 July, St James's Day, Rupert and Albemarle led their great line of ships, almost ten miles long, out to sea. The fleets met almost where they had last crashed together, off the Galloper shoals. This time the English line was better disciplined, with more ships and guns, and the victory was clearly theirs. A week later, Henry Savile, now a Groom of the Bedchamber to the Duke of York, told his brother George, 'the noise of our victory does daily encrease and the Dutch are said to have lost such quantity's of men as they will hardly recover, unless they recruit with landsmen'.[21] Winning a battle, however, did not mean winning the war. As the Venetian envoy reported to the Doge and Senate, 'The two maritime and warlike nations' were still contesting to whom 'the empire of the seas shall belong'.[22]

Charles was equally concerned as to who should rule the United Provinces, the States General or his nephew the Prince of Orange. But in August, while people were still rejoicing over the St James's Day victory, a bizarre error by a passionate Orange supporter, the Sieur de Buat, set back the Orange cause irrevocably. By mistake, thinking it was another letter altogether, Buat had handed de Witt a long message from Arlington laying out English plans for levering the Prince of Orange into power. Buat was speedily tried and executed, but not before he had given the names of sixty powerful allies in Holland, many of whom fled the country. The English intelligence system was shattered, de Witt's own position was immeasurably strengthened, and the people rallied behind him.[23]

There was a final act to the sea war of 1666. Hoping to exploit their July triumph, the English admirals seized on the comment of a Dutch informer that merchant ships unloaded their stores on the islands of Vlie and Terschelling at the mouth of the Zuyder Zee, and also waited there, fully laden, on their outward voyages. Captain Holmes was given a squadron and sent to find them. On 8 August, with the help of a Dutch pilot, he found more than 160 richly laden merchantmen riding at anchor in the Vlie channel, guarded by only two men-of-war. The next day he sent fireships in, and burned all the ships except two. 'They burned likewise the whole town of Schelling,' wrote Clarendon soberly, 'which conflagration, with that of the ships, appearing at the break of day so near Amsterdam, put that place into that consternation that they thought the day of judgement was come.'[24] The Amsterdam merchants had thought their ships safe, and now their losses amounted to over a million pounds. The Dutch public were enraged at the callous attack on the village, and de Witt himself boarded the Dutch flagship and sailed for England, vowing revenge.

In the state bedchamber, an optimistic Charles could gaze up at John Michael Wight's ceiling painting of the goddess Astraea returning to earth, bringing a golden age, while cherubs waft his own image to the clouds.

The two miniatures by Samuel Cooper show a world-weary Charles in his Garter robes, and a fragile Catherine, wearing the statutory rope of pearls.

The cool, reserved Henry Bennet, Earl of Arlington, with a black plaster on his nose hiding an old civil war scar.
John Maitland, Duke of Lauderdale, hulking giant of Scottish politics, with his equally formidable wife Bess, Countess of Dysart.

Lely's double portrait of James, Duke of York, and Anne Hyde. James's marriage to Anne, Clarendon's daughter, provoked a scandal at the start of Charles's reign, while his Catholic faith caused uproar in the later years.

The attractive, ill-fated James Duke of Monmouth, Charles's much-loved son by Lucy Walter, who was supported by many as the Protestant heir to replace the Catholic James.

An unknown English artist reconstructs the drama of the Great Fire, looking
through Ludgate to old St Paul's, as whole streets explode in flames and crowds
laden with possessions scurry from the burning city.
The burnt-out ruins of a transept of St Paul's, sketched around 1673,
seven years after the fire.

The Dutch raid on the Medway in June 1667, showing the capture of the *Royal Charles*. The flagship was later towed away, crowning the humiliation of the English navy. The flags in the sea on the left mark the line of ships sunk in the vain hope of creating a barrier to the Dutch attack.

THREE BEAUTIES BY SIR PETER LELY

The one that got away. Frances Stuart, the model for Britannia, painted by Lely as a
modern-dress Diana, holding her bow. Charles fell in love with her when she was a
girl at court, but she resisted his advances and later eloped to marry the Duke of
Richmond and Lennox.

Nell Gwyn, the irresistible actress with fine legs, unfashionable tawny hair, snub
nose and Cockney wit, depicted as a model of pastoral innocence.
Nell's rival, Louise de Keroualle, who became Charles's mistress in the early 1670s.
In court undress, Louise, nicknamed 'Fubbs' for her chubby cheeks, adopts the pose
of a Renaissance Venus.

Dover in the 1660s, the fishing village below the castle, where the secret treaty with
Louis XIV was signed.
Henriette-Anne, Minette, 'Madame de France', around 1670. One of the chief
negotiators of the treaty, his sister Minette was perhaps the only person whom
Charles wholeheartedly loved.

'Holmes's Bonfire'. The English fleet under Sir Robert Holmes enter the Vlie Roads in August 1666, using fireships to attack Dutch ships and also burning the undefended town on the island of Terschelling.

But although the fleets caught sight of each other on 1 September they were kept apart by easterly gales, blowing relentlessly across the sea and land. The east wind had blown all summer, and all over Britain, the country people were waiting for it to turn, longing for the rain-carrying westerlies. For ten months the rainfall had been unusually low and there was widespread drought, even in Scotland. In Oxford in late July, Anthony Wood wrote, 'This year 1666 a dry year or summer: rivers almost dry, rivulets quite drye, notwith-standing divers violent flashes of rain and haile. The like hath not bin knowne in the memory of man, or at least for 60 years. Plentiful year of corne. To the great impoverishment of the boatmen.'[25] The Thames was so low that no boats could pass the locks. There were sudden freak thunderstorms, with hailstones the size of eggs. Those among the sects who believed in the power of the number 666, or who shivered over the prophecies in the almanacs, were waiting for the judgement to fall.

27 Conflagration

I am for living where no fires affright,
No bells rung backward break my sleep at night;
I scarce lie down and draw my curtains here,
But straight, I'm roused by the next house on fire;
Pale and half dead with fear, myself I raise
And find my room all over in a blaze.

JOHN OLDHAM, *A Satyr in Imitation of Juvenal*

LONDONERS WERE USED TO FIRES. When Sir Thomas Bludworth, the Lord Mayor of London, was called to one in Pudding Lane at the house of Mr Farryner, the king's baker, at three o'clock in the morning on Sunday 2 September 1666, he was not impressed. 'Pish!' he said, 'a woman might piss it out.'[1] The Fire of London had started an hour earlier. Before he went to bed, Farryner had gone through the house checking every hearth. There was a fire in only one room, and here he carefully raked up the embers. Yet somehow, perhaps from a spark smouldering beneath the floorboards on the edge of the stone hearth, the flames caught hold. They reached the faggots piled up for the day's baking, and soon the building was ablaze. All around stood wooden-frame pitched houses, densely packed together, dry as kindling after the drought. Within an hour, the easterly gale that prevented the British fleet engaging the Dutch was sweeping the fire through the streets.

One river of flame rushed northward towards the city, another south to the Thames. At London Bridge the great waterwheel under the most northerly arch was set alight, slipping off its axle into the mud, ending hopes of pumping water from the river. As day broke, those citizens who had not already been roused from their beds awoke to see clouds of smoke above the City. Pepys, who lived in Seething Lane, east of the Tower, was woken in the small hours by their servant Jane, telling him she saw flames. Like Bludworth, he decided this was nothing to worry about and went back to sleep – it was too far away and fires were common. But when he woke again at seven, and heard that three hundred houses had been burned near London Bridge, he dressed hurriedly and walked over to the Tower to get a clear view. What he saw over the next hour prompted him to take a boat upriver to Whitehall. He reached the river stairs about eleven o'clock and when the dismayed courtiers heard his news, they took him to the king. Immediately, Charles sent him back with orders to the Lord Mayor ordering him to pull down houses to create firebreaks, and offering to provide soldiers to help, an offer that went against all City traditions to accept no troops other than its own Trained Bands.

The conflagration was so sudden and fierce that it seemed to many onlookers as though the authorities hardly stirred to quench it, and men and women and children ran crying through the streets as if distracted. The chaos blinded them to the desperate efforts that were indeed being made. The magistrates organised rosters of hosepipes and buckets – as effective as throwing teaspoons of water on a bonfire. More practically, from early Sunday morning until midday, Bludworth sent the Trained Bands out to demolish houses to create firebreaks. But the gaps were too small, the wind too strong and the fire too fierce. Sailors from the Tower offered to blow up more houses with gunpowder, but the mayor was held back by fears that angry owners would demand compensation, and 'who will pay the charge?'[2] By mid-morning he had reached the limits of his strength and patience. When Pepys reached him with the king's message, 'he cried like a fainting woman, "Lord, what can I do? I am spent! People will not obey me. I have been pulling down hous- es. But the fire overtakes us faster than we can do it."'[3]

A fire on this scale was something that Charles had long dreaded. Eighteen months before, in April 1665, he had written to the mayor and aldermen of London warning them that the narrowness of the streets made a large-scale fire a real danger, and authorising the imprisonment of those who broke the new building regulations. But the advice had been ignored, and the cheap buildings now so vulnerable to the flames had continued to rise. By noon on this first day, having ordered companies of the King's Guard to stand by outside the City, Charles and the Duke of York were on their way downriver. They landed at the Three Cranes in Vintry, climbing to the roof to see the extent of the blaze. Urgently, Charles ordered yet more demolition, and went on by water to the Tower to see that the surrounding houses were torn down, and to remove the gunpowder stored in the White Tower.[4]

As the fire rushed down the streets it sucked in air, so that a burning wind heralded its path. After laying low the houses at the north end of London Bridge, it reached Thames Street, separated from the river by webs of narrow alleys full of stores and cellars and by huge warehouses packed with goods from the Baltic, the Mediterranean and the East: 'oils, pitch, tar, turpentine, brimstone, saltpetre, gunpowder, cordage, resin, wax, butter, cheese, brandy, sugar, honey, hops, tobacco, tallow, rope, hemp, flax, cotton, silk, wool, furs, skins and hides'.[5] Beyond these stores lay the wharves where coal and timber and wood were piled high. All were fodder for the flames.

Fire swept through the timber houses and shacks of the fish market, devouring the Fishmongers' Hall, the Watermen's Hall and the Steelyard, the old hall of the German merchants of the Hanseatic League. More slowly, the flames crept up the alleys heading north from Thames Street into the City. In the evening, Pepys looked across from a little alehouse on the south bank and saw the fire leap from corner to corner, between churches and houses, 'in a most horrid malicious bloody flame'.[6] As he watched, a great arc of flame, a mile wide, curved like a bow over the whole of the city. Overnight, people got ready to flee, hiding their valuables in cellars, placing them for safety in churches, staggering through the streets in their nightclothes, their arms laden with precious goods.

*

Next day, Monday, Charles rose at dawn. Setting aside the vaunted independence of London, he took personal control. The Duke of York was given supreme authority over the City, above the Lord Mayor. Charles summoned the Privy Council and set up a special committee, headed by the Yorkshire soldier Lord Belasyse, with headquarters at Ely House, Holborn. A semicircle of five fire posts, each with a hundred men and thirty soldiers, with an allowance of £5 for bread and beer, was established outside the ring of flame, curving from Smithfield to Temple Bar. Three courtiers were attached to each post, with the power to override the aldermen if they thought that more houses should be destroyed, and to hand out a shilling 'to anyone who are diligent all night'.[7] Within this, a nearer ring was organised by parish constables. The Lords Lieutenant of neighbouring counties were asked to send their militia to replace the exhausted London bands, and sailors were brought in from Woolwich and Deptford to help the demolitions.

James began his work at Fetter Lane, organising defences and dousing houses against the expected flames. Meanwhile Charles went by barge to Queenhithe to work with the men pulling down the market stalls and houses, and then rode around the inner ring of fireposts, encouraging and exhorting, carrying a bag of silver – some said golden – sovereigns to persuade townsfolk not to flee but to stay and fight the fire. The two brothers worked all day, as one Londoner, Henry Griffith, reported to his relative Seth Biggs, a Shrewsbury draper. He described

his Majesty's and the Duke of York's singular care and pains, handling the water in buckets while they stood up to the ankles deep in water, and play-ing the engines for many hours together, as they did at the Temple and Cripplegate, which people seeing, fell to work with effect, having so good fellow labourers.[8]

The flames roared on. At one point they built suddenly to a single wall of flame, fifty feet high, consuming everything it met. All along the riverside, as far as the medieval bulk of Baynard's Castle, the oil and resin of the chandlers' shops and the piles of ropes and timber went up like straw. To the north the fire licked along Cannon Street and Eastcheap, and then up Gracechurch Street towards Lombard Street. In Cornhill, Monmouth led a troop of the King's Guard, clearing anxious owners from the street. As the flames reached the Royal Exchange, the heart of London's mercantile power, they swept the balconies, cracked the columns and filled the courtyard with a lake of fire. The burning spices of the East India Company, packed in the crypt, filled the air with incense and rainbow-coloured flames. The statues of England's kings, from William the Conqueror on, all tumbled from their niches: only Gresham's statue stayed intact.

When the Exchange finally fell, with a deafening, roaring crash, said the Revd Thomas Vincent:

Then, then the city did shake indeed, and the inhabitants did tremble, and flew away in great amazement from the houses, lest the flames should devour them. *Rattle, rattle, rattle*, was the noise which the fire struck upon the ear round about, as if there had been a thousand iron chariots beating upon the stones: And if you opened your eye to the opening of the street, where the fire was come, you might see in some places whole streets at once in flames, that issued forth, as if they had been so many great forges from the opposite windows . . . and then you may see the houses *tumble, tumble, tumble*, from one end of the street to the other with a great crash, leaving the foundations open to the view of the heavens.[9]

The people fled. Some ran west and north, to the open fields. Others took their families to Westminster and beyond. The roads were jammed with coaches, carts, drays and packhorses, laden with boxes, blankets, vats of wine, babies' cradles, bedcurtains and even the beds themselves. A cart that cost a few shillings to hire could now command any price: ten, twenty, thirty, forty pounds. Carts were also pouring into the city from the countryside, driven by people anxious to make a profit or simply to help. There were jams at all the gates and on Monday the magistrates ordered them to be shut to any incoming traffic, a well-intentioned but disastrous move that led to desperate fights for the few remaining coaches. Many people also took to the river, piling their household goods into skiffs and wherries. The better off tried to save prize possessions. Some carried their new pictures, in gilded frames. Some buried their money, and Pepys buried his Parmesan cheese. (He never tells us why, or what it was like when he dug it up.)

The scene was lit by the lowering red of the fire shining on the underside of the cloud of smoke. 'All the skie were of a fiery aspect, like the top of a burning Oven,' wrote Evelyn. It seemed to him as if he saw ten thousand houses,

all in one flame, the noise & crakling & thunder of the impetuous flames, the shrieking of Women & children, the hurry of people, the fall of towers, houses & churches was like an hideous storme, & the aire all about so hot and inflamed that at the last one was not able to approach it.[10]

As he left the city in the evening he was reminded of the burning of Sodom, the Day of Judgement, the sack of Troy. 'London was,' he wrote, 'but is no more.'

By next morning clouds of smoke were streaming far over the countryside, like the plume from a volcano. Ash and charred embers and half-burnt scraps of paper drifted down on lanes and fields and parks miles from the city. In London, the fire surged along the Thames through the slums of Blackfriars, consuming the grain stored in the empty Bridewell prison. Further north it reached Cheapside, the home of the goldsmiths. Up in smoke went the great halls of the Merchant Taylors and the Drapers. Next came the medieval Guildhall, with the offices of the mayor and aldermen. Its structure of old oak timbers was so strong that even after the fire engulfed it the skeleton stood whole for several hours, outlined 'in a bright shining coal, as if it had been a palace of gold, or a great building of burnished brass'.[11] Luckily the floor was equally strong: beneath it lay all London's ancient records, untouched by smoke or flame.

To the west, the fire raged past Newgate and the Old Bailey and down Ludgate Hill towards the Fleet River. The wind was blowing it inexorably towards Whitehall and Westminster. The alarm was raised at court. The Exchequer was despatched to Nonsuch where it had taken refuge from the plague, and Charles ordered the roofs stripped from the new houses that Denham had built in Scotland Yard, to create a break before Whitehall itself. Throughout the night and most of the day James directed workmen at the Fleet river, pulling down sheds and wharves, 'handling buckets of water with as much diligence as the poorest man that did assist', and summoning all the nearby counties to send workmen with their tools.[12] The aim was to create a long firebreak stretching from the Thames to Holborn, where the Earl of Craven had his team, to stop the flames jumping across the Fleet from Ludgate Hill to Fleet Street.

Meanwhile, filthy, smoke-blackened and tired, Charles toured the fireposts, wielding buckets and shovels with the men. Many contemporary accounts mention his bravery and energy, 'even labouring in person, & being present', as Evelyn put it, 'to command, order, reward, and encourage Workmen; by which he shewed his affection to his people, & gained theirs'.[13] The king and duke, wrote Clarendon,

who rode from one place to another, and put themselves in great dangers among the burning and falling houses, to give advice and direction what was to be done, underwent as much fatigue as the meanest, and had as little sleep or rest; and the faces of all men appeared ghastly and in the highest confusion.

Where citizens had fled, Charles and James took charge themselves, exposing themselves to flames and smoke and the danger of falling buildings.

When the Great Fire roared down Ludgate Hill it swept into a printing house in King's Head Court, off Shoe Lane. John Ogilby's entire stock went up in flames, including the manuscript of his twelve-book epic *Carolies* – 'the pride, divertisement, business and sole comfort of my age'.[14] Many booksellers and publishers, whose shops clustered around St Paul's churchyard, were ruined the same day. Some had placed their stock in Christ Church and Stationers' Hall, where the loss amounted to over £150,000. Others had taken their books and the sheets ready for binding to St Faith's Church, in the cathedral crypt. The great private library of Samuel Cromleholme, High Master of St Paul's School, was also stored here. It was thought to be safe, but the burning roof timbers crashed through the floor into the vault and the tightly packed books burned for a week. Wren's mentor John Wilkins, who had been rector of St Lawrence Jury since 1662, lost his house, his possessions and the manuscript of the *Essay towards a Real Character and a Philosophical Language* on which he had been working for years, and which he had to reconstruct from a proof.[15] Richard Baxter reported that the libraries of most of the ministers in the City were burnt and from his home, six miles from London, he could see 'the half burnt leaves of books' whirling in the wind.[16] Pepys's favourite bookseller Kirton lost his house, shop and thousands of pounds' worth of books. He died a year later, having never recovered from the shock.

One great monument remained. Around St Paul's, all the houses were burning, but so far the cathedral itself was untouched. Crowds of people had taken their goods there and were sheltering inside, believing it could never fall.[17] But now the fire began to lick the wooden scaffolding which had been put up in preparation for long-discussed repairs, like a pyre around a martyr's stake. Above the cathedral the smoke-cloud was so dense that it caused a local thunderstorm, with jagged lightning forking down to the burning buildings around. At eight in the evening the roof caught fire. As the crowd inside rushed for the doors, the roof timbers blazed above their heads. The scorched stones cracked and whistled through the air like grenades and molten lead poured in streams from the roof, turning the pavements into glowing hearths.

Charles watched St Paul's burn. Only now, when he returned to Whitehall, did he give orders for the court to leave for Hampton Court next morning. But that evening the wind changed, blowing more from the south. Gradually, too, the force of the gale lessened and the sparks no longer flew across the yawning gaps made by the demolished streets. Whitehall was saved.

*

The following day thousands of Londoners were out dousing the embers and quenching the fires that remained. In the eastern part of the city, the flames still roared around Cripplegate, north-west of the Guildhall, reducing the Barber Surgeons' Hall to ashes. Charles and James were both here, directing the fight. Once again, the king was compared, approvingly, to a common labourer.

Although Pepys walked through Cheapside and Newgate market, in many places the glowing ruins were still too hot to approach. When Evelyn ventured through the burned-out areas, clambering over mountains of smoking rubbish, the ground under his feet was still so hot that it burnt the soles of his shoes. All the City's finest buildings and churches had vanished: men were bemused and lost, lacking the familiar landmarks. Even the waters in the broken fountains seemed to boil, and evil-smelling smoke swirled up from wells and cellars like fumes from hell. The great chains that were used as barriers to close the City streets, the hinges and bars of the prisons, the bells from the churches, all lay on the ground, melted and twisted. In the narrow alleys the intense heat singed the hair on one's head.

It was a scene of horror, but also one of wonder, a natural curiosity drawing the observant men of the Royal Society. In the broken tombs in St Paul's, they observed the mummified bodies of bishops buried two centuries before, while in the tomb of Dean Colet, a more recent burial, his lead coffin was found to be full of a curious liquor that had conserved the body. 'Mr Wyle and Ralph Greatorex tasted it and it was a kind of insipid taste, something of an ironish taste. The body felt, to the probe of a stick which they thrust into a chink, like brawn.'[18]

PREVIOUS PAGES In December 1666 the Lord Mayor and Common Council of the City appointed John Leake and his team of surveyors to make an 'Exact Surveigh' of the damage. This was engraved by Wenceslaus Hollar, as the *Map of the Destruction wrought by the Great Fire of London*, 1667. The numbers on the map refer to the many parish churches lost, and other important buildings such as the Baynard's Castle (160), the Stocks Market (165) and the Royal Exchange (166).

28 Blame

Now nettles are growing, owls are screeching, thieves and cut-throats are lurking.

A sad face there is now in the ruinous part of London: and terrible hath the voice of the Lord been, which hath been crying, yea roaring in the City, by these terrible judgements of the Plague and Fire, which he hath brought upon us.

THOMAS VINCENT, 1667

THE GREAT FIRE destroyed five sixths of the city, cutting a swathe half a mile wide and a mile and a half long. Over 13,200 houses were burned, with eighty-seven churches and fifty company halls. No one knows how many people died. Thousands took refuge on the outskirts, on St George's Common south of the river, in the fields of St Giles and Soho to the west, Moorfields, Islington and Highgate to the north and Goodman's Field to the east. Some sheltered in tents, while others put up rough huts. Several of London's wealthiest citizens were here, without a rag or a bowl to their name.

By the fourth morning, many of those who had fled had been without food since the fire began. Charles ordered the local Lords Lieutenant to send all bread and provisions that could be spared to London. He also set up temporary markets and decreed that churches, chapels and schools should be opened as communal storehouses. Army tents were provided and stocks of ship's biscuits from naval stores were also distributed in Moorfields (although these hard, weevil-filled objects were widely declined as inedible). Outside London, Charles commanded all cities and towns to accept refugees and to allow them to operate their trades, regardless of the rules of local guilds, pledging that they would not be a burden on the parishes that took them in after the immediate crisis.[1]

Among these refugees, on Wednesday night a new rumour spread, that fifty thousand French had invaded, taking advantage of the devastation, and were coming to cut their throats and seize what goods remained. 'Many citizens,' wrote Revd Vincent, 'having lost their houses, and almost all they had, are fired with rage and fury and they begin to stir themselves like lions, or like bears bereaved of their whelps; and now *Arm! Arm! Arm!* doth resound the fields and suburbs with a dreadful voice.'[2] Grabbing whatever arms lay at hand, people poured back into the city, falling upon any foreigner they met. Troops were sent to quell the riots and drive the crowds back into the fields, where they were guarded until dawn broke.

Ever since fires caused by wind-blown sparks began to flare up simultaneously in different places, people had been convinced that the blaze was set deliberately. The first suspects were the Dutch and French. Even those who had lived in a neighbourhood for years were abused, beaten, kicked, dragged to the magistrates and thrown into gaol. William Taswell, a schoolboy from Westminster, who was sent into the City with his classmates to carry water-buckets, remembered how a blacksmith, 'meeting an innocent Frenchman walking along the street, felled him instantly to the ground with an iron bar'.[3] After the foreigners, suspicion fell on the local Catholics, who were forced to cower indoors, said Clarendon, despite the threat of the fire, 'and yet some of them, and of quality, were taken by force out of their houses, and carried to prison'.[4] Near Newgate, a crowd seized a servant of the Portuguese ambassador, accusing him of pulling a fireball out of his pocket and hurling it into a house across the street. When examined, he explained that he had picked up a piece of bread, put it in his pocket and then laid it on a shelf in the next house: 'which is a custom or superstition so natural to the Portuguese, that if the king of Portugal were walking, and saw a piece of bread upon the ground, he would take it up with his own hand, and keep it till he saw a fit place to lay it down'.[5] Luckily, Lords Hollis and Ashley, who were in charge of this area, returned to the scene and found the bread, but kept the man in prison for his own safety. Such strange, small incidents were rife. Some were comic, like the Frenchman in Moorfields who was set upon because he was thought to be carrying a box of bombs, that turned out to be tennis balls. Others were horrific, like the Frenchwoman carrying small chicks in her apron that were thought to be fireballs, set on by a mob who clubbed her and cut off her breasts.[6]

Charles's most urgent fear now was of riot, escalating from the attacks on foreigners and Catholics.[7] Seeking to calm things, on Thursday 6 September, he handed back control of the City to the Corporation, and ordered the troops and militia that had been called in from elsewhere to stand down. On the same day he rode out to Moorfields, accompanied by only a few courtiers. With St Paul's still smoking in the background, he addressed the crowd gathered on the fields littered with their belongings. He spoke firmly:

The judgement that has fallen upon London is immediately from the hand of God and no plots by Frenchmen or Dutchmen or Papists have any part in bringing you so much misery. Many of those who have been detained upon suspicion I myself have examined. I have found no reason to suspect connivance in burning the City. I desire you all to take no more alarm. I have strength enough to defend you from any enemy and be assured that I, your King, will by the Grace of God live and die with you and take a particular care of you all.[8]

Four days after the fire subsided, the fields that had been so crowded with people were empty. Everyone went home as fast as they could, finding shelter in the suburbs or the unburned areas of the City. 'And very many', added Clarendon, 'set up little sheds of brick and timber upon the ruins of their own houses.'[9] But for weeks London still burned. When cellars were opened, the rush of air fanned smouldering ashes into flame. Fires flared sporadically until a downpour doused the City in October.

Everyone had stories, details that haunted their minds at the time and have been repeated down the centuries in all histories of the fire: John Locke seeing strange red sunbeams as far away as Oxford;

Pepys watching the pigeons circling, unable to land on their lofts, until they fell, with charred wings, into the smoke; William Taswell hunting for souvenirs in St Paul's churchyard and stumbling over the charred bones of an old woman who had sought shelter by the cathedral wall.[10] For months, the sleep of many Londoners was troubled by dreams of fire and falling buildings. People also lived in dread of robbers. Many houses had been looted and in mid-September Charles issued an optimistic proclamation for 'restoring goods embezzled during the late fire and since'.[11] This noted that great quantities of plate, money, jewels, household goods and building materials were found daily in the rubble: all must be returned to the Armourer's House within eight days or those hoarding them would face the full penalties of the law, including death. The looting, however, continued and the abandoned houses sheltered thieves and foot-pads. When men rode through the town at night or were driven in their carriages, they carried drawn swords.

Not everything was dark. A great sum was raised in the provinces and sent to the mayor and aldermen to help the homeless. The City officials moved into Gresham College, ousting the professors (except for Hooke) and filling the courtyard with tents. Here they opened a ledger where householders could record their title deeds, to estimate what was lost and what must be rebuilt. Gresham also became a temporary Exchange and observers marvelled at how quickly the guilds and livery companies who had lost their great halls began trading again. Not one merchant went bankrupt. A month later, a newsletter reported the Dutch to be dumbfounded that 'after the late ruin of London all men continue amongst us so merry and hearty, no sign of any such mischief, when they expected we should have been wholly ruined and lost'.[12] The corporation let tradesmen operate from tents and booths on public land, and commanded householders to clear the rubble from the foundations and surrounding streets. In a few weeks the theatres reopened, having agreed to give part of their profits to help those rendered destitute by the blaze.

The City was ready to start again.[13] On 11 September, less than a week after the fire ended, Wren, as deputy surveyor, submitted his plan for a new city. Evelyn and Hooke were almost as fast. Other plans were later submitted by the topographer Richard Newcourt, who proposed a grid plan rather like Hooke's, and by the army captain Valentine Knight, who suggested the building of a new canal from Billingsgate to the Fleet, for which the King could charge fees and finance the rebuilding. (Charles was horrified by the idea that the crown might benefit from the calamity, and Knight was arrested for his pains.) All proposed a modern city of avenues and squares, open markets, brick-built houses. With the loss of the old crooked, overcrowded, medieval London, it seemed that a new spirit would emerge, rational, individual, competitive, forged in fire. From the desert of ruin and death, Charles dreamed that a new London would arise, a phoenix from the ashes.

After the fire, Charles asked the Privy Council to sit morning and evening to examine all the allegations of conspiracy. Their conclusion was that 'Nothing had been found to argue the Fire in London to have been caused by other than the hand of God, a great wind and a very dry season.'[14] Sadly, their efforts to clear foreigners were largely overturned when a young Frenchman, a watchmaker's son from Rouen named Robert Hubert, made a public confession, claiming that he had been hired in Paris to set the fire. His story was so disjointed and nonsensical that none of the justices believed him, while the captain of the ship that had brought him swore that he had not even landed until two days after the fire began.[15] Yet Hubert was adamant, and because he could lead the justices to the exact place that the fire had started – which was hardly difficult as this had been widely reported – he was put on trial. The jury convicted him, and he was hanged on 27 October. Clarendon's explanation, that Hubert's fatal stance was effectively suicide, rings horribly true.

Hubert's confession heightened suspicion that the Fire was a papist plot. On 25 September parliament set up a committee of

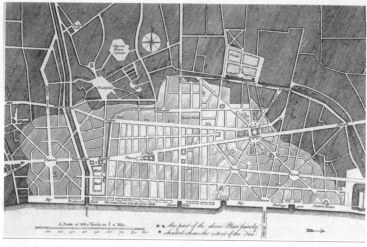

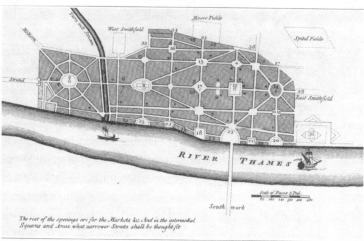

Plans for rebuilding the City by Christopher Wren (above) and John Evelyn.
Wren's plan has bold avenues, radiating out from circular piazzas, and a new
quay along the Thames from Bridewell to the Tower. Evelyn, like Wren, has an
octagonal piazza on Fleet Street, with avenues linking twelve squares and piazzas.
He also planned to move the Royal Exchange to the riverside.

inquiry. A month later, before the committee had even gathered all its evidence, the House of Commons asked Charles to issue a proclamation banning Catholic priests. Anxious to appease protestant anger, he agreed with alacrity. The following day Andrew Marvell reported to the Mayor of Hull that the king had decreed 'that all Popish priests and Jesuites (except those attached to Queen Mother and Queen) be banisht in 30 days or else the law to be executed upon them'.[16] The justices were also ordered to put the existing laws against Catholics into execution.

The parliamentary committee's report, published on 22 January 1667, was very different from the Privy Council's, finding clear 'evidence' that French Catholics and Jesuits were involved. As Marvell reported with his usual diligence, that day the House 'heard the report of the Fire of London full of manifest testimonys that it was by a wicked design'.[17] The fear of a conspiracy spread to the provinces, where local people hunted down all those labelled as potential incendiaries, sectaries in the north (where memories of the 1663 rebellion were still strong) but Catholics almost everywhere else. From this point on, the paranoia about Catholic designs would grow in strength, culminating in the hysteria of the Popish Plot a decade ahead.

Partly due to the finger pointed so fiercely at the French and the Catholics, Charles was also blamed. Pamphlets and lampoons cursed the sins of the nation, and particularly the Francophile court, with its Catholic queen, for rousing the wrath of God and bringing down sickness, fire and war as a judgement. William Sancroft, Dean of St Paul's and later Archbishop of Canterbury, preached a solemn sermon on this theme. The portents of nature continued. In October people saw a bright comet fly low over the Midlands sky, while gales and strong winds blew down trees, tore off roofs and damaged church spires, and torrents of rain flooded the fields.[18] On 10 October, when Charles instituted a general fast, Evelyn described it lugubriously as intended 'to humble us, upon the late dreadfull conflagration, added to the Plage & Warr, the most dismall judgments could be inflicted, & indeede but what we highly deserved for our prodigious ingratitude, burning Lusts, dissolute Court, profane & abominable lives'.[19]

The poster for Dean Sancroft's sermon,
with Hollar's engraving of St Paul's in flames.

In the eyes of his critics, Charles's record was not good. When the London poor were being shovelled into plague pits, he went to Newmarket and set up a prize for an annual race. When war with France was declared, he was off to Newmarket again. His tendency to turn to pleasure at moments of crisis could be seen as icy cool, or a symptom of strained nerves. Either way it pleased no one. His court was damned not only for its French connections but also for its excessive luxury. Even in the King's Theatre, the criticism continued, in a self-mocking, lighthearted vein, a kind of inoculation against the disease. In October 1666 in James Howard's *The English Monsieur* (there were four Howard playwrights, Robert, James, Ned and Henry), Nell Gwyn portrayed a wealthy widow in love with her servant. It was John Lacy, however, who took the plaudits, playing the 'Monsieur', Mr Frenchlove, a courtier obsessed with all things Gallic, an anticipation, perhaps, of Etherege's ludicrous Sir Fopling Flutter.

Noting all this, Charles decided a gesture was needed to counter the slurs. Thus was born the strange episode of the 'Persian Vest'. In October, while Howard's play was still running, Charles banned French fashions from court. Instead of a stiff collar, doublet and cloak he adopted a loose knee-length tunic of black cloth with white silk trimmings, with an open coat like those in Persian miniatures,

A fashionable man wearing the long coat and tunic
of the Persian vest style in their richest form.

with a girdle or sash. Below this 'the legs were ruffled with black riband like a pigeon's leg', observed the admiring Pepys (who had his own vest for Sunday best, but was afraid he would catch cold in it).[20]

Charles's new style was intended, he told the Privy Council, to teach the nobility thrift. John Evelyn was delighted, having recommended a similar style in a pamphlet, *Tyrannus*, which he had given to the king, 'an invective against . . . inconstancy & our so much affecting the French fashion'.[21] To other observers, however, it merely suggested the king's frivolity in the face of his people's sufferings. That autumn there were masquerades, plays and parties every night at Whitehall. In November, when a magnificent ball was held for Catherine's birthday, Charles's own version of the vest was hardly thrifty, being made of rich cloth with a silver lining. The regulations for court mourning were relaxed, and the ballroom was ablaze with silver, silks, gold lace and jewels. (The most beautiful of all the women was Frances Stuart, wearing black with white lace, her head and shoulders dressed with diamonds.) A hundred courtiers wore their new Persian coats, each costing £100. As the New Year came there were dances and comedies, and in February a wrestling match for a prize of £1,000, between teams from the north and the west, before a huge crowd of lords, ladies and commons, at which 'greate sums were abetted'. That evening there was a ball, where Evelyn admired the dancers, and especially the men 'in their richly embroidred, most becoming Vests'.[22]

Charles swore never to drop his Persian style, prompting sardonic courtiers to lay bets as to how long this vow would last. He did indeed wear it from time to time for the next five years, and the slim coat over a long waistcoat gradually became the standard pattern for the elegant gentleman's dress well into the next century. But in its bolder form its death blow as a major court fashion was dealt by Louis XIV who found the style so comical, according to London gossip, that he dressed all his servants in it and ordered his noblemen to do the same, 'which, if true, is the greatest indignity ever done by one prince to another. And would incite a stone to be revenged.'[23]

Hollar's 'The Swan and the Stork', from Ogilby's *Aesopics*, 1668
with the newly fashionable coat lording it over the old-style cloak.

While the French court laughed, the British public – if they
noticed at all – felt that a sartorial gesture was unlikely to solve the
court's finances, let alone appease the Almighty, or to protect the people. If plague and fire were acts of God, the mismanagement of the
war was clearly the work of men. Their critics were ready to pounce.

29 The Trick Track Men

Draw next a pair of Tables op'ning, then
The House of Commons clatt'ring like Men.
Describe the *Court* and *Country*, both set right,
On opposite points, the black against the white.
Those having lost the Nation at *Trick track*,
These now advent'ring how to win it back.
The Dice betwixt them must the Fate divide,
As Chance does still in Multitudes decide.
  ANDREW MARVELL, *Last Instructions to a Painter*

IN LATE 1666 Charles faced onslaughts from all quarters: hostility in parliament, disapproval of his court, unrest in Scotland and Ireland, and war with Holland and France. Although the great companies revived so quickly after the Fire they had lost trade during the war, while landowners and farmers saw their profits devoured by high taxes. The price of coal had risen steeply, as the Dutch targeted the coastal ships from Newcastle, and the poor were perishing from cold. Everywhere Charles turned, the arrows flew.

When the Commons met on 21 September, ranging themselves according to loyalties, Marvell compared them to the 'men' in trick track, or tic tac, a popular version of backgammon. Their mood was distressed and wary. The division between the 'court' party, who supported the king, and the 'country' party was beginning to be clear. In particular the country MPs were ready to question the expenditure of every penny raised in taxes. And Charles was once more appealing desperately for money. The plague had stopped the collection of taxes and the Fire had halted loans from London companies and goldsmiths. Meanwhile the sailors were still unpaid and the ships again needed refitting.

The Commons were ready to grant funds, but this time they asked to see accounts to estimate what was needed, irritating the King and throwing the Navy Board into a minor panic about the poor state of their books. However, after Sir William Coventry persuasively laid out the case for increased grants to the navy, the Commons voted yet another £1,800,000. But then fiery arguments followed as to how this should be raised, delaying other parliamentary business by about three weeks. The Privy Council and their pet MPs argued not for a tax on land but a general excise duty. This in turn was fiercely resisted as a universal tax that ruined trade, the dread Dame Excise,

> A thousand Hands she has and thousand Eyes
> Breaks into Shops and into Cellars pryes.[1]

Critics thought it would breed a swarm of officials and that it was merely an excuse for a standing army, needed to enforce it. In the end, it was decided, reluctantly, that some of the money would be found from an assessment on property, some from a tax on legal documents, and the rest from a new variation on the poll tax.

In the autumn of 1666, after the Fire, Buckingham returned to court. At the start of the war the duke had been incensed when he was denied command of a flagship and refused a place on the Naval Council. He had turned, instead, to industry, building a huge, innovatory glassworks at Lambeth, until Charles sent him north to arrange coastal defences against the Dutch; he and his deputy lieutenant George Savile were both given commissions to raise a troop of horse in Yorkshire. But this summer he had also begun a fatal, obsessive affair with Anna Maria Brudenell, Countess of Shrewsbury, a fiery beauty already famed for her lovers. He filled his commonplace book with broodings on love, fate and women – 'Their power is so absolute, that I think the Devil's promise was made good to women, when he said, You shall be like gods' – and returned to London fired up, eager to plunge back into court intrigue.[2]

Buckingham was now nearly forty. His face was puffier and more

Anna Maria Brudenell, Countess of Shrewsbury

jowly, his elegant figure lost, but his wit was as keen as ever and his desire for revenge strong. In early October he took his seat in the Lords, attended all the debates and won seats on the key committees. From the start he set out to forge a link between groups in the House of Lords and others in the Commons, and to lead the growing opposition, particularly the criticism of the government's handling of the war. He seduced all critics, thought Clarendon, and astonished those who knew him by his application in gathering these allies.

The Duke of Buckingham took more pains than was agreeable to his constitution to get an interest in all such persons, invited them to his table, pretended to have a great esteem of their parts, asked counsel of them, lamented the king's neglecting his business, and committing it to other people who were not fit for it; and thus reported all the license and debauchery of the court in the most lively colours, being himself a frequent eye and earwitness of it.[3]

'It cannot be imagined', continued the appalled Clarendon, considering the loose life Buckingham led, how powerful his influence was, and how many in both houses of parliament 'would follow his advice and concur in what he proposed'.

Buckingham's adherents were a motley crowd, ranging from presbyterians keen for toleration to royalists unhappy with the Restoration settlement and the ways of the court. As well as the angry royalist Sir Richard Temple and the playwright Robert Howard, they included the eloquent speakers John Vaughan and Sir Thomas Littleton, and two young men, Edward Seymour and Thomas Osborne. Both these men were destined for power, Seymour as Speaker of the House, and Osborne as Earl of Danby, one of Charles's most powerful ministers. In the Lords, Buckingham had the support of Ashley. He managed to unite his followers by focusing their complaints on the suspicion that the crown was moving more towards French-style absolutism, and encouraged them to damn the heavy taxation, hint at corruption among officials, and attack the squandering of resources that denied honest seamen their pay.

Behind all this, Buckingham also had a personal agenda, the desire for revenge on Clarendon and Ormond, the grand old men who had criticised his wildness since the early days of exile and whom he blamed for his current disfavour at court. At this precise moment he had a new grudge against Ormond, whose second son, the Earl of Arran, had just married Buckingham's niece Mary, daughter of the Duke of Richmond and Lennox. As he had no children himself, a child of this marriage would not only inherit the Richmond estates in Scotland, but would be heir-at-law to all his own Villiers estates. The thought of his land passing to Ormond's family was intolerable. As it happened, Mary died the following July, aged eighteen, but in the autumn of 1666 the threat seemed real, and was deeply resented. The Duke's first target therefore was Ormond, and Ireland.

Most English MPs saw Ireland as a nuisance, a drain on the revenue. In the early 1660s they were more worried about the poverty of the English countryside than about the Irish landlords and peasants. To protect England's farmers, in 1663 the Commons had passed a partial restriction on importing cattle from Ireland, limiting the trade to certain months. They later tried to extend this, but when it reached the Lords Charles declared firmly that he would never give the royal assent. This autumn, when Charles's position was weakened by his need for money, the Commons reintroduced the bill in a more extreme form, banning the import of Irish cattle outright. It was a controversial measure, backed by the members from the 'breeding party' in Wales and the northern and western counties, who wanted to raise the prices of local-bred cattle and prevent rents from falling, but opposed by those who represented the 'feeding' counties, of East Anglia, and by Londoners who wanted cheap meat.

The Irish were appalled and Charles resisted the bill firmly, knowing that the cattle trade was Ireland's one hope of relief. Without it the economy would be devastated and the Irish government reliant on English subsidies. The Dublin treasury was already so empty that Ormond was reduced to paying the troops out of his own pocket. When there was mutiny among the garrison at Carrickfergus, he rode there himself at the head of four hundred men, but even these troops had not been paid for seven months, and he feared that they too might join the rebels.[4] If they did so, when the French had landed there would be no one to oppose them (This was no fantasy: passing through Paris the following year the Earl of Essex was horrified to find Henrietta Maria trying to mediate between Louis and Irish Catholics seeking money and troops.)[5] The passing of the bill, said Ormond, might stir yet more unrest.

In direct, almost jubilant opposition, the Buckingham clique picked up the Irish Cattle Bill and ran with it. Temple pushed the bill forward in the Commons, and it was passed after only three weeks, with a key clause, added by Seymour, describing the trade as a 'common and public nuisance', a technicality that prevented Charles from using his prerogative to reinstate it. Then came a month of acrimonious argument in the Lords, where Buckingham and Ashley (who had investments in Scottish cattle and hated Ormond and the Irish) faced Clarendon, Anglesey and the bishops and Catholic peers, eager to win royal favour. During one debate, Buckingham quipped, amid much 'mirth and laughter', that those who opposed the bill 'had either an Irish interest or an Irish understanding'. (Which, noted Pepys, 'is as much as to say he is a fool'.[6]) Enraged at this slight, Ormond's son Ossory challenged Buckingham: both men were sent to the Tower for three days until they apologised to the House. The quarrel threatened to spread. Arlington was apparently 'so warm in defence of Ossory' that if the House of Lords had not interposed, a new challenge would have 'sprang out of the embers of the former'.[7] A month later came another row, in which Ossory taunted Ashley for his past Cromwellian loyalties, and called Buckingham a liar.

Finally the Irish Cattle Bill was voted through the Lords, but with Seymour's nuisance clause removed. The angry Commons promptly reinstated it. At the same time, urged by Howard and the disgruntled royalist William Garraway, they added a proviso to the Poll Tax Bill, which decreed that new money should only be raised if the government gave parliamentary commissioners an account of all funds spent since the war began. This was an extremely worrying development, the first time the Commons had asserted their right to examine and question royal expenditure. On the night of the final Commons vote, Charles allegedly ordered the Lord Chamberlain to send to the playhouse and bawdy houses to make all the court MPs go back to parliament and vote to get rid of the clause.[8] The vote still went against him. He was saved, briefly, when the House of Lords then rejected the proposed parliamentary commission and petitioned the King to name his own team of inquiry. At this the Commons were outraged again.

While the Poll Tax Bill was still being debated, and Charles was not yet sure of his supply, the Buckingham faction in the Commons pushed forward yet another divisive issue. This concerned Lord Mordaunt, Charles's spymaster during the exile. In November the House received a petition claiming that as Constable of Windsor Castle, Mordaunt had illegally tried to evict a castle official, sending in troops, who hurled out his furniture and frightened his son so badly that he died. Mordaunt, it was said, had thrown the official into prison and had also tried to rape his daughter. In December, the Commons drew up articles of impeachment, a process that had not been used for twenty years. When the House rose for the Christmas holiday Mordaunt's future looked bleak.

A further issue, this time a direct onslaught on Clarendon, concerned the Canary Patent. Trade with the Canaries had been established since Tudor times, and when he was ambassador in Madrid in the 1650s Clarendon had become convinced that the wine growers were exploiting the competitive English market by pushing up their prices. After the Restoration he persuaded seventy British merchants to ask for a charter of incorporation, so that they could combine together and offer the Spaniards a single price 'which they would have to take or leave'.[9] In 1665, despite protests from merchants left out of the favoured group, and from the City of London, a charter was given to the 'Governor and Company of Merchants trading to the Canary Islands', to regulate the trade. But the sailings had been challenged by private carriers and badly affected by the war and the Fire and by opposition in the Canaries themselves, and the merchants found themselves in difficulties. Aggrieved traders who had been excluded claimed that Clarendon had been bribed to set up the patent. There were several petitions to parliament against the charter, which was bound, sooner or later, to be overturned.

In the run-up to Christmas, Westminster had become tense and unruly. In the Commons, MPs turned up drunk and would not stop talking. In the Lords, on 19 December Buckingham deliberately jostled the Marquess of Dorchester, a small man known for his hot temper, provoking a stand-up fight. Wigs were lost, hair was pulled, blows were exchanged, and both were briefly sent to the Tower.[10] Buckingham began to seem out of control. A few days after his release, he leant across the table at a meeting, grabbed the Marquess of Worcester by the nose and 'pulled him about'. Charles intervened and Buckingham was despatched to the Tower again. Observers were baffled by Charles's patience with him. It was not loyalty to childhood memories, since although Charles could be sentimental, he was no fool. Certainly some of his decisions were tactical, but he seems almost to have admired the duke's manic brilliance. He provided a kick of adrenalin, like the other things Charles loved – sailing in a hard wind, fierce games of tennis, racing, sex. The aura of imminent danger added to his allure.

Meanwhile the navy was on the verge of disintegrating. When some sailors were sent to Newgate for 'discontented words', several hundred armed seamen gathered in the city to break into the prison to release them, and Albemarle was forced to march his troops to Wapping. At the end of 1666 Pepys wrote disconsolately, 'Public matters in a most sad condition. Seamen discouraged for want of pay, and are become not to be governed. Nor, as matters are now, can any fleet go out next year. Our enemies, French and Dutch great, and grow more, by our poverty.'[11]

The winter frost was violent and intense. In January a sudden thaw filled London streets with mud and slush, and then two more months of freezing weather followed, bringing the coldest days in living memory. The people shivered, complaining loudly of the scarcity of coal and the extortionate prices. The need for money was so urgent that Charles took Arlington's advice, against that of the Duke of York, Clarendon and Sheldon, and told the Lords to accept the Irish Cattle Bill, including the nuisance clause, and the Poll Tax Bill. But instead of immediately discussing the grant, the Commons returned to Mordaunt's impeachment, which he answered in the

Lords this month. Charles would pardon him the following July, but a year or so later, Mordaunt resigned his offices and retired. For stalwarts like Clarendon and Ormond the precedent was ominous. It was the first time in Charles's reign, discounting Bristol's wild attempt, that a serious move was made to impeach a peer.

The session of parliament left Charles bruised. He had surrendered over the Cattle Bill but had still not obtained his money. In mid-January he addressed both houses in angry tones:

My Lords and Gentlemen: I have now passed your Bills; and I was in good Hope to have had other Bills ready to pass too. I cannot forget that within a few days after your coming together in September both Houses presented me with their vote and declaration, that they would give me a Supply proportionable to my occasions; and the confidence of this made me anticipate that small part of my Revenue which was unanticipated for the payment of the same. And my Credit hath gone farther than I had reason to think it would; but it is now at an end.

This is the first day I have heard of any Money towards a Supply, being the 18th of January, and what this will amount to, God knows. And what Time I have to make such preparations as are necessary to meet Three such Enemies as I have, you can well enough judge . . . [12]

He blamed the delay partly on Buckingham, with whom he had finally completely lost patience. On 25 February, almost as soon as the parliamentary session ended, Charles ordered a warrant to be put out for his arrest. The charge, manufactured by Arlington, was that he had arranged to have the king's horoscope drawn up by an astrologer.[13] Since a horoscope implied the old offence of 'imagining the king's death' it could be categorised as treason. Faced with the prospect of such an accusation, Buckingham went into hiding. His post as Lord Lieutenant of Yorkshire was taken over by Lord Burlington, his protégé George Savile was dismissed, and he was stripped of the lucrative patents for his glassworks.

But if Charles could not control his nobles, his subjects, his sailors or his parliament, he could at least try to make a deal with his enemies. Early in 1667 he began to sue for peace.

V SPADES / *piques*

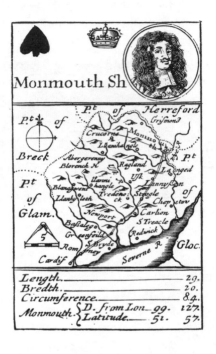

Monmouth Sh.

Pt of Herreford
Pt of
Breck
Grysmond
Crucorne
Llanihangle
Monmo th
Pt
Abergeveny
Blorench H.
Ragland
Langed
of
Blangwen
llanvi hangle
Tredene ck
Vsk
Sfannyston
Glam.
Llanhylech
Chep stow
Newport
Carlion
Basaleg
Greensfield
Redwick
S Treacle
Rom ney
S Bryde
Severne R.
Gloc.
Cardif

Length. _____ 29.
Bredth. _____ 20.
Circumference. _____ 84.
Monmouth { D. from Lon 99. 127.
Latitude. 51. 57.

King of Spades from *The English Counties*, by Robert Morden, 1676.
The medallion for the King of each suit showed Charles II, while the Queen
was depicted by Catherine of Braganza. Clubs showed the Northern counties,
Hearts the Eastern, Diamonds the Southern and Spades the Welsh.

30 Breathing Spaces

> What buying and selling, what dealing and chaffering, what writing
> and posting, what toil and labour, what noise, hurry, bustle and
> confusion, what study, what little contrivances and overreachings,
> what eating, drinking, vanity of apparel, most ridiculous recreations;
> in short, what rising early, going to bed late, expense of precious time
> is there about things that perish!
>
> WILLIAM PENN, *No Cross, No Crowne*

IN DEFERENCE to the sombre mood after the Fire, there were no
great Christmas festivities in Whitehall. But as the New Year came,
with its fierce frost and snow, new singers arrived to entertain the
court. 'This evening I heard rare *Italian* voices', wrote Evelyn, '2
Eunuchs & one Woman, in his Majesties greene Chamber next his
Cabinet.'[1] The singers also appeared at the Theatre Royal, including
a beautiful soprano, who, Killigrew warned all admirers, adamantly
refused to be kissed. This year too, young Pelham Humfrey, later
Purcell's mentor, returned from France to inject some Gallic brio into
the King's music.[2] A new card game, too, had arrived from France in
the middle of the war. This was basset, or *bassette*, which became an
obsessive court pastime, considered only fit for those of high rank
since the gains and losses could be so huge. It was a game of pure
chance, where the banker, the *talliere*, assisted by the *croupiere*, sat with
his bank of gold on the table before him and the rest of the players put
forward their cards one by one, with their stakes upon them, hoping
to multiply this through a mass of complex rules, but almost bound to
lose, since all the advantage was with the bank. (Louis XIV decreed
that the banker must be the son of a nobleman of the first rank, and
eventually banned the game altogether, fearing court bankruptcies.)

While fortunes were being lost at court, more serious things were happening outside. Soon work began on rebuilding London. Immediately after the Fire, Charles had ordered that no rebuilding should start until the damage was properly estimated. He warmed to the plans of Evelyn and Wren, with their new quays along the Thames and geometric grid of avenues, vistas and squares, bringing memories of the Paris of Mansart and Le Vau that he had admired in his exile. But to implement these he would have to raze the old network of city streets, and such high-handed grandeur would smack of absolutism, an affront to the rule of the City fathers. Much as he liked the plans, they had to be laid aside. On the other hand, he could lay down basic rules for rebuilding without a political storm. A swift royal proclamation declared that new houses should be of brick or stone; the old overhanging storeys must go; roads should be widened to get rid of the web of alleys and lanes, and paved to allow easier traffic, 'convenient and noble for the advancement of trade of any city in Europe . . . both for use and beauty'.[3] Even this early statement made it clear that every stage of planning and building was to be a collaboration between the crown and the Lord Mayor and aldermen. It was vital for Charles to work with the City, to capitalise on the goodwill he had won during the Fire, and to squash the gossip that some courtiers – notably the ever tactless Bab May, his current Keeper of the Privy Purse – had actually rejoiced that the 'rebellious city' had been brought to its knees.[4]

At booths around the City, landlords and tenants registered their legal claims, and a commission was set up to survey the burnt areas. The court appointments included Christopher Wren and the royal architects Roger Pratt and Hugh May, while the City put forward their surveyor, Peter Mills, and builder, Edward Jerman, and also Robert Hooke, who had delivered his proposed plan not to Charles, but directly to the City Corporation at Gresham House.[5] In the bitter, stormy winter the commission drew up their plans and costings. In February 1667 parliament passed two acts. One set up Fire Courts, dealing with wrangles between landlords and tenants who were ruined, or reluctant to rebuild. (Business was so heavy that there was still a waiting list after a year, and the courts sat all day.) The other was the first Rebuilding Act, which laid down the provisions for standardising houses, widening streets, arranging compensation and relaxing guild rules to allow immigrants to swell the army of labourers. The work was to be paid for by a ten-year tax of a shilling on each chaldron of coal (just over a ton) brought into the Port of London. Soon the City passed its own Act of Common Council, laying down rules for establishing disputed boundaries.

Work could now begin. At the end of February, Sir Robert Vyner and the Lord Mayor came to ask directions from Charles about measuring out the streets. Everyone had a view. The best way, according to Pepys's friend Captain Cocke, would be to sell the whole area to a commission, then let them sell it again, giving preference to the old owners, so that it could be built as the trustees desired, 'whereas now, great differences will be and the streets built by fits'.[6] The commission, however, could not do anything so bold and the streets, as Cocke prophesied, were indeed built in bursts as money and men became available. First, though, they had to be surveyed. In March and April, when the weather was still so icy that no leaf appeared on the trees, Hooke and Mills began the Herculean task of staking out the line of the new streets. With a small team of workmen they covered the entire area in nine weeks. In late March, Pepys wrote, he went out with Sir William Penn 'to my shoemaker's, cutler's, tailor's . . . and in my going do observe the great streets in the City are marked out with piles drove into the ground; and if ever it be built in that form, with so fair streets, it will be a noble sight'.[7] (At the end of the year, Pepys heard that William Penn junior, who would warn people so passionately against this greedily material world, had lately returned from Ireland, as 'a Quaker again, or some very melancholy thing'.[8])

Hooke was appointed surveyor for the City, and became a local hero, greeted warmly wherever he went. For years the streets would be a mess of scaffolding, ropes and piles of bricks and timber. Roads were widened and the gradients were lowered on the steepest hills, making them easier for carriages and carts. Entrepreneurs made fortunes out of new brickworks, and the price of land rocketed. By the end of 1667, in the centre of the City, where a new road was planned from the Guildhall to Cheapside, ground worth fourpence a foot before the fire was now valued at fifteen shillings.[9] Speculators flourished, like Nicholas Barbon, who first set up a fire insurance business and then began buying back leases from landlords who did not wish to redevelop their land themselves. With astonishing speed, Barbon built up a property empire, building terraces of houses from St Paul's to St James's. His new wealth seemed remote from his family's old faith: he was the son of the preacher Praise-God Barebones, who had christened him not Nicholas, but 'If-Jesus-Had-Not-Died-For-Thee-Thou-Hadst-Been-Damn'd'.[10]

For many people, as for Barbon, money came before religion. The Exchange was rebuilt before the churches. In October crowds watched as Charles rode in procession to the sound of kettledrums and trumpets to lay the first stone of the new building.[11] It was reopened two years later, with all its shops and wonderful arcades. But the churches came next. In May 1667 a second Rebuilding Act listed fifty-one parish churches to replace the eighty-seven churches and six chapels lost in the fire. These would slowly rise over the coming decades, their spires inscribing the vision of Wren, Hooke and Hawksmoor on the skyline.

The argument over the design of St Paul's took longer. The remains of the charred tower and crossing were pulled down stone by stone in the late summer and autumn of 1668. Crowds gathered to see the walls tumble, and gaze into the great vaults of St Faith's, where the booksellers' stock had burnt. But it was not until a year later, when Charles appointed Wren as surveyor general, that any real plans were made. Even then it took another three years for the walls to be demolished, and Wren's design for a cruciform neo-classical building with a cupola, displayed as a model to the King, was compromised by the demands of the Church for something more traditional. The foundation stone was eventually laid in June 1675. The work was finished stage by stage under Charles, James and William and Mary, until it was finally completed in 1711, in the reign of Queen Anne, with the aged Wren the only survivor of those who had begun this great project.

London came to life again fast, with all the 'noise, hurry, bustle and confusion' that the young Quaker Penn so disliked. The theatres reopened, and the booths and freak-shows, the dancing horses and 'Pulchinello' were back at Bartholomew Fair in Smithfield in late August. The Post Office was up and running and stage-coaches clattered into the great galleried inns in the suburbs. Messengers and porters were back at their posts on street corners, with the great white scarves that they used to carry parcels tied across their chests, ready to run errands through the half-built streets. The number of hackney carriages was much lower than the four hundred authorised by law that had crammed the streets before the Fire, but the river was crowded with skiffs carrying people from bank to bank. The taverns and coffee-houses and brothels were packed. As if the conflagration had never happened, Londoners walked in the parks, played on the bowling greens and laid bets on bull- and bear-baiting and cock-fights. If anything, the mood was even wilder. Pepys was horrified by the young gallants in Spring Gardens, forcing themselves on any woman who walked by.

In this time of reconstruction the city moved westward. The ecclesiastical courts moved to Essex House in the Strand, and the Excise Office to Bloomsbury Square, built by the Earl of Manchester on land granted at the Restoration, its fine houses now nearly complete. While the old Exchange was out of action, the New Exchange in the Strand became the great shopping centre, an alternative to the theatre as a place of entertainment. It had two long double galleries of drapers' and mercers' shops, where customers were served by well-dressed women or smart apprentices selling silks and gloves, walnut cabinets and gilded mirrors, everything the heart could desire. Nearby, a 'great new ordinary' was built by Adam Lockett at Charing Cross, much admired by Pepys when he ate his grilled pigeons there, and immortalised as 'Lockett's' in the plays of the next generation.[12]

The Royal Society, still exiled from Gresham House, also moved west. Henry Howard, Duke of Norfolk, invited the Fellows to move into Arundel House in the Strand, and prompted by Evelyn, he also donated the great library collected by his grandfather, the famous virtuoso, whose collecting trips on the continent were an early forerunner of the Grand Tour. Soon all was as before. 'We had divers Experiments for improving Pendule Watches,' wrote Evelyn on 8 January, '& for winding up huge Springs by force of powder; with an invention for the letting down, & taking up any earth, Corall, or what ever it met with at the bottome of the sea.'[13] The noisy, dangerous gunpowder trials continued, to the Fellows' evident enjoyment, and so did the gruesome medical experiments, transfusing blood from a sheep into a dog 'till the sheep died, the dog well, & was ordered to be carefully looked to'.[14] In a lighter mood, there was a demonstration of a newly invented calash, a light, four-wheeled carriage with a folding hood, with which Charles was particularly pleased.

His Majesty was also pleased this spring by a striking visitor with strong views on experimental philosophy. The Duke of Newcastle had finally raised enough funds to buy back the house that he had built in Clerkenwell in the 1630s, and he and his duchess drove down in state from the country in April 1667. Although Newcastle's relationship with Charles had been awkward ever since he requested permission to leave court and live in the country, Charles was among their first visitors. A host of nobles and old friends from the days of exile followed, crowding into Newcastle House over the next month. Margaret Cavendish, now in her forties, fascinated all those who came. 'The whole story of this lady is a romance, and all she doth is romantic,' wrote Pepys, who pursued her coach all over town to get a glimpse of her.[15] She talked volubly to cover her shyness, about her books, her ideas on religion, her poetry, her views on science. 'My tongue runs fast and foolish,' she had once confessed, uttering 'so much, and fast, as none can understand'.[16]

The Duchess was a poet, a writer of successful plays and the author of provocative essays. In *Observations upon Experimental Philosophy*, in 1666, she had attacked Boyle and Hooke and the high value that the Royal Society put upon experiment. Like Hobbes and other critics she objected that their experiments revealed only superficial wonders, and their observations were often distorted. She was now extremely keen to visit the society, so they made a great exception to their rule against women and invited her to a meeting, displaying the air-pump and other wonders. At the time she seemed overcome, and could say nothing except that she was 'full of admiration, full of admiration'.[17] But with her usual energy Margaret thought over everything she had seen and diligently reworked her ideas in *The Grounds of Natural Philosophy*, published the following year. In all her work she sought a way of using reason that acknowledged the limitations of human intellect, and remained humble before the mysteries of nature. Since order was clearly visible in the natural world she concluded that a vacuum could not exist in nature, as it would 'destroy nature's unity and create disorder'. The cosmos worked, she decided, not by one body forcing another into motion, but by free will, 'general agreement', the 'consent of associating parts'. In the climate of the late 1660s, amid musing about the power of king and people, and debates about the place of men and women, this argument from 'consent', even in cosmic terms, seemed to shimmer with a political and personal resonance.

While Margaret Cavendish astonished with her ideas, she startled even more by her appearance. She wore no make-up, but covered her face with patches. She also designed her own clothes. 'I took great delight', she wrote, 'in attiring, fine dressing, and fashions, especially such fashions as I did invent myself . . . I always took delight in a singularity, even in accoutrements of habits.'[18] Her outdoor dress combined silken gowns with a man's coat and a broad, plumed, Cavalier hat; her court dress was stiff and heavy, like something from an earlier age, with a train of alarming length. When she and the duke went to see his comedy, *The Humorous Lieutenant*, at Lincoln's Inn Fields, she wore a classical-styled 'antique' dress, with bared breasts and scarlet-trimmed nipples – unfortunately more like an actress than an Amazon. At one court ball, when a woman appeared with 'at least sixty ells of gauze and silver tissue about her, not to mention a sort of pyramid upon her head, adorned with a hundred thousand baubles', Charles stopped for a moment to think. 'I bet,' he said, 'that it is the Duchess of Newcastle.'[19]

Charles was impressed as well as amused by the duchess. When the Newcastles paid their formal visit to court, he directed them to the queen's rooms after their audience with him had finished, and later joined them there, something that was considered most unusual. Like the heroine of her fantastical, feminist fiction, *The Blazing World*, which had been published – all too aptly, given its title – in 1666, Margaret Cavendish was proud of being different. She was, she wrote, 'as ambitious as ever any of my sex was, is, or can be'. Although she could not be Henry V or Charles II she could be '*Margaret* the *First*'. She could not conquer the world like Alexander or Caesar: 'Yet rather than not be mistress of one, since Fortune and the Fates would give me none, I have made a world of my own: for which no body, I hope, will blame me, since it is in every one's power to do the like.'[20]

In *The Blazing World*, carried off to sea by a ruthless merchant Margaret's heroine is saved by Providence, in the shape of a storm that carries her beyond the Arctic ice-floes, beyond the Pole to the region of animal-men – walking Bear-men, Fish-men, Bird-men, Spider-men and a host of others, who treat her as a goddess. As empress of her new world, she thinks, discusses and plans her state with care, joining with these wondrous creatures in scientific and philosophical debate. Charles's court circles abounded in strong women, not all of them brilliant, but many of them brave. But

Margaret Cavendish stood out, even in an age when women in many spheres made their mark: as mistresses of estates and court politicians behind the scenes, as actresses and writers, as printers and publishers and businesswomen and scientists.

The frontispiece to Margaret Cavendish's *Plays, Never before Printed,* 1668, uses a portrait of her on a pedestal, engraved ten years earlier, and shows her attended by Minerva, huntress and goddess of the arts, and Apollo, in his guise as god of poetry.

Charles's capital was humming and the women of all classes were a chief adornment. On May Day, Pepys was walking to Westminster 'in the way meeting many milk-maids with their garlands upon their pails, dancing with a fiddler before them; and saw pretty Nelly standing at her lodgings' door in Drury-lane in her smock sleeves-and bodice, looking upon one – she seemed a mighty pretty creature'.[21] Nell Gwyn was a stage star, but the London streets were a perpetual theatre. Every feast day had its show, from the milkmaids and maypoles on May Day to the Lord Mayor's procession in October and the marches of the guilds on their saints' days. Every square saw jugglers and acrobats and quack medicine-sellers setting up their stages and booths. Every district rang to the street-cries of the traders.

For the king, at odds with his parliament and anxious about the war and his empty treasury, there was no real breathing space. From time to time in this chilly spring of 1667 his habitual cool seemed to crack. He was unsure how to play his hand. This was seen in his abrupt attack on Buckingham in February over the business of the horoscope. And in the same month, Charles also suffered from a crisis in his affair with Frances Stuart. She was now eighteen. He offered to make her a duchess, promised her lands and swore he would banish Barbara, but still she refused him. She was in a difficult position, since her reputation was tarnished simply by his public attention, and this spring she told one courtier that she felt that she could no longer stay at court 'without prostituting herself to the King, whom she had so long kept off, though he had liberty more than any other had, or he ought to have, as to dalliance'.[22] She had come to such a pass, she said, 'as to resolve to have married any gentleman of 1500l a year that would have had her in honour'.

The man Frances found was another Charles Stuart, the third Duke of Richmond. Still in his twenties, he had been married twice, drank, gambled and was hopeless with money. His marriage to his second wife, Margaret, was furiously acrimonious and within weeks of her death in late 1666, like a man set free, he was courting Frances. Charles already disliked Richmond for his work in Middleton's now disgraced administration in Scotland. He was also irritated by a duel in 1665, for which Richmond was imprisoned in the Tower. It was alleged, although it says little for Richmond's reasoning powers, that he first became friendly with Frances because he wanted to get back into Charles's favour. By early February, when Pepys saw her wearing her hair in a new fashion, 'done up with puffes', they were meeting secretly. Later that month, after a tip-off, allegedly from Barbara Castlemaine, Charles entered Frances's room to find her in bed, with Richmond seated at her pillow.[23]

Richmond fled, and after an angry exchange with the King, Frances appealed tearfully to the queen, explaining that she and Richmond wanted to marry. Sensible and tactful, Catherine persuaded Charles to accept the marriage. But since Richmond was a relative, he required the King's permission to marry, and Charles stalled obstinately.[24] Despairing of an end to this obstruction, on a stormy night at the end of March Frances crossed London Bridge to meet the duke at the Bear at the Bridge-Foot. They eloped and were married at his estate in Kent. Scrupulously, but insultingly, she left behind the jewels Charles had given her, including a pearl necklace worth over £1,000. On 3 April the couple returned to London, to stay at the lodgings of Frances's mother, in Somerset House, hoping for forgiveness from court. None came.[25] The personal and political were always linked. Wry jokes were made when people saw the new medal for the Peace of Breda, for which Frances had sat as the model for Britannia, encircled by the motto *Favente Deo*, 'By God's Favour'.

Charles found that other small humiliations hit home. In mid-April he arrived at a Privy Council meeting to find no paper laid out for him on the table. The man responsible explained that he could provide it no longer: he was not well off, had already spent four or five hundred pounds of his own, and had not been paid since the

The Peace of Breda medal 1667. The front of the medal showed a portrait of Charles II, with the image of Britannia on the reverse, modelled from Frances Stuart, so accurately that both Pepys and Evelyn thought one could recognise her at first glance.

king was restored. After being snubbed by a servant, Charles was then attacked in his own theatre. He had shrugged off uncomfortable plays written by friends before, including Orrery's *Mustapha* in 1665, with its evil counsellor, threatened succession and infatuated king. Ned Howard's *The Change of Crownes*, which Charles watched with Catherine on 25 April, should have been standard fare, containing a double plot in which two usurpers, a brother and sister, repent and marry the legitimate rulers. Unfortunately, in the sub-plot, Charles's favourite comedian John Lacy acted 'the Country Gentleman come up to Court, who doth abuse the Court with all the imaginable wit and plainness, about selling of places and doing everything for money'.[26] As if the script was not provocative enough, Lacy added his own impromptu gags. Icy with rage, Charles had the actor confined to the porter's lodge, the theatre closed and the playbill torn down. The play was withdrawn and in the ensuing rows Lacy hit Howard with his cane, shouting that the playwright was 'more a fool than a poet'. The hierarchies of court and theatre were well and truly ruffled.

Observers thought Charles was behaving wildly. A week after his outburst over the play, on 22 April, the eve of St George's Day, there was a sumptuous banquet for the Garter knights. This was followed next day by a service, when the knights processed in solemn order, a ceremony mounted with extra show to impress the Swedish ambassador. Four days later Charles and his crew put their Garter robes back on, fooled around the court all day and even rode with them on into the park, 'which is a most scandalous thing', thought Pepys, 'so as all gravity might be said to be lost among us'.[27]

The frivolous, rushing, material world that dismayed the men of faith was returning. Yet ten days before the Garter feast, a work of eloquent gravity, in all senses, appeared in the bookshops. *Paradise Lost* passed the censor with hardly a whisper of protest. It was published by Samuel Simmons, the nephew of Milton's old friend and publisher, next door to the Golden Lion at Aldersgate, where the poet had lived during the early days of the Civil War. (Milton was paid £5 when he signed the contract, and another £5 when the first print run of thirteen hundred copies was sold.) Like the note of a great organ, heard faintly at first, his epic slowly found its readers. His former colleague Marvell wrote a sober, moving tribute and before Milton's death in 1674, Dryden approached him for permission to turn his poem into an opera for the stage, an impossible project. Charles took note. Around this time, according to Betty Milton, her husband 'was applied to by message from the King, and invited to write for the Court, but his answer was, that such behaviour would be very inconsistent with his former conduct, for he had never yet employed his pen against his conscience'.[28]

In his earlier prose Milton had written with eloquent power of the virtues of the republic, the right to freedom of speech, the need for easier divorce. In his epic he turned to battles in Heaven and joys in

Eden, to the Fall, and the promise of redemption from a corrupt world. But if the Good Old Cause and the rule of the saints were behind him, they were not forgotten. His poem was a cry to the nation to defy tyranny and to reject corruption and luxury. Moreover the fallen world that the Archangel Michael shows to Adam and Eve could appear a direct criticism of Charles II's court:

> The brazen Throat of war had ceast to roar,
> All now was turn'd to jollitie and game,
> To luxurie and riot, feast and dance,
> Marrying or prostituting, as befell,
> Rape or Adulterie, wher passing fair
> Allurd them; then from Cups to civil Broiles.

Driven from Eden by their own sin, banished by the angel's flaming sword, Milton's fallen couple enter a world where the future is all uncertain. But they still have the power to choose their way 'with Providence their guide'.

Charles rejected the guidance of Providence, and thought he could make his own luck. But this proved hard. It seemed a dark hour, yet in this space of winter and spring, between the Fire and the warmer days when the fleets might set out again and threaten war, a powerful sense of life revived flowed through his capital. Its clashing voices were full of energy, from Wren's grand plans to Margaret Cavendish's ambitious imaginings, from the experiments of the Royal Society to the sonorous, severe yet lyrical visions of Milton. These too, like the tributaries that flowed into the Thames, mixing their streams and blending at last with the sea, were part of the currents and counter-currents of Charles's first decade.

31 The Dutch in the Medway

There our sick ships unrigg'd in summer lay
Like molting fowl, a weak and easy prey,
For whose strong bulk earth scarce could timber find,
The ocean water, or the heavens wind –
Those oaken giants of the ancient race,
That rul'd all seas and did our Channel grace.

MARVELL, *Last Instructions to a Painter*

THE DUTCH WERE QUICK to see the Fire of London as God's judgement for English sins, including 'Holmes's bonfire' which had consumed their merchant ships in the Vlie Roads. They too were badly battered by the war. In September 1666 Aphra Behn wrote, 'Things are in so universal a disorder, that if God give our fleet good success at sea we shall see strange things.'[1] But when Charles tried to negotiate a peace, the States General held out for terms that would take English possessions back to before the war.

This had its bright side, as Louis held the view that the obsinacy of the Dutch freed him from his agreement with them. In secret he began to approach Charles about terms for peace. Despite this, French privateers continued to attack traffic in the Channel, damaging British customs and excise duties. In February 1667 the Navy Board gave the Duke of York a forthright account of their plight. They could place no contracts for supplies since they had only been able to pay £1,315 out of the £150,000 due to suppliers. They owed the sailors £930,000, of which they had paid £140,000.[2] They needed half a million pounds immediately, or there would be no fleet at all. In this situation Charles could take only the minimum action. He sent squadrons out to the West Indies to retake Surinam, which had been lost to the Dutch, and to Antigua and Montserrat, which had been seized by the French. Privately, he ordered James, as High Admiral, to mothball the warships and use smaller boats to police the coast, to keep privateers away and harass enemy ships. He was probably advised by Sir George Carteret, the treasurer for the navy, but this was his own decision, made outside the Privy Council, which still – like most of the public – expected the fleet to set sail. Instead of building and repairing, Charles and James concentrated on fortifying the coastal towns and ports, building new defences at Harwich and Portsmouth. Charles himself drew up plans to fortify Sheerness, on the Isle of Sheppey, guarding the mouth of the river Medway, where most of the fleet was laid up in Chatham dockyards. He also went down to talk to the engineers.

It was a gamble, but Charles argued that this policy was the only way he could play the poor cards left in his hand. There was no way he could repair the whole fleet. Even if all the new grant was collected, the money was already committed to pay existing bills. After that, the treasury was bankrupt. The run of play, and of luck, had gone against him and all he could do now was sue for peace. And of course, if peace was in the offing, he would have no need for a new battle fleet anyway.[3] Yet he might still have been able to raise funds if he had appealed to the City, and his decision would later be seen as an inexplicable lapse of judgement.

When he dismissed parliament in February Charles said, 'I must tell you, that if any good Overtures be made for an Honourable Peace, I will not reject them.'[4] In fact talks had already begun. Louis's attack on the Spanish Netherlands would be helped by English neutrality, and he had hinted to St Albans, Henrietta Maria's burly, card-playing chief adviser and close companion, that he would make peace if Charles promised not to enter into any alliances contrary to French interests (in other words with Spain) for at least a year. In return France would restore the English possessions seized in the West Indies, and broker a good peace deal with the Dutch.

In February, encouraged by Clarendon, Charles secretly signed these terms, which were formally agreed in early April.

Charles made no public statement for fear of deterring his anti-French parliament from raising money. But news of the 'underhand' treaty leaked out, reaching the Dutch. This was awkward, as in Holland Arlington was negotiating with de Witt on opposite lines, offering to help protect the Spanish Netherlands against the French, in return for the island of Pulo Run and compensation for English losses. In his approaches to de Witt, Arlington suggested that their peace talks be held in the Hague. This offer to meet on their enemies' home ground was partly a symbolic gesture, implying that England really did want peace, contrary to the propaganda of the States General. But the Hague was also a good place for the supporters of the House of Orange to make their presence felt, and for that very reason, de Witt turned the suggestion down. Eventually, after much to-ing and fro-ing, it was settled that they would meet at Breda. The English delegates, Denzil Holles and Henry Coventry (William Coventry's brother), set off in late April, arrived on 4 May and began their talks ten days later. Charles was optimistic and instructed his ambassadors to press hard for the terms he wanted. The Dutch, however, had other plans. That winter, de Witt had already persuaded the States General to grant money for preparing an even stronger fleet, but when agents reported this to London it was seen simply as a move to strengthen the Dutch at the conference table: 'Som will have it best to make peace with the sword in the hand.'[5]

De Witt certainly had sword in hand, and was determined to show his strength, both to avenge the Vlie raid and to force concessions from the English delegates. The Dutch commander Van Ghent sailed over to Scotland and on 1 May led a squadron into the Firth of Forth, hovering opposite Leith harbour, alarming the local people. But this was only a warning: the real target was the Thames. Among the prisoners of war in Holland de Witt had found two English pilots who knew the tricky shores and shoals of the Thames estuary, and had recruited English sailors from among the exiled republicans. An English dissident, the mysterious Thomas Dolman, mustered a large force of troops and marines. On 4 June these troops joined the Dutch fleet and set sail. De Witt's brother Cornelis sailed with them, on board Admiral de Ruyter's flagship.

So confident was Charles that the Dutch wanted peace that he and his councillors largely ignored reports about the movements of their fleet. They were worried enough, however, for Arlington to warn the Lords Lieutenant of coastal counties to keep their militia on the alert. As for the Medway, the government were relying on Charles's detailed orders for fortifying Sheerness. The only action they took was to place a heavy chain across the river, protecting the warships laid up at Chatham. They had no doubt that these defences would hold.

On 1 June Charles was at Greenwich, watching tests of new cast-iron grenades. By then Van Ghent had sailed down from Scotland to meet de Ruyter, and on Friday 7 June watchmen spotted a large Dutch fleet off the North Foreland. Over the next three days, although hampered by slackening winds, the Dutch moved slowly towards their target. First Van Ghent led his squadron along the Thames estuary's north coast, landing briefly on Canvey Island, burning barns and killing sheep for his ships' stores. The threat was clear, and desperate actions were taken, all too late. The Duke of York ordered an alarm sent to all the dockyards, frantic work took place in Plymouth and Portsmouth, militia were sent to the Isle of Wight and a Scottish regiment was despatched to Margate, to fend off any invasion. Charles hastily borrowed £10,000 from the City to pay for new defences along the Thames, and ordered Albemarle to take charge in Chatham. Then he sent Rupert to Woolwich to supervise defences, and commanded Coventry to organise fireships. The naval officials scurried down to Deptford, wrote Pepys, 'and pitched upon ships and set men to work but Lord! to see how back-wardly things move at this pinch'.[6] The Dutch prizes, and the merchantmen that lay at anchor at Chatham, were moved further up the river and guard-ships were placed in the creeks to defend the chain. But when the first guns were heard Albemarle was still at Gravesend, 'with a great many idle lords and gentlemen, with their pistols and fooleries'.

On Tuesday 11 June, riding the incoming tide, the Dutch surged up the Medway. The much-vaunted Sheerness defences had never been finished and the Dutch took the fort easily, capturing its guns and valuable stores and landing eight hundred men. English troops arrived too late and were confused about their orders – many spent their time looting the houses that terrified occupants had abandoned. The precious fireships, so rapidly assembled, were sunk to blockade the narrow channels. It was no use. Next morning Van Ghent's ships passed Sheerness and marshalled at the mouth of the Medway. Albemarle arrived to find the local workmen in a panic. There was hardly any ammunition, either at Chatham or at Upnor Castle on the opposite bank, and every small boat had been taken to carry away the goods of frightened householders. The Dutch hacked their way slowly through the ships that had been sunk to defend the chain, destroying and setting fire to the guard-ships. The following morning, 13 June, with their canvas taut against the wind, they sailed on upriver, exchanging shots with the guards at Upnor Castle and with Sir Edward Spragge's battery on the southern shore. Then they broke through the chain as if it was a rope of straw, and burst into the sheltered reach of Chatham where the big warships were moored. Rounding the river bend they took the grounded *Sancta Maria* and went on to capture their supreme prize, the flagship the *Royal Charles*. When Cornelis de Witt wrote his report to the States General, he headed his letter 'In the Royal Charles . . . about two in the afternoon, lying in the River of Chatham'.[7]

Standing on the shore, Albemarle watched the ships burn. The General was, as Clarendon said, 'of a constitution and temper so void of fear, that there could appear no sign of distraction in him: yet it was plain enough that he knew not what orders to give'.[8] When the Dutch broke the chain Albemarle even thought of taking a ship out himself, with a group of volunteers, but was soon persuaded that he would merely be leading them to their deaths. All that he and Commissioner Pett could do was to send out longboats to help the sailors who were trapped. He knew that the main body of the fleet under de Ruyter still lay off the coast, and might be back the next day.

Sure enough, on the next morning's tide the Dutch returned, sailing with astounding bravery under the batteries of guns that Albemarle had now organised. This time they sent fireships into the Chatham docks, blasting three more ships of glorious names, the *Royal James*, the *Royal Oak* and *Loyal London*. All on board fled, except for the Scottish soldier Archibald Douglas, who stayed alone on the *Royal Oak* until it went down in flames – the one act of heroism of the whole episode. 'Fixt on his Shipp, he fought the horrid day', wrote Marvell, 'And wondred much at those who ran away.'[9] Everyone was running away, although after abandoning a sketchy attack on the Chatham dockyard itself, the Dutch left the river, deciding that the sunken ships that Albemarle had put in their way made any further sally too risky. Displaying a bravado and skill that made all on land marvel they steered the *Royal Charles* downriver through the shallow waters, braving difficult tides and contrary winds. Their triumph was complete.

There was panic in London. It was rumoured that the Dutch had landed and the drums were sounded to raise the Trained Bands. People sent their families into the country with all their valuable goods, plate and reserves of cash. There were reports of English sailors going over to the Dutch and in Wapping the seamen's wives cried, 'This comes of your not paying our husbands.'[10] When a fire broke out at Deptford, the town was in uproar, believing the Dutch were already there. Arlington's secretary, Joseph Williamson, received alarmed letters from across the country. James Bentham, for one, wrote from East Anglia, 'The beacons are on fire, and some say that Harwich, Colchester and Dover are burned, and the King gone out of town or out of the world.'[11] Anxious letters from Devon,

A panoramic view, looking upriver to Chatham and Rochester, and bringing
together the events of all three days. In the centre, the masts of sunken ships mark
the point where the chain was strung across the river, and in the foreground the
Royal Charles is being towed away.

Hull and Chester voiced the same refrain, 'All conclude that there
was treachery in the business, and hope the contrivers will receive
the reward due to those who betray King and country.'

In the wake of this humiliation, on 25 June Charles summoned
parliament to meet in late July, breaking into its summer recess.
During the Medway alarm he had ordered an army to be raised,
twelve regiments under the command of old Commonwealth generals, including Marsden and Fairfax. The troops were ready within three weeks. He wrote to the East India Company pleading for
contributions to pay the navy and begged the nobility and gentry
to support the new land forces. But instead of appeasing critics, this
move roused fears of an old bogey, a standing army under royal
control. When parliament assembled, member after member
demanded that the troops be dismissed, in a sequence of angry
speeches.

On 21 July, the Treaty of Breda was signed. As soon the news was confirmed four days later, Charles briskly dismissed the MPs, asserting the crisis was over. They had met for only four days, and many had just unpacked their bags after their journey from the country. 'The parliament', wrote Clarendon, putting it mildly, 'that had been so unseasonably called together from their business and recreations, in a season of the year that they most desired to be vacant, were not pleased to be so soon dismissed.'[12] To win them over, Charles ordered the new army to be disbanded within a month, while to soothe the MPs' anti-Catholic fears, Catholics were purged from civil and military offices by being compelled to take the Oath of Allegiance and Supremacy. They were also banned from court, and British subjects were forbidden to attend mass in any ambassadors' chapels.[13]

The Treaty of Breda itself was curiously anti-climactic. Both countries kept their conquests, England forfeiting its claim to Pulo Run and losing the West African forts except Fort James and Cape Coast Castle, but gaining New York and New Jersey. Until the treaty was finally ratified on 24 August, the Dutch kept up the pressure, cruising coolly off the English coast. People were relieved that trade was now free to flourish, but everywhere there was a feeling of let-down, a sense that England had submitted weakly, and dishonourably. The revelation that the French had known of the planned raid on the Medway added to the feeling that Louis had been playing with English interests all along, lulling Charles with false promises.[14]

When people heard that on the day of the Medway attack, Charles had not stayed with his troops but had come back to London and spent the evening playing at trivial party games after dinner with Barbara Castlemaine, the Duke of Monmouth and others, they were quick to compare him to Nero. And after the treaty was signed Pepys noted that the merchants at the Exchange did not seem glad, 'but rather the worse, they looking upon it as a peace made only to preserve the king for a time in his lust and ease'.[15] It was widely believed, he added, that 'the king and court were never in the world so bad as they are now for gaming, swearing, whoring and drinking, and the most abominable vices that ever were in the world – so that all must come to naught'. All through the summer, he filled his diary with reported conversations linking the licence of the courts to the national disasters. Even the royal chaplain Dr Creighton, he noted, preached a sermon against adultery, 'over and over instancing how for that single sin in David, the whole nation was undone', and then moving swiftly to the lack of ammunition at Chatham.[16]

Gossip about the court rippled through the bitter post-mortem on the war. In particular a deluge of satire was prompted by two long, pro-government narrative poems. The first was Edmund Waller's *Instructions to a Painter, for the Drawing of the Posture and Progress of his Majesties Forces at Sea, under the Command of his Highness Royal* which celebrated the Duke of York's naval victories in 1665. Waller's imitation of a Venetian poem, in which the poet had celebrated a naval victory over the Turks by instructing a painter how to depict the battle, immediately provoked parodies, offering acid revisions of the heroic accounts. These included *The Second* and *Third Advice to a Painter*, circulated in manuscript in 1666.

In answer to these attacks, Dryden published his *Annus Mirabilis: The Year of Wonders*, which he had been composing since 1665 and which tried to counter the 'Advice' poems and prodigy-ridden *Annus Mirabilis* pamphlets by painting the battles and the Fire in epic terms. Just as Dryden had described Charles as a potential Augustus in 1660, now he portrayed him as Aeneas, concerned for his people and the fate of his country. He even took on the assertion that the disasters were a judgement on the King and his court, giving Charles a dramatic prayer during the Fire, in which he asks to be made a sacrifice for the ills of his people.

> Or if my heedless Youth has stept astray,
> Too soon forgetful of thy gracious hand
> On me alone thy just displeasure lay,
> But take thy judgments from this mourning Land.

We all have sinn'd, and thou hast laid us low,
As humble Earth from whence at first we came:
Like flying shades before the clowds we show
And shrink like Parchment in consuming flame.[17]

Annus Mirabilis was a fine poem, rich in effects and feeling, but in 1667 such rhetoric merely roused scorn. The hollow laughter grew louder after the publication of Marvell's devastating *Last Instructions to a Painter* in the same year, adding to its sharp picture of the idiocies of the war a blow-by-blow account of the stupidity of factions in parliament.

Andrew Marvell

Instead of lauding their courage, the satires showed the government and its naval and military leaders – with the exception of Albemarle and the brave Captain Douglas – mired in cowardice, chaos, negligence and greed. The printing was actively aided by Marvell and by his patron, the puritan Lord Wharton, and when the 'Advice' poems were published in a single volume, the unlicensed printers were rounded up (including Elizabeth Calvert).[18]

But the poems could not be written off as the work of sectarian conspirators. Most dissenters had been stoutly loyal during the war. The satires were a trenchant critique of government incompetence, mirroring the despair of the whole nation. Furthermore, they showed the first stirrings of a publicly voiced opposition, a new dynamic that would in time replace court intrigue as the nation's political driving force, leading, through the Whigs, to the party politics that have defined public life ever since.

After the plague and the Fire, who would take the blame for the Medway disaster? The naval commissioners Sir William Coventry and Peter Pett, who was in charge of Chatham dockyard, and Sir Edward Spragge, nominally in command of the ships in the Medway (and doubly under suspicion as an 'Irish papist'), were all abused for incompetence. There were even mutterings about the doubtful loyalty of the Chatham dock-workers. On 17 June Pett was arrested and taken to the Tower, to be interrogated by a committee of the Privy Council. Coventry's nephew George Savile, by now Earl of Halifax, wrote to his brother Henry, 'He is most undoubtedly to be sacrificed; all that are the greater lay the fault upon him in hopes that he is to bear all the blame; the town has no mind to be so satisfied.'[19] He was right on both points. The government certainly hoped that the sacrifice of Pett would calm the public rage. The day after Pett's arrest, Arlington wrote to Ormond, 'if he deserve hanging, as most thinke he does, and have it, much of the staine will be wip'd off the Government which lyes heavily upon it'.[20]

That autumn in parliament, a committee of inquiry was appointed into the miscarriages of the war, looking at mishaps as far back as 1664–5. Henry Brouncker, for example, was questioned about taking false orders to Sir John Harman to lower sails and thus let the Dutch get away after the Battle of Lowestoft. The following April, Brouncker was dismissed from the Commons in disgrace.[21] Sir William Penn was threatened with impeachment for his part in sharing and selling the cargoes of the East Indiamen that Sandwich had captured. Raising more recent matters, William Coventry, an eloquent speaker who, with his brother Henry, had practically been Leader of the House during the last two years, tried to blame Albemarle for the Medway disaster, but was firmly rebuffed by the General's supporters.

Pett, however, was the first victim. When he appeared before the Commons committee he made a miserable impression and Albemarle's statement, accusing him of negligence down to the smallest detail – in not providing sufficient tools and boats, and using deal planks instead of oak boards, so that the shots whistled through them – was devastating.[22] The final charge, that he had not taken the *Royal Charles* further upriver as ordered, sealed his fate. 'It is believed he will prove a very great criminal,' wrote Sir John Milward, who was following each day's debate with furrowed brow, 'but very much friended by the old gang.'[23] Despite his powerful friends, Pett was the handy scapegoat, a point that Marvell hammered home in *Last Instructions to a Painter* in angry, echoing rhyme.

> After this loss, to relish discontent,
> Someone must be accused by Punishment.
> All our miscarriages on Pett must fall:
> His name alone seems fit to answer all . . .
> Who all our Seamen cheated of their debt?
> And all our Prizes, who did swallow? *Pett.*
> Who did advise no Navy out to set?
> And who the Forts left unrepaired? *Pett.*[24]

Articles of impeachment were drawn up, but when parliament was dismissed in November the matter was dropped. The following February Pett was formally dismissed as commissioner of the navy; he retired into obscurity, dying four years later, never clearing his name. But Arlington's hope that Pett's disgrace might shield other government figures proved vain. The public rage was not so easily slaked. And in their mind the chief culprit, among all those deemed responsible, was the Lord Chancellor, Edward Hyde, Lord Clarendon.

32 The Blows Fall on Clarendon

> Pride, lust, ambition, and the people's hate,
> The kingdom's broker, ruin of the state,
> Dunkirk's sad loss, divider of the fleet,
> Tangier's compounder for a barren sheet,
> This shrub of gentry, married to the Crown
> (His daughter to the heir), is tumbl'd down.
>   ANON., 'The Downfall of the Chancellor'[1]

CLARENDON'S PALATIAL HOUSE in Piccadilly, said to have been paid for with bribes from the sale of Dunkirk and built with the stones put aside to mend St Paul's, was still rising, a visible symbol of his overweening power. Charles had been loyal to Clarendon through earlier efforts to unseat him, like Bristol's attempt at impeachment in 1663. But he had now become irritated. In a haunting passage in *Last Instructions*, Marvell deftly implied the ruthless calculation and knowledge of his courtiers that lay beneath Charles's mask. In his dreams the king is accosted by a pale and beautiful Britannia (a figure he eyes lustfully, of course, until he sees she is a phantom) and then by the ghost of his grandfather Henry IV and his father Charles I, with the 'purple thread about his neck'. Dawn breaks.

> The wondrous night the pensive King resolves,
> And rising straight on Hyde's disgrace resolves.
> At his first step he Castlemaine does find,
> Bennet, and Coventry, as 'twere designed;
> And they, not knowing, the same thing propose
> Which his hid mind did in its depths enclose.[2]

Charles could let this designing crew do the work, without any effort on his part. Clarendon had become a problem. He was increasingly pompous in defending tradition and blocking measures advocated by new ministers like Arlington and Coventry. Worse, he had lost his old skill at manipulating parliament. In the winter of 1666 he had failed to win the Commons round over the Irish Cattle Bill, and had enraged them by his stubbornness over the Canary Patent. He was so dominant in the council chamber, Downing reported, that the king 'doth call the Chancellor that insolent man and says that he would not let him speak himself in council'.[3]

At the start of 1667, Clarendon was ill and tired. After the Fire he had moved from Worcester House, where his lease was almost up, to stay with his son Laurence's parents-in-law, the Burlingtons, at Berkshire House, opposite St James's Palace. They were kind and considerate, but as winter drew in he felt out of place, dreading the gout that always came with the cold. It arrived as he expected and while he was laid up, from January to March, forces mobilised against him. Clarendon was fifty-six, but seemed older than his years, tetchy and overbearing, his natural impatience inflamed by stress and pain. And although Charles's affection for him endured, he had become tired of his lectures and of hearing courtiers joke, 'There goes your schoolmaster!' As Thomas Carte put it, 'The king was weary of a minister, of whom from his earliest youth he had learned to stand in awe, and who still seemed to keep up an authority over him by the remonstrances which he made to him on all occasions and with little ceremony.'[4] This impatience is still heard in a story remembered many years later. Charles, it related, seeing a man in the pillory, asked what his crime was. It was libelling Lord Clarendon, he was told. 'Odds fish! crys the King, why did not the Fool go on libelling of mee, he must now certainly suffer for libelling this great man.'[5]

The last straw was the idea that Clarendon had interfered in his relationship with Frances Stuart. Charles knew that Clarendon wanted to prevent an affair and he became suspicious when he bumped into Clarendon's son, Cornbury, who was taking Frances a message from the queen, on the very night that he discovered

Frances and Richmond together. Cornbury, wrote Burnet, 'met the
king in the door coming out full of fury', and Charles 'spoke to him
as one in a rage, that forgot all decency, and for some time would
not hear Lord Cornbury speak in his own defence'.[6] His opponents
whispered that Clarendon had forwarded the Richmond marriage
because he feared that Charles might divorce Catherine and marry
Frances; their children would then block his own grandchildren's
route to the throne.

The idea that involvement in the Richmond marriage was to
blame for Clarendon's downfall is far-fetched. But it may well be
that Charles's resentment blocked any remaining impulse to protect
his chancellor from the coming storm. Clarendon was undoubtedly
shaken by the king's anger, and during the summer, more blows followed. In May his two young grandsons died, James, Duke of
Cambridge, and Charles, Duke of Kendal, aged three and one. His
old friend Southampton died in the same month and to his distress,
instead of appointing a new Lord Treasurer, Charles made the bold
decision to put the Treasury in commission. There were six commissioners: Ashley, Clifford and Coventry (all of whom Clarendon
loathed), as well as Albemarle, Sir John Duncombe and Downing,
as treasury secretary. Together they scrutinised the creaking work-
ings of the old system and put in place fundamental reforms. The
old order was passing. Clarendon poured out his anxieties in long
letters to Ormond, as if he feared that he too would desert him.
Writing of Southampton's death, he lamented, 'I have lost a frende,
a fast and unshaken frende, and whether my only frende or not, you
only know.'[7] Would Ormond, the last of the old crowd, stand by him
'against all temptacions and assaults'?

After the attack on the Medway in June, Clarendon found himself
the prime target of popular fury. The trees in front of his Piccadilly
house were lopped down, his windows were broken, and a gibbet
was painted on his gate. His enemies were gathering. Buckingham
had been in hiding since the order for his arrest for commissioning
the horoscope in February. But his battles in the last parliament had

Clarendon House

made him a hero to many, and after the Medway disaster he was sure that the government would not risk more public anger by pressing charges against him. He now came out of hiding and gave himself up. On 28 June he asked Robert Howard to take a letter to Charles, begging forgiveness. Clarendon insisted on a formal surrender, but when he was taken to the Tower, Buckingham staged a triumphal rather than penitential progress. He stopped on the way to dine at the Sun Inn in Bishopsgate with powerful supporters – Lords Rivers, Buckhurst, Vaughan and the Duke of Monmouth. Here 'he showed himself to a numerous body of spectators with great ceremony from the balcony, openly threatening his accusers, and that Parliament should execute vengence on his enemies'.[8]

Such public theatre was a blatant assertion of Buckingham's power. In July he was released from the Tower, partly as a sop to his supporters in parliament, who were smarting at their abrupt summons and dismissal after the Breda treaty. In a brief Privy Council hearing, the horoscope charges were dismissed almost as a formality.

Buckingham was so confident that he felt able to toss off a careless jibe without fear. 'It is said,' wrote Pepys,

that when he was charged with making himself popular (as endeed he is, for many of the discontented Parliament . . . did attend at the Council-chamber when he was examined), he should answer that whoever was committed to prison by my Lord Chancellor or my Lord Arlington could not want being popular.[9]

Pepys may have been right that it was Buckingham's popularity which had most angered Charles in the spring. At that point Charles had not yet fallen out with Clarendon, and he rushed to show the Chancellor the depositions, including the letters to the duke from an astrologer, which, he said, 'gave him the style of prince, and mentioned what great things his stars promised to him, and that he was the darling of the people, who had set their hearts and affections and all their hopes upon his highness, with many other foolish and fustian expressions'.[10] This dangerous ambition was now forgotten, or at least overlooked. When Barbara Castlemaine pleaded for her cousin in July, Charles was not quite ready, and she 'so far solicited for him', wrote Pepys, 'that the King and she are quite fallen out; he comes not to her nor hath for some three or four days, and parted with very foul words, the King calling her a whore, and a jade that meddled with things she had nothing to do withal'.[11] But shortly afterwards, Barbara arranged a meeting between Charles and Buckingham at her apartments. The duke was allowed to kiss the king's hand and return to court. After a quickly staged rapprochement with Arlington he was ready to do battle with Clarendon again.

In the same month Clarendon's wife Frances fell ill. She died on 9 August, 'so sudden, unexpected and irreparable a loss, that he had not courage to support'.[12] She was buried in Westminster Abbey a week later, and Charles visited Clarendon to offer his sympathy and support. But there was hardly time for private grief. Before another fortnight had passed Clarendon's son-in-law the Duke of York came to see him, looking troubled. Charles, said James, was concerned at reports that when parliament met the Commons were planning to start proceedings towards impeaching the Chancellor, 'who was grown very odious to them'. Once proceedings began, Charles would no longer be able to divert them or protect him. The only course, the king believed, was for Clarendon to surrender his seals of office, and go.[13] Or, as an anonymous poet put it pithily in the voice of Charles,

> I will have my Chancellor bear all the sway,
> Yet if Men should clamor I'll pack him away.[14]

As soon as the news leaked that Clarendon had been asked to resign, his family and supporters rallied round. His daughter Anne, Duchess of York, appealed to Charles in tears and his son Cornbury openly blamed Arlington. On 25 August, Charles sent Albemarle to talk to him, and persuade him to give up the seals. Again, Clarendon refused. The next day, around ten o'clock Clarendon went to his room at Whitehall. He had not been there long before the king and Duke came in, by themselves. At once Clarendon went on the offensive. What fault had he committed that Charles should be so severe? Even in Clarendon's own third-person telling one can almost hear Charles's indrawn breath, and exasperation. In reply, the king said that he 'must always acknowledge', wrote Clarendon, 'that he had always served him honest and faithfully, and that he did believe that never king had a better servant, and that he had taken this resolution for his good and preservation'. James, Charles asserted, agreed. James demurred, huffed, and contradicted, but Charles talked on. If impeachment began, he insisted, Clarendon would no more be able to defend himself against parliament than his father's minister Strafford had been all those years ago, whereas if he went now, Charles could at least guarantee his safety. The mention of Strafford, who had been impeached and executed after Charles I signed his death warrant in tears, was a clear warning.

Charles and Clarendon talked for two hours, during which the Chancellor argued strongly that giving in to demands for his dismissal would irrevocably weaken the position of the crown in parliament. Then, fatally, he began to lecture Charles about Barbara Castlemaine, 'and in the warmth of this relation he found a seasonable opportunity to mention the lady with some reflections and cautions, which he might more advisedly have declined'.[15] Charles rose without speaking and left the room. Even James was taken aback. In an oft-described scene, like a climax in Shakespeare, Clarendon walked out into the Privy Garden, where a crowd of courtiers had gathered and, 'the lady, the Lord Arlington, and Mr May, looked together out of her open window with great gaiety and triumph, which all people observed'.[16] It was obvious from the King's demeanour and from Clarendon's expression that he would now be dismissed. Barbara, so Pepys heard, leapt from bed and ran into the aviary in her smock, 'and stood herself joying at the old man's going away'. Four days later, on 30 August, Charles sent Orlando Bridgeman to collect the Great Seal.

A few days after the dismissal of his Lord Chancellor, Charles had a long meeting with Buckingham. 'My lord of Buckingham has made but few visits to court since he came out of his trouble,' wrote Henry Savile, 'but was yesterday two hours alone with the King in his closet.'[17] By the end of September, Buckingham was restored to the Privy Council and to his position close to Charles, as a Gentleman of the Bedchamber. He also patched up his quarrels with Barbara, who was eager for an ally in her fight against the Chancellor.

Buckingham, Clarendon's deadliest opponent, now had the ear of the king, the Lords and the Commons. He was there, in the House of Lords, when parliament met again on 10 October. Almost before proceedings began, his allies, including William Coventry, suggested that both houses should thank the king for removing the Chancellor. Charles assured them that Clarendon would never be employed on official business again. He clearly wanted him to stand down and go to the country. But Clarendon stayed and fought his corner, using all his old legal training. His defiance began to infuriate Charles, already pressured by the Commons' attack on the handling of the war. On 20 October 1667, bowing to the Commons' will, he agreed to Clarendon's impeachment. By early November, Buckingham and Bristol – who had suddenly reappeared to gloat over his old enemy after three years lying low and out of favour – had drawn up seventeen articles of impeachment. These ranged from collecting bribes in relation to the Irish land settlement and the Canary patent, to the sale of Dunkirk, the division of the fleet before the Four Days Battle, and the plan for a standing army. Crucially, he was even accused of divulging secret information to the French, and this highly dubious charge, based only on a casual remark of the Austrian ambassador, Lisola, was tantamount to treason.

One by one, the MPs spoke, with mounting bitterness. In the notes on the debate, one can feel their resentment of Clarendon as a man who had held the reins of power too tight, for too long, infuriating MPs by his apparent contempt for them. Charles offered no support, and in November Clarendon wrote him an impassioned letter, declaring that he was so broken under the signs of his displeasure, that he did not know what to do or to wish for. He was innocent in every respect, he pleaded, including involvement in the marriage of Frances Stuart and Richmond, where he was as free of guilt as an unborn child. He asked the King's pardon for any 'saucy or overbold expressions' he might have used, and begged him, appealing to the memory of his father Charles I, to 'put a stop to this severe persecution against me'.[18] Charles, Clarendon later recorded in neutral tones, was in his cabinet when the letter was brought to him. As soon as he read it he burned it in the flame of a candle standing on the table, and said 'that there was somewhat in it that he did not understand, but that he wondered that the chancellor did not withdraw himself'.

Clarendon still refused to flee, sure of his innocence and determined to beat his foes. It was now becoming too late to retreat to his country house, where he could easily be arrested. At this point Charles sent another old friend to see him, the gentle Bishop

Morley, accompanied by the Bishop of Hereford, who brought assurances of safe passage if he would leave the country. He replied that he was too ill to travel fast, and that he must have a safe pass from the king to save him from arrest while still in England. Buckingham's ally Edward Seymour had already taken the indictment to the House of Lords, asking them to order Clarendon's committal. The Duke of York was absent from the Lords, recovering from a mild bout of smallpox, but Ashley, Sheldon and most of the bishops spoke on Clarendon's behalf, while Bristol, Albemarle, Arlington and Ossory, the son of his old friend Ormond, all spoke against him. On 20 November Buckingham protested vehemently against the Lords' reluctance to try the Chancellor on a general charge of treason, a charge which, if he were found guilty, brought the penalty of death. When they refused to impeach him, dismissing Lisola's remark about his dealings with the French, Clarendon was triumphant.

Opposed by his own House of Lords, Charles smarted with rage. Word spread that he would soon dismiss parliament and arrange for Clarendon to be tried by twenty-four of his peers, in a special court, chaired by Buckingham. Such a court would almost inevitably sentence him to death. The French ambassador offered him refuge (a promise that would later prove problematic), and the Duke of York persuaded Morley to visit him again and tell him that he must leave at once.

Morley saw Clarendon on the morning of 30 November. Later that day, Evelyn found him 'at his new built Palace sitting in his Gowt wheel charyre' gazing at the gates and the fields to the north, where 'he looked & spake very disconsolately'.[19] Evelyn took his leave, and next morning heard that he was gone. A friend had arranged for a custom cutter to wait for him down the Thames at Erith, and when darkness fell Clarendon clambered into his coach, accompanied by two servants. His two sons rode with him. An hour later they said their farewells and the boat cast off, only to be becalmed as the wind slackened and carried briefly back upstream by the tide. At last, the cutter sailed down the Thames, past the marshes of Kent and Essex, into the King's Channel and then south, to France. Three days later Clarendon was in Calais. After many months of illness and adventures, he settled in Montpellier, where he lived until his death in December 1674. He occupied his time in writing his *Life*, a continuation of the *History of the Great Rebellion* that he had written during his first long exile. He never relinquished his hopes of returning home.

33 The Triple Alliance

Nay, he could sail a yacht both light and large,
Knew how to trim a boat and steer a barge;
Could say his compass, to the nation's joy,
And swear as well as any cabin-boy.
But not one lesson of the ruling art
Could this dull blockhead ever get by heart.
BUCKINGHAM, 'The Cabin-boy'

DESPITE BUCKINGHAM'S SCORN in this verse, full of the bile of later battles, Charles had in fact learnt the rudiments of the ruling art. He wanted to steer his ship of state alone, and Clarendon's fall allowed him to go ahead with changes he had been pondering for some time. He wanted to loosen the control of the Privy Council, which he had sometimes found as irksome as that of the House of Commons. He also wanted to handle his own money, freeing the Privy Purse from the rule of the Exchequer. In late August 1667, when he demanded the chancellor's seals from Clarendon, he had a team at the ready. He was determined that no one councillor would dominate as Clarendon had done, almost as if he took note of Marvell's accusation that his advisers were cutting him off from the nation:

Bold and accurs'd are they that all this while
Have strove to isle our Monarch from his isle,
And to improve themselves, on false pretence
About the common Prince have rais'd a fence.[1]

His decision to gamble on being more open, and to display his majesty in public rather than letting his people judge him through

salacious rumours, showed in small but significant things. He began
to dine in public again in the state apartments, a practice that had
been abandoned in the economies of 1663. In early August, after
noting a trivial chat with the king about swimming, a delighted
Evelyn wrote, 'Now did his Majestie againe dine in the Presence in
antient State, with Musique and all the Court ceremonies which had
been interrupted since the late warr.'[2]

In politics, his decision to take a personal, public lead meant that
courtiers and officials felt even less secure. In particular Charles set
about juggling carefully between the men of the moment, Arlington
and Buckingham. These two were seen as the leaders of a new inner
group of five. The others were Ashley, Clifford, and Lauderdale,
now firmly ensconced in Edinburgh. But despite the neat shorthand
of their initials – Clifford, Arlington, Buckingham, Ashley and
Lauderdale – there was no coherent 'Cabal'. They were not natural
allies. Arlington and Buckingham could not stand each other,
Lauderdale was preoccupied with Scotland, Clifford was a near-
Catholic, while Buckingham sympathised with the dissenters, and
so did Ashley, who also retained much of his earlier republican loyalties. This was not a team that would form a policy based on
shared principles. Instead their approach was pragmatic, reacting to
events more than guiding them. If Charles himself had a long-term
aim, it was carefully concealed.

In late 1667, as recriminations about the war echoed through
Westminster, Charles's main concern was to put the humiliations of
the Medway attack and the Breda treaty behind him. It was as if he
narrowed his eyes and looked at Europe as a chequerboard spread
out before him and worked out the odds, placing groups of counters
in different combinations and seeing what advantages they might
bring. He needed a pause to work out his next direction.

The increasing power of France at sea, and Louis's bold sweep
across the Spanish Netherlands on land, made Charles seek conciliation with the French as soon as possible. This tack was favoured by

Buckingham, who was keen to join the French in a booty-taking war against Spain. Arlington, by contrast, had been pro-Spanish and anti-French since his time in Madrid in the 1650s, so his instinct was to forge a Dutch treaty first. This inclination was bolstered by his surprise marriage in April 1666, in the middle of the war, to Isabella van Beverweerd, daughter of Lodewyck van Nassau, head of the Dutch embassy to Britain at the Restoration. At a quiet wedding at Arlington's country house, Moor Park, the bride was given away by Ormond's son Ossory, who had married Isabella's sister Aemilia in the last days of exile. Isabella brought important connections, not only with Ossory and Ormond: her father was an illegitimate son of Prince Maurice of Orange and she was thus cousin to William of Orange. She also brought a dowry of a hundred thousand guilders to add to Arlington's income from fees and from the Post Office, of which he became head in December 1666. On a personal level, she was a skilful hostess, as serious and discreet as her husband. Their only child, the adored 'Tata', was born in 1667. At the Restoration Arlington had come back from Madrid with virtually nothing, but he was now a man of substance, owning Euston Hall in Suffolk (handy for Newmarket), and Goring House, at the end of St James's Park, on the site of the later Buckingham Palace. He could not yet rival Buckingham, but with Isabella he made Goring House a centre for London's polite society. He was a power in the land and, he hoped, in Europe.

At the end of November 1667, in uneasy partnership, Arlington and Buckingham met the French ambassador, Henri de Massue, marquis de Ruvigny.[3] They offered to recognise Louis's conquests in the Spanish Netherlands in return for an alliance against the Dutch, and British control of the ports of Ostend and Niuewpoort. Arlington was on crutches, limping from an accident when his coach was overturned, and as they left and he struggled ahead, so that he would not hold up their coach, Ruvigny grabbed Buckingham and urged him to persuade Charles to a French deal.[4]

The omens looked promising but although he wanted the treaty,

Louis, secure in his conquest, rejected Charles's particular demands. Without a quiver, Charles immediately did a swift volte-face and discreetly approached the Dutch. Although they had so recently been England's enemies, this line was more likely to be popular at home, where outrage at French 'perfidy' was loud. The first move had come, rather surprisingly, from Holland, when Johann de Witt hinted that the Dutch were alarmed at French aggression in Flanders: an alliance with England might, perhaps, be possible, its aim being to stop the war between France and Spain in the Low Countries. The twists and turns continued. Three days after Buckingham and Arlington talked with Ruvigny the Privy Council sent Sir William Temple, a man of immense energy and commit-ment, to make approaches to de Witt. He carried with him the min-utes of the meeting with the French ambassador, subtly edited by Arlington to show how the French were manoeuvring against their supposed Dutch allies. 'You shall plainly tell Monsieur de Witte', Arlington told him, that the Privy Council would like to know if England and Holland could form a league to protect the Spanish Netherlands, 'and if the interests of both Nations shall require it, even against France itselfe'.[5] Temple was also specifically instructed to say that although Charles still felt 'all possible kindness for his nephew, the Prince of Orange', this should not interfere with 'the great interest betwixt the nations, which must ever be superior to that particular one'.[6] At the cost of family loyalty, one major cause of friction was therefore shelved.

Arlington was still slightly concerned that de Witt might be using the threat of an English alliance to force concessions from the French. He therefore worked hard to ensure that British merchants' fears about a Dutch monopoly were recognised, demanding that the Dutch should not block access to independent trading districts by building forts, or make exclusive contracts with local peoples. Not all the demands were met, but nonetheless, in early January, Temple and de Witt worked out a deal with lightning speed, and Charles signed the agreement on 13 January. In London, 'with the sincerity of a great actor throwing himself into a new role', Charles charmed the Dutch ambassador with his zeal for the new alliance.[7] Glibly, he justified his actions to Minette: 'finding my propositions to France receave so cold an answere, which was in effect as good as a refusal, I thought I had no other way but this to secure my selfe'.[8]

The Swedish ambassador in London had also been brought into the talks, and at the end of January a triple alliance was signed between England, Holland and Sweden. Charles was intent, it now seemed, on establishing himself as a thoroughly protestant prince. Louis was infuriated and a distinct coolness arose between London and Paris.

The new allies were committed, as part of the agreement, to endeavouring to end the fighting between France and Spain. The first course was to weaken support for France, and in April, after long, hard work, Sandwich finally negotiated a peace between Spain and Portugal, thus depriving Louis of his Portuguese allies. (Charles was pleased, but so angry with Sandwich on grounds of protocol, because he had signed the treaty second, after the Spanish ambassador, that he froze his expenses.) Louis fought on regardless, taking the Spanish-owned Franche-Comté, on the eastern borders of France, which he then cleverly used as a bargaining counter; in the Treaty of Aix-la-Chapelle in May he handed it back to Spain in return for keeping his gains in Flanders. This new treaty was greeted with bonfires in Paris and audible relief in London. Sir John Reresby, who had been busy rebuilding his house in Yorkshire, took his family down to the capital this spring, 'where the Court and town', he found, 'were in great joy and galentry, peace being now concluded with France, Denmarke, and the States-Generall, and also with Spain'.[9] Ambassadors were dashing to and fro across the Channel, he noted, 'and received with great splendour to confirm the same between the said princes'. But despite the gallantry and celebrations, the protestant allies rubbed along uneasily, and the Royal Africa Company and East India Company were still demanding government support in their quarrels with the Dutch. When the

William III

jubilation over the triple alliance had died down Clifford wrote prophetically, 'Well, for all this noise, we must yet have another war with the Dutch, before it be long.'[10]

While their eyes were on the threat from France, both de Witt and Charles overlooked the fact that a new, quiet player had joined their table. Neither appreciated how cool and strong William of

Orange was becoming. He was now eighteen, but both still thought of him as a boy. At the end of the war, William had been admitted to the Dutch Council of State, but since the old post of stadtholder of Holland had been abolished, he could never hope to become head of the whole kingdom. Calmly, he began to reassert his position, beginning by persuading the states of Zeeland that as Margrave of Flushing and Vere, he should be 'first noble' in the province, and therefore its stadtholder. (Arlington rushed to persuade de Witt that Charles had no hand in the affair.) And in the late 1660s he also began looking at his accounts, working out how to recover the vast sums that the House of Orange had lent to the Stuarts during the Civil Wars and the exile. Combined with a large chunk of his mother's dowry which had never been paid, the debt added up to around £250,000. Soon he intended to come to London to demand it.

34 Buckingham's Year

Boabdelin. See what the many-headed Beast demands.
Curst is the King whose Honour's in their hands.
In senates, either they too slowly grant,
Or saucily refuse to aid my want:
And when their Thrift has ruined me in Warr,
They call their Insolence my want of care.
Abenamar. Curst be their leaders who the Rage foment;
And vail with publick good their discontent.

  DRYDEN, *The Conquest of Granada*

DURING THE MONTHS of convoluted talks with the French ambassador, Charles had been keen to impress on Louis that although the constitutions of their two countries were different, in Britain as in France, the king was the ultimate power. In March 1668 he wrote to his sister, countering her anxiety about factions in parliament. He was, he admitted, in debt after the war and it would take time to get out of it, but his position was secure:

I will not deny but that naturally I am more lazy than I ought to be, but you are very ill informed if you do not know that my treasure, and in deede all my other affaires, are in as good a methode as our understandings can put them into. And I think the peace I have made between Spaine and Portugal and the defensive league I have made with Holland, should give some testimony to the world that we think of our interest heere. I do assure you that I neglect nothing for want of paines. If we faile by want of understanding there is no helpe for it.[1]

Later in the letter he added tersely, 'I do assure you that my Lord of Buckingham does not governe affaires here.' He was not 'a slave to Buckingham' or anyone else.

The disclaimer was needed because Buckingham was very much

in the public eye in 1668. It was a year of duels and dissenters. In the parliamentary debates after the Dutch war, a real battle was fought over who ruled the nation. When court audiences watched Dryden's *Conquest of Granada* a couple of years later, many royalists thought that Charles, like Dryden's King Boabdelin, had been too merciful to his enemies, with the result that a powerful opposition was growing in parliament. At its heart stood Buckingham, with Ashley beside him. This spring, however, Ashley fell dangerously ill, suffering from a liver ulcer that turned into a festering tumour, a plight from which he was rescued by a young doctor and scholar from Oxford, John Locke.

Anthony Ashley Cooper, later Earl of Shaftesbury

The balance between the crown and parliament, which Locke would later examine in his *Two Treatises of Government*, was increasingly uneasy. Charles's game plan was to rule as much as he could on his own, making policy in the Privy Council and more secretly, with his inner cabinet and his Gentlemen of the Bedchamber. But parliament held the purse strings and had the power to crush any bills he wished to push through. Parliament's drive to make the monarch accountable was also growing more vocal, both in their demand to see accounts and in the enquiries into mismanagement of the war. The nascent court and country parties, Marvell's 'Trick track men', were preparing the way for the emergent Whigs and Tories later in the reign. But the factions that worried Minette also upset many MPs. Pepys's cousin Roger, speaking for the independent country gentlemen, said he 'never knew what it was to be tempted to be a knave in his life, till he did come into the House of Commons, where there is nothing done but by passion and faction and private interest'.[2]

As Charles saw it, managing parliament was now his biggest challenge. The Commons were delighted at the removal of Clarendon but they were still bristling, fearful of the threat of a standing army, and wary of the king's use of the money they had granted. It seemed, at first, that Buckingham, with his energy and popularity, would be a useful tool, if he could be converted to working for the government rather than against it. In the autumn of 1667 he and his supporters had enjoyed the taste of battle, demanding public accounts, demolishing navy officials, attacking Mordaunt and, most of all, trying to impeach Clarendon.[3] A signal that his group was gaining favour came when his right-hand man, George Savile, was created Baron Savile of Eland and Viscount Halifax, in January 1668. Outside parliament, Buckingham cultivated former republicans, and intellectuals like John Wilkins and his chaplain Thomas Sprat, historian of the Royal Society. Marshalling his forces, he may have felt that he was using Charles, rather than the other way round. Once more, the issue was one of what exactly it meant to rule, to be in control.

While Buckingham drew the public gaze, it was Arlington, stouter now but still with his odd black plaster over his nose, who gained most by Clarendon's fall. Cautiously, he picked his way through the mess that followed the wars. He would be the most potent minister of state for the next five years, and a considerable influence for a decade to come. Charles was careful to put Arlington's protégés into positions where they actually had some effective power, while appeasing Buckingham by letting him buy the non-political position of master of the horse, at a huge price. (This was doubly clever, since Buckingham's Yorkshire stables added good blood-stock to the royal stud.)

Charles watched both his ministers coolly, as Halifax, who served him later, could see. 'He lived with his Ministers as he did with his mistresses,' Halifax wrote; 'he used them, but he was not in love with them. He shewed his judgment in this, that he cannot properly be said ever to have had a *Favourite*, though some might look so at a distance.'[4] His later courtier Ailesbury was equally sure that there was a ruthlessness in the way Charles watched favourites sparring and noted that he often quoted the maxim, 'When rogues fall out, then the master is like to know the truth.' By the same maxim, added Ailesbury, the King 'rather fomented underhand than otherwise the two parties of Whig and Tory'.[5]

By keeping Buckingham in favour, Charles would make Arlington wary and more dependent, and stop him becoming too powerful.[6] At the same time, making Buckingham work on the government side should divert the dangerous energy that had stirred up the previous session. The only risk in this ploy lay in Buckingham's volatility. Many people felt he was unstable, including, with hindsight, Gilbert Burnet. 'He had no principles', decided Burnet, 'of religion, virtue, or friendship. Pleasure, frolic, or extravagant diversion, was all that he laid to heart. He was true to nothing, for he was not true to himself. He had no steadiness nor conduct: he could keep no secret, nor execute any design without spoiling it.'[7] This judgement resembles Dryden's baleful picture of Buckingham during the Exclusion Crisis of 1679–81, as Zimri in *Absalom and Achitophel,*

> A man so various that he seemed to be
> Not one, but all mankind's epitome.
> Stiff in opinions, always in the wrong,
> Was everything by starts, and nothing long;
> But in the course of one revolving moon
> Was chemist, fiddler, statesman and buffoon.

Dryden was writing with both political and personal hostility, aggravated by Buckingham's caricature of him as the foolish playwright Bayes in *The Rehearsal.* But even in 1668 Buckingham was Dryden's 'blessed madman', thinking up a new scheme every hour, a compelling orator with no middle course:

> Railing and praising were his usual themes
> And both, to show his judgement, in extremes.[8]

Buckingham badly wanted to stay in high office, needing the revenue from fees and gifts to pay the interest on his staggering debts. When Magalotti was collecting gossip for sketches of leading courtiers, he drew Buckingham as a total contradiction, eloquent and brilliant, yet 'atheistical', depraved and especially violent to his male, as opposed to female, lovers. (Buckingham, when accused of sodomy, replied neatly, 'God knows, I have much to answer for in the plain way, but I never was so great a Virtuoso in my lusts.'[9]) But at the start of 1668, 'in the 'plain way', he was already teetering on extremes: 'a man of no more sobriety than to fight about a whore', decided Pepys.[10] The previous September his mistress, Anna Maria Brudenell, Lady Shrewsbury, had suddenly left England and gone to live in a convent in France. A month later, when Harry Killigrew insulted her at the theatre, Buckingham lost his temper and hit Killigrew over the head with the flat of his sword. Once again, Charles took his side. Killigrew had already damaged his standing with Charles by making slurs on Barbara Castlemaine's reputation and by his mounting debts, and after this fracas he was virtually banished to France. Anxious that this should not be misinterpreted as approving of Lady Shrewsbury, Charles wrote to Minette, sending his letter via Buckingham's sister, the Dowager Duchess of Richmond, who was about to become Henrietta Maria's Lady of the Bedchamber. 'Though I cannot commende my Lady Shrewsbury's conduct in many things,' he wrote firmly, 'yett Mr Killigrew's carriage towards her has been worse than I will repeate, and for his demele with my Lord of Buckingham he ought not to brag of, for it was in all sorts most abominable.' Forestalling any criticism she might hear when Killigrew put his side of the story, he added that Minette should not believe 'one word he says of us here, for he is a most notorious lyar, and does not want witt to sett forth his storyes pleasantly enough'.[11]

Although Lord Shrewsbury had been complaisant about his wife's earlier lovers, in January 1668 he issued a challenge to Buckingham. They gathered their seconds, Bernard Howard and Sir John Talbot supporting Shrewsbury, and a Mr Jenkins and Robert Holmes backing Buckingham.[12] When Charles heard that a duel was planned, full of alarm, he told Albemarle to try to keep Buckingham indoors, and at least make sure that he did not fight. The General, misunderstanding, or mishearing, and thinking his role was only to be an informer, did nothing. On 21 January the duellists met at Barn Elms. Howard ran furiously at Jenkins and stabbed him fatally, Holmes slashed Talbot across the arm, and Buckingham dodged, feinted, and plunged his sword into Shrewsbury's chest. Shrewsbury's seconds bundled him into a coach, soaked in blood, and drove to Arundel House.

A doctor said that although the wound was grave, Shrewsbury would live. Six days later he received a royal pardon for indirectly causing Jenkins's death. Buckingham and his seconds were also pardoned by 'immediate warrants' authorised by Charles's signature alone, rather than by the Privy Seal, Lord Robartes, who might not have been so lenient.[13] At the next council meeting, Charles had to argue his case forcefully, invoking the services to the crown of everyone involved, and promising 'the extreme penalty' in the case of another duel. It seemed that Buckingham could do anything. On 10 February he was at the opening of parliament, his popularity only slightly dented by the duel. But during these weeks, while Buckingham spoke passionately in favour of toleration, or enjoyed himself watching Etherege's new play, Shrewsbury was slowly weakening from septicaemia. Six weeks later he died.

All this time, Lady Shrewsbury had stayed in France. Yet this did not stop the stories that she had gone to the duel dressed as a page, holding her lover's horse, and then spent the night with him, his shirt drenched with her husband's blood. After Shrewsbury died she returned to London, mourning with theatrical grief. Buckingham himself was shocked, but spellbound. 'Her sadness became her so well', he wrote sardonically, 'that it bred delight in everyone else,' and, even more tartly, ''Twas her husband grieved whilst he was living, 'tis reasonable she should do it now he is dead.'[14] Despite his sarcasms Buckingham was still obsessed. When Harry Killigrew came back from France, still sneering that the countess was any man's for the asking, she hired a gang of footpads and watched from her coach as they waylaid Killigrew, killed his servant, and stabbed him nine times, leaving him for dead. At court, Buckingham defended her, saying the gang only meant to scare Killigrew and that his wounds were his own fault, as he had run at them with his sword. James and Rupert both suggested Buckingham was part of the conspiracy to attack him, but Charles did not listen.

Even more defiantly, in May Buckingham moved Lady Shrewsbury openly into his own house. As the newsmongers reported, when his wife protested that she could not share a house with his mistress, he answered, 'Why Madam, I did think so; and therefore have ordered your coach to be ready to carry you to your father's.'[15] Which, noted Pepys, 'was a devilish speech, but they say true; and my Lady Shrewsbury is there it seems'. Even sharper gasps of horror were heard when he had their child christened in Westminster Abbey.

Again, Charles did not blink. He needed Buckingham in the House of Lords, and he needed his allies in the Commons. A deal was hatched whereby particular men would act as 'undertakers' in parliament, working to get the king a good grant of money in return for offices. One of the things Charles hoped for in the spring session was that these undertakers, in addition to securing his funds, would speak for the nonconformist interest, arguing for greater liberty of conscience. He still smarted from the failure in 1663 of his Declaration of Indulgence, and this strategy would finally let him fulfil his Breda promises, and, he hoped, pacify the growing discontent among protestant nonconformists. Charles's renewed interest was also driven by a desire to snub the bishops, nearly all of whom had backed Clarendon and blamed his fall on Barbara Castlemaine. When Charles tried to consult Sheldon about Clarendon, the Archbishop had merely said, 'Sir, I wish that you would put away this woman that you keep.' This time he went too far. Charles removed him from the Privy Council and would not let him preach at Whitehall.[16] He never regained his previous power.[17]

Buckingham's own attachment to the idea of toleration was genuine and enduring, despite the vagaries of his life. In a private justification, he later wrote that he had always inclined 'to some moderate way in matters of Conscience', not out of hatred of the Church, 'but only because I thought that to be the surest way to settle the Church and unite the Nation'.[18] A toleration bill for protestant dissenters had been drafted in October 1667 to soothe anti-Catholic fears after the Fire and the raid on the Medway, especially to appease the rich dissenting merchants. But the bill was set aside while parliament continued to pick over the mishandling of the war.[19] The delay gave Sheldon time to gather his supporters. That autumn a spate of pamphlets appeared, revealing sharp differences of opinion even among the would-be reformers. Some thought that the best course was comprehension, relaxing the strict law on services and doctrine so that presbyterians could feel at ease within the Church of England itself. Others opted for toleration, keeping the Act of Uniformity as it stood, but accepting different forms of worship outside the church. Despite these differences, both protestant dissenters and Catholics were full of anticipation. 'The Catholics', reported a puzzled Magalotti, 'say that their number increases daily, and that the Act of Comprehension would be the truest means of establishing religion in the kingdom. The Presbyterians promise themselves the same advantage . . . I do think I can say that the nobility would be catholic and the rich men Presbyterians'.[20]

Over the Christmas holiday, Orlando Bridgeman, Keeper of the Seals, consulted with Richard Baxter and the London presbyterians. At the same time the remarkable John Wilkins, now a royal chaplain and soon to be Bishop of Chester, marshalled the moderate Anglican divines.[21] Wilkins had a two-hour conference with Charles, and won his support for a set of proposals based on the Breda declaration. He also suggested that those who could not accept a broader, more inclusive church should be allowed to worship separately in licensed meeting houses. Catholic services, however, would still be forbidden and extreme sects would be denied a licence. By the end of January 1668, the Privy Council had accepted the idea, and a comprehension bill was drafted by the distinguished lawyer Sir Matthew Hale.[22]

Charles needed Buckingham's men to push Hale's bill through parliament. That was why he pardoned his duel so swiftly. When he opened parliament in February, he first announced the signing of the triple alliance, which was greeted with enthusiasm, then turned to his vision of a broader church which might reunite English protestants.[23] But here he badly misjudged the Commons' mood. They had already talked before the king arrived and it took them only half an hour to make a stand. 'This day the vote was passed', wrote John Milward, 'to prevent the bringing in the bill of comprehension, which will be brought in and countenanced by very great persons.'[24] Far from accepting the bill, the angry MPs called for firmer enforcement of the current laws.

The debates over the next few weeks were fierce and wide-ranging but there was no doubt that the idea of comprehension was dead.[25] In the House of Lords, the whole argument about freedom of debate and the state's rule over religious matters was revived again. Hobbes's works, in particular, were attacked as giving heart to dissenters. The bishops refused to let *Leviathan* be reprinted, and copies were soon selling second-hand at ten times their original price. The publication of Hobbes's new work, *Behemoth*, was stopped, and his Latin translation of *Leviathan*, with a long appendix defending himself from the charge of heresy, had to be published abroad, in Amsterdam. Charles knew that this persecution was also aimed partly at himself. While one camp damned him as a papist, another feared him as a Hobbesian atheist. On his birthday the previous year, he had been halted in his long stride through Whitehall by the sight of some graffiti, topped with a royal crown, on the wall of one of the corridors:

> Hobbes his Religion, Hyde his Moralls gave
> And this day birth to an ungrateful knave.[26]

He merely asked for the wall to be cleaned. But he now detached himself from Hobbes, as he had done from Hyde.

Since the comprehension bill had failed, the only relief for dissenters was that the Conventicle Act of 1664, which forbade religious meetings, was due to relapse at the end of the parliamentary session. A new bill was rapidly introduced, but delays and adjournments kept it from being passed before parliament was prorogued. For a time the dissenters could meet together without fear. The reprieve was brief, since a new, even sterner act would be passed in 1670, described by Marvell as 'the Quintessence of Arbitrary Malice'. Marvell, with his low-church sympathies and puritan friends, had always supported comprehension. When parliament closed he even drafted an address begging Charles to act separately, to use his prerogative in ecclesiastical affairs – as he had tried to do in 1663 – 'for the better composure and union of the minds of his protestant subjects'.[27] It is strange to find this stalwart, satirical, anti-absolutist MP appealing to the King to overrule parliament, but perhaps this direct action was what Marvell had meant when he begged Charles to ignore those advisers who were cutting him off from his people.

Realising that they could expect no help from parliament, the dissenters appealed with increasing vehemence to the liberty of 'individual conscience'. People must be allowed to choose their own religion, according to an inward persuasion. In *Paradise Lost*, now in readers' hands, Milton's Archangel Michael had forewarned Adam that in human history some so-called Christian ministries would seek to impose spiritual laws by force 'on every conscience':

> What will they then
> But force the Spirit of Grace it self, and binde
> His consort Libertie; what, but unbuild
> His living Temples, built by Faith to stand,
> Thir own Faith not anothers.[28]

With this idea of the individual 'living Temple' went the realisation that each person's definition of their faith might be subtly different. Writers began to argue, almost like Fellows of the Royal Society, for an unbounded intellectual perspective, so that religious truth, like the truth of 'other sciences', could develop freely 'into variety of Thoughts and Principles'. And if variety of thought was accepted, there could be no possibility of imposing 'uniformity' except as an act of repression.[29]

In the spring of 1668, once the religious reforms were defeated, the MPs returned to their tireless wrangling over the war. Marvell caused uproar in a debate on the shambolic intelligence system, when he not only condemned its inefficiency but implied that Arlington had bought his way to power and title. The money allowed for intelligence was so small, he fumed, that 'the intelligence was accordingly – a libidinous desire in men for places makes them think themselves fit for them – the place of Secretary ill gotten, when bought with £10,000 and a barony'. He was called to explain himself, but 'said the thing was so plain that it needed not'.³⁰ Many MPs were as angry as Marvell, if less outspoken. The situation was chaotic. 'God almighty sett all our heades right,' Arlington wrote to Ormond in February, 'for there are few that are not verry giddy!'³¹ In the same month Pepys scribbled morosely, 'The house is in a most broken condition':

nobody adhering to anything, but reviling and finding fault; and now quite mad at the 'Undertakers', as they are commonly called – Littleton, Lord Vaughan, Sir R. Howard, and others that are brought over to the Court and did undertake to get the King money; but they despise and will not hear them in the House, and the Court doth do as much, seeing that they cannot be useful to them as was expected.³²

In this climate, Sir Richard Temple's promotion of a new Triennial Bill, which sought to flatter the Commons by restricting the time that the King was allowed to prorogue parliament, was 'condemned by all moderate men', declared John Milward, as being 'composed of strange and very dangerous heads to take away the King's power'.³³ The backbenchers resented being managed by the undertakers even more than they minded directions from the crown.

Having lost face by supporting the court, Buckingham and his gang – Temple, Osborne, Seymour and Howard – now turned against it. Far from getting Charles a good supply, as they had promised, they now argued that the house should not vote any money at all until there was a full investigation of the war. Fearful civil servants decided the only course was to stall and delay. When Henry Brouncker, facing the allegations of incompetence at Lowestoft, pleaded with Charles to save him, 'with tears in his eyes the King did say he could not, and bid him shift for himself at least until the House is up'.³⁴ Charles dared not alienate the Commons until he had his money. At last, the Commons voted £300,000 to pay for the navy, as long as the money was not raised by a land tax or excise. The preference was for taxes on foreign goods, French commodities and especially wine (with a jovial proviso from one MP that a tax should be put on spirits 'to prevent excessive drinking, but not upon anything to hinder good hospitality').[35]

As the session ended, however, a political storm of a different kind erupted in the capital. On 10 March Charles responded to the Commons' fury over the comprehension bill by issuing the proclamation that they demanded, to enforce the Act of Uniformity and accompanying laws.[36] The London dissenters, who had been hoping for a relaxation of the law, were outraged. On Easter Monday, 23 March, a fine spring day, the City apprentices gathered to attack a favourite holiday target, the bawdy houses. This was an old tradition, but this time it was given a new slant. If the King was going to persecute honest people by applying the religious laws strictly, the apprentices implied, then they would persecute him – and all his whoring courtiers – by enforcing the laws against sexual licence, the creed by which the court lived.[37]

The trouble began in Poplar where the mob's first target was a brothel run by Damaris Page, 'the great bawd of the seamen'. Next day riots spread rapidly through Moorfields, Smithfield, Shoreditch and Holborn. By Wednesday, thousands of young men were on the streets – some said forty thousand – armed with iron bars and staves, organised into 'regiments', wearing the colour green, and led by captains, in the fashion of the City's trained bands. An anxious Charles asked the Lord Mayor to gather the militia, and also sent in troops of his own, commanded once again by the excitable Lord Craven 'riding up and down to give orders like a madman'.[38]

Some of those involved said openly 'that they did ill in contenting themselves in pulling down the little bawdy-houses and did not go and pull down the great bawdy-house at Whitehall'.[39] During the days of rioting, three satires appeared, pointing at the vices of the court, and specifically at Charles's 'Catholic whore', Barbara Castlemaine. The first attack, *The Poor Whore's Petition*, written as an appeal from the prostitutes of the town, recorded Barbara's lubricious rise to power and asked sardonically for her protection against the apprentices ruining their business, and, by implication, threatening hers. The second and third satires, in manuscript and print respectively, were Castlemaine's 'answer'.[40] The printed *Gracious Answer* was particularly devastating since it was clearly written by someone who had watched Barbara recently at the theatre at Whitehall, dripping with jewels, 'which the (abhorred and undone) people of this kingdom have paid for'.[41] She was made to speak like a vain, self-regarding woman, gloating over the provision for her children, and a self-satisfied Catholic, blithely attacking the Church of England and presenting the Privy Council as pimps for the papist interest. If they had their way, she promised, the sects would be crushed but court Catholics would be spared since 'venereal pleasure, accompanied with looseness, debauchery and prophaneness are not such heinous crimes and crying sins'.

Charles and the council saw at once that the riots and pamphlets were less about sex than about the church and political power. Among the slogans shouted were 'Liberty of Conscience!' and the promise that the next popular holiday, May Day, would be a 'bloody day'. When the leaders were arrested they were not charged with pulling down brothels but with treason, and their attempts at reform of manners smoothly reinterpreted by the Chief Justice Kelyng (the man who had tried Bunyan in 1660) as usurping 'regal authority'.[42]

Buckingham had nothing to do with these riots, yet his popularity in the City was well known and his hand was suspected. In several ways his efforts during the past months had backfired. The intense debates in the Commons had revealed a curious pattern. While almost everything pushed by Buckingham's 'undertakers' failed, their efforts had nudged the MPs, in opposition to their pressure, into more and more open declarations of support for the king. In reaction, Buckingham snarled. He attacked former allies like Sir William Coventry and Lord Anglesey, who was soon deprived of his post as treasurer to the navy. Then he turned on old enemies, including Ormond. Scenting trouble, Ormond dashed to London. Days later, on 9 May, Charles dissolved the Commons.

Buckingham's ambitions, many thought, verged on the dangerous. Soon he and Ashley were implicated in plans to oust the Duke of York from the succession by making Monmouth the legal heir. In the autumn of 1668, at Whitehall, Pepys's friend Povey told him that people thought the duke 'hath a mind rather to overthrow all the Kingdom and bring in a Commonwealth, wherein he may think to be General of the Army, or to make himself king; which he believes he may be led to by some advice he hath had with conjurers which he doth affect'.[43] Charles's bid to make use of him had brought unforeseen consequences. By the end of the year, Buckingham's magic was once again suspect.

35 Loving Too Well

He spends all his Days
In running to Plays
When in his Shop he shou'd be poreing;
And wasts all his Nights
In his constant delights
Of Revelling, Drinking and Whoreing.
ANON., 'Upon his Majesties being made free of the
Citty'

IN 1668 MAY DAY was foul and cold. The ribbons on the may-poles flapped in the rain, and the dancers' feet were muddy. Only a few bedraggled coaches took part in the annual procession round the ring at Hyde Park. People could not even shelter in the play-house, at least not in the Theatre Royal, where the rain came spit-ting into the pit through the badly glazed cupola. The only place to take refuge was in the tavern or the coffee-house.

On 9 May Charles dissolved parliament for the summer, signing off, said Pepys, with a 'short silly speech'.[1] He seemed restless and distracted. At Whitehall he ordered a new range of rooms, which became known as the Volary Buildings since they were built on the site of the old aviary. His new apartments, with fine river views from their novel sash-windows, were near the queen's, so that people could come and see him more informally when they visited her. They also had a private entrance which was handy for more private meetings, organised by the invaluable and slightly sinister William Chiffinch. William had taken over when his older brother, Thomas Chiffinch, Keeper of the King's Closet, died suddenly in 1666, and his wife Barbara also became laundress to the queen. The couple arranged everything from meetings with ministers in the

Bedchamber to a rota for walking the royal dogs. Their apartment was next to Charles's rooms, opening onto the back stairs down to the river, a route taken by visitors who did not want to be seen, like French ambassadors – and young, ambitious actresses.

As if the pent-up energy which he controlled so carefully in his public life had to find release, Charles was more mobile and unsettled this summer than ever before. He hunted at Windsor, Bagshot and in the New Forest; he visited the ports and sailed his fast yachts; he stayed at Audley End (which he soon bought from the bankrupt Earl of Suffolk), to be near Newmarket. The excuses that he gave to Minette for not answering her letters were often of this kind: he has just come back from the sea, he has been hunting all day, he is off to the races next week.

Thousands flocked to Newmarket for the race-meetings and from now on Charles went regularly in summer and autumn. His father had a hunting lodge there, but this had been almost completely demolished by the regicide Colonel Okey, and Charles had not bothered with repairs, apart from rebuilding the stables. This year he bought an old timber-framed house, with bays overhanging the High Street, and commissioned the architect William Samwell to convert it. The small courtyard behind was surrounded by unpretentious but comfortable suites of rooms for Charles and Catherine, the Yorks and Monmouth.[2] The Lord Chamberlain's office was next door, and many of the court had lodgings nearby, including the Chiffinches. When Evelyn visited the house on a trip to East Anglia in July 1670, he was disappointed. Not only was it full of awkward angles, low ceilings and poky rooms but it was 'placed in a dirty Streete; without any Court or avenue, like a common Burger's: whereas it might & ought to have been built at either end of the Towne, upon the very Carpet where the Sports are Celebrated'.[3]

The stables, Evelyn thought, were far more impressive, with many fine horses kept 'at vast expense, with all the art & tendernesse Imaginable'. Racing, like sailing, became one of Charles's passions. He employed four jockeys, expanded his stables and set up a stud.

He also improved the race-course (moving the site of the summer course, because the sun got in his eyes), introduced the idea of racing in silk colours, and gave purses and trophies. In the early mornings he could be seen watching the training, and when the races began he often galloped alongside to cheer the winner at the post. Sometimes he raced himself, and in 1671 won the Town Plate which he had established six years before, with a purse of £32.

Francis Barlow's engraving of the last horse race before the king below Windsor Castle, drawn on the spot in 1684 and engraved three years later. This is thought to be the first English drawing of a horse race.

It was at Newmarket that he was given the name of 'Old Rowley' after a favourite stallion, a dig at his womanising. He was popular in the town, wandering through the streets in his old clothes. John Reresby, recording a later race-meeting, noted his informality, slightly disapprovingly:

The King was soe much pleased in the countrey, and soe great a lover of the diversions which that place did afford, that he lett himselfe down from majesty to the very degree of a country gentleman. He mixed himself amongst the croud, allowed every man to speak to him that pleased, went a-hawking in the mornings, to cock matches in afternoons (if there were

noe hors race), and to plays in the evenings, acted in a barn and by very
ordinary Bartlemew-fair comedians.[4]

Outsiders were still astonished by the King's accessibility and his
habit of being charming to all. His courtiers explained this to
Magalotti as being a hangover from his days in exile, and he concluded that Charles's courtesy and affability were 'not so entirely
due to the effect of royal magnanimity that some little part of them
may not be due to the habit formed in his youth of adopting the
humble manners of a poor and private nobleman'.[5] In 1668 the
young Italian, open-eyed at the intrigues of London, stayed mostly
with scientific friends from the Royal Society, and gathered gossip
from them and from members of the court. His portrait of Charles
suggests the effects of the strain of the past years. He had a fine figure, he decided, 'and is free and attractive in his person and in all his
motions'. His complexion was swarthy, his hair black, his eyes
'bright and shining, but set strangely in his face', his nose large and
bony:

His mouth is wide, with thin lips, and he has a short chin. His cheeks are
marked across under the eyes with two deep and prominent lines or wrin-
kles that begin near the middle of the nose and go towards the corners of the
eyes, getting thinner and thinner and vanishing before they get there. He
wears a wig, almost entirely black, and very thick and curly above the forehead, which makes him look sadder, but without giving him any trace of
grimness; on the contrary his appearance is sad but not grim. Indeed a certain smiling look coming from the width of his mouth so greatly clears and
softens the roughness of his features that he pleases rather than terrifies.[6]

The king was, he learned, lighthearted about religion, clever but
lazy. In private life he was a good friend, with a dread of seriousness. As a lover, he was sensual but not 'bestial', and generous to his
mistresses, especially in the first flush of infatuation.

Like all observers, Magalotti was fascinated by anything he could
learn of Charles's sex life. The very public nature of Charles's sexu-
ality was both a bonus and a drawback. On the one hand it implied
an almost supernatural virility and potency; on the other it certainly

diminished his dignity. Both points would later be made by Rochester in his famous lines about Charles's sceptre and his prick being 'of a length'. This could mean nothing if he needed dextrous cajoling even to get it up, and, then, could never be satisfied:

> Restlesse he roalles about from Whore to Whore
> A merry Monarch, scandalous and poor.[7]

In terms of the body politic as opposed to the body private, the identification of his prick with his power was potentially dangerous. If one drooped, then by implication the other might also collapse. In 1667–8, said Magalotti, Charles was thought to prefer friendship to 'bodily relations'. During the Dutch crisis, wrote Pepys, 'the King's greatest pleasure hath been with his fingers, being able to do no more'.[8]

If conflict made him impotent or dulled his desire, when the war ended he found release in an unusual burst of promiscuity. So far Charles had been known as a one-woman man, or at least one at a time. In the next few months he was linked to a circle of names: to the maid of honour Winifred Wells, about whom Buckingham was so cruel; to Jane Roberts, a clergyman's daughter down on her luck, who was imbued ever after with a deep sense of guilt, caught the pox and suffered in the same sweating-houses as Rochester. He was bracketed, too, with Maria Knight, the singer with the heavenly voice; with the beautiful Elizabeth, Countess of Kildare; and with Mary, Countess of Falmouth, the widow of his beloved Berkeley and the future wife of his friend from the circle of wits, Charles Sackville, Lord Buckhurst.

Buckingham was well aware of Charles's sensual enjoyment of women and as soon as he was back in favour he began trying to direct Charles's sex life as well as his political fortunes. He could see that he was weary of Barbara. While the war was at its height she had been seen constantly again with the ugly, frog-faced yet oddly attractive Henry Jermyn. Charles had crushed their earlier flirtation, but it was now accepted that they were lovers. When she thought she was pregnant again, however, she asked Charles to acknowledge the child. He would not, he said, given that he had no memory of sleeping with her in the last six months. 'God damn me! but you shall own it,' was her reply. If the baby was not christened at Whitehall, she would dash its brains out before him on the Gallery wall, and parade his bastard children outside his door.[9] When Charles stood firm Barbara left to stay in Covent Garden with her friend Elizabeth, Lady Harvey, a member of the ubiquitous Montagu family and co-fighter against Clarendon. True to habit Charles begged forgiveness; true to custom, Barbara returned. Nothing more was heard of the controversial pregnancy.

In February 1668, while critics were poring over the state accounts, Barbara was gambling so deeply that she apparently won £15,000 in one night's play, and lost £25,000 the next – betting £1,000 or more on one throw of the dice. She had also quarrelled with Buckingham, now that their alliance against Clarendon had ended. In Buckingham's view, Charles needed a protestant mistress to counter Barbara's Catholicism, a woman who would link him to the people, rather than the despised, licentious court. And where better to find one than the theatre.

Two actresses who had leapt to fame in recent seasons were Moll Davis at Lincoln's Inn Fields and Nell Gwyn at the Theatre Royal. Moll had been on stage since childhood and was famed for her singing and her light-as-air dancing. Her first great hit was *Sir Martin Mar-All*, a farcical collaboration between Dryden and Newcastle (Pepys went three days running, it made him laugh so much), and George Etherege then wrote a madcap role for her as Gatty in *She Would if She Could*, complete with song and jig. In this play, as she and her companion Ariana spy their gallants, the language of naval warfare that the court knew so well is turned into the jargon of dalliance:

Ariana. Now if these should prove two men of War that are cruising here, to watch for Prizes.
Gatty. Would they had courage enough to set upon us; I long to be engag'd.

Ariana. Look, look yonder, I protest they chase us.
Gatty. Let us bear away then; if they be truly valiant they'll quickly make
more sail, and board us.[10]

A little later, as the mad Celania in a revival of Davenant's *The
Rivals*, Moll appeared in a more winsome vein, singing a plaintive
song:

> My lodging it is on the cold ground,
> And very hard is my fare
> But that which troubles me most is
> The unkindness of my dear.
> Yet still I cry, O turn love,
> And I prythee, love, turn to me,
> For thou art the man that I long for,
> And alack what remedy.

She performed this so charmingly before the King, wrote the
prompter John Downes, 'that not long after, it Rais'd her from her
Bed on the Cold Ground, to a Bed Royal'.[11]

In the autumn of 1667, Buckingham had been dangling both
young actresses before Charles, having decided, said Burnet, that 'a
gayety of humour would take much with the king'.[12] Both girls were
guided secretly up the Whitehall back-stairs, but Nell ruined her
chances of becoming a royal mistress by asking for £500 a year.
Instead Charles took Moll. One of the satirists' favourite stories was
that Nell tried to put Charles off Moll Davis by dosing her, when
she was about to dine with the King, with a drastic purgative called
jalap, made from the pounded root of a Surinam herb and given to
her by her friend Aphra Behn. If so, it was not effective, or at least
not in the way she planned. In early 1668 it was confidently asserted that Charles had taken a house for Moll in Suffolk Street and
bought her a ring worth £600, more than Nell had asked as an
annual fee.

Oblique comments were made about Charles's affairs in the theatre
itself. In February 1668 Robert Howard's dark new play, *The Great*

Moll Davis

Favourite, or the Duke of Lerma, featured a disgraced favourite – an implied attack on Clarendon – who tried to prostitute his daughter to the King of Spain. (Nell played Maria, the daughter whose integrity foiled her father's dastardly plans.) Pepys sat nervously in the pit. Seeing that the play 'was designed to reproach our King with his mistresses', he wrote, 'I was troubled for it, and expected it should be interrupted; but it ended all well, which salved all.'[13] In public at least, Charles took no notice.

Shortly afterwards, perhaps hoping to compete with Moll, Barbara Castlemaine herself went on the stage, taking a starring role in a glittering court performance of Corneille's *Horace*. The translation was by the Welsh prodigy Katharine Phillips, 'the matchless Orinda', another exceptional woman, a friend of the Ormonds and Boyles and the poet of friendship and devotion between women. Katharine had died of smallpox in 1664, aged thirty-two, and her translation of Corneille was published after her death. The play was a success, with magnificent costumes and superb dancing, but Barbara should have known that she could never match an actress on the stage. This spring she was parading with the actor Charles Hart, as if tossing her head at the king for taking an actress lover. But Charles could not really care. After the apprentice riots and *The Poor Whore's Petition*, she had begun to seem coarse. 'Paint Castlemaine in colours that are bold', wrote Marvell, 'Her, not her picture, for she now grows old.' Even devoted admirers found she had lost some of her glamour. In early May 1668 Pepys watched her at the theatre, seated in the balcony with several great ladies. Not caring who was watching, she called to one of her women and borrowed a patch off her face 'and put it into her mouth, and wetted it and so clapped it upon her own by the side of her mouth, I suppose she feeling a pimple rising there'.[14]

Less than a week later, Pepys heard that Barbara was to leave Whitehall. Charles settled a pension on her of £4,700, paid out of Post Office profits through her uncles, Viscount Grandison and Colonel Villiers. Her new home was Berkshire House, for which Charles borrowed £4,000 from the ever-obliging Edward Backwell. Ironically this was the very house where Clarendon had taken refuge after the Fire, on the other side of the Park from Whitehall, but directly across the road from St James's Palace, the home of the Yorks, who seemed to have forgiven her for her scheming against Clarendon and were becoming her closest friends. Her two eldest children, Anne and Charles, now aged seven and six, were currently in Paris but the three youngest, Henry, Charlotte and baby George, moved across the Park with their mother. Charles dropped in every day to see them, 'as a good friend' only, reported Ambassador Ruvigny.[15]

Barbara's reign was over. At the end of the year, when the court attended a performance of *Macbeth*, Pepys was shocked to see Moll Davis lounging in a box just above the King's. He watched Moll look down on Charles, and saw him look up at her, 'and so did my Lady Castlemayne once, to see who it was; but when she saw her, she blushed like fire'.[16]

In May 1668, between dismissing parliament and setting off on his summer journeys, when he pensioned off Barbara, Charles made a series of such personal decisions, an emotional clearing of the decks. The catalyst was probably not the actions of his mistresses but a problem with his queen. When Magalotti tried to fathom Catherine's nature, he jotted down notes about her liking for playing ombre and chatting with her women, her constant praying and her habit of lauding Portugal above all other nations. But he also liked to think that there was a wild, sensual creature within this small, plain woman. Catherine, he wrote, was thought to be 'unusually susceptible to pleasure':

She finds the king provided by nature with implements most suitable for exciting it, and it is said that her ecstasy is then so extreme that after the ordinary escape of these humours that the violence of pleasure presses even from women, blood comes from her genital parts in such great abundance that it does not stop for several days.[17]

If there were such alarming reports, and Catherine did bleed abundantly, this almost certainly says less about Charles's performance than about her frail reproductive system. Charles never mentioned her miscarriage in Oxford in 1666, and may have believed that that pregnancy was a false alarm. But he had not yet abandoned hope of her bearing children and was delighted, early this year, when she announced that she was pregnant. Almost inevitably she miscarried, at dawn on 7 May. 'And though I am troubled at it', Charles told Minette, 'yet I am glad that 'tis evident she was with childe, which I will not deny to you, till now, I did feare she was not capable of.'[18] He added that the doctors had put her on a course of physic, 'which they are confident will make her holde faster next time'.

As if looking afresh at his life, within days of Catherine's miscarriage Charles set aside Barbara. Later in the month, when the weather turned from cold wind and rain to sudden heat, he left for two days in Newmarket. Back in town, he was kind to his wife, who grieved bitterly over her lost child, yet although he dined with her often he had not really changed. Catherine, as usual, knew just what was happening. At the end of May, when Moll Davies was about to dance her jig during a play at Whitehall, Catherine rose and left the room, 'which people do think it was out of her displeasure at her being the King's whore, that she could not bear it.'[19]

Charles's affair with Moll would last on and off for the next six years and they had a daughter, Mary, in 1673.[20] But she hardly touched his heart: in 1668 his deepest feelings were still for Frances Stuart. The previous year, after peace was proclaimed and he could write to Minette again, he had tried to explain why he acted so harshly towards Frances, whom Minette had been fond of since she was a girl in Paris:

I do assure you that I am very much troubled that I cannot in everything give you that satisfaction I could wish, especially in this business of the duchesse of Richmonde, wherein you may thinke me ill natured, but if you consider how hard a thing 'tis to swallow an injury done by a person I had so much tendernesse for, you will in some degree excuse the resentment I use towards her.[21]

Before he wrote the word 'tendernesse' he first wrote 'love' then crossed it out. He saw Frances's behaviour as a direct provocation, a breach of friendship and faith, 'therefore I hope you will pardon me if I cannot so far forget an injury which went so neere my hart'. Minette begged him to take her into favour again, but his pride was hurt. A poem survives in his hand, an easy exercise in courtly pastoral:

> I pass all my hours in a shady old grove,
> But I live not the day when I see not my love;

I survey every walk now my Phillis is gone,
And sigh when I think we were there all alone;
O then, 'tis then, that I think there's no hell
Like loving, like loving too well.

This is conventional enough but with regard to Frances the sentiment rings true. Charles had loved her.

Frances spent the months after her marriage looking after the Richmond estate at Cobham in Kent, while her husband raised troops in Dorset amid the fears of a French invasion.[22] After the war ended the couple thought of going to France, where Richmond, as duc d'Aubigny, had estates in Berry, and where Frances could attach herself to the household of Henrietta Maria. But in the end Frances decided to come to London and join her mother at Somerset House. When she arrived there at Christmas 1667, her old friends from court flocked to see her. Charles, however, scotched any rumours of a reconciliation. 'You were misinformed in your intelligence concerning the Duchesse of Richmond,' he told his sister. 'If you were as well acquainted with a little fantastical gentleman called Cupide as I am, you would neither wonder, nor take ill, any sudden changes which do happen in the affaires of his conducting, but in this matter there is nothing to be done in it.'[23] And then, in the early spring of 1668, Frances contracted smallpox. His anger forgotten, Charles dashed to see her.

Frances's illness hardly marred her beauty and it saved her friendship with Charles. In May, the month of Catherine's miscarriage and Barbara's move from Whitehall, Charles appointed Richmond Lord Lieutenant of Kent. Pepys noted that while the King supped nightly with Catherine, it seemed that he was 'mighty hot upon the Duchess of Richmond'.[24] One night, rather than taking a coach to see her at Somerset House, he impetuously took a scull and rowed downriver alone. Since the garden door was shut, he climbed over the wall to see Frances. There was no talk of an affair, but Charles admitted to Minette that being with her, and worrying about her illness, made him completely forget to write, 'and I must confess this last affliction made me pardon all that is past, and cannot hinder myself from wishing her very well'.[25] With affectionate concern he fretted about Frances's scars and problems with her eyes and hovered over her progress to recovery.

Catherine had always remained friends with Frances, and later that year, after the Richmonds gave 'a grand dinner for their majesties', she appointed her a Lady of the Bedchamber.[26] The Richmonds moved into rooms by the bowling green in Whitehall, and Frances was back among her friends and family. (Her sister Sophia, a dresser to Henrietta Maria, also became one of Catherine's attendants, and married the son of Charles's Master of the Household.) Barbara was said to be so furious at her reinstatement that she refused to have supper with the king, who took to dining instead with Monmouth, Buckingham and Rupert at the Duchess of Monmouth's. (He was always kind to Monmouth's young duchess, who had dislocated her hip while dancing at court and walked with a limp for the rest of her life.)

Visiting Frances became one of the few untroubled areas of Charles's life. Her husband, however, remained a problem, intemperately demanding overseas posts and getting into brawls. In 1672 Richmond was sent to Denmark as ambassador, where he splashed out on furs, ran up debts and complained loudly of the dullness of the Danes. After a few months, in the winter snows, despite everyone's advice, he rowed out for a drunken evening with the captain of an English frigate moored off Elsinore. In the darkness he missed his step between ship and boat and plummeted into the icy waters. He died the same evening. Frances did not remarry, but stayed at court with the queen. Since she had no children, after her husband's death the Richmond and Lennox title reverted to the crown: in 1675 Charles would bestow it on his son by his mistress of the next decade, Louise de Kéroualle.

Charles's many children were all dear to him, although his favourite was always Monmouth, now a handsome, wayward and easily influenced teenager. In early 1668, when Monmouth was in Paris, Charles asked Minette to look after him for, he confessed, 'I do love him very well'. He was anxious that she should keep him from joining Louis's army in Flanders, where he might be plunged into a 'hot campaign'. When Monmouth went back again to France in June, he wrote an amused paternal letter: 'He intendes to put on a perriwig againe, when he comes to Paris, but I believe you will thinke him better farr, as I do, with his short haire.'[27]

James, Duke of Monmouth in his glamorous teenage years

For the last two years rumours had been circulating that Charles was thinking of making Monmouth legitimate and even of acknowledging a marriage with Lucy Walter, a course strongly urged by Buckingham and Ashley. These hints caused friction between Charles and James, who were never as close as they had been after Clarendon's fall. Here was another split around which factions could grow. James's anxieties about the succession were also heightened by Charles's sudden interest in divorce. In 1669 he personally attended the hearings in the House of Lords when John Manners, Lord Roos, appealed for a private act of parliament to obtain a divorce from his wife Anne. Roos had already won an ecclesiastical separation on the grounds of Anne's adultery, and a private act bastardising her children. But a civil divorce would mean that he could remarry and produce a legitimate heir. The case gripped the news-devouring public, firstly because of the revelations about Anne's promiscuity, but also because an act allowing the husband to marry again would set a crucial precedent, challenging the indissolubility of marriage. The bill was promoted in the Lords by John Wilkins, now Bishop of Chester, who pointedly remarked that divorce might be granted not only for adultery but also for 'immundicity of the womb, which is given forth to [be] the queen's condition'.[28] Charles's influence undoubtedly helped the passing of the bill in 1670.

Charles himself said that he followed the Roos case simply because, as he put it, the revelations were as good as a play. It was partly true. And it was also true that in his current unsettled mood, plays offered the best escape from the strains of his life. And players, too, he thought, could offer such release, a freedom from any real commitment.

36 Sweet Ladies

Chance, not prudence, makes us fortunate.
GEORGE ETHEREGE, *She Would If She Could*

CHARLES'S ACTRESS MISTRESSES linked him to the world of the theatre and the Wits, masters of street and court performance. Buckingham had dabbled with the stage since his adaptation of Fletcher's *The Chances* in 1661, and *Sir Politic Would-Be* two years later. Among the playwrights, Etherege was slowly drawing nearer to the court, being made a Gentleman of the Privy Chamber in 1668. In February that year his new play, *She Would if She Could*, drew such a crowd at the Duke of York's Theatre that scores of people were turned away in the rain. Buckingham, Buckhurst and Sedley sat with him in the crowded pit, and although to Etherege's fury the play was not a success (he blamed the actors), it set a new style in the comedy of manners that would soon sweep the stage. Three months later, the same quartet took their seats to watch Sedley's first comedy, *The Mulberry Garden*, so keenly awaited that the doors opened two hours early. A silly play, Pepys thought, noting that the king did not laugh from beginning to end.

He did not laugh either at the off-stage performances of the libertine crew – at Buckingham's duel, at Rochester having his clothes stolen in a brothel, at the arrest of Sedley and Buckhurst for 'running up and down all the night with their arses bare through the streets, and at last fighting and being beat by the watch and clapped up all night'.[1] The last jape was made worse to many minds by the fact that the constable who arrested them was reprimanded and imprisoned.

Although Charles could be impatient with these rule-breakers, sometimes he joined them. Normally a temperate drinker, unlike most of his court, in this disturbed spring he got drunk with Sedley and Buckhurst in Suffolk, and was said to go incognito with them to London brothels. In an intensified form they reflected his own scepticism, his belief that God would not damn a man for taking a little pleasure. Rochester said of this period that he was completely drunk for five years (which makes sense of the comment on his courageous dash in the Four Days Battle, that no sober man would have done it). Yet there was logic, and often genius, in his self-destructive madness. To Rochester, man was a material creature, his existence bounded by birth and death. If life was a perpetual flux then change was natural and constancy was not. To deny 'natural' instincts went against all sense. Pleasure, seizing the moment, was an obligation. During one of his frequent banishments from court Rochester disguised himself as an Italian mountebank and set up in Tower Street, 'where he had a Stage', selling quack medicines: other disguises included a porter or a beggar. And when he returned from these adventures, he entertained the court with scabrous accounts of his doings, a parodic parallel to Charles's repeated stories of his wanderings after Worcester.

The king in disguise is a trope of theatre, the good monarch walking among his people and watching their lives. With Nell Gwyn, even more than with Moll Davis, Charles could again play this role. Nell was open in her manner, but she too, in some sense, was in disguise. She kept very quiet about her origins. Actresses often liked to suggest some upper-class blood (Moll was described variously as the daughter of a blacksmith or of the Earl of Berkshire), and in Nell's case the most common story, still often baldly stated as fact, was that she was born in Oxford, the daughter of a royalist officer, Captain Thomas Gwynn, and granddaughter of a dean of Christ Church. At the time, many people doubted this. As a cruel lampoon, 'The Lady of Pleasure: a Satyr', put it,

> No man alive could ever call her daughter
> For a battalion of arm'd men begot her.[2]

This was a dig at her mother Helena, a larger-than-life figure well known in London as a drunken, pipe-smoking, quarrelsome broth-el-keeper, always bragging about her fine girls. One of Nell's most challenging roles was playing the company whore in Lacy's comedy *The Old Troop* (a part said to be based on Helena). This drama of cor-rupt royalist soldiers billeted on resentful villagers, drawn from Lacy's own Civil War experience as a lieutenant with a troop of horse, full of bawdy jokes and ludicrous mock-French from the com-pany chef 'Monsieur Raggou', was a dazzling hit – if uncomfortably close to Nell Gwyn's own past.

All that is known for sure, apart from her mother Helena's address in Coal Hole Lane, off Drury Lane (a place that makes Nell an irre-sistible type of Cinderella), is that she had a sister called Rose. This was almost certainly the 'Rose Gwyn' who begged Harry Killigrew to present her petition to the Duke of York in 1663 to help her get out of Newgate, where she was held for theft. Rose claimed, as so many petitioners did, that her father had lost everything in the serv-ice of Charles I. Harry Killigrew was the son of Tom Killigrew of the King's Theatre, and by this point Rose and Nell, who was then about thirteen, were probably both working there as orange girls.[3]

Nell was almost illiterate – all her life she marked, rather than signed her name – but Hart and Lacy must have taught her to read, or to learn from dictation. At fourteen she had small roles on stage, including a bit-part in Orrery's *Mustapha* in April 1665, a play whose numbing dullness was relieved for Pepys by the presence of the king and queen and Barbara Castlemaine, 'and pretty witty Nell'. From then on, in play after play, Nell and Hart entranced the crowds as the combative 'mad couple'. In early 1667 Nell acted in a re-run of Buckingham's *The Chances*, and in March Charles and James saw her play Florimell to Hart's Celadon in Dryden's *Secret Love, or the Maiden Queen*. After its bawdy prologue, Dryden's serious plot, in solemn rhyme, told the story of the Queen of Sicily, whose love for her courtier threatens to tear the court and country apart (another warning to Charles about inappropriate passion). By contrast, in the 'mad' sub-plot, Nell and Hart played an independent-minded woman and suitor, engaged in constant, lively jousting. Pepys burst out in his diary:

... so great performance of a comical part was never, I believe, in the world before as Nell doth this, both as a mad girle, and then, most and best of all, when she comes in like a young gallant; and hath the motions and carriage of a spark the most that ever I saw any man have. It makes me, I confess, admire her.[4]

Charles admired her too, declaring *Secret Love* 'his play', and commanding a court performance, for which he provided costumes.[5] When Davenant died the following year, he appointed Dryden as Poet Laureate.

The part of Florimell was written specially for Nell, and it conjures up her unusual good looks: 'Ovall face, clear skin, hazle eyes, thick brown Eye-browes, and Hair.'[6] She stood out among the dark-haired, sloe-eyed beauties with her unfashionable tawny hair and turned-up nose, and she was petite and curvy, with tiny feet and extremely fine legs. Charles liked good legs, as the earlier incident with Frances Stuart showed, and in an age when breasts were often on display, in paintings, in deep-necked ball gowns and particularly on stage, legs had a particular charm.

In *Secret Love* Nell's legs and her confident, breezy style were shown off to advantage when she admired herself proudly in her disguise as a French-obsessed fop:

If cloathes and a bon meen will take 'em, I shall do't. – Save you *Monsieur Florimell*: Faith methinks you are a very *janty* Fellow, *poudré* & *adjusté* as well as the best of 'em. I can manage the little Comb – set my Hat, shake my Garniture, toss about my empty Noddle, walk with a courant slurr.[7]

She was fun, and the witty promises of the play's closing contract also had their appeal, implying a new kind of relationship between men and women, and certainly between a king and his mistress. Florimell and Celadon will agree to give each other their liberty and never to interfere in each other's lives or ask awkward questions:

Nell Gwyn, painted by Simon Verelst around 1670

Celadon Provided always, that whatever liberties we take with other people,
we continue very honest to one another.

Florimell As far as will consist with a pleasant life.

Celadon Lastly, Whereas the names of Husband and Wife hold for nothing
but clashing and cloying, and dullness and faintness in their significa-
tion; they shall be abolish'd for ever betwixt us.

Florimell And instead of those, we will be married by the more agreeable
names of Mistress and Gallant.[8]

The summer after this success Nell briefly disappeared from London as the mistress of Charles Sackville, Lord Buckhurst – her second Charles she called him, Charles Hart being her first. Entranced by the sight of her legs as she tumbled across the stage, Buckhurst had promised her £100 a year, but the affair did not work out as planned. After a month or so in Epsom, where Buckhurst shared a house with Sedley, and was visited by Buckingham and Rochester, Nell was back on stage. Playing to almost empty houses in the dusty days of late August, before the season had fully begun, she fended off Buckhurst's hints that he had dropped her because she asked for money, and ignored the lewd suggestions that all his friends had shared her favours. By autumn she was back on top form, playing in Howard's *The Mad Couple* with all her old brio, mocking Moll's 'cold lodging' song and flaunting her youthful independence. When the fiddlers arrived on stage she jumped up and declared roundly:

> A Fiddle! Nay, then I am made again;
> I'd have a dance, if I had nothing but my
> Smock on. Fiddler strike up and play my jig
> Call'd *I care not a pin for any man*.[9]

Moll Davis had her house and her ring, but Charles's affair with her was no grand passion. From the start, he had his eye on Nell. In one story, in April 1668, soon after he set Moll up in Suffolk Street, Charles took a box at a performance of *She Would if She Could*. This time Nell was in the audience rather than on stage, and Charles flirted with her as she sat in the next box with a Villiers cousin of Buckingham. Afterwards he and the Duke of York, both incognito, took them to a tavern, but when the reckoning came, Charles and James turned out their empty pockets and poor Villiers had to pay. Another version has it that Nell herself paid, imitating the King's idiom perfectly, sighing, 'Ods fish! But this is the poorest company I ever was in!'[10]

Charles watched this irreverent beauty on stage and off and soon all theatregoers knew of their flirtation. When Nell played Jacintha in Dryden's *An Evening's Love, or the Mock Astrologer*, she openly teased the audience with her lines about the staircase of love:

Wildblood: Then what is a Gentleman to hope from you?
Jacintha: To be admitted to pass my time with, while a better comes: to be the lowest step in my Stair-case, for a Knight to mount upon him, and a Lord upon him, and a Marquess upon him, and a Duke upon him, till I get as high as I can climb.[11]

An Evening's Love was an exuberant Spanish intrigue in which Wildblood and Bellamy, gallants from chilly London, wandered bewildered through Madrid in carnival time. The contrasting cultures let the Town laugh at itself, as in Bellamy's good-natured definition of his own status: 'I am a Gentleman, a man of the Town, one who wears good Cloathes, Eates, Drinks, and wenches abundantly; I am a damn'd ignorant, and senceless fellow.'[12] Pepys found the play smutty, but Nell seemed at home in this carefree world, with its happy accidents, disguises and random encounters, and its view of life as a game, where love hung on the throw of a dice.

At the end of 1668 Barbara and Nell came face to face in a curious episode. Barbara had always exploited her theatrical contacts, and still called on Charles's backing in her many quarrels. She was currently in the middle of a row with her friend, Elizabeth, Lady Harvey, largely caused by her tense relationship with Lady Harvey's ally Buckingham, and her new friendship with the opposing clique surrounding the Duke of York. That December Barbara denounced Elizabeth as a 'hermaphrodite' and claimed that she was only angry because Barbara had refused her advances. To which Elizabeth replied quickly that she was 'amazed that Barbara, who did not refuse anyone, should say such things'.[13] This was followed by a full-scale feud.

There was a new fashion for Roman plays (less for the opportunity of Ciceronian eloquence than the chance to create bloodcurdling villains) and at the time of this row, Nell was playing an Amazon in a revival of Jonson's *Catiline Conspiracy*, and delivering the prologue as a blatantly sexy Cupid. But this time it was not Nell who caused a sensation. Before the play opened, Barbara coached the actress Katherine Corey, who played the ageing courtesan and would-be stateswoman Sempronia, to mimic Elizabeth Harvey in every drawling tone and gesture. Corey's accurate, exaggerated impersonation made the audience gasp, fall silent, then burst into loud, delighted applause. And when Cicero was asked, 'What will you do with Sempronia?' Barbara leapt to her feet and shrieked 'Send her to Constantinople!'[14] There was uproar in the pit, since everyone knew that Charles had just sent Elizabeth's husband as ambassador to Turkey, at her request, to get him out of her way.

Elizabeth counter-attacked, getting her cousin, Ned Montagu (who as Lord Chamberlain was in charge of licensing the theatres), to have Corey arrested. In response Barbara persuaded Charles to overrule Montagu, free the actress and command another performance. Both Barbara and Charles were there. But this time Lady Harvey was prepared, organising her supporters to hiss and fling oranges at the stage. Whitehall was abuzz, and the gossip was that 'my Lady Castlemayne is now in a higher command over the King then ever; not as a mistress, for she scorns him, but as a tyrant to command him'.[15]

While Barbara played the tyrant off-stage, the new hit in the playhouse was Dryden's baroque verse drama, *Tyrannick Love, or The Royal Martyr*. This was another roaring Roman epic, the tyrant being the cruel and lustful Emperor Maximin, who orders the torture and death of Catherine of Alexandria, because she refuses to submit to him. Dryden dedicated the play to the Duke of Monmouth, but the portrayal of the martyred St Catherine was, of course, a tribute to the Queen, and the royal couple attended the opening performance. Dramatic and excessive, *Tyrannick Love* played for a fortnight, an almost unheard-of run for a serious play. It was full of absurd, rhetorical speeches, including Maximin's sadistic gloating over Catherine's pierced breasts and torture. It also demanded spectacular effects: during her torture, the stage direction read, '*Amariel descends swiftly with a flaming Sword, and strikes at the Wheel, which breaks in pieces; then he ascends again.'*[16]

The miniature beauty Margaret Hughes played Catherine, while Nell played Maximin's well-intentioned daughter, Valeria. She was not good at serious parts, but she was always remembered for this play. At the end, Valeria (like most of the cast) died in suitably gory fashion. But as her bier was carried off, Nell rose again. 'Hold, are you mad?' she shouted to the bearer, 'you damned confounded Dog,/ I am to rise, and speak the Epilogue'. Then she cheekily turned to the audience, in her own person:

> I come, kind gentlemen, strange news to tell ye,
> I am the Ghost of poor departed Nelly.
> Sweet ladies, be not frighted, I'le be civil,
> I'm what I was, a little harmless devil . . .
> Oh Poet, damn'd dull Poet, who could prove
> So sensless! To make Nelly dye for Love;
> Nay, what's yet worse, to kill me in the prime
> Of *Easter*-Term, in Tart and Cheese-cake time!

Even while *Tyrannick Love* was running, Nell had her tart and cheese-cake, being invited to a banquet to honour Prince Cosimo, heir to the Grand Duke of Tuscany. In the spring of 1669 Charles took her to Newmarket. Back in London. she would slip into the coach that the Chiffinches sent to carry her from the theatre to Whitehall, and run round to the private stairs. Courtiers and civil servants were shocked that Charles should defy custom and choose a common orange girl as his mistress, but this was sound politics as well as sex. Nell was a girl from the people, the only one of his mistresses whom the crowd loved.

In summer Charles left the stench of London for the cool of Windsor. Up to now, the old castle had been used as a base for the garrison and for housing political prisoners. But when Mordaunt resigned in 1668 after his impeachment, Charles appointed Rupert constable in his stead and he began to repair it. The following August, Evelyn still thought it 'exceedingly ragged and ruinous'. He was also startled by the 'curious and effeminate pictures' in Rupert's bedchamber, so different from the warlike armour and guns and martial scenes in the public rooms 'which presented nothing but Warr & horror'.[17] The martial Prince had mellowed. He had never been a natural courtier, and had always been known for his temper, his unkempt dress and habit of eating in 'ordinary public taverns, paying his bill like everyone else'.[18] But now he fell in love with the actress Peg Hughes, formerly Sedley's mistress. The court agreed that Peg 'brought down and greatly subdued his natural fierceness'.[19] Their daughter, Ruperta, was born in 1673, and when Rupert died he left them most of his fortune.

Charles spent much of the summer in Windsor, hunting in the park, where Nell allegedly taught him to fish, up to now a sport of commoners not kings. This summer she became pregnant and at the end of the year she left the stage. Charles set her up first in a house at Newman's Row, to the north of Lincoln's Inn Fields. It was hardly a secret meeting place but it was a private one, and the French ambassador Colbert de Croissy was often summoned there. He reported back to Louis XIV on Charles's new domesticity, finding him and Nell playing cards among friends, eating pigeon pie and drinking Canary wine.[20] Nell returned to the stage briefly in late 1670 – perhaps a hint to her royal lover that she needed more cash – but then she moved permanently to Pall Mall, graduating from a small house at the far end to a larger one nearer Whitehall. Although she never received lodgings at court, and was not treated with the respect accorded to Barbara Castlemaine or Frances Stuart, Nell did well. Within three years Charles had spent £60,000 on his irrepressible actress, whom Burnet called 'the indiscreetest and wildest creature that ever was in a court . . . She acted all persons in so lively a manner, and was such a constant diversion to the King, that even a new mistress could not drive her away.'[21]

Nell was jokingly proud of her status, and enjoyed her rivalry with Charles's next mistress, Louise de Kéroualle, in the years to come. Nell's wit in this Anglo-French rivalry was much enjoyed, as in the famous, if apocryphal story of the time her coach was stopped by an an anti-papist mob during the Exclusion Crisis who took her for Louise. Unperturbed, Nell leaned from the coach window and shouted, 'Pray good people be civil; I am the *Protestant* whore.'[22] Nell was loyal to her friends, including Buckingham, Rochester and Monmouth, and never ashamed of her background or her body. She made Charles laugh. She was one of his good bets, part of his life until he died, and part of his legend thereafter.

37　Troublesome Men

Sir Cautious Trouble-all. You must know Sir Gravity, that upon the
model of an Oyster table, I have plodded out a Table for business.
Sir Gravity Empty. Y'gad that's very neat, what model can this bee?
. . .
Sir Cautious. . . . 'tis only thus: if enemies opposite, one here t'other
there, if friends – close touch – So I never trouble myself with reading newes books or Gazets, but go into my chamber, looke upon my
Table, and snap, presently I'le tell you how the whole world is disposed.

    ROBERT HOWARD, *The Country Gentleman*

AFTER CHARLES DISMISSED parliament in May 1668 he did not
call it to Westminster again for eighteen months. The work of government and diplomacy – Arlington's sphere – was directed through
the Privy Council and its four main committees, for naval and military affairs, foreign affairs, trade and 'Complaints and Grievances'.[1]
In Scotland, Lauderdale's rule increased in strength; in Ireland
Ormond's power hung in the balance. And in Whitehall, as in parliament, Charles used Buckingham to clear the board of those he
thought dangerous. His deployment of Buckingham is puzzling,
unless one considers that his policy with regard to troublesome men
was threefold. He wanted to clear away the men associated with the
Dutch war and put a new team in charge of the navy; to get rid of
any lingering supporters of Clarendon, whom many people (Charles
included) felt was still capable of stirring up trouble from exile; and
to rule out any chance of political uprising by dissenters.

    The first man to be brought down was Sir William Coventry. The
men Coventry worked with, including Pepys, liked his directness

and his refusal to curry favour, but the former naval commissioner and secretary to the Duke of York had many enemies, especially the country MPs, who suspected him of feathering his nest from selling places in the navy. His blunt criticism, especially of the court's carelessness with money, made Charles so impatient that during one encounter the king turned angrily on his heel and stalked away. But he was not an easy man to dismiss. That would be an affront to a leading family – the Coventry brothers, William and Henry, were uncles to George Savile, Viscount Halifax (who was now firmly separating himself from the Buckingham camp), and Henry Savile, Rochester's rakish friend. William Coventry had led Charles's triumphant entry into London on 29 May 1660, and since the middle of the decade he and his brother had dominated the House of Commons. 'A man of great notions and eminent virtues,' Burnet called him, 'the best speaker in the house, and capable of bearing the chief ministry.'[2] And although he had outraged the Duke of York by his attacks on Clarendon, he was still seen as a member of his camp.

The opportunity to oust him came from a crisis of Coventry's own making, when a rumour spread that he was about to be ridiculed on the stage. The theatre was fast becoming an accepted arena for courtiers to attack their enemies. *The Duke of Lerma* had implicitly demolished Clarendon; Shadwell's *Sullen Lovers* had caricatured Robert and Ned Howard as 'Sir Positive At-All' and 'Poet Ninny'; Barbara Castlemaine had caused uproar by arranging the mockery of Lady Harvey. Most recently, Kynaston's spectacular mimicry of Charles Sedley in Newcastle's *The Heiress* had won the actor a vicious beating from Sedley's hired thugs. Charles well understood the tactic of demolition through performance. Buckingham's burlesque of Clarendon had been an effective means of reducing the courtiers' respect, and later this year, Ralph Montagu, ambassador to Paris, wrote to Arlington in alarm, when a French nobleman told him that Paris was abuzz with (false) rumours of Arlington's disgrace. Apparently, said Montagu, everyone had heard 'it is a custom in England that when the King is angry with anybody, that he makes them be acted, and that my Lord Buckingham and Bab May had acted you to the King, and endeavoured to turn you *en ridicule*.[3]

In March 1669, Coventry heard that Buckingham and Robert Howard were planning to ridicule him in their new play, *The Country Gentleman*, as 'Sir Cautious Trouble-All'. The name stemmed from Charles's own frustration with Coventry's pessimism and despair over royal carelessness with money. Coventry had told Pepys the previous December that he was 'represented to the King by his enemies as a melancholy man, and one that is still prophesying ill events, so as the King called him *Visionaire*'.[4] He learnt that in the play, Sir Cautious would be discovered sitting in the middle of a huge circular table (like one that Coventry actually owned), turning round on his chair, fluffing through papers taken from drawers labelled 'Affairs of Spain', 'Affairs of France', 'Affairs of Holland'. When Coventry angrily complained to Charles, the king sent for the play but claimed he could find nothing in it – unsurprisingly since the scene had been cut from the script he was shown. Unappeased, Coventry sent an angry challenge to Buckingham. The duke stalled, unwilling to risk another duel after the Shrewsbury affair. Meanwhile rehearsals continued, coming to a halt only when Coventry told Tom Killigrew that he would slit the actors' noses if they performed it.

As soon as Charles heard about the challenge to Buckingham, he seized on it as a pretext for excluding Coventry from the council. As he explained to Minette:

I am not Sorry that Sir Will: Coventry has given me this good occasion by sending my Lord of Buckingham a challenge, to turn him out of the Council. I do intend to turn him also out of the Tresury. The truth of it is he has been a troublesome man in both places, and I am well rid of him.[5]

One wonders if Charles had not been an accomplice all along.

Coventry was sent to the Tower, where his many friends rushed to see him, blocking the roads with their coaches. (There were near duels in the Tower itself, the Duke of Richmond drawing his sword

Sir William Coventry, by John Riley

on James Hamilton, with Halifax and Rochester in attendance.⁶) On 6 March Coventry petitioned the King for a pardon, and when Charles returned from Newmarket two weeks later he set him free. It was a brief imprisonment, but it was the end of Coventry's government career. Coventry himself could not care less, he said, about being stripped of office. He had had enough of court intrigues. He retired to his home at Minster Lovell in Oxfordshire, keeping his place as an MP and speaking out in parliament against court policies and any alliance with the French.

The Country Gentleman was not acted but the text shows how absurd it made Coventry look, with his 'oyster table' and his papers in piles, forming an instant guide to the alliances and ambitions of all foreign powers. Quite apart from this particular target, the whole play was a scathing satire on the secrecy and cabals of the court, the greed of the new-moneyed men, and the neglect of British virtues and English goods in favour of foreign ways and imports. Country gentlemen, Howard argued, should fight against corrupt placemen and self-seeking plotters, wherever they could be found.⁷ Sadly, this was exactly what Coventry himself thought, although he belonged to a different faction. The most significant impact of his dismissal was to thrust the royal brothers even further apart. It seemed that Charles was allowing Buckingham to have his way, at the expense, in particular, of the Duke of York. In a strange scene, just after Coventry was imprisoned, Pepys came across the duke and duchess dining at the navy treasurer's house at Deptford, with Barbara Castlemaine and the Duchess's maids of honour. All the ladies were sitting on the carpet playing 'I love my love with an A', rivalling each other in their wit.⁸ Their main toast at this picnic, however, was 'to the union of the two brothers' – Charles and James.

Charles could afford to shrug off criticism. But if Coventry was a disposable nuisance in Whitehall, as Clarendon had been, there were more difficult problems in the administration of Ireland. The country had been bedevilled for years by the deficit in government funds – something that Coventry, ironically, had tried to solve. The situation there was doubly precarious because of the hostility between Ormond, as Lieutenant Governor, and Roger Boyle, Earl of Orrery. In theory, the Irish treasury was controlled by Orrery's older brother, the Earl of Cork and Burlington, but he was rarely in Ireland and in practice, since Ormond disliked dealing with money, it was managed by the vice-treasurer, Arthur Annesley, Earl of Anglesey. He proved wholly inadequate to the job, his worst blunder being a drastic underestimate of army pay. Although he left the post in 1667 when he was appointed treasurer of the navy, by then the damage was done. The only good financial brain in the Irish administration was Orrery's, and he fumed at this incompetence, especially at the inadequate payments to his own Munster troops. A man who was always unable to keep still, or to keep quiet, he complained constantly to Ormond in lengthy letters, which Ormond brushed off with late, short replies. At the same time, Orrery began to build up a close relationship with Buckingham, and seeing this, scenting danger, Ormond came hot-foot to Whitehall in May 1668, to make sure nothing would happen behind his back. A month later Orrery also arrived, to prepare a direct attack.

Charles set up a commission of inquiry into the Irish finances, its members drawn from both factions. Anglesey's accounts were criticised and his fudging answers led Charles to suspend him as navy treasurer (another convenient cleansing of the Navy Board.) When Anglesey rashly challenged the King's right to dismiss him, Charles immediately removed him from the Privy Council and banished him from court. (Unlike Coventry, Anglesey chose to serve the court side in parliament, and was reinstated on the council two years later.) In the vacant post of treasurer to the navy, Charles appointed not one but two new commissioners, balancing both camps: Arlington's candidate, Sir Charles Lyttleton, and Buckingham's supporter, Osborne. When the two men came to kiss the king's hand at court, Pepys was careful not to join the throng surrounding them, 'that I might not be seen to look either way'.[9]

With Anglesey gone, attention turned to Ormond himself. Charles had always admired the duke, and was fond of him, but his staunch support of Clarendon and his lordly ways with Orrery and Buckingham did him no favours. In Ireland itself, there was no doubt that his record in some respects was good. Apart from scattered instances, he had kept the country peaceful and had shown true concern for the welfare of the Irish. After the disaster of the Cattle Bill, he helped Irish farmers turn to 'salt beef, butter and sheep', which led to a brisk trade with the colonies and the continent, and he banned imports of linen from Scotland, thus spurring the local linen trade. He also persuaded Charles to assign the Dublin government some of the prize money from captured ships, and urged the Privy Council to allow Irish merchants freedom of trade.[10] But Ormond's manner had not made him popular. His regal lifestyle in Dublin, his part in implementing the unpopular land settlement, his tolerance of Catholic worship and his use of his son Ossory as a deputy when he himself was away in England, all made people feel that he saw Ireland as a fiefdom, to be ruled solely by the Butler family.

Ormond's dismissal as Lord Lieutenant soon seemed inevitable, although his allies in parliament tried to mount a pre-emptive attack on Orrery, who was fiercely defended by the Buckingham group. To save his pride, Charles softened the blow by saying that Ormond's advice was now needed at Whitehall as Lord Steward, and by giving him a seat on the inner committee of foreign affairs.[11] The new Lord Lieutenant was the ineffective Lord Robartes, 'a sullen and morose man', who was attached to no faction, but upset everyone in Dublin by his cynicism, severity and lack of tact.[12] He lasted less than a year before he was replaced by the older, genial Lord Berkeley. Ormond remained out of favour during the next decade, and deeply in debt, but he maintained a dignified calm until he was needed, being recalled to Ireland as Lord Lieutenant again in 1677.

As far as Ireland was concerned, with Ormond gone, Charles could feel secure that there would be no over-mighty subject in charge.

The opposite was true of Scotland, where Lauderdale was now increasing his power. Lauderdale was a passionate, if self-serving, Scottish patriot, but paradoxically, for that very reason he was also a ferociously loyal supporter of the crown. His aim was to build Scotland into a strong 'citadel', a bulwark of monarchical strength, which would bring it revenue and help it progress. He was also useful to Charles, in dealing with the most intractable Scottish question, religion.

To begin with, when the Earl of Rothes took over from Middleton as Charles's commissioner to the Scottish parliament in 1663, backed by Archbishop James Sharp as head of the kirk, Lauderdale had mostly remained in Whitehall. But the Dutch war placed a great drain on Scottish resources and at the same time Archbishop Alexander Burnet of Glasgow persuaded Rothes to implement a fierce crackdown on covenanters, depicted as potential rebels. The administration expelled ministers and imposed draconian fines on all who attended conventicles, sending out troops to collect them and hunt down illegal meetings. The troops were led by the ruthless Sir James Turner, whose searches became even more brutal when it was feared that covenanters might collude with the Calvinist, republican States General. In November 1666, in reaction to Turner's raids, and prompted by a passionate exhortation from John Brown, an exiled minister in Holland, rebels gathered in the south-west of Scotland. Affirming their oath to the covenant, they captured Turner at Dumfries and marched on Edinburgh. But they were not strong enough to take the city, and as they turned back to the south they were trapped at Rullion Green in the Pentland Hills. Gilbert Burnet (no relation to the Archbishop), who was twenty-three at the time, and had already written a polemic against the repressive policy of the Scottish bishops, reported the scene in the hills before the rebels faced the government troops:

Their ministers did all they could by preaching and praying to infuse courage into them: and they sung the seventy-fourth and the seventy-eighth Psalms. And so they turned on the king's forces. They received the first charge that was given them by the troop of guards very resolutely, and put them in disorder. But that was all the action; for immediately they lost all order, and ran for their lives. It was now dark: about forty were killed on the spot, and a hundred and thirty were taken.[13]

Ironically, Rothes was in London, assuring Charles of the security of his northern kingdom, when the rising broke out. Now he came scurrying back with a new title, as general-in-chief of the army. In their interrogation of the prisoners, and in their hunt for conspirators in the country, Rothes's men used torture (which was banned by law in England but remained legal in Scotland) to obtain information. This horrified all who heard of it and many people risked their lives to save the rebels. The leaders were tried, convicted and strung up in groups on the gallows, still refusing to renounce the covenant. 'For all the pains of torture,' wrote Burnet, describing the death of the young preacher Maccail, he 'died in a rapture of joy':

His last words were, Farewell sun, moon and stars, farewell kindred and friends, farewell world and time, farewell weak and frail body; welcome eternity, welcome angels and saints, welcome saviour of the world, and welcome God the Judge of all: which he spoke with a voice and manner that struck all that heard it.

According to this account, Archbishop Burnet watched the men hang, deliberately keeping a reprieve from the king in his pocket. Charles had sent an urgent message, saying that he thought enough blood had been shed: all prisoners who agreed to obey the law should be released, and those who refused should be sent to the Plantations. But the king and the cleric had different notions of justice. Charles was pragmatic, wanting just enough judicial murder to stop further risings, but not enough to create martyrs. The Archbishop simply wanted revenge.

Lauderdale was appalled by the brief, tragic Pentland Rising and its consequences, but used it swiftly to increase his own influence. In early 1667, with the usual help from Robert Moray, who talked over affairs with Charles in the privacy of his Whitehall laboratory,

Lauderdale persuaded Charles, correctly, that Rothes himself had in fact provoked moderate dissenters into becoming hard-line rebels by his clampdown on conventicles. First he turned Charles against Archbishop Sharp, whom the King had never liked, then slowly undermined Rothes's power. In September, since Charles, said Lauderdale, found it so hard 'to say bleak things', he had personally drafted the letter revoking Rothes's appointment as commissioner. The leading noble in Scotland was now Lauderdale's close friend the Earl of Tweeddale, and soon Lauderdale himself held the post of commissioner, which he had coveted for so long.[14]

With regard to nonconformity, of whatever kind, Charles was simply concerned to keep the peace as far as he could in all his three kingdoms, distinguishing conscientious religious dissent from republicanism and sedition. Thus in Ireland, Robartes and Berkeley were instructed to follow Ormond's tolerant line, bolstering the strength of the Church of Ireland, encouraging Catholic clergy who supported the crown and reining in those who were difficult or obstructive. In Scotland, in 1669 (at the same time as he was attempting to suppress the more extreme dissenting meetings in England), Charles was asking Lauderdale to take a line of appeasement, while still urging that extremists should be ruthlessly weeded out. On 7 June Charles granted the 'First Indulgence', by which a long-discussed idea was finally put into practice, allowing moderate Scottish presbyterian ministers to be reappointed to their former parishes or to empty livings. When Archbishop Burnet and his followers objected, and sent an address to the king, Moray managed to slant their protest so that it looked like an attempt to force his arm. Charles, angry, ordered the Archbishop to resign. During this time, he told Moray, 'in most pungent and unanswereable terms', that he profoundly disliked the persecution of people for their religious beliefs.[15] His motivation was purely politcal.

In England, Charles's attempt at comprehension had been a tactic to impose his authority as Supreme Head of the Church, disciplining the bishops and disarming dissent. But after the failure of that effort, his policy was straightforward: woo the moderates and crush the extreme sects. There were inevitable confrontations, the most significant of these being with the Quakers, and their new spokesman William Penn. In Ireland, the young Penn had helped Ormond put down the Carrickfergus mutiny but while there he had been impressed by Quaker meetings at Cork, and had returned to London (to the alarm of his father Sir William and the disgust of Pepys) as a member of the Society of Friends. Trained as a lawyer, Penn was an eloquent spokesman and skilled polemicist. His uncompromising attitude was shown by the title page of *Truth Exalted*, in 1669, written, it declared, 'By William Penn the Younger, whom Divine Love constrains in a holy attempt to trample on Egypt's glory, not fearing the King's wrath, having beheld the Majesty of him who is invisible'.

In 1669 Penn also published a Quaker critique of the Restoration court and its culture in *No Cross, No Crowne*, and the following year he would make his first stand as a political activist when he defied the new Conventicle Act, writing *The Great Case of Liberty of Conscience*, addressed directly to Charles. When he and his colleague Richard Meade were tried for addressing a 'tumultous assembly' in Gracechurch Street, in court Penn defended his right to freedom of religious conscience as the right of every English citizen. Both Penn and Meade were acquitted, setting a key precedent in English law.[16] Tumult followed. The angry Lord Mayor imprisoned the jury, who were then released by the Chief Justice of the Court of Common Pleas, Sir John Vaughan, establishing yet another principle, the independence of juries.

In late 1669, when Penn made his protests in defence of liberty of conscience, the new Scottish parliament, persuaded by Lauderdale, passed a series of acts. One was an Act of Supremacy, drafted by Moray, recognising Charles's authority over the Kirk, something that was deeply resented both by the presbyterians and the Scottish bishops. Another was a new militia act, which gave the

King authority to raise twenty thousand men in Scotland. A third piece of legislation was a ferocious act against conventicles. 'Never was King soe absolute as you in poor old Scotland,' Lauderdale told Charles in November 1669.[17]

Since the end of the Dutch war, in which Scotland faced high taxes and lost many men, with little hope of reward from the trade that the war was supposed to save, Lauderdale had aimed at stabilising Scotland's position. The best way, he thought, would be through a more formal union with England, so that Scotland too would benefit from the Navigation Acts, and other protective legislation. By the end of 1669, thanks to Lauderdale's management of the Scottish legislators, Charles had come round to the idea of union, and put the proposal to the Westminster parliament. Immediately, he met opposition, partly due to the spectre of the 20,000 Scottish troops that he could now supposedly call on at any time, but more because of the deep-rooted English distrust of the Scots, born of the two Civil Wars. Despite this opposition, Charles did appoint commissioners to examine the possibility, but in November 1670 he told them to set it aside, and meet 'later'. It would be thirty-seven years until the union was actually achieved, in 1707.

The reaction to 'Gyant Lauderdale . . . This haughty monster with his ugly claws', and his ideas of union (which were seen as pimping his own mother nation for the King), was uniformly harsh. Satirists drew him as an absolutist, a chapbook villain, who

> Sets up in Scotland *alamode de* France,
> Taxes Excise and Armyes does advance.
> This Saracen his Countryes freedom broke
> To bring upon our Necks the heavier yoke:
> This is the Savage Pimp without dispute
> First brought his Mother for a Prostitute:
> Of all the Miscreants ever went to hell
> This Villin Rampant bares away the bell.[18]

Lauderdale also roused enmity because of his flamboyant personal style. In 1669, the year he was campaigning for union with England, he took up again with an old flame from the 1650s, Elizabeth, 'Bess of Dysart', now a red-haired, dynamic woman in her forties. In reaction, Lauderdale's wife Anne went to Paris in disgust. When she died there in 1671, he married Bess. She had great beauty, thought Burnet, but it was her clever conversation and passion that made her stand out:

She had studied not only divinity and history, but mathematics and philosophy. She was violent in everything she set about, a violent friend, but a much more violent enemy. She had a restless ambition, lived at a vast expence, and was ravenously covetous; and would have stuck at nothing by which she might compass her ends.[19]

The Lauderdale establishments in Edinburgh and at Ham House in Richmond were notoriously sumptuous and extravagant. Bess was a political force in her own way, and it was under her influence that Lauderdale dropped his allies, Moray and Tweeddale, early in the next decade.

The careers of Ormond and Lauderdale followed opposite curves. While Ormond fell in the late 1660s and waited in the wings to be recalled, Lauderdale soared into power. In 1672, on the eve of the third Dutch War, Charles made him a duke, and then a knight of the Garter. He clung to his power like a tyrant, and Charles backed him in all his repressive measures. But while Ormond was restored in the mid-1670s, and remained Lord Lieutenant of Ireland until Charles's death, by the end of that decade it was clear that Lauderdale had over-reached himself and must fall. Ousted from office and disabled by a stroke, he died in 1682, three years before his king.

38 Charles and Louis

There is all the reason in the world to join profit with honour, when it
may be done honestly . . .
     CHARLES II to Minette, 1669

BEHIND THE SCENES Charles was brooding again over his country's position in Europe, and its control of the seas. What would be
his best move? Ostensibly he was still firmly behind the protestant
triple alliance with the Dutch and the Swedes, but privately he had
not forgiven the Dutch and still saw them as the great competitors,
who must be checked if British trade was to flourish. The triple
alliance was an interim move, to prove his strength and independence of his cousin Louis. Charles admired and envied Louis, for his
style, his wealth, his palaces, his official mistresses, his balls and ballets, fetes and fireworks. He envied him even more for his obliging
officials, his vast standing army, his overflowing treasury, and above
all for his freedom to rule without being weighed down by parliament, like a shackle around the leg. He too would have liked to say
'L'Etat, c'est moi.' But while he may have had a hankering for absolutism, Charles's style was very different. He was by nature more
informal, more humorous, more sceptical. Recognising the changes
that the Interregnum had brought, and the ideas that had inspired
the Commonwealth, he accepted that things had changed. A British
monarch must now rule with parliament.

Charles was concerned for his country's honour but had only a
touch of Louis's obsession with glory, or his notions of the divinity
of kingship. While Louis desired to be the 'Most Christian King' of
a Catholic nation that tolerated no heresy, Charles felt religion was
a personal matter, although one of great concern to the state where

it challenged the regime's power. And although Louis held a far better hand, Charles's pragmatic approach and willingness to bluff gave him certain advantages.

Louis XIV could be seen as the supreme embodiment of the Age of Absolutism, while Charles II, with all his faults and failures, was a monarch of the dawning Age of Reason. Below the surface, France was riven by division, and its trade and industry were stifled by the control and restrictions of the state, while the fluid conditions in Britain fostered an individualism that helped the growth of a commercial and industrial nation. Louis's far-sighted minister, Jean-Baptiste Colbert, recognised the problems. In 1660 nearly all the produce from French colonies had been carried in Dutch or English ships, but from the middle of the decade Colbert began reorganising the state finances, setting up state industries, like the great textile factories, and attempting to find some way for France to share in the expanding global trade. Trading companies were formed in quick succession: La Compagnie des Indes Orientales in 1664, des Indes Occidentales, 1665, du Nord, 1669, du Levant, 1670. To support these, Colbert strengthened the navy, and fortified the ports.

Louis, however, was more concerned with his army and his ambitions on land, expanding his boundaries to bolster the security of his dynasty. His ambitions, and his thirst for *la gloire*, as well as his anger with the Dutch for interfering in his campaigns in Flanders, seemed to offer Charles the chance of a favourable alliance. The intermediary, as before, was his sister Minette. During the spring and summer of 1668 their letters were full of court gossip and of concerns for Minette's health. One enduring theme was the atrocious state of her marriage and the intrigues in the French court, which made those of Whitehall seem like village flirtations. Despite his own infidelities and his overwhelming devotion to the unscrupulous chevalier de Lorraine, Minette's husband, the duc d'Orléans, was ferociously jealous, to the point of implying that Minette might even be having an affair with the nineteen-year-old Monmouth. She herself was not innocent. In the early years of her marriage she had encouraged the beau of the court, Armand, comte de Guiche, at the expense of another suitor, the marquis de Vardes. When the latter complained to Louis, the King sent de Guiche to a military post far from Paris. As de Vardes, encouraged by this success, grew increasingly insolent, Minette turned for help to her mother, to Charles, and to Louis, who reacted (or overreacted) by banishing him to the Camargue for twenty years. De Vardes's revenge came through his friend, the chevalier de Lorraine, who virtually took over Minette's house. She was feeling anxious and lonely, consoled only by Charles's suggestion that they might meet again soon. He asked Monmouth, on his second trip to France that year, to try to arrange a visit which, he promised his sister, 'if we can bring to passe, will be the greatest happiness to me imaginable'.[1]

In August 1668 a new French ambassador was sent to London, Colbert's younger brother, Charles Colbert, marquis de Croissy. As before, reams of letters flowed between London and Paris, as Colbert sifted court gossip and reported on factions and feuds. Charles did not trust him and became still more firmly resolved to settle matters privately, cousin to cousin, king to king. This time he was in a stronger position, since he was working closely within the triple alliance and discussing the inclusion of other protestant states. So when Louis offered the terms Charles had asked for in 1667 (payment for troops during any war, and control of Ostend and Nieuwpoort), he shifted the ground. Politely expressing his sincere desire for closer union, but citing the alarm of his people, he asked that Louis abandon the strengthening of his navy and remove the protectionist tariffs.[2] Louis, as Charles suspected, was bound to decline.

Now that Louis was making overtures, Charles played hard to get. To begin with, he proposed a treaty of commerce. This, he explained to Minette, was where they must begin, 'because I must enter first upon those matters which will render the rest more plausible here, for you know that the thing which is nearest the harte of the nation is trade and all that belongs to it'.[3] Beyond this, he suggested a treaty of friendship, its terms as yet unspecified. By December 1668, matters had become so delicate that Charles sent his sister a cipher to use in future letters. One complication was that Buckingham, always keen on a French alliance, was feeding information to Colbert and promising him that he could swing the deal within a year. Buckingham's supporter Sir Ellis Leighton ('a mad frieking fellow' according to Pepys) carried urgent letters to Paris, addressed to Minette, Henrietta Maria and St Albans.[4] Charles watched every move, keeping his own approaches secret. When Colbert told him of Leighton's visit to Paris, he expressed intense surprise and annoyance, as if he knew nothing of it at all.

Determined to break the triple alliance, and making little headway with Charles, in early 1669 Louis approached the Dutch, seeking an agreement on trade and assurances that they would not interfere more in Flanders. But de Witt too was now arguing from strength, and the talks came to nothing. Meanwhile Charles wrote to Louis, as he told Minette, assuring him of 'the desire I have to enter into a personall frindship with him':

and to unite our interests so, for the future, as there may never be any jealousys between us. The only thing which can give any impediment to what we both desire is the matter of the Sea, which is so essenciall a point to us here, as an union upon any other security can never be lasting.[5]

It was vital, he stressed, that no word should get out about these negotiations, so that no advances he made towards France 'may ever turn to my prejudice'. This time, he suggested that any alliance between them could be kept secret, so that he could still maintain the façade of the triple alliance. He waited for a response. But even as he waited, he had a further move in mind. In return for a large sum of money, he would declare himself a Catholic.

Before he committed himself to making such a dramatic and fateful promise, Charles needed to create the right diplomatic team to support it. Bluff or not, in order to convince Louis, it was important that this team themselves should all be convinced of the sincerity of his desire to convert. He needed people who would be fired by zeal for the Catholic cause, and ask no awkward questions. According to his brother James, on 25 January 1669 – the Feast of the Conversion of St Paul – Charles called a private meeting. Those present included James himself; Arlington, a Catholic sympathiser despite his Dutch wife; his loyal, pro-Catholic right-hand man Clifford; and the elderly Catholic courtier Lord Arundell of Wardour, who was Master of the Horse to Henrietta Maria and would therefore have a good excuse for frequent trips to Paris. James himself still conformed outwardly to the Church of England, but he had already come to believe that salvation could only be found in Roman Catholicism. In James's recollection, at this meeting Charles declared his longing to proclaim his Catholic faith, 'with tears in his eyes'. Moved, the group came up quite independently with the novel idea of approaching Louis XIV.

James's 'memoirs', compiled by others from his notes in the nineteenth century, are embroidered with hindsight and confused about timing. While some see his account as fantasy, most accept that the meeting happened (though some cavil at Charles's tears), and one or two suggest that his conversion was genuine.[6] Yet it rings true of Charles as consummate actor and dissembler, and also as a man who, despite his scepticism, longed for lost certainties. He had little time for doctrine and no evident fear for his soul, but he would have been a Catholic if he could, for the sake of community and family. It was imperative for this group to believe him sincere. It was important too, that Minette should accept his desire to convert as genuine. Despite her fashionable ways, she was pious, and while she could be Machiavellian in her understanding of strategy, and was keenly alert to the danger of Charles making any public avowal, the religious aspect of the secret deal became crucial to her. Charles needed France, she once wrote revealingly, 'to ensure the success of the design about R', as if that were his main aim.

The negotiations continued. Charles deliberately used unlikely couriers to carry his letters and seems to have actively amused himself in choosing them. One night in February 1669, shortly after

Coventry was arrested and Ormond had been dismissed from his office in Ireland, Charles was dining at the Dutch embassy. After dinner, according to the ever knowing Pepys, 'they drank and were pretty merry'.[7] In their cups, Tom Killigrew outraged Rochester by teasing him about keeping his wife in the country and not letting her see London. When Killigrew complained, Rochester gave him a box on the ear, at which Charles 'very angerley called my Lord R. an impertinent fellow and bad him be gon'.[8] Technically, for Rochester to cast a blow in front of the King, was *lèse-majesté*, or treason. This time it had happened publicly, and embarrassingly, in a foreign embassy. But not only did Charles cheerily pardon Rochester ('which doth give much offence to the people here at Court, to see how cheap the King makes himself'), next day he walked up and down with him 'as free as ever'.[9] Rochester ruined this reprieve almost at once by joining in the duel while Coventry was in the Tower and as a token banishment Charles sent him off to Paris, carrying a letter to Minette. 'You will find him not to want witt', he told her drily, 'and did behave him selfe, in all the duch warr, as well as anybody, as a volunteer.'[10]

When he wrote this, Charles was in Newmarket. Instead of travelling decorously he had delayed his departure and had to rush, early on the morning of 8 March. The day before was a Sunday, and there was good news as Sir Thomas Allin had finally concluded an agreement with the Algerians, who had taken a ship hostage at Tangier.[11] Charles and James met at Arlington's house, ostensibly to discuss the Tangier deal. But was this really the subject of their abrupt Sunday meeting? On the same day, Charles finally sent Arundell to Minette, carrying a detailed offer to Louis. His cover was attending Henrietta Maria, and Minette should on no account, Charles told her, suggest he had any mission from himself. Respecting his sister's interest in English affairs, he explained, too, his irritation with Coventry, and brushed off her enquiry about Ormond by explaining that he did, of course, still trust the Duke and the reasons for his dismissal were 'too long for a letter'.[12] Then he signed off hastily, 'and so my dearest sister good night, for tis late, and I have not three howers to sleepe this night'.

After that brief sleep, Charles and James, with Rupert and Monmouth, set off for Newmarket at three in the morning. In the rush, their coach overturned at King's Gate in Holborn, 'and the King all dirty, but no hurt'.[13] The cause was a mystery, except that it was dark 'and the torches did not, they say, light the coach as they should do'. There were rumours of a plot but this was, it appeared, a simple accident. The next ten days at Newmarket were free of incident, except for the entertainment provided by the Abbé Pregnani, Louis's incompetent courier and spy. Pregnani was an amateur astrologer who had worked out a foolproof system for finding winners by the stars. To Charles's amusement he lost on every race, and the Duke of Monmouth, following his tips, lost even more.

Charles's bid was now on the table, waiting for Louis to respond. Charles's terms were that the triple alliance would remain in place, but England and France would make a private alliance, both offensive and defensive. As part of this, Louis should agree to drop his naval expansion, and if there was a war (which Charles did not yet accept) England should receive money, ships and men. The most startling clause followed. If Louis gave £200,000 to make his position safe, Charles would declare himself a Catholic.

After initial shock, the French response to 'the Grand Design' was encouraging. Louis stopped his negotiations with de Witt, agreed to abide by the Treaty of Aix-la-Chapelle (keeping the peace with Spain that the triple alliance had worked for), and promised to build no warships for a year. On the issue of trade, he agreed that there might be grounds for commercial co-operation. And as for the religious issue, he would send Charles the money he asked for to support his Catholic conversion. But he too now laid down a condition: any agreement must be founded on a war with the Dutch. At present this was the last thing Charles wanted. For a few months, the negotiations stopped.

Nanteuil's portrait of Louis XIV, 1664, with the armour beneath his fine cravat
hinting at the ruthless calculation beneath his elegance

Charles's offer to convert to Catholicism may, perhaps, have been
intended largely to support his brother. James was clearly drifting
towards Catholicism, and disastrous as Charles felt this to be, it
would make sense to have Louis's support in place if trouble arose
about his claim to the throne. Buckingham and Ashley had already
been campaigning behind the scenes against James, expressing their

determination to have a protestant heir. Charles advised Minette, in heavy code, to write to Buckingham warmly to keep him sweet, but 'pray have a care you do not say any thing to him which may make him thinke that I have employed anybody to Louis'.[14] It was vital that he should not suspect 'that there is something of Catholic interest in the case'.

The problem of the succession was currently uppermost in Charles's mind. That spring, less than a year after her last miscarriage, Catherine fell pregnant again. Charles gave Minette all the details, anxiously, but also with the briskness of a man who had fathered several children. She had missed her periods twice, he reported:

and she had a kind of colic the day before yesterday which pressed downwards and made her apprehend she should miscarry, but today she is so well as she does not keep her bed. The midwives who have searched her say that her matrix is very close, though it be a little low; she has now and then some little shows of *them*, but in so very little quantity as it only confirms the most knowing women here that there is a fair conception.[15]

Two weeks later he ended another heavily enciphered letter with this news. 'I have no more to add, but to tell you that my wife, after all our hopes, has miscarried again, without any visible accident.'[16] The denial of an accident referred to rumours that Catherine had become frightened when Charles's pet fox suddenly appeared in her bedroom. He would take no blame, but nor would he entertain any more hopes. 'The physicians are divided whether it were a false conception or a good one, and so good night, for 'tis very late.' James would, after all, be his heir.

In May, plans for Minette's visit had to be postponed because she too was pregnant. As she sweltered heavily in the summer heat, bedridden for much of the time, she longed for a son. Her daughter Marie Louise was now six, but her infant son, the duc de Valois, had died of a fever three years before. Since then she had suffered a miscarriage. She longed to produce an heir, largely as her duty to

Monsieur would then be done. At midnight on 27 August she gave birth to a girl, Anne Marie. Exhausted, she sank into depression.

A fortnight later came the news that Henrietta Maria had died suddenly. Frail and unable to sleep, she had defied her doctors' advice and taken a large dose of opium, sleeping never to awake. Despite her move to Paris Henrietta Maria had been very much a part of British court life, and with her death an era ended. She had made no will, and Charles was her sole heir. He gave Minette her mother's rope of pearls and her house at Colombes, but many jewels and fine paintings now made their way to Whitehall. When she died, Minette's daughter Marie Louise and the Yorks' daughter Anne, who was receiving treatment for her eyes in Paris, were both staying with their grandmother. Now they came to Minette. The nursery at St Cloud was full of girls, instead of the longed-for boys. But in time two of these three girls would be queens – Marie Louise as Queen of Spain and Anne Queen of England – and the baby Anne Marie would be Duchess of Savoy.

Minette's knowledge that Henrietta Maria had passionately wanted her sons to become Catholics made her support the religious element of the Anglo-French agreement even more strongly. As the letters went back and forth, over the summer Charles shored up his bargaining position. Forty warships patrolled the coast in ostentatious fashion. His diplomats worked hard within the triple alliance and his envoys scurried across Europe, arranging talks with the princes of Germany and the Scandinavian governments, canvassing alliances, mediating in disputes and arranging commercial treaties. He was in a strong position when the autumn arrived, bringing a new round of diplomatic juggling. Once again, Louis approached the Dutch, and once again Charles approached Louis. This time Charles was less hostile to the idea of a war, following Minette's cynical advice that he should simply agree with Louis's demands for a war, take the spoils of victory, and then ruthlessly use his alliances with German princes and with Spain to contain French power. Thoughtfully, he placed new demands on the table.

*

This was the position when parliament met again in October 1669, ignorant of the dealings behind the curtain. Hoping that both the Commons and the Lords would finally have put the disasters of the Dutch war behind them, Charles greeted them in his most affable and charming style, asking for funds to continue his successful foreign policy with the triple alliance. To his dismay, the Commons plunged back into old disputes, Buckingham attacking Arlington's friend Sir George Carteret, treasurer of the navy during the war, and Arlington and Ormond attempting to impeach Buckingham's ally, the Earl of Orrery. Sir John Verney kept a score, as if this were a tennis match:

13 Oct. Bucks and Arlington are still pecking one the other.
10 Nov. Bucks and Arlington were made friends on Saturday last, and long it will last.
16 Nov. Bucks and Arlington are broke out again.[17]

When the Commons finally proposed a grant of supply, not only was it too low but there were fierce arguments about how it should be raised. Throwing up his hands, on 11 December, Charles abruptly prorogued parliament until February. The move was shrewd. Greeting the MPs and Lords at the opening of the session on Valentine's Day 1670, Charles was friendly but severe: 'One thing I must earnestly recommend to the prudence of both Houses: that you will not suffer any occasion of difference between yourselves to be revived, since nothing but the unity of your minds and counsels can make this meeting happy, either to me or to the nation.'[18]

The farcical disputes were dropped. The break had allowed Charles's naval officials to work out a way of planning for the future and their proposals were accepted. Treading carefully, Charles now worked to keep both houses sweet. He agreed to the Commons' demand for a new Conventicle Act (the blow to the dissenters that would prompt the defiance of Penn), but insisted that the act should carry a clause, like the one that Lauderdale had steered through in Scotland, affirming that the king had supreme authority over Church affairs. This, he believed, would allow a window of hope for him to introduce more toleration in the future. Treading carefully, he backed the Commons in their dispute with the Lords over who had jurisdiction in such cases as *Skinner* vs *the East India Company*, the subject of long debates that had blocked the previous session. And lest that decision in favour of the Commons should offend the Lords, he made a conspicuous point of attending debates in the House of Lords personally, including the discussion of Lord Roos's divorce. The strategy worked. With minimum fuss parliament granted £400,000, to be raised by new taxes on wine and vinegar.

This amicable agreement allowed Charles to continue his own complicated dealings, hidden from Westminster. Early in November Louis had demanded that Colbert de Croissy be informed of all the terms of the treaty under discussion, including the religious clause. This was done, but Ralph Montagu, now ambassador in Paris, was kept in the dark, lest word should leak back to London. Negotiations in Paris were therefore carried on by Minette. By December Charles had come round to the prospect of another Dutch war, but the new terms he offered Louis were staggering. He asked for £1 million down, and then £600,000 a year until the war ended (this was not, in fact, inflated, being roughly the sum that the Navy Board judged essential to pay existing debts and keep a large fleet afloat). In territory, if Holland was defeated, Charles asked for three ports controlling the trade entering the Rhine. Louis would keep faith with the Treaty of Aix-la-Chapelle, thus allowing Charles to remain, in this respect, true to the triple alliance. If Louis continued with any further plans to dismantle the old Spanish empire, then Britain must have a share in South American territories. Charles must affirm his Catholicism before any Dutch war was begun, but Louis must pay the money he had promised for this act of conversion within six months of the treaty, even if no declaration had been made.

Swallowing his shock, Louis reduced the number of warships that he had calculated the English would need to contribute to the proposed war, thus cutting the giant sums requested. Eventually the two sides ironed out their differences: Charles would send sixty ships and forty thousand soldiers; Louis would pay nearly £250,000 for the ships and fund the troops himself. Any prizes that English vessels took would belong to Charles.[19] It seemed that Charles had nothing to lose. He would get the money for his conversion, but could delay the war indefinitely by delaying the announcement of his Catholicism, which both sides had agreed would come first, but for which no date had been set.

After more talks and secret meetings, more letters, more dextrous web-weaving, Charles and Louis finally reached an agreement. Thomas Clifford drafted papers, the Irish peer Richard Belling translated them into French and Arlington led the negotiations. In April Colbert and Arlington wrangled over the final details. Charles was in Newmarket again, and in a desperate last attempt to get him to soften requested restrictions on the French navy, Colbert rushed up to Suffolk to see him. He would not budge, and a weary Colbert finally advised Louis that he must give in or call the whole thing off. On 2 May the deal was done.[20]

Minette's visit was now imminent. Louis had suggested that she come over from Dunkirk while the French court was touring through the conquered territories in Flanders, thus making it look simply like a convenient trip to see her brother. The problem was the hostility of Monsieur to such a visit. Over the past year, he had persuaded Louis to deprive his wife of her two closest friends, imprisoning Bishop Cosin and banishing her children's governess, the Countess of Chaumont (who had both been involved in Minette's plots to disgrace the chevalier de Lorraine). Ralph Montagu, who was devoted to Minette, wrote passionately from Paris to Arlington and to Charles, who protested firmly.[21] Louis took note. In the ensuing arguments he found a pretext to have the

A Dutch print from the early 1670s, showing Louis XIV chasing Charles, offering him gold, while French troops attack Holland. Allegorical figures of peace and trade stand on the left, but on the right battle rages.

chevalier arrested for slander and in mid-winter, in a furious sulk, Monsieur whisked his wife off to virtual banishment in their gloomy country house at Villers-Cotteret, near Soissons.

In this mood Monsieur was adamant that Minette should not leave France. To appease him, Louis released the chevalier from prison and sent him to Italy, granting the two men permission to correspond. But even so, Monsieur raged violently about Minette's visit, threatening to come with her and demanding a reciprocal trip by the Duke of York to Paris. This was averted by Louis's stern words and Charles's insistence that James could not leave the country. Grudgingly, Monsieur gave in. By the end of March, Minette was back at court, in intense talks with Louis. A month later they set off to Flanders.

This was a progress in the old style, on a grand scale, ostensibly designed to show Maria Teresa 'her' new territories, but really to show the people the grandeur and might of the French King.[22] Most of the court accompanied them, including Mademoiselle de Montpensier (the 'Grand Mademoiselle' who had rejected Charles during his exile) and Louis's current *maîtresse en titre*, Madame de Montespan. With them rode thirty thousand troops, while dozens of carts carried gold and silver plate, hangings and carpets, paintings and provisions. But the food they ate off their gold plate was appalling and Minette, weak after the trials of recent months, could drink nothing but milk. Every day the rain poured down, and they were stopped on their route by the flooded river Sambre.[23] According to Madame de Montpensier, the courtiers huddled in their coaches, and when Louis arranged for them to move to a two-room farmhouse nearby, Maria Teresa had hysterics and refused to abandon her coach. At last, the grandees trudged through the mud into the farm, sleeping together on the floor on hard mattresses, in the freezing damp.

After these uncomfortable adventures, Minette left the party at Courtray, accompanied by the French and British envoys, and escorted by six hundred horsemen. At dawn on 25 May she set off in her coach, riding west to Lille and Dunkirk, where Sandwich was waiting with his fleet, just as he had waited for Charles at Scheveningen, almost exactly ten years before. She arrived at the port after sunset and her entourage boarded their ships during the night, ready to sail with the tide in the early morning.[24]

The Prince of Orange landing

A political pack, produced *c.* 1690

39 Dover and Beyond

All my past life is mine no more:
The flying hours are gone
Like transitory dreams given o'er,
Whose images are kept in store
By memory alone.

Whatever is to come is not:
How can it then be mine?
The present moment's all my lot,
And that, as fast as it is got,
Phillis, is wholly thine.
ROCHESTER, 'Love and Life: A Song'

IN DOVER, Charles, James, Monmouth and Rupert were waiting
for Minette to arrive. Charles had planned to sail down the Thames
and round the coast, but slack winds forced him to land at
Gravesend and dash by coach across the downs of Kent. Early on
16 May he saw sails in the distance and set off in the royal barge to
meet his sister when her ship anchored. When they landed, he
escorted Minette up the steep hill to the castle, the old Norman bas-
tion with its Roman lighthouse, glaring across the Channel at
France. The royal apartments were in the upper storeys of the inner
keep, and on the lead-covered roof above were scratched 'footprints
of some people inscribed with their names, amongst them those of
Charles II, which he had marked there when he landed at Dover'.[1]

Minette had not travelled alone. Although Charles had advised
her to bring a small retinue, this amounted to 237 people, including
cooks and hairdressers, musicians and doctors.[2] Her intimate *suite
d'honneur* included the maréchal du Plessis, the Bishop of Tournai

and the Count and Countess of Gramont – Elizabeth Hamilton of old. Sandwich had taken Sir Winston Churchill with him, from the royal household, to arrange provisions on the short voyage, and Lord St Albans to escort the French nobles, whom he knew well. The English court had descended from London to greet them. Catherine and the Duchess of York arrived, 'with a numerous train of ladies'. Charles's ministers came too, complaining that they hardly had time to pack their bags, and the French and Dutch ambassadors brought their own retinue. The Venetian ambassador, who stayed in London, puzzled over the sudden flurry. He was, he reported at first, unable to penetrate deeper into the motives for the visit, since everyone had left town and no one had yet returned. A week later he decided that Madame's arrival was prompted only by family affection, although he continued, shrewdly, to suspect 'secret transactions'.[3]

Dover was a small port, where the chalk cliffs fell 'horribly into the sea', or so visitors thought. Fishing boats went out every day, and the fires along the beach were not bonfires of welcome, but local people burning seaweed to get ashes for their fields. The followers of both courts were billeted through the town, in small houses in the winding streets. It was a place full of emotion for the king and his sister.

The main business was indeed the secret treaty. Minette's final contribution to this was to cajole Charles into agreeing to support the French in war with the Dutch whenever Louis was ready, and not insist on them waiting until he had made his dangerous declaration of faith. She won the support of Clifford and Arlington for this move, helped, in Arlington's case, by her persuading Charles to agree to the betrothal of Arlington's three-year-old daughter 'Tata' to Henry Fitzroy, his second son by Barbara.[4] On 22 May, Arlington, Clifford, Arundell and Belling signed the treaty for England, ready for Minette to carry it back to be ratified in France.[5]

The treaty seemed a coup for Charles, but better was to come. Buckingham and most members of the Privy Council had no idea of the signing of the agreement. At Dover, keen to keep Buckingham as a friend, Minette was always completely charming towards him, and his enthusiasm for a French alliance increased still more. He was backed in this by Lauderdale and by Ashley, who had harboured considerable doubts about any rapprochement with France, until he realised that concessions on trade could only be won from the Dutch by force. Two months later, in July, Buckingham proposed that when he visited Paris he should suggest a secret alliance to Louis. With some amusement, Charles, James and Arlington agreed at once. Buckingham set off, taking with him as a 'proposal' the exact terms of the Treaty of Dover, but without the conversion clause. Charles had no great hopes of this hoax, but back Buckingham came, triumphantly bearing a draft treaty.

With a serious face, Charles promptly renegotiated the terms to his advantage, much to Louis's irritation. The money secretly designated for Charles's declaration of faith was now written in as a general 'subsidy', which would be paid whether there was a war or not, and at Ashley's and Lauderdale's insistence two more islands at the mouth of the Scheldt and Rhine were added to English claims if the war was won.[6] With a flourish, Buckingham and the other members of the Cabal – Clifford, Arlington, Ashley and Lauderdale – signed the 'Secret Treaty of London' on 21 December 1670. The bluff had worked. If any news leaked out about a secret treaty – as it eventually did – this would be the one that was discovered. The Dover pact that lay behind it was not known until its terms were published in the *History of England* by the Catholic historian John Lingard in 1826. Details were still coming to light in Clifford's papers in the 1930s.[7]

Louis had followed Minette to Dunkirk, where he stayed three days, inspecting the fortifications, as if he could influence events by beaming his will across the channel. Messengers sailed back and forth, and to her surprise and delight, Louis gave Minette permission to stay an extra ten or twelve days, in defiance of Monsieur's wishes.

The treaty signed, she and Charles enjoyed themselves. Charles had ordered the leading officers of the court to attend him to entertain Minette, a newsletter reported, 'and the Duke's Company and the King's private music are ordered thither for her "divertissement"'.[8] Since Monsieur had adamantly refused to let her go to London – although several of her entourage went up to see the sights – the royal party rode over the downs to Canterbury. It was May, and the tall hedges were once again white with hawthorn. Kent's labourers were the best paid in England, and between Dover and Canterbury, in the deep valleys that cut into the downs, lay orchards and hop gardens, and pastures full of sheep. As they came down the hill towards the gates the bells pealed from the city's sixteen churches. The small cathedral city was a busy, prosperous place, its timbered houses crammed within encircling walls, its gardens watered by branches of the Stour, 'the sweetest river', as Cosimo of Tuscany had called it the year before. At its heart was the cathedral, beautifully restored since Charles had held his first Privy Council there, encircled by the houses of the close like a jewel in a box.

In Canterbury Charles and Minette attended a great banquet in the hall of St Augustine's Abbey. During her stay in England, they also watched a comedy performed by the company of the Duke's Theatre, and a ballet. The English court were on holiday, and some even took the chance to go over to Calais 'to satisfy their curiosities and see a glimpse of that country'.[9] On Whitsunday, the king and all the Garter knights, in their full robes and regalia, attended Dover parish church. Only the Duke of York was missing as he had dashed to London to help the Lord Mayor, since there was fear of trouble from the 'fanatics'. Charles himself sent firm instructions to the Lord Mayor and the Earl of Craven, as Lord Lieutenant of Middlesex and Southwark, to contain all trouble.[10] But the day passed without uproar in London, and the court celebrated without anxiety on 29 May, Charles's fortieth birthday and the tenth anniversary of his arrival in London. Though pale and thin, Minette was radiant, her happiness giving her energy. She went to all the feasts and balls and enchanted all who met her. The cold May rain stopped, and they sailed out into the Channel in the royal yachts, with three men-of-war standing by.[11]

Before she left, Charles gave Minette money for her expenses and two thousand crowns to build a chapel to their mother's memory at Chaillot. In return, so the legend goes, she opened her mother's jewel box and asked him to choose the jewel he liked best. Jokingly, he said that there was only one he would really like, the young woman standing nearby, her Breton maid of honour, Louise de Kéroualle. Minette, who was responsible to Louise's parents, firmly refused. But Charles did not have to wait long. When Buckingham went to France in July he was charged with bringing Louise back with him. They set out together, but for some reason, never explained, he left her behind at the port, for which she never forgave him: Arlington instead arranged her voyage. With her round face and curls (Charles called her 'Fubbs', for her chubby cheeks), Louise brought a new vitality to court, instead of worldly languor. Since Nell was regarded as Buckingham's protégé, Arlington was particularly glad to see Louise installed. Colbert de Croissy breathlessly reported his views:

For although his Majesty is not disposed to communicate his affairs to women, nevertheless as they can on occasion injure those whom they hate, and in that way ruin many affairs, it was much better for all good servants of the King that he was attracted to her, whose humor is not mischievous, and who is a lady, rather than to comediennes and the like, on whom no honest man could rely, by whose means the duke of Buckingham was always trying to entice the King, in order to draw him away from all his Court and monopolize him.[12]

Louise must learn to manage Charles well, Colbert added, 'not to speak to him of affairs, and not to show any aversion to those who are near him, and, in short, to let him find only pleasure and joy in her company'. She became Charles's mistress in late 1671, and gave birth to their only son nine months later – the new Duke of Richmond, last of the acknowledged royal bastards. 'She studied to please and observe him in every thing,' wrote Burnet, 'so that he passed away the rest of his life in a great fondness for her.'[13]

No one really wants to know the future, Charles warned Minette, joking about her interest in astrology. He had no patience with prophets; 'I give little credit to such kind of cattle and the lesse you do it the better, for if they could tell any thing tis inconvenient to know ones fortune before hand whether good or bad.'[14] Despite his Catholic protestations he may, like Rochester, have agreed with Hobbes: 'The present only has a being in nature. Things past have a being in the memory, only. But things to come have no being at all, the future being but a fiction of the mind, applying the sequels of actions past to the actions that are present.'[15] Hobbes had also declared that experience of things past could endow a man with foresight. But in May 1670, with the future, at least in Charles's mind, settled by the Treaty of Dover, the present was all that counted.

40 Sailing

Not caring to observe the wind,
Or the new sea explore,
Snatched from myself, how far behind
Already I behold the shore!
EDMUND WALLER, 'Of Loving at First Sight'

ON 3 JUNE, carrying the treaty, and accompanied by her court,
Minette sailed for France. The treaty was ratified on 4 June, and
twelve days later she celebrated her twenty-sixth birthday. Towards
the end of the month she wrote her only known letter in English,
her spelling as vivid as a spoken voice. The note was to Clifford,
asking him to remind Charles of the promise he had made about the
marriage of Arlington's little daughter:

When I have write to the King from Calais I praid him to tel milord
Arlington an you what he had promised for mi bothe. His ansers was that
hi gave me againe his word, that hee would performe the thing, but that hi
did not think it fit to exequte it now . . .

This is the ferste letter I have ever write in inglis. You will eselay see it bi
the stile and tograf [autograph] prai see in the same time that I expose mi
self to be thought a foulle in looking to make you know how much I am
your frind.[1]

By this time Minette had left Paris to stay at St Cloud, where she
could sit in the shade and stroll in the gardens by moonlight, listening to the fountains and talking to her friends. On the afternoon of
29 June, complaining of a pain in her side, she drank a glass of iced
water, flavoured with chicory. Immediately she cried out in agony,
fearing she was poisoned. For the next few hours she was in terrible
pain. People rushed to her side, including Ralph Montagu, and

Louis himself, bringing with him the queen and his rival mistresses, both of whom had been Minette's maids of honour. Ralph Montagu arrived just after she made her last confession.[2] After sending last messages to Charles, and asking Montagu to retrieve her very private letters to her brother, Henriette-Anne, 'Madame', duchesse d'Orléans, died at three in the morning on 30 June 1670. According to Montagu, her last thoughts were with her brother. 'I have loved him better than life itself,' she whispered, 'and now my only regret in dying is to be leaving him.'[3]

The royal doctors pronounced the cause of death as 'cholera morbus', and the accepted view now is that she probably died of peritonitis as a result of a burst duodenal ulcer. But rumours that Minette had been poisoned by allies of the chevalier de Lorraine circulated fast. An hour after she died Montagu wrote to Arlington to tell him the news, adding 'God send the King, our master, patience and constancy to bear so great an affliction. Madame declared she had no reluctancy to die, but out of the grief she thought it would be to the King, her brother.'[4] Sir Thomas Armstrong, who had also been present at her death, travelled without stopping to bring the news to Charles. Shouting in pain and rage, 'Monsieur is a villain', Charles turned and shut himself in his bedroom. Convinced that his sister had been poisoned, he refused to see Colbert de Croissy, or Louis's official envoy. (Rochester, who was back at Whitehall, told his wife that the King was enduring 'the highest affliction imaginable', before thanking her for some cheeses and signing off cheerily 'tarara'.[5])

Charles emerged after five days. He sent Buckingham to Paris for Minette's state funeral, carrying with him, to Charles's bitter amusement, the fake 'secret treaty'.

The Treaty of Dover that Minette had helped Charles to achieve was the biggest gamble of his reign. It paid off, in the sense that the money from Louis paid over the years relieved the pressure of being totally reliant on parliament. But the sum was less important than the security of having Louis on his side in case of crisis. It was not uncommon for monarchs to receive subsidies from foreign rulers – indeed Richard Cromwell had asked for a large sum from Mazarin in 1658. As to his religious promise, if he had really meant to pronounce his Catholicism and reinstall the faith, now would have been the moment to act, backed by Louis's arms and money. But Charles knew that one virtue of his restoration was that it had taken place without bloodshed, and without help from foreign armies. He was no man of stubborn principle, like his father and his brother James. Furthermore, he had cleverly agreed only to his *own* conversion, not that of his country. As far as this was concerned, he said tactfully to Minette that he was not yet satisfied with the Catholic truth. When the papal nuncio visited in November, there was no word of conversion.[6]

It was the secrecy of the treaty that was so significant. For a king who had intended to be so open and accessible, this was an admission that he must now rule in a different way. His assertion at the Restoration that he wanted to rule with his parliament was implicitly denied, and his actions were the forerunner of many later deals, when heads or cabinets of allegedly democratic states commit their nation to action without the knowledge or full agreement of parliament and people. To modern eyes, the treachery may lie less in 'the design about R', which so shocked his contemporaries, than in Charles's committing his country to fight a pointless war in which thousands of lives might be lost.

The people who gathered on the Dover shore in May 1660, and the crowds that greeted him in London or petitioned him from all his three nations, had expected their lives to change. And so they had, not always for the best. The euphoria of regime change did not last long. Many royalists won back their lands, but others did not, and those that had were often crippled by loans and mortgages. Trade survived, even flourished, and the rising 'middling class' were buying newly fashionable walnut furniture, paintings and books, but the poor did not benefit and the prisons were full of debtors. The people welcomed him as a prince of peace and plenty, only to experience a decade of war, plague and fire. They had sought stable government and lower taxes, but the factions still fought and the taxes were higher than ever. And there was one great gulf that Charles could not bridge. At the restoration the traditionalist Anglicans had hoped for a strong, united, state church to which all must conform, while those who held other views, from the presbyterians within the Commonwealth church to the Catholics and the sects outside it, had hoped only to be allowed to worship in peace. No group had achieved what they desired, and after the struggles of the 1660s those whose tender consciences Charles had vowed to respect now found themselves outside the law.

The events of 1670 drew a line in the sand, which marked the end of all the experiments of that first decade. Defeated in his attempts at comprehension the year before and unable to get funds from parliament, Charles had turned his back on the would-be reformists, and embraced the old Anglican, royalist faction. When he signed the Treaty of Dover, his future track was set. From now on, although the surface charm remained, he became increasingly wary and withdrawn, his thinking even harder to fathom, his course with regard to parliament and the public ever more duplicitous. In the parliamentary session from October 1670 to the following April, the Commons granted yet another huge sum, supposedly to boost the navy in the face of France's increasing strength, but actually to fight the Dutch.

For Charles, his family came first, even more than his nation. His loyalty to his brother James – the only one of his siblings still alive – would bedevil the rest of his reign. If one takes a whirlwind view forward, dashing through time like the comets that swooped over England in the mid-1660s, this becomes all too clear.

James had decided to become a Catholic in 1668. A month before Minette landed at Dover, he told Colbert de Croissy that his wife Anne (who had practised confession since she was twelve) planned to convert and that both were keen for the secret treaty to be signed so that they could declare their faith.[7] Anne was received into the Catholic Church this winter. At Charles's request, James kept her conversion secret.

Alarm flared in 1672, when Charles issued his second Declaration of Indulgence to fend off opposition among powerful dissenters in the country and the city to the coming war with the Dutch. This not only allowed dissenters to open meeting houses but freed Catholics to worship in their homes. It was supported by Buckingham and by Ashley, who was made Earl of Shaftesbury and Lord Chancellor. At the outbreak of war, Charles was seeking support on all sides, but despite Louis's promises, funds were desperately short, so much so that Charles agreed to Clifford's drastic suggestion of a Stop of the Exchequer, which meant that government loans were no longer to be repaid. 'The Robbery at the Exchequer', satirists called it, pointing to yet another arbitrary action by the crown. Small lenders were ruined and the bankers who had lent a fortune to the crown, including Backwell, Robert Vyner and Francis Child, lost many thousands.

The war opened with French successes, although neither the English nor the Dutch fleets could claim victory at sea. In Holland, an Orangist coup, in which the de Witt brothers were removed from power and murdered by the mob, made William of Orange stadtholder at last. When William rejected peace terms – thus making a mockery of any claim from Charles that the war had been fought to aid his cause – rumours circulated that Britain had only been dragged into war at France's behest. As before, anti-French and anti-Catholic feeling grew strong. Under this pressure, Charles switched tack once again, withdrawing the Declaration of Indulgence and agreeing to the passing of the Test Acts by which all public office-holders must deny Catholic doctrines.

After the Test Acts, James's resignation as Lord Admiral made his Catholic allegiance public. His wife Anne had died two years before, and now he married the Catholic Mary of Modena and stayed away from Anglican communion. It was clearer than ever that if Charles had no legal offspring, Britain faced the prospect of a Catholic dynasty. In response a powerful opposition grew around Buckingham and then around Shaftesbury: 'For close designs and crooked counsels fit', as Dryden described him, 'Sagacious, bold and turbulent of wit'.[8] The protests in parliament were vehement, and, at James's request, Charles dismissed Shaftesbury. This was an error, since when parliament met again Shaftesbury's supporters tried to impeach Buckingham, Lauderdale and Arlington. The threat was stopped, but the power of these ministers faded: by the end of 1674 Buckingham was finally dismissed, Arlington demoted to Lord Chamberlain, and Lauderdale was losing ground in Scotland. Once again Charles had to shore up his position and settle vast debts, which he did with the help of Buckingham's former supporter Thomas Osborne, who was created Earl of Danby.

Secretly, Charles obtained more subsidies from Louis, but publicly, in two gestures of protestant appeasement, he signed the peace with Holland and began negotiating for James's daughter Mary to marry William of Orange. But this was still not enough and in 1677, the year of William and Mary's marriage, many agreed with Marvell, when he wrote in his *Account of the Growth of Popery and Arbitrary Government*, that for 'divers years' there had been a plot to change the 'Lawful Government of England into an Absolute Tyranny', and to convert the lawful Church into 'down-right Popery'.[9] A year later, their fears seemed confirmed when the 'Popish plot' was 'discovered' by the criminally mendacious Titus Oates.

According to Oates and his followers, as part of this plot, Catholic families would rise up and massacre protestant Londoners in their beds; incendiaries would fire the city; the king would be mugged by Irish ruffians, stabbed with knives, shot with silver bullets in St James's Park – and poisoned by the queen's physician. Charles was dismissive, but Oates persuaded the Privy Council, and when the magistrate Sir Edmund Berry Godfrey was found murdered, the country panicked. With backing from

Shaftesbury, the charges proliferated beyond reason. The Jesuits were blamed as instigators and the Archbishop of Dublin, the Pope and even the queen were implicated. In the hysteria that followed there were 'Pope burnings' across the country. Apprentice gangs carried arms, and one cutler was said to have sold three thousand knives in a day. And despite Charles's belief that the whole thing was a fabrication, he let twenty-four 'plotters' go to the scaffold, unwilling to contest with the courts and the popular will. Many other suspects were imprisoned, including, briefly, Samuel Pepys.

A contemporary playing card showing scenes from the Popish Plot

Amid this passion, in 1679 the Commons brought in the Exclusion Bill, voting that James should be excluded from the succession, which should pass instead to the Duke of Monmouth. At this point, Charles finally dissolved the Cavalier Parliament that had served him since 1661. He sent James and Mary to Brussels, eventually bringing his brother back but giving him a post in Scotland, away from the centre of power. From the ensuing struggle came the ragged birth of party politics, with Shaftesbury's supporters dubbed Whigs (from the name the Scots had given to their covenanter rebels, 'Whiggamores' – 'whigg' being Scots for sour milk) and Danby's known as Tories (from the Irish '*toraidhe*', the pro-royalist Catholics who had turned bandits, or 'bog-trotting brigands', in the civil wars). But Shaftesbury's power was greater, and although Charles tried hard to save Danby, eventually he was committed to the Tower, where he spent the next five years.

Over these years, as the pressure mounted, so Charles's resolve stiffened. He tried still harder to protect his family, not only recalling James, but also briefly allowing the return of Monmouth, the son he loved, until Monmouth's actions led to a final banishment. In 1680 the situation reached a crisis, as a new parliament brought in a new Exclusion Bill, which was only defeated in the Lords after a famous duel of speeches between Shaftesbury and the eloquent Halifax. Parliament was summoned to meet at Oxford, away from the Whig-dominated City of London, in 1681. Old battles of authority were fought again. Sir Robert Filmer's *Patriarcha*, written during the conflicts of the 1640s, was now published, arguing that kingship was a 'divine and natural law' model of government, like that of a father in the family, instituted by God in the person of Adam: the king alone could be the maker of laws. In opposition, John Locke drafted a reply. Ten years later, Locke's two *Treatises of Government* would replace both the patriarchal law of Filmer and Hobbes's theory that submission to arbitrary power was vital to protect society, with a new, contractual argument, in which the right of any government to rule depended on the consent of the people. But the crisis of 1681 was not a moment to utter such thoughts. For a moment, civil war hovered like thunder – people saw visions of pikemen fighting in the sky. Finally, when Shaftesbury not only suggested that Monmouth be declared legitimate, but asserted that parliament could legislate to encompass this without royal consent, Charles stood firm. 'My Lords', he said, 'let there be no self-delusion':

I will never yield, and will not let myself be intimidated. Men become ordinarily more timid as they grow old; as for me, I shall be, on the contrary, bolder and firmer, and I will not stain my life and reputation in the little time that, perhaps, remains for me to live. I do not fear the dangers and calamities which people try to frighten me with. I have the law and reason on my side. Good men will be with me.[10]

Just as the Commons were about to pass the bill, Charles summoned the MPs to the Lords, who were sitting in Christ Church. Unknown to anyone, he had smuggled in the full robes and regalia that he wore to the formal opening and closing of a parliament. When the Commons squeezed into the hall, they were confronted by a king in his glory. It was a dazzling piece of theatre. In one sentence, and with one gesture, Charles ordered parliament dismissed. It was the last parliament of his reign. In a declaration, he then appealed directly to his people, many of whom, with memories of the civil war, already felt that parliament had gone too far. His direct appeal was another great gamble, a brilliant propaganda coup. Gradually the tide turned back towards him. The fraudsters of the Popish Plot confessed, one by one, and Shaftesbury was charged with treason. The London jury, full of exclusionists and Whigs, was unable to decide and the charges were dismissed with a plea of *ignoramus*, 'we do not know', but in 1682 Shaftesbury would flee to Holland, where he died within a year. Oates was arrested (cruising for boys) and then charged with perjury. After three years in prison he was released – to become a Baptist preacher.

This was the time of 'the Stuart Revenge', when a wary Charles was 'watchful, voracious, ready to spring'.[11] Using carefully legal methods, his ministers bullied corporations – including the City of London – removed unhelpful judges and handed out places. In the last years of his reign, with the people quiet and parliament dismissed, the king seemed, astonishingly, to be on the brink of reasserting absolute power almost by sleight of hand. One further plot remained, the Rye House Plot, designed to assassinate both Charles and James on their way back from Newmarket, and to give the throne to the Duke of Monmouth. When it failed (a fire in his lodgings at Newmarket had made Charles leave early), a group of leading Whigs were arrested, although it is doubtful whether their involvement was more than mere talk. The Earl of Essex, who had fought for Charles I in the Civil War, slit his throat while imprisoned in the Tower. Lord William Russell, Algernon Sidney (whose trial was loaded against him by Judge Jeffreys) and the former Leveller John Wildman were executed for treason, becoming known as the famous 'Whig martyrs'. Here, as in the executions during the Popish Plot, Charles might have intervened. His 'laziness', to use Halifax's term, with regard to judicial vengeance, is a measure of his political ruthlessness, a counter to his personal warmth.[12]

Why was there so little resistance in Britain to Charles's personal rule? Partly perhaps the fear of civil war, so fresh in people's memories; partly the apathy that comes with prosperity – in the early 1680s taxes were light and there was a boom in trade. Despite the Dutch war and the panic over exclusion, the initiatives of his first decade went on from strength to strength. The Royal Society continued their work and the Royal Observatory was founded at Greenwich. The theatre flourished, bringing the great age of Restoration comedy, whose wit belies the darkness of the time. Whatever the reason, people closed their eyes to the fact that no parliament was sitting, no checks were operating on Charles's power.

In those troubled years Charles's complicated personal life was relatively serene; its even temper interrupted only by the tempestuous stay of the flamboyant, lushly beautiful Hortense du Mancini, niece of Cardinal Mazarin and cousin of Mary of Modena, thought by many to be yet another French spy. Catherine, his queen, found a way of living in Charles's hectically amorous court. During the row over the Test Acts she sheltered his mistress Louise, now Duchess of Portsmouth, by including her name among those of her own

women. Barbara Castlemaine had long ago been set aside, made
Duchess of Cleveland. Nell and Louise stayed by Charles to the
end. Nell, never a duchess, lived in her house in Pall Mall, Louise in
her Whitehall apartments draped in tapestries depicting French
royal palaces, her rooms crammed with vases, mirrors and silver.
Charles's many children were also well cared for: rattles and cradles
figure in the royal accounts, looking glasses and laundry-maids as
the children grew older.[13] He paid for weddings, and gave dowries
and allowances. He gave dukedoms to six sons, and made his
daughters' husbands lords. But his affection went beyond material
generosity – he teased them, worried over them, loved them. His
first son, James, Duke of Monmouth, whom he had doted upon in
his childhood and youth, broke his heart by his ambition, his kingly progresses and his involvement in the schemes of Shaftesbury
and the Rye House Plot. Banished from court, by the mid-1680s
Monmouth was in exile in the Hague.

Charles still loved his pleasures and plans. He never had enough
money to rebuild Whitehall as he had dreamed, and after 1670 his
ambitious new building at Greenwich lay boarded up and unfinished. But in the bitter winter of 1683, the coldest ever known, he
was planning a new palace at Winchester. He went racing, he went
to the playhouse, he walked his spaniels in the park. And to the end,
his court remained his strength and his weakness. On Sunday 25
January 1685, John Evelyn pursed his lips at the sight of its 'unexpressable luxury, & prophanesse, gaming and all dissolution, and as
it were total forgetfulnesse of God'. The king was 'sitting, & toying
with his concubines', Louise de Kéroualle, Barbara and Hortense
Mancini, with the 'French boy singing love-songs, in that glorious
Gallery, whilst about 20 of the greate Courtiers & other dissolute
persons were at Basset round a large table, a bank of at least 2000
in Gold before them'.[14]

'Six days later was all in the dust', Evelyn added with a righteous
sigh. A sudden fever struck, followed by a stroke. When Charles
neared death – although it is unclear whether he was conscious or

comatose – he turned to the Catholic Church. He was received into the faith, and the last rites were administered by Father Huddleston, the priest whom he had met in hiding after the Battle of Worcester, now a chaplain to the queen. Had Charles's Anglicanism, or his scepticism, been bluffs all along? Or was his confession an honourable fulfilment of his promise to Louis? Or a judicious last gamble, with nothing to lose? Certainly, he received Huddleston with a cry of pleasure, was granted absolution and received the sacrament. He listened to the prayers for the dying and asked Huddleston to repeat the act of contrition, with its final request 'Mercy, Sweet Jesus, Mercy'. He asked for the curtains to be opened, so that he could see the dawn on the river. On 6 February 1685, at noon, when the tide was high, Charles II died peacefully in his bed, loved by most of his people. A week later he was buried very simply in Westminster Abbey. He had achieved a supreme balancing act, ruling a divided people for twenty-five years. His brother James, that darker mirror image, fled the country after only three.

Present becomes past, past becomes 'history'. It is different, although less easy to analyse, if we turn it into lives, whether they be farmers and seamstresses, writers and artists, or kings and queens. The gambles Charles II took to stay on his throne succeeded, with the help of subsidies from Louis and a ruthless reliance on, and sacrifice of, his ministers. But in the larger game that continued when he left the table, he lost. He had overestimated the flexibility of James, and the security offered by Louis. And he had underestimated one player, his nephew, William of Orange. When William came over to England in 1670, a few months after the Treaty of Dover, attempting to claim the money owed to his family, Charles arranged for Backwell to repay him over four years, against the security of receipts from the Customs. He treated him with due respect as his sister Mary's son, giving him precedence over Prince Rupert. But he could not take him seriously. William was too young, too solemn, too Dutch. He disliked the wild court and bitterly resented being made to seem foolish by drink. Charles continued to patronise him as a junior relation, even when he became captain-general of the Dutch forces, and then stadtholder and the husband of his niece Mary. Yet this was the man – cautious and steely – who would topple the Stuarts in the Glorious Revolution of 1688. Clarendon's grandchildren, Mary and Anne, did, as the Chancellor's opponents had feared long ago, eventually become queens of England.

James II and Mary of Modena slipped out of London on the day that William of Orange reached the capital in 1688. Only the Catholics of Ireland rose to support James, and in his bloody attempt to regain his throne, he was defeated at the Battle of the Boyne. He returned to France, becoming a virtual recluse at St Germain. He died there in 1702. His heart was taken to his mother's chapel at Chaillot, his brain to the Scots College, and his body

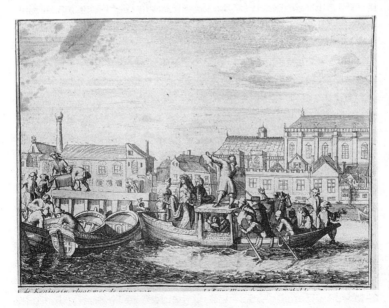

James II and Mary of Modena leave Whitehall in 1688

was buried in the English Benedictine church in Paris – temporarily – until his bones could be brought to England. This never happened. During the French Revolution his tomb was vandalised and his corpse displayed for crowds to gaze at. Then it was destroyed.

Many of those who shone or struggled in the 1660s, like Danby, and Halifax, and Dryden, lived on and made new careers in the reigns of William and Mary and Anne. Others had long departed. Some deaths were quiet, some public and tragic. Rochester died five years before Charles, who had pardoned him so often. They were together at Newmarket at the races in spring 1680, and then Rochester, already ill and nearly mad with a concoction of venereal diseases, went home to Woodstock Park. There he underwent a typically intense, spiritual conversion, declaring his sins dramatically until he died in July. By contrast the sober Arlington died quietly five months after his king, calling, like Charles, for a Catholic confessor on his deathbed. Monmouth died in the Tower in the same month. He had landed in Lyme Regis a month before, in his ill-fated attempt to remove James from the throne, and after his ragged army was defeated at Sedgemoor, he was found hiding in a ditch and carried to London. He died in agony, from five blows of the axe, his death so bungled that those watching would have torn the executioner to pieces, said Evelyn, if he had not been protected by a guard.[15] Buckingham died in Yorkshire two years later from a chill caught out hunting, having run through his estate and lost most his friends. He was buried, with a splendour and panache that he would have appreciated, in the Henry VII Chapel in Westminster Abbey.

Catherine of Braganza slowly recovered from a profound depression after Charles's death. Very bravely, she pleaded with James II to spare the life of Monmouth, whom she had been so fond of when he was a boy. She spent some time in the convent that she had founded in Hammersmith and then moved to Somerset House for almost a decade. In 1692 she went home to Portugal, where she lived quietly, until in 1704 she was called to act as regent to her ill brother, Pedro II. Several victories over Spain were won under her rule and she was Regent when she died a year later, at the palace of Bemposta.

Frances Stuart remained with Catherine until 1688 then retired to her home, to spend her last years playing cards with her friends and looking after her cats. She died in 1702. Barbara Castlemaine lived abroad in France for a while to cut costs, but her life remained full of intrigue and scandals, including a bigamous marriage to a young rake, who treated her abominably. She died in Chiswick, of dropsy, in 1709. Louise de Kéroualle, Duchess of Portsmouth, survived into a grand old age, dying in Paris, rather broke and down on her luck, in 1734. By then Nell Gwyn, London's Cinderella, had been dead for more than half a century. 'Be well to Portsmouth,' Charles asked James on his deathbed, and 'Let not poor Nelly starve.'[16] But James only had to pay Nell her pension for two short years. She died in 1687, aged thirty-six. Her estate went to her surviving son by Charles, the Duke of St Albans, but she left money to her sister Rose and to the debtors of the parish, plus £20 to release debtors from prison on Christmas Day. Nell, at least, understood that there were deep rifts that must be healed. Her will also left £50 to poor Catholics 'for showing my charity to those who differ from me in Religeon'.[17]

All these deaths and departures are now part of history, a past that lies not in memory but in dusty documents. From these we learn that in May 1670, his treaty accomplished, Charles said goodbye to Minette as if he would never see her again. It was another fine day in the Channel, and Minette set sail while the forts on the coast saluted the royal yachts with their guns. Charles sailed with her part of the way. He could hardly bear to part from her, and came back three times to say goodbye, before sailing again for the Dover shore.

Acknowledgements

I have been working on this subject for several years, and have many people to thank, primarily the historians from whose books, articles and arguments I have learned so much, and the archivists and librarians who have guided me through complex material and have made the research so enjoyable. I hope that my debts to both these groups are fully acknowledged in my notes. I am particularly grateful to Professors John Barnard, Lisa Jardine and Neil Keeble, who generously read through drafts and made many invaluable comments, corrections, as well as giving me their warm support.

I would also like to thank Norma Clarke, Mary Evans, Deborah Rogers, Alison Samuel, Ruth Scurr, Francis Spufford and Stella Tillyard, for many lively conversations, Hannah Uglow for scenting out good archives, Pamela Clark for steering me through the Royal Archives, and Philip Winterbottom for showing me how to read early banking ledgers. The Faber team, as usual, have been wonderful, especially my editor Julian Loose, Kate Murray-Browne, Anna Pallai, my copy-editor Eleanor Rees, proofreader Peter McAdie, indexer Alison Worthington, and Kate Ward, painstaking production manager. My thanks also go to Melanie Jackson and Jonathan Galassi in New York. Thanks too to Kate Metcalfe of How Foot, the perfect writer's escape. And finally, as always, my heartfelt thanks go to Hermione Lee, best of readers, and to my family, especially Steve.

Abbreviations and Sources

Some archives and sources are abbreviated throughout, as listed below. For all other books and articles a full reference is given the first time a work is listed in each chapter; thereafter it is in a short form.

BL   The British Library
Bod.   The Bodleian Library, Oxford
CA   Archives de France, Archives du Ministère des Affaires Etrangères,
            Correspondance Politique: Angleterre.
CCL   Canterbury Cathedral Library
CS   Camden Society
HMC   Historical Manuscripts Commission
NA   National Archives, Kew (formerly PRO, The Public Record Office)
PM   Pierpont Morgan Library, New York
RA   Royal Archives, Windsor
RBS   Royal Bank of Scotland Archives, Backwell and Vyner papers

Ailesbury – *The Memoirs of Thomas, Earl of Ailesbury written by himself*, ed. W. Buckley, 2 vols (1890)

Aubrey – *Aubrey's Brief Lives*, ed. Oliver Lawson Dick (1958); see also *Brief Lives*, ed. John Buchanan-Brown (2000)

Aylmer – Gerald Aylmer, *The Crown's Servants: Government and Civil Service under Charles II, 1660–1685* (2002)

Barbour – Violet Barbour, *Henry Bennet, Earl of Arlington* (1914)

Barnard and Fenlon – T. Barnard and J. Fenlon, eds, *The Dukes of Ormonde 1610–1745* (2000)

Baxter, *Autobiography* – *The Autobiography of Richard Baxter* (1974 edn)

Bell – Walter G. Bell, *The Great Fire of London in 1666* (1920)

Bernstein – William Bernstein, *The Birth of Plenty* (2004)

Birch – T. Birch, ed., *The History of the Royal Society of London*, 4 vols (1756–7; 1968 facsimile)

Black and Gregory – Jeremy Black and James Gregory, eds, *Culture, Politics and Society in Britain 1660–1800* (1991)

Boyle, *Works* – Michael Hunter and Edward B. Davis, eds, *The Works of Robert Boyle*, 14 vols (1999–2000)

Browning, *Historical Documents* – Andrew Browning, ed., *English Historical Documents*, vol. 6, 1660–1714 (1966, 1996)

Browning, *Osborne* – Andrew Browning, *Thomas Osborne, Earl of Danby and Duke of Leeds, 1613–1712*, 3 vols (1951)

Buccleugh MSS – HMC *15th Report*, Appendix VIII, *Calendar of the Manuscripts of the Duke of Buccleugh*, 3 vols (1899–1926)

Buckingham – Robert D. Hume and Harold Love, eds, *Plays, Poems and Miscellaneous Writings Associated with George Villiers, Second Duke of Buckingham*, 2 vols (2007)

Burnet – M. J. Routh, ed., *Burnet's History of His Own Time*, 2 vols (1833)

Burnet, *Some Passages* – Gilbert Burnet, *Some Passages in the Life and Death of the Earl of Rochester*, in John Jebb, ed., *Bishop Burnet's Lives, Characters and an Address to Posterity* (1833)

Burnet, *Supplement* – H. J. Foxcroft, ed., *Supplement to Burnet's History of My Own Time* (1902)

Cal. Clar. SP – W. D. Macray and H.O. Coxe et al., eds, *Calendar of the Clarendon State Papers Preserved in the Bodleian Library*, 5 vols (1869–1932)

Carte – Thomas Carte, *History of the Life of James, Duke of Ormonde*, 3 vols (1736)

Carte MSS – Carte manuscripts, Bodleian Library

Cavendish, *Life* – Margaret, Duchess of Newcastle, *The Life of William Cavendish, Duke of Newcastle*, ed. C. H. Firth (1886)

Chandaman – C. K. Chandaman, *The English Public Revenue, 1660–1688* (1975)

Cibber – *An Apology for the Life of Colley Cibber*, ed. B. R. S. Fone (1968)

CJ – *The Journals of the House of Commons*, vol. 7 (1651–9); vol. 8 (1660–7); vol. 9 (1667–87)

Clar. *Life* – Edward Hyde, Earl of Clarendon, *The Life of Edward, Earl of Clarendon . . . in which is included a Continuation of his History of the Grand Rebellion*, 3 vols (1827)

Clar. *Hist.* – Edward Hyde, Earl of Clarendon, *The History of the Rebellion and Civil Wars in England*, ed. W. D. Macray, 6 vols (1888)

Clay, *Fox* – Christopher Clay, *Public Finance and Private Wealth: the Career of Stephen Fox 1627–1716* (1978)

CSPD – *Calendar of State Papers, Domestic Series*

CSPV – Allen B. Hinds, ed., *Calendar of State Papers and Manuscripts* (1916–35)

CTP – Joseph Redington, ed., *Calendar of Treasury Papers 1556/7–1696* (1868)

Downes – John Downes, *Roscius Anglicanus*, ed. Montague Summers (1929, 1968)

Dryden, *Poems* – *Poems of John Dryden*, ed. Paul Hammond (1995)

Dryden, *Works* – *The Works of John Dryden*, ed. E. N. Hooker, H. T. Swedenberg Jr. and Vincent A. Dearing, 20 vols (1956–2000)

EHR – *English Historical Review*

Evelyn – *The Diary of John Evelyn*, ed. E. S. de Beer, 6 vols (1955)

Fanshawe – J. Loftis, ed., *Diaries of Anne, Lady Halkett and Ann, Lady Fanshawe* (1979)

Fox – Frank Fox, *Great Ships: the Battlefleet of Charles II* (1980)

Fraser – Antonia Fraser, *Charles II* (1979)

Gazette – *The London Gazette*

Glassey – L. K. J. Glassey, ed., *The Reigns of Charles II and James VII and II* (1997)

Grammont – [Anthony Hamilton], *Memoirs of the Count de Grammont*, trans. Horace Walpole, with notes by Sir Walter Scott and others (1876 edn)

Greaves – Richard L. Greaves, *Deliver Us from Evil: The Radical Underground in Britain, 1660–1663* (1986)

Green – I. M. Green, *The Re-Establishment of the Church of England 1660–1663* (1978)

Grey, *Debates* – *Debates of the House of Commons from the year 1667 to the year 1694*, collected by . . . Anchitell Grey, 10 vols (1763)

Grove – Richard H. Grove, *Green Imperialism: colonial expansion, tropical island Edens, and the origins of environmentalism, 1600–1860* (1996)

Halifax, *Works* – *The Works of George Savile, Marquis of Halifax*, ed. Mark N. Brown, 3 vols (1989)

Hamilton, *Castlemaine* – Elizabeth Hamilton, *The Illustrious Lady: a Life of Barbara Villiers, Countess of Castlemaine and Duchess of Cleveland* (1980)

Harris, *London Crowds* – Tim Harris, *London Crowds in the Reign of Charles II* (1999)

Harris, *Politics* – Tim Harris, *Politics under the Later Stuarts: Party Conflict in a Divided Society 1660–1715* (1993)

Harris, *Restoration* – Tim Harris, *Restoration: Charles II and His Kingdoms, 1660–1685* (2005)

Harris, *Sandwich* – F. R. Harris, *The Life of Edward Montagu, K.G., First Earl of Sandwich (1675–1672)*, 2 vols (1912)

Harris, Seaward and Goldie – Tim Harris, Paul Seaward and Mark Goldie, eds, *The Politics of Religion in Restoration England* (1999)

Hartmann, *Madame* – C. H. Hartmann, *Charles II and Madame* (1934)

Hartmann, *King My Brother* – C. H. Hartmann, *The King My Brother* (1954)

Hastings MSS – HMC *Report on the Manuscripts of the late Reginald Rawdon Hastings Esq.*, 4 vols (1928–47)

Hatton Corr. – *Correspondence of the Family of Hatton being Chiefly addressed to Christopher, Viscount Hatton AD 1601–1704*, ed. Edward Maunde Thompson, 2 vols CS NS 22, 23 (1878)

History of the Book – John Barnard and D. F. Mackenzie, ed., *The Cambridge History of the Book in Britain*, vol. 4 (2004)

HJ – *The Historical Journal*

HMC Ormonde – *HMC 14th Report, Appendix Part VII*, Calendar of the Manuscripts of the Marquess of Ormonde, 7 vols (1895–1920)

Hobbes, *Leviathan* – Thomas Hobbes, *Leviathan* (1651) ed. C. B. Macpherson (1968 edn)

Holmes – Geoffrey Holmes, *The Making of a Great Power, 1660–1722* (1993)

Houston and Pincus – Alan Houston and Steve Pincus, eds, *A Nation Transformed: England after the Restoration* (2001)

Howe – Elizabeth Howe, *The First English Actresses: Women and Drama 1660–1700* (1992)

Hunter, *New Science* – Michael Hunter, *Establishing the New Science* (1989)

Hutton, *CII* – Ronald Hutton, *Charles II: King of England, Ireland and Scotland* (1989)

Hutton, *Restoration* – Ronald Hutton, *The Restoration* (1985)

Intelligencer – *The Kingdome's Intelligencer*

Jackson, *Scotland* – Clare Jackson, *Restoration Scotland, 1660–1689* (1997)

Jardine, *Going Dutch* – Lisa Jardine, *Going Dutch: How England plundered Holland's Glory* (2008)

Jardine, *Hooke* – Lisa Jardine, *The Curious Life of Robert Hooke* (2003)

Jardine, *Wren* – Lisa Jardine, *On a Grander Scale: the Outstanding Career of Sir Christopher Wren* (2002)

Jones, *CII* – J. R. Jones, *Charles II: Royal Politician* (1987)

Josselin – *The Diaries of Ralph Josselin 1616–83*, ed. Alan Macfarlane (1967)

Jusserand – J. J. Jusserand, *A French Ambassador at the Court of Charles the Second* (1892)

Keay – Anna Keay, *The Magnificent Monarch: Charles II and the Ceremonies of Power* (2008)

Keeble, *Restoration* – N. H. Keeble, *The Restoration: England in the 1660s* (2002)

Keeble, *Literary Culture* – N. H. Keeble, *The Literary Culture of Nonconformity in Later Seventeenth-Century England* (1987)

Kenyon – J. P. Kenyon, *The Stuart Constitution 1603–1688: documents and commentary* (1986)

King's Works – Howard Colvin, ed., *The History of the King's Works*, 6 vols (1963–82)

Kishlansky – Mark Kishlansky, *A Monarchy Transformed: Britain 1603–1714* (1996)

Lansdowne, *Works* – *The Genuine Works in Verse and Prose of the Right Honourable George Granville, Lord Lansdowne*, 2 vols (1736)

Lauderdale Papers – Osmund Airey, ed., *The Lauderdale Papers*, CS 34, 36, 38 (1884–5)

Le Fleming – HMC *12th Report*, Appendix VII, *The Manuscripts of S. H. Le Fleming Esq. of Rydal Hall* (1890)

Letters – A. Bryant, ed., *The Letters, Speeches and Declarations of King Charles II* (1935)

Leviathan and the Air-pump – Stephen Shapin and Simon Schaffer, *Leviathan and the Air-pump: Hobbes, Boyle and the Experimental Life* (1985)

Lister – T. J. Lister, *Life and Administration of Edward Hyde, Earl of Clarendon*, 3 vols (1888)

LJ – *Journals of the House of Lords*, vol. 11 (1660–6); vol. 12 (1666–75)

Ludlow, *Voyce* – Edmund Ludlow, *A Voyce from the Watchtower* Part V, *1660–1662*, ed. A. B. Worden, CS 4th series, 21 (1978)

Maclean – Gerald Maclean, *Culture and Society in the Stuart Restoration* (1995)

Macray – W. D. Macray, ed., *Notes Which Passed at Meetings of the Privy Council* (1896)

Magalotti – W. E. Knowles Middleton, trans. and ed., *Lorenzo Magalotti at the Court of Charles II: his 'Relazione d'Inghilterra' of 1688* (1980)

Magalotti, *Travels* – Count Lorenzo Magalotti, *Travels of Cosmo the Third Grand Duke of Tuscany through England* (1669; 1821 edn)

Margoliouth – H. M. Margoliouth, ed., *Poems and Letters of Andrew Marvell*, 2 vols (3rd edn. rev. 1971)

Marshall, *Faction* – Alan Marshall, *The Age of Faction: Court Politics 1660–1702* (1999)

Marshall, *Hamilton* – Rosalind K. Marshall, *The Days of Duchess Anne: Life in the Household of the Duchess of Hamilton, 1656–1716* (1973)

Marshall, *Intelligence* – Alan Marshall, *Intelligence and Espionage in the Reign of Charles II, 1660–85* (2003)

McClain, *Beaufort* – Molly McClain, *Beaufort: the Duke and His Duchess, 1657–1715* (2001)

McKeon, *Domesticity* – Michael McKeon, *The Secret History of Domesticity* (2007)

Mignet – F. A. M. Mignet, *Négotiations Relatives à la Succession d'Espagne*, 4 vols (1835–42)

Miller, *CII* – John Miller, *Charles II* (1991)

Miller, *James II* – John Miller, *James II* (1978, rev. edn 2000)

Milward – *The Diary of John Milward*, ed. C. Robbins (1938)

Newcastle, *Advice* – Thomas P. Slaughter, ed., *Ideology and Politics on the Eve of the Restoration: Newcastle's Advice to Charles II* (1984)

Norrington – Ruth Norrington, *My Dearest Minette: the letters between Charles II and his sister Henrietta, Duchesse d'Orléans* (1996)

ODNB – *Oxford Dictionary of National Biography*

Ogg – David Ogg, *England in the Reign of Charles II*, 2 vols (1934)

Ogilby, *Relation* – John Ogilby, *The Relation of his Majesties Entertainment Passing through the City of London to his Coronation* (1661, new edition as '*The Entertainment of His Most Excellent Majestie . . .*, 1662)

Oldenburg Corr. – A. R. Hall and M. B. Hall, trans. and eds, *The Correspondence of Henry Oldenburg*, 13 vols (1965–86)

Ollard, *Clarendon* – Richard Ollard, *Clarendon and his Friends* (1987)

Ollard, *Image* – Richard Ollard, *The Image of the King: Charles I and Charles II* (1979, 1993)

Painted Ladies – C. MacLeod and J.M. Alexander, eds, *Painted Ladies: Women at the Court of Charles II*, National Portrait Gallery (2002)

Peck – Linda L. Peck, *Consuming Splendor: society and culture in seventeenth-century England* (2005)

Pepys – *The Diary of Samuel Pepys*, ed. Robert Latham and William Matthews, 11 vols (1970–83)

Picard – Lisa Picard, *Restoration London* (1997, 2001 edn)

Pincus – Steven C. A. Pincus, *Protestantism and Patriotism: ideologies and the making of English foreign policy, 1650–1688* (1996)

POAS – [General ed. G. F. de Lord], *Poems on Affairs of State: Augustan Satirical Verse, 1660–1714*, 7 vols (1963–75), vol. I *1660–78*

Rawdon Papers – Edward Berwick, ed., *The Rawdon Papers* (1819)

Reresby – *Memoirs of Sir John Reresby*, ed. Andrew Browning (2nd edn, 1991)

Ribeiro – Aileen Ribeiro, *Fashion and Fiction: Dress in Art and Literature in Stuart England* (2005)

Robertson – Geoffrey Robertson, *The Tyrannicide Brief* (2005)

Rochester, *Works* – *The Works of John Wilmot, Earl of Rochester*, ed. Harold Love (1999)

Rochester, *Letters* – *The Letters of John Wilmot, Earl of Rochester*, ed. Jeremy Treglown (1980)

Rodger – N. A. M. Rodger, *The Command of the Ocean: a Naval History of Britain, 1649–1815* (2004)

Rogers – P. D. Rogers, *The Dutch in the Medway* (1970)

Roth – Cecil Roth, *A History of the Jews in England* (1964 edn)

Rugg – W. L. Sachse, ed., *The Diurnal of Thomas Rugg 1659–1661*, CS 3rd series 91 (1961)

Sandwich, *Journal* – *The Journal of Edward Montagu, First Earl of Sandwich and General at Sea,* ed. R. C. Anderson (1929)

Savile Corr. – W. D. Cooper, ed., *Savile Correspondence*, CS OS 71 (1863)

Schellinks, *Journal* – M. Exwood and H. L. Lehmann, eds, *The Journal of William Schellinks' Travels in England 1661–63*, CS 5th series 13 (1993)

Scott – Eva Scott, *The King in Exile* (1905)

Seaward, *Cavalier Parliament* – Paul Seaward, *The Cavalier Parliament and the Reconstruction of the Old Regime, 1661–67* (1989)

Shapiro, *Wilkins* – Barbara Shapiro, *John Wilkins, 1614–1672: An Intellectual Biography* (1969)

Smith – Nigel Smith, *The Poems of Andrew Marvell* (2003)

Smuts – Malcolm R. Smuts, ed., *The Stuart Court and Europe* (1996)

Sorbière – Samuel Sorbière, *A Journey to England in the Year 1663* (1707 edn)

Spencer, *Rupert* – Charles Spencer, *Prince Rupert, the Last Cavalier* (2007)

Sprat – Thomas Sprat, *The History of the Royal Society of London*, ed. Jackson I. Cope and H. Whitmore Jones (1667, 1958 edn)

Spurr, *Restoration Church* – J. Spurr, *The Restoration Church of England, 1646–1689* (1991)

Spurr, *Post-Reformation* – J. Spurr *The Post-Reformation: Religion, Politics and Society in Britain, 1603–1714* (2006)

State Trials – *A Complete Collection of State Trials and Proceedings for High Treason and Other Crimes and Misdemeanours*, ed. William Cobbett, 28 vols (1809–20)

Steinman – G. Steinman, *A Memoir of Barbara, Duchess of Cleveland* (1871)

Strickland – A. Strickland, *Lives of the Queens of England*, vol. 8 (1845)

Stuart Courts – Eveline Cruickshanks, ed., *The Stuart Courts* (2000)

Summers – Montagu Summers, *Restoration Theatre* (1934)

Taaffe Letters – T. Crist, ed., *Charles II to Lord Taaffe: Letters in Exile* (1974)

Tedder – A. E. T. Tedder, *The Navy of the Restoration* (1916)

Thirsk and Cooper – Joan Thirsk and J. P. Cooper, eds, *Seventeenth-Century Economic Documents* (1972)

Thomas – Keith Thomas, *Religion and the Decline of Magic* (1971, 1991 edn)

Thurley, *Lost Palace* – Simon Thurley, *The Lost Palace of Whitehall* (1998)

Thurley, *Whitehall* – Simon Thurley, *Whitehall Palace: An Architectural History of the Royal Apartments, 1240–1690* (1999)

Tinniswood, *Wren* – Adrian Tinniswood, *His Invention So Fertile: A Life of Christopher Wren* (2001)

Tomalin – Claire Tomalin, *Samuel Pepys: The Unequalled Self* (2003)

Verney MSS – 'The Manuscripts of Sir Harry Verney, Bart.', *HMC Seventh Report* (1879)

Vincent – Revd Thomas Vincent, *God's Terrible Voice in the City* (1666, 1811 edn)

Walker, *Circumstantial Account* – Edward Walker, *A Circumstantial Account of the Preparations for the Coronation of His Majesty King Charles the Second . . . to which is Prefixed an Account of the Landing, Reception and Journey of His Majesty from Dover to London* (1820)

Weber – Harold Weber, *Paper Bullets: Print and Kingship under Charles II* (1996)

Weiser – Brian Weiser, *Charles II and the Politics of Access* (2003)

Whitaker – Katie Whitaker, *Mad Madge: Margaret Cavendish, Duchess of Newcastle* (2003)

Williamson – W. D. Christie, ed., *Letters to Sir Joseph Williamson*, 2 vols, CS NS 8, 9 (1874)

Wilson – C. H. Wilson, *Profit and Power: A Study of England and the Dutch Wars* (1957)

Winn – James Anderson Winn, *John Dryden and His World* (1989)

Wood – Andrew Clark, ed., *The Life and Times of Anthony Wood*, 5 vols (1891–1900)

Notes

PROLOGUE: THE REPUBLIC TRUMPED

1 *Letters* 37
2 9th version, Rochester, *Works* 294
3 Evelyn, IV 405, 4 February 1685
4 Burnet II 480
5 Gilbert Burnet in L. von Ranke, *History of England* (1875 edn) VI, Appendix, Second section, III 78–9
6 Ibid.
7 Burnet I 167
8 November 1659; Tim Harris, 'Understanding popular politics', Houston and Pincus 130
9 J. Tillotson, *Works* (1798) I 95
10 See *The Cambridge Companion to Lucretius*, ed. Philip Hardie (2007); Paul Hammond, 'Dryden, Milton and Lucretius', *Seventeenth Century* 16 (2001) 158–76
11 Margaret Cavendish, 'Of Many Worlds in this World', *Poems and Fancies* (1653)
12 Hobbes, *Leviathan*, Part I, Ch. 13, 186
13 Ibid. Part II, Ch. 18, 231
14 Ibid. Part I, Ch. 5, 105
15 Thomas Hobbes, *De Cive* (1642), ed. H. Warrender (1983) 177–8

1 SAILING

1 Previously attributed to Marvell, but this is now generally doubted; see Smith
2 Evelyn III 149–50, 9 April 1655
3 Fox 69
4 Sandwich, *Journal* 75–7, reporting message from Monck
5 Pepys I 136, 13 May 1660
6 Ibid. 153, 22 May 1660
7 Quoted in Charles Fitzroy, *Return of the King* (2007) 198
8 Ian Roy, *ODNB*. For Elizabeth of Bohemia, see the project on her voluminous correspondence at CELL (Centre for Editing Life and Letters), Queen Mary, London, www.livesandletters.ac.uk; for Rupert see Rupert Kitson, *Prince Rupert: Admiral and General-at-sea* (1998) and Charles Spencer, *Prince Rupert: The Last Cavalier* (2008)
9 Burnet I 52
10 *Cal. Clar. SP* II, Appendix lxiv
11 Burnet II 466
12 Pepys I 155, 23 May 1660
13 Ibid. 156, 23 May 1660

2 LANDING

1 Pepys I 156–7, 24 May 1660
2 Jardine, *Going Dutch*, 172–3

3 Pepys I 157, 24 May 1660
4 Fanshawe, 140–1
5 Josselin, 17 November 1650. See Pincus, *Protestantism and Patriotism*, passim
6 CII to Elizabeth of Bohemia, Cottrell transcripts, RA 5/2/1
7 6 March 1658, Scott 2. For background see also Geoffrey Smith, *The Cavaliers in Exile 1646–60* (2003)
8 Pepys I 45, 7 February 1660
9 *The Complete Prose Works of John Milton* (1953) VII 353
10 *Letters* 83, CII to Monck, 27 March 1660
11 *Letters* 86–8, CII to the Speaker, Lenthall, 4 April 1660: Clar. *Hist.* VI 227–9. For the Declaration, see Browning, *Historical Documents* 57
12 Sir William Killigrew to CII, 8 April 1660, PM, R of E Box 9, 003
13 Pepys I 121, 1 May 1660
14 Rugg 79
15 Hutton, *Restoration* 5
16 Clar. *Hist.* VI 256; see Evelyn III 245, 24 May 1660
17 Pepys I 143, 16 May 1660
18 Clar. *Hist.* VI 262
19 Sandwich, *Journal* 78
20 Pepys I 158, 25 May 1660
21 Ibid. I 159. Also W. Blundell, *Crosby Records*, ed. T. E Gibson, 1822, 90; Margaret Blundell, *Cavalier: Letters of William Blundell* (1933) 92

3 HOW TO BE KING

1 *Manner of the Most Happy Return* (1660)
2 Cavendish, *Life* 127
3 *CSPD* 1659–60, 448, 28 May
4 *CSPD* 1660–1,109, 3 July
5 *Letters* 92, CII to Minette, 29 May 1660
6 *CSPD* 1659–60, 447
7 Giavarini, *CSPV* 1659–61,151; Fitzroy 203
8 For the procession, see *Mercurius Publicus*, 339–42, 24–31 May 1660; Rugg 85–6, Edward Walker, *A Circumstantial Account* 11–15
9 Evelyn III 246, 29 May 1660
10 *Letters* 92–3
11 Clar. *Hist.* VI 234
12 Sir Samuel Tuke, *A Character of Charles II* (1660); Hutton, *Restoration* 111
13 Tuke, op. cit.
14 Margaret Willes, *Reading Matters: Five Centuries of Discovering Books* (2008) 47. See also 'News and Partisan Politics', Weiser 95–125, and John Miller, *After the Civil Wars. English Politics and Government in the Reign of Charles II* (2000) Ch. 4
15 See David H. Solkin, 'Isaac Fuller's Escape of Charles II: A Restoration Tragicomedy', *Journal of the Warburg and Courthauld Institutes* 62 (1999) 199–240
16 Evelyn III 259, 29 October 1660
17 Canon David Lloyd (often attrib. to Sir Richard Fanshawe), *Eikon Basilike . . . or the true pourtraiture of Charles II* (1660). For later parodies of these books see McKeon, *Domesticity* 566
18 Francis Gregory, *David's Return from His Banishment*, 1660. CCL
19 See Katharine Gibson, '"Best Belov'd of Kings": The Iconography of King Charles II', PhD thesis, Courtauld Institute, University of London, 2004; Ribeiro 218
20 *Mercurius Publicus*, July 1660; Picard 79. See also Pepys I 182, 23 June 1660. See Keay

112–8; Raymond Crawfurd, *The King's Evil* (1911); Marc Bloch, trans. J. E. Anderson, *The Royal Touch: Sacred Monarchy and Scrofula in England and France* (1973)

21 Aubrey, *Miscellanies* (1890 edn) 128; Thomas 230
22 *CSPV* 1659–61 32, 74
23 RA, Establishment Book 1660
24 Schellinks, *Journal* 60
25 Thurley, *Lost Palace* 42
26 Magalotti 126
27 Newsletter, 9 June 1660, HMC *5th Report*
28 Pepys I 222, 15 August 1660
29 *CSPV* 1661–4, 42
30 Establishment Book, RA EB 55/ ff. 133–47
31 Macray 11, 5 October 1660
32 Evelyn III 256, 13 September 1660
33 '. . . it has since been Disputeable among the Judicious, whether any Woman that succeeded him so Sensibly touch'd the Audience as he'. Downes, 19; Cibber 71
34 Warrant granted to Killigrew and Davenant, 21 May 1660; D. Thomas, ed., *Theatre in Europe: Restoration & Georgian England* (1989) 11–12. BL Add. MS 19,256, f. 47
35 Evelyn III 399–400, 9 February 1665
36 Waller, 'On St James's Park, As Lately Improved by His Majesty' (1661), *The Poetical Works of Edmund Waller and Sir John Denham*, ed. George Gilfillan (1877) 75–6
37 Reresby 22
38 Randle Holme, *The Academy of Armoury* (1688); Picard 126–34
39 Pepys II 66, 6 April 1661
40 Holme, *Academy of Armoury*; see Richard Corson, *Fashions in Hair* (1980), 219–20
41 Pepys III 157–8, 19 August 1663
42 Carte IV 451
43 *Mercurius Publicus*, 28 June 1660. With thanks to Francesca Beauman, who quotes this in *Shapely Ankle Preferr'd: A History of Lonely Hearts Advertisements* (forthcoming 2011)
44 Ailesbury I 93

4 THREE CROWNS AND MORE

1 For the administration see Aylmer, *Crown's Servants*
2 Fanshawe, 140
3 Clar. *Life.* I 77–8
4 Burnet I 171
5 Macray 5
6 For background, see Harris, *Restoration* 21–38, 85–138
7 Miller, *CII* 137
8 Burnet I 186
9 Ibid. 205
10 For his debts, see G. E. Aylmer, 'The First Duke of Ormond as Patron and Administrator' in Barnard and Fenlon; also J. C. Beckett, *The Cavalier Duke: a Life of James Butler, 1st Duke of Ormond, 1610–88* (1990)
11 Carte II 240–1
12 Macray 65
13 Ormond to Orrery, 9 September 1661, Hastings MSS IV 109
14 See David Watts, *The West Indies* (1990). Barbados sugar exports rose from seventy-five tons in the early 1650s to 190 tons a decade later, with an additional thirty tons from the Leeward islands and ten from Jamaica.

15 Willoughby's report on the islands of the West Indies, CSP Col., *America and W. Indies* V (1661–8) 586
16 Grove 67, 277; PRO, CO1/21, 'Memorial of the Island of Tobago' (1667)

5 THIS WONDERFUL PACIFICK YEAR

1 See Holmes, 27–43
2 Jusserand 100, Cominges to Louis XIV, 4 February 1664
3 *Act for Confirming Judicial Proceedings* 1660
4 *Act to Preserve the Person and Government of the King* 1661
5 Keeble, *Restoration* 79
6 J. Gibson, *The Hearth Tax and other later Stuart Tax Lists*, Federation of Family History Societies (1996). The tax was levied on households worth more than 20s, whose occupants contributed to the church tithes and poor rates.
7 Pepys IV 373–4, 9 November 1663
8 Baxter, *Autobiography* 92
9 *Letters* 85
10 Baxter, *Autobiography* 148
11 Ibid. 155
12 Browning, *Historical Documents* 365–70
13 Evelyn III 247, 4 June 1660; Weiser 55
14 Newcastle, *Advice* 289
15 *A Character of England* (1659), *An Apology for the Royal Party* (1659) and *The Late Newes from Brussels Unmasked* (1660). For Evelyn's life see Gillian Darley, *John Evelyn: Living for Ingenuity* (2006)
16 Hutton, *Restoration* 134–5
17 Pepys III 42–3, 7 March 1662
18 Evelyn III 250, 5 July 1660; J. Tatham, *London's Glory* (1660)
19 Weiser 128, PRO, CO 389, 2

6 FAMILY MATTERS

1 Jardine, *Wren* 168; Scott 95
2 Clar. *Hist.* VI 95–7
3 Norrington 78, CII to Minette, 28 March 1664
4 Jardine, *Going Dutch* 170–1. Jardine dates the baby's birth as 1648, revising the accepted 1650.
5 Pepys VIII 182 (reporting conversation with Evelyn), 26 April 1667
6 *Taaffe Letters* 21–3, 29; Jardine, *Going Dutch* 73
7 Halifax, 'Character of Charles II', *Works* II 490
8 Wilson 115; *Taaffe Letters* 39
9 Steinman 16
10 Halifax, *Works* II 493
11 Pepys I 199, 13 July 1660
12 Sandwich, *Journal* 82, 20 September 1660
13 Clar. *Life* I 325
14 *Grammont* 174–5
15 Those named included the Earl of Arran, Charles Berkeley, Harry Jermyn, Richard Talbot and Harry Killigrew. See Miller, *James* II 44–5
16 Pepys I 261, 7 October 1660
17 *Grammont* 104
18 Pepys I 265–6, 14 October 1660; IX 342, 30 October 1668.

19 Pepys II 3, 1 January 1661
20 Sir John Lawson, 26 January 1661, included in Sandwich, *Journal* 84

7 BLOOD AND BANNERS

1 John Milton, *Paradise Lost*, VII, 24–8
2 'Astraea Redux', Dryden, *Poems* I 51–2
3 See Winn, 12–53
4 *Letters* 100–1, Speech to the House of Lords, 27 July 1660
5 Robertson 285
6 This offence, in relation to the treason trials of the 1790s, is discussed in John Barrell, *Imagining the King's Death: Figurative Treason, Fantasies of Regicide, 1793–6* (2000). For the trials see Robertson 290–353; *An Exact and Most Impartiall Account of the Indictment, Arraignment, Trial and Judgement . . .* (1660); Gilbert Mabbutt, 'A Perfect Narrative', *State Trials* IV; Rugg 116–40 and the *Intelligencer* and *Mercurius Publicus*, October 1660
7 Robertson 326
8 Evelyn III 259, 17 October 1660
9 *Lauderdale Papers* 135, Lauderdale to Moray, 23 June 1663
10 PM, R of E Box 08, Charles II, Part I, 009
11 William Fuller to John Bramhall, Bishop of Armagh, 18 February 1661; Hastings MSS IV 103
12 Schellinks, *Journal* 72
13 Newcastle, *Advice* 44 (modernised spelling)
14 Ibid. 290
15 Jardine, *Wren* 31–45
16 Fraser 197; Evelyn III 276, 18 and 19 April 1661
17 Hamilton Archives; Marshall, *Hamilton* 88
18 Pepys II 86, 22 April 1661 (with Sir William Batten and family, and Sir William Penn and his son)
19 Elias Ashmole, *Brief Narrative of His Majesties Solemn Coronation* 1662, CCL H/M 12–2
20 *Intelligencer* 29 April 1661; see Ogilby, *Relation* (1661) and *Entertainment* (1662), Walker, *Circumstantiall Account*, and Rugg 173–5. For the rituals, see Lorraine Medway, '"The Most Conspicuous Solemnity": the Coronation of Charles II', *Stuart Courts* 141–57
21 L. G. W. Legg, *English Coronation Records*, 286–96 (1901). See also Roy Strong, *Coronation: A History of Kingship and the British Monarch* (2005) and Keay 5, who notes that the crown is still used for coronations today.
22 Ashmole, op. cit. 78
23 Ludlow, *Voyce* 287
24 Pepys II 87, 23 April 1661
25 Evelyn III 284, 24 April 1661
26 Margoliouth 31, Marvell to Mayor Richardson, 15 June 1661
27 Sermon, 29 May 1661, CCL H/A 5–9
28 Macray, 29 July 1661; *Cal. Clar. SP* III xlvi

8 WHITEHALL

1 Thurley, *Lost Palace* 40
2 Thurley, *Whitehall* 106
3 RA 84770–94, Cash book 1663–4
4 Hutton, *CII* 133
5 BL Stowe 562, 1; Weiser 26. See also Susan Foreman, *From Palace to Power* (1995)
6 Weiser 29: PRO, LC 5/137

7 Ibid. 39–45
8 Thurley, *Lost Palace* 29–33
9 Clay, *Fox* 30–5; Jardine, *Wren* 343–6
10 Pepys VIII 201; Paul Hammond, 'The King's Two Bodies: Representations of Charles II', in Black and Gregory 22
11 Macray 21
12 Carte MSS 59; Aylmer, 'The First Duke of Ormond', 120 n.
13 *CSPD* 1660–1, 30–1. In May alone, 179 petitions were received for posts in the Lord Chamberlain's and Lord Steward's departments.
14 Neil Cuddy, 'Reinventing a Monarchy', *Stuart Courts*, 63
15 Kate Colquhoun, *Taste: the Story of Britain through its Cooking* (2007) 154–63; for the continental banquets see Roy Strong, *Feast* (2002) 211–65
16 *CSPD* 1660–1, 6; for the Dutch gift, see Jardine, *Going Dutch*, 139–45, Arthur Macgregor, *Curiosity and Enlightenment, Collectors and Collecting from the Sixteenth to Nineteenth Centuries* (2008); S. Gleissner, 'Reassembling a Royal Art Collection', *Journal of the History of Collections* 6 (1994) 103–15
17 *CSPD* 1660–1, 190, 14 August 1660

9 COURTIERS AND ENVOYS

1 Clar. *Hist.* III 381
2 Jusserand 29
3 Evelyn III 310, 10 January 1662
4 Ailesbury 23, 86
5 C. H. Hartmann, introduction to *Memoirs of the Comte de Grammont*, trans. Peter Quennell (1930)
6 Ronald Hutton, *ODNB*; see C. H. Hartmann, *The King's Friend: A Life of Charles Berkeley, Viscount Fitzhardinge, Earl of Falmouth, 1630–65* (1951)
7 *Grammont* 95
8 *Cal. Clar. SP* II, 319, 1928 and Hyde to Nicholas 18 March 1650; *Cal. Clar. SP* III 13, 46, 69
9 Joseph Spence, *Anecdotes, Observations, and Characters, of Books and Men* (1820), 102
10 V. da Sola Pinto, *Sir Charles Sedley, 1639–1701: A Study in the Life and Literature of the Restoration* (1927) 54
11 Willa McClung Evans, *Henry Lawes: Musician and Friend of Poets* (1941), 227
12 Pepys I 297–8, 20 November 1660
13 Jonathan Keates, *Purcell* (1995) 20
14 *Grammont* 186
15 Jusserand 84, Cominges to Lionne 15 February 1663
16 Magalotti 74
17 Evelyn III 334, 1 September 1662
18 *Grammont* 93
19 See H. J. Habbakuk, *Marriage, Debt and the Estates System; English Landownership 1650–1950* (1994)
20 Clar. *Life* III 118–19
21 Pepys III 170–1, 19 August 1662; see also *Grammont* 113
22 PM MSS, 'The reprehension of the Lords Bridgewater and Middlesex', endorsed by Clarendon 7 February 1663
23 Evelyn III 308, 6 January 1662
24 Jusserand 19, Louis XIV to d'Estrades, 25 January 1662
25 Quoted in Sheila Russell, 'Restoration Londoners', *Apollo*, August 2006 49. See Rugg 111

26 Ibid. 21
27 Pepys II 188, 30 September 1661
28 John Parker to John Bramhall, Archbishop of Armagh, Hastings MSS IV 113
29 Jusserand, d'Estrades to Lionne, 13 October 1661
30 Macray 42, 11 October 1661
31 Evelyn III 299, 3 October 1661
32 *CSPV* 1661–4, 2 June 1662

10 THE COMING OF THE QUEEN

1 Pepys II 80, 20 April 1661; II 174, 7 September 1661
2 Burnet I 299–300; for a counter to Burnet, see also 'Vindication of General Monck' Lansdowne, *Works* II 177–184
3 Macray 14
4 Schellinks, *Journal* 35, 21 July 1661
5 Palmer/Morice letter, Hamilton, *Castlemaine* 42
6 Ibid., 8 November 1661
7 Pepys III 15, 22 January 1662
8 Ibid. 60, 6 April 1662
9 [Samuel Hinde], *The Lusitanicum; or the Portugal Voyage* (1662). For Catherine, see also Edward Corp, 'Catherine of Braganza and cultural politics' in Clarissa Campell Orr, ed., *Queenship in Britain 1660–1837: Royal Patronage, Court Culture and Dynastic Politics* (2002)
10 Thurley, *Whitehall* 115
11 Pepys III 87, 21 May 1662
12 Schellinks, *Journal* 85–6
13 CII to Hyde 21 May 1662, BL Lansdowne MS 1,236, f. 124
14 Burnet I 315
15 *Letters* 126; Hartmann, *Madame* 43
16 *Letters* 126–7
17 Reresby 41
18 Wood II 440
19 Schellinks, *Journal* 90
20 *King's Works* 153
21 Evelyn III 321, 30 May 1662
22 Pepys III 87, 21 May 1662
23 Ibid.
24 Clar. *Life* 173
25 Ibid. 180
26 Ibid. 177
27 Hartmann, *Madame* 49
28 Lister III 202
29 Clar. *Life* III 184–5
30 See Willis Bund, ed., *Diary of Henry Townshend* (1920) 92–3
31 *King's Works* 141–5
32 Evelyn III 300–1, 313, 6 October 1661, 24 January 1662
33 450,000 whole bricks, and 750,000 brickbats: *King's Works* 145
34 Evelyn III 331, 17 August 1662
35 Ibid. 333, 23 August 1662
36 Pepys III 175, 23 August 1662
37 Edward Weston to his wife, 15 November 1662, Capt. Stewart MSS, HMC *10th Report*, App. IV, 111

11 LAND

1 *Cal. Clar. SP* 3 Feb 1663; Bod. Clar SP v. 79
2 Lucy Worsley, *Cavalier* (2007)
3 Whitaker 244
4 McClain, *Beaufort* 116
5 See E. A. Wrigley and R. Schofield, *Population History of England 1541–1871: a Reconstruction* (1989)
6 See Thirsk and Cooper 490, 'Wool Smuggling on the Kent Coast' 1669, House of Lords report
7 Alice Clark, *The Working Life of Women in the Seventeenth Century* (1982 edn) 66–9
8 H. C. Darby, *A New Historical Geography of England after 1600* (1978)
9 Worlidge, *Systema Agriculturae*: see D. Macdonald, *Agricultural Writers 1200–1800* (1908) 116
10 J. V. Beckett, *Coal and Tobacco: the Lowthers and the economic development of East Cumberland* (1980); for towns see Holmes 47, 54–5
11 J. Thirsk, ed., *The Agrarian History of England and Wales* (1985), V ii 315
12 Cavendish, *Life* 136
13 Darby, op. cit. 28
14 See Paul Hartle, *ODNB*; A. I. Dust, ed., *Charles Cotton: Works 1663–65* (1992); J. Beresford, ed., *Poems of Charles Cotton* (1923) 260
15 Margaret Cavendish, *Sociable Letters* (1664), 167; Whitaker 245–6

12 TENDER CONSCIENCES

1 Published 1666, *POAS* 303
2 Schellinks, *Journal* 72
3 Peter Holman, *Four and Twenty Fiddlers: the Violin at the English Court, 1540–1690* (1993); Pepys I 195, 275–6, 8 July, 14 October 1660
4 Pepys IV 393–4, 22 November 1663
5 Evelyn III 347, 21 December 1662
6 E. H. Plumptre, *Thomas Ken* (1888) I 157–8
7 Burnet I 158–9, 475; II 22
8 See J. R. Jones, *The Restored Monarchy* (1979) 33, and I. M. Green, *The Re-establishment of the Church of England* (1978)
9 *An Act for Retaining the Queen's Subjects in their Due Obedience*. See *A Relation of the Imprisonment of Mr John Bunyan*
10 Keeble R, 144, quoting *Grace Abounding*
11 Proclamation 10 January 1661
12 Magalotti 49
13 *Reliquiae Baxterianae*, quoted in Keeble, *Richard Baxter: Puritan Man of Letters* (1982) 184–5
14 Pepys I 174, 7 September 1661
15 George Wild, Bishop of Derry to John Bramhall, Archbishop of Armagh, Hastings MSS IV, 131
16 Evelyn, 310–12,12 January 1662; *Mercurius Publicus* 16 Jan 1661/2, 31
17 Pepys III 15, 22 January 1662; *CJ* VIII 349
18 *CSPD* 1661–2, 281
19 Pepys III 39, 18 February, n. 1, citing Rugg II f12r. See also *Mirabilis annus secundes* (1662) and *A full and certain account of the last great wind* (1661/2)
20 *Rawdon Papers*, ed. Ed Berwick (1918), 138
21 For the Commissioners, see *LJ* 25 March 1661. The copy of the King Edward the Sixth Book of Common Prayer, 1604, and the small book with the six hundred manuscript

alterations, which had both been thought lost, turned up in a cupboard during building work in the House of Lords in the nineteenth century. HMC *1st Report* (1874) 3

22 *Letters* 124, 1 March 1662
23 Seaward, *Cavalier Parliament* 180
24 Holmes 149
25 George Fox, *Summ of Such Particulars as are Charged against George Fox* (1660), quoted in Keeble, *Restoration* 144
26 Halifax, *Works* 139

13 ALL PEOPLE DISCONTENTED

1 Thomason Coll 669, f. 25, in William E. Burns, *An Age of Wonders: Prodigies, Politics and Providence and in England, 1657–1727* (2002) 23
2 Ogg 98
3 *Leviathan and the Air-pump* 288
4 *POAS* I xxxiii
5 Keeble, *Restoration* 148–50
6 See D. F. Mackenzie, 'Printing and Publishing 1557–1700: Constraints on the London Book Trade', in *History of the Book* 553–67
7 *POAS* I xxxiii
8 See Michael Winship, *Seers of God; Puritan Providentialism in the Restoration and early Enlightenment* (1996), also, generally, Ian Green and Kate Peters, 'Religious Publishing in England 1640–1695', in *History of the Book* 67–93
9 *Truth and Loyalty Vindicated*, 56–8; Ariel Hessayon, *ODNB*. See also Frank Smith's *Narrative* (1680); *State Trials* VI 520–70; *CSPD* 1662, 1663–4. In 1660 the Baptist bookseller and minister Francis Smith (Bunyan's publisher, known as Elephant Smith, for his shop near Elephant and Castle) had been imprisoned three times for publishing *The Lord's Loud Call to England*, a list of providential signs reasserting the need for a republic.
10 Pepys III 127, 30 June 1662
11 Wood II 465
12 Baxter, *Autobiography* 176
13 Evelyn III 331, 17 August 1662
14 Schellinks, *Journal* 127
15 M. R. Watts, *The Dissenters: from the reformation to the French revolution* (1978) 219
16 Greaves, *Deliver Us from Evil* 112–29. See Marshall, *Intelligence* 142–50
17 Hutton, *Restoration* Ch. 2; Jackson, *Scotland* passim
18 Anne Creighton, 'The Remonstrance of December 1661 and Catholic Politics in Restoration Ireland', *Irish Historical Studies* XXXIV, No. 133 (May 2004) 16–41
19 Bunyan, *Christian Behaviour* (1663), Keeble, *Restoration* 137
20 Pepys IV 372, 9 November 1663
21 *Letters* 140, 18 February 1663
22 Ailesbury I 93; Burnet, Supplement 50
23 Ollard, *Image* 109; Halifax, *Works* II 490
24 Carte IV 111
25 Ollard, *Image* 107–8
26 Jusserand 116, 12 April 1663
27 Magalotti, 28

14 THE KING STREET GANG

1 Carte MSS 33, f. 118, O'Neill to Ormond [July 1662]
2 See *Painted Ladies* 116–35

3 Ibid. 40
4 Clar. *Life* II 256
5 Sir William Temple, *Works* (1814) II 492
6 Burnet I 182
7 Carte MSS 32, f. 3, O'Neill to Ormond, 2 September 1662
8 Carte MSS 32, f. 26, O'Neill to Ormond, 13 September 1662
9 Ibid.
10 Pepys III 227, 17 October 1662
11 *CSPD* 1661-2, 545-6, 561
12 RA 84770-94, Cash book 1662-3, February 1663. For the queen and queen mother's circle and the drawing room, see Keay 126-30
13 Lister III 244
14 *Letters* 140, 18 February 1663
15 J. P. Kenyon, *The Stuart Constitution* (1966) 403-6. For the Lords' proviso, see HMC *7th Report*, Appendix 162-3
16 Carte MSS 47 f. 52, 6 June
17 Clar. *Life* III 258
18 Jusserand 107, Cominges to Lionne, 8 October 1663
19 Ollard, *Clarendon* 242; Hutton, *Restoration* 193

15 GOVERNED AS BEASTS

1 McClain, *Beaufort* 72; BL M287 (Alnwick MSS) 18, f. 71
2 Carte II 261
3 Keeble, *Literary Culture* 72
4 Clar. *Life* 279. For the northern rebellions see Greaves, *Deliver Us from Evil*, and Marshall, *Intelligence* 107-14
5 Reresby 49
6 Pincus 234; CII to Sir Godfrey Copley, 24 February 1664, PRO, SP 44/17, 11
7 Ibid. 233; Humphrey Gyfford to George Oxenden, 25 March 1664
8 Ibid. 151; Geoff Kemp, *ODNB*
9 George Kitchin, *Sir Roger L'Estrange* (1913) 113
10 *CSPD* 1664, 587, 15 May 1664
11 Bunyan, *Miscellaneous Works, ed. Roger Sharrock* (1975) VI 42. See Keeble, *Literary Culture* 78-92, 203; also Kate Peters, *Print Culture and the Early Quakers* (2005), and *History of the Book* IV 60-75; and for the continuing struggle between L'Estrange and the radical press, see Weber, and Richard L. Greaves, *Enemies Under his Feet: Radicals and Nonconformists in Britain 1664-67* (1990) 167-84
12 Milton, *Paradise Lost*, XII 587
13 Carte MSS 45, f. 151
14 *Act to Prevent and Suppress Seditious Conventicles* (16 Car II c. 4)
15 *CSPD* 1664, 487
16 *Act for Restraining Non-Conformists from inhabiting in Corporations* (17 Car II c. 2) For legislation and context see Keeble, *Restoration*; Harris, Seaward and Goldie; and Spurr, *Restoration Church* and *Post-Reformation*

16 THE SPRING OF THE AIR

1 Aubrey 231
2 *Leviathan and the Air-pump* 97-8
3 Boyle, 'Prenomial Essay', *Leviathan and the Air-pump* 68
4 Gordon Cragg, *From Puritanism to the Age of Reason* (1950) 100; Worden, 'The question of

secularization', Houston and Pincus 22
5 Robert Hooke, *Micrographia* (1665) Preface
6 Declaration, Kenyon 357
7 Evelyn III 260–1, 1 November 1660
8 See Jardine, *Going Dutch*, 267–90
9 Aubrey 232
10 Jardine, *Ingenious Pursuits: Building the Scientific Revolution* (1999)
11 Marjorie Hope Nicolson, ed. *Conway Letters: The Correspondence of Anne Viscountess Conway, Henry More, and their Friends, 1642–1684* (1930). For the women more generally, see L. Hunter, 'Sisters of the Royal Society; the circle of Katherine Jones, Lady Ranelagh', and Frances Harris, 'Living in the neighbourhood of science: Mary Evelyn, Margaret Cavendish and the Greshamites', in L. Hunter and S. Hutton, eds, *Women, Science and Medicine 1500–1700* (1997)
12 Ibid. 27; Boyle to John Dury, 3 May 1647, Boyle I xxxix. The intellectual ferment is described in C. Webster, *The Great Instauration: Science, Medicine and Reform 1626–60* (1975)
13 Jardine, *Wren* 118–19
14 Jardine, *Wren* 64–8; Tinniswood, *Wren* 28; W. Pope, *Seth, Bishop of Salisbury* (1697) 29
15 Evelyn III 110–11, 13 July 1654

17 ROYAL SOCIETY

1 Samuel Sorbière, *A Journey to England . . . Also Observations on the Same Voyage by Dr Sprat* (1709) 35
2 Jardine, *Wren* 166
3 Ibid. 142
4 Evelyn, library catalogues, BL Add. MS 78632
5 Sprat 53
6 Hunter, *New Science* 35; Birch I 3. See also Hunter's other books: *Science and Society in Restoration England* (1981) and *The Royal Society and its Fellows 1660–1700: The Morphology of an early Scientific Institution* (1999), and Lisa Jardine, *Ingenious Pursuits: Building the Scientific Revolution* (1999)
7 Tinniswood, *Wren* 68–9; see also Wood, *Life and Times* I, 201, 472–3
8 Birch I 8
9 Pepys II 21–2, 23 January 1661
10 Evelyn III 268, 16 January 1661
11 Pepys III 9, 12 January 1662
12 Jardine, *Going Dutch* 200–3
13 Evelyn III 272, 6 March 1661; Birch I 37–41
14 Robert Boyle, *The Sceptical Chemist*, in Boyle, *Works* II 208, 211
15 Stephen Wren, *Parentalia* (1750, repr. 1965), 210–11; cit. Jardine, *Wren*, 176
16 Birch I 10,17
17 Evelyn III 288, 14 May 1661
18 Ibid. 330, 13 August 1662
19 Birch I 271
20 Ibid. 272
21 Ibid. 289
22 Sorbière, *Voyage* 39–40
23 Ibid. 36–8. Louis XIV judged that Sorbière had been indiscreet in making libellous remarks about British ministers and banished him to Brittany, and Charles asked that he should be pardoned. Charles also stopped the society from framing an answer which would spark more Anglo-French animosity.

24 See Keeble, *Restoration* 202–3
25 Hunter, *New Science* 85. See Peck, Ch. 8, 311–45, on the Royal Society and luxury goods, and on Henry Howard and North Africa 143–51
26 *Oldenburg Corr.* III 525
27 Quoted in Shapiro 74
28 Sprat 111–13
29 Ian Roy, *ODNB*
30 Birch I 281
31 Ibid., quoted in D. C. Martin, 'Sir Robert Moray' in Sir Harold Hartley, ed., *The Royal Society: Its Origins and Founders* (1960) 246–7
32 Pepys V 32–3, 1 February 1664; Hunter, *Science and Society* (2002 edn) 131
33 Birch II 463, 1671. See Middleton, 'What did Charles II call the Fellows of the Royal Society?', *Notes and Records of the Royal Society* 32 (1977) 13
34 *Leviathan and the Air-pump* 33

18 CARD HOUSES

1 Pepys III 191, 7 September 1662
2 Evelyn III 347, 1 December 1662
3 Pepys III 297, 29 December 1662; Evelyn III 349; *Mercurius Publicus* 5 Jan 1663, 13–16
4 Ibid. 293, 25 December 1662
5 Ibid. 301, 31 December 1662; *Grammont* 171; Evelyn III 346
6 Jusserand 91
7 *Grammont* 126
8 Thurley, *Lost Palace* 42–4
9 Pepys IV 1, 1 January 1663
10 *Grammont* 116
11 Pepys IV 37–8, 8 February 1663
12 *Grammont* 190
13 Ibid. 344
14 C. H. Hartmann, *La Belle Stuart* (1924) 55
15 *Grammont* 339
16 Jusserand 89; *Grammont* 297
17 *Savile Corr.* 6, Henry Savile to Lady Dorothy Savile, May 1665
18 Pepys IV 136–7, 15 May 1663
19 Ibid. 216, 4 July 1663
20 Ibid. 230, 13 July 1663
21 *Newes* 14 July, *Intelligencer* 18 July
22 Pepys V 209, 15 July 1664
23 Hartmann, *La Belle Stuart* 150
24 *Letters* 145
25 Earl of Anglesey to Ormond, HMC *Ormonde* NS III 78, 174–5; Carte MSS 221, f. 77, Bennet to Ormond, 22 August 1663, 143, 175–6. For the economies, see *CSPD* 1663–4, 264. See Andrew Barclay, 'Charles II's Failed Restoration: Administrative Reform Below Stairs, 1660–64', *Stuart Courts* 164–5
26 *Moneys received and paid for the Secret Service of Charles II and James II*, CS, 1851, vi–viii
27 Cash book, 1663–4, RA 84770–94
28 HMC *Hastings*, 142–3. For the tour, see Hutton, *CII*, 210; *CSPD* 1663, 264, 271; Carte MSS 33 ff. 69,118; *Intelligencer* 31 August, 7, 28 September, 5 October; *The Newes* 10 September, 1 October. For Avebury, John Aubrey, *Topographical Collections*, ed.

Jackson (1862), 316; For the Herberts, see McClain 68: Wilts RO 1300/503 Duchess of Devonshire

29 Schellinks, *Journal* 105

30 Oldenburg to Evelyn, 16 April 1663, quoted in Jardine, *Wren* 215

31 This version from Brown's *Miscellanea Aulica* (1702) 306: *Grammont*, n. 153

32 Jusserand 88

33 Fraser 213; Strickland 560; Pepys IV 339, 19 October 1663

19 BEAUTIES

1 Jusserand, Lionne to Cominges, 5 August 1663; for language, see 52

2 *Grammont* 106

3 Ibid. 115

4 Norrington 80, CII to Minette, 2 June 1664

5 Sonya Wynne, 'The Brightest Glories of the British Sphere', in *Painted Ladies* 37–8

6 Norrington 53–4, Minette to CII, 4 January 1662

7 Keay 132

8 Ibid.

9 Diana Dethloff, 'Portaiture and Concepts of Beauty in Restoration Painting', in *Painted Ladies*, 25

10 Horace Walpole, *Anecdotes of Painting* (1762) II 27

11 *Grammont* 117

12 Norrington 72, CII to Minette, 10 December 1663

13 Jusserand 85, 90

14 Pepys IV 4, 5 January 1663

15 *Grammont* 214

16 *King's Works* 15

20 PERFORMANCE

1 Wood II 476

2 Pepys IV 209, 17 July 1663

3 Pepys III 34, 22 February 1662; 36, 25 February 1662

4 Harold Love, *ODNB*; Matthew Prior, *Poems on Several Occasions* (1718)

5 Burnet I 485

6 Magalotti 77. Sermon from the Canticles, Pepys IX 264, 18 July 1668

7 Dryden, *Works* (*Essay of Dramatic Poesie*), XVII 39

8 Summers 82–3

9 Etherege, *She wou'd if she cou'd* (1668); Summers 45

10 Proclamation 1663; Summers 50–1

11 See Nancy Klein Maguire, *Regicide and Restoration:English tragicomedy 1660–1671* (1992)

12 Dryden, *Works* XVII 35

13 Orrery to Ormond, 23 January 1662, Winn 146

14 Dryden, *Works* XVII 56

15 John Barnard, *ODNB*

16 28 March 1663, Summers 16

17 *Grammont* 86–90

18 Jeremy Collier, *Short View of the Profaneness of the English Stage* (1698) 13; Howe 93

19 John Barnard, ed., Etherege, *The Man of Mode* III i

20 Cibber, *Apology* (1925 edn) I 79

21 Pepys VII 76–7, 19 March 1666

22 Halifax, *Works* II 495

23 *Remarques on the Humours and Conversations of the Town* (1673)

21 MONEY-MEN AND MERCHANTS

1 Ogilby, *Entertainment* 107; Weiscr 121
2 'The Royal Exchange', *Old and New London* I (1878) 494–513
3 Fraser 218. See Roth 167–96
4 Minutes to 1665, BL Add. MS 25,115
5 PRO, CO 389-1, in Weiser 128
6 Weiser 137–8
7 Josiah Child, *Brief Observations*; in Bernstein 130
8 See R. D. Richards, *The Early History of Banking in England* (1929) 23–64, and for the goldsmiths' dealings with the Treasury and Exchequer, 65–91
9 Dorothy K. Clark, 'A Restoration Goldsmith-Banking House: the Vine on Lombard Street', *Essays in Modern History in Honour of Wilbur Cortez Abbott* (1941) 7
10 RBS EB1/1/1663 ff. 84, 137
11 RBS CH/194/1–6
12 Holmes 58
13 See, for example, David Harris Sacks, *The Widening Gate: Bristol and the Atlantic Economy, 1450–1700* (1991)
14 Dudley North, *Observations and Advices Oeconomical* (1669); Adrian Tinniswood, *The Verneys* (2007) 302
15 See 'The Levant Trader', Tinniswood, *Verneys*
16 Bernstein 152
17 Weiser 147
18 William Dalrymple, *White Mughals* (2002) 22, and illustration. See the earlier study by S. A. Khan, *The East India Trade in the Seventeenth Century: its Political and Economic Aspects* (1923), and John Keay, *The Honourable Company: A History of the East India Company* (1991)
19 Weiser 152; B. E. Sainsbury, *Calendar of the Court Minutes etc. of the East India Company* (1929) 310
20 Magalotti, *Travels* 326–7
21 Wilson 19 (Charles's Council of Trade had already drawn on Mun's ideas to recommend that he agree to the East India Company's request to export bullion; Weiser 127)
22 See, for example, the reading of Samuel Tuke's *Five Hours* (1663) in Richard W. Kroll, *Restoration Drama and the 'Circle of Commerce'*, 58–63
23 *Cal. Clar. SP* 357, 358, 373, 377
24 See Sonia Anderson, *An English Consul in Turkey: Paul Rycaut at Smyrna 1667–1678* (1989)
25 Kate Teltscher, *India Inscribed: European and British Writing on India 1600–1800* (1995) 51

22 ONE MUST DOWN

1 Thomas Killigrew m. Charlotte van Hesse-Piershil, daughter of an Orange courtier, in 1655. In 1659 the Earl of Ossory m. Aemilia, daughter of Lodewyck van Nassau, heer van Beverweerd, whose father was an illegitimate son of Maurice of Orange. Arlington m. her sister Isabella, 1666. Alexander Bruce, Earl of Kincardine, m. Veronica van Aerssen van Sommelsdijck, daughter of a powerful politician, in 1659.
2 See Pincus 200–4
3 Bernstein 144
4 Petty, *Political Arithmetic*, in C. A. Hull, ed., *Economic Writings of Sir William Petty* I 258; Ogg I 222
5 K. G. Davies, *The Royal African Company* (1975) 42, 64. See Weiser 159
6 Tomalin 180; Pepys III 95, 30 May 1662

7 Picard 179; see F. O. Shyllon, *Black Slaves in Britain* (1974) and G. A. Clay, *Economic Expansion and Social Change 1500–74* (1982)

8 Pepys VI 43, 129. For Holmes see Richard Ollard, *Man of War: Sir Robert Holmes and the Restoration Navy* (1969)

9 Jardine, *Going Dutch* 284; 'Captain Robert Holmes his Journalls of Two Voyages into Guynea', Pepys Library Sea MS No. 2,698

10 Pepys III 125, 28 June 1662

11 Simon Schama, *The Embarrassment of Riches: An Interpretation of Dutch Culture in the Golden Age* (1987; 1991 edn) 229

12 Hutton, *CII* 215

13 Pepys V 35, 2 February 1664

14 For contrasting arguments about the prime causes of the Second Dutch War see: Sir Keith Feiling, *British Foreign Policy 1660–1672* (1930) 3–4, trade, and continuity of foreign policy from Commonwealth; Wilson 20, economic competition; J. R. Jones, *Britain and the World 1649–1815* (1980), anti-Clarendon factions at court; Hutton, *Restoration* 215–16, economic aggression among courtiers; and Pincus, ideological differences and support of Orange faction, 195–8. See also Pincus 237–9

15 Pepys V 107, 1 April 1664

16 Weiser, 134

17 Pincus, 237; *Newes* 5 May 1664

18 Wilson 126

19 Jusserand 87, Cominges to Louis XIV, 16 November 1663

20 Norrington 80, CII to Minette, 2 June 1664

21 Ibid. 84, CII to Minette, 27 June 1664

22 Ibid. 95, CII to Minette, 24 October 1664

23 Jusserand 92, Cominges to Louis XIV, 18 August 1664

24 For radical conspiracies see Greaves, *Deliver Us from Evil*, also his *Enemies under His Feet: Radicals and Nonconformists in Britain, 1664–1677* (1990). For spies and informers generally, see Marshall, *Intelligence*.

25 Bod. Clar. MSS 108, ff. 79–80

26 CSP Col: *W. Indies and America* (1664), 215

27 For the ships, see Fox *passim*

28 Clar. *Life* II 303

29 Hutton, *CII* 220; Keeble, *Restoration* 100–1; Margoliouth I 143–6; Lister II 386–8

30 Clar. *Life* II 310

31 Sandwich, *Journal*, 26 January 1665

32 Evelyn III 387, 2 February 1665

33 Norrington 110, CII to Minette, 9 February 1663

34 Ibid. 107, CII to Minette, 5 January 1665

35 Pepys VI 42, 23 February 1665

36 Autograph draft, 22 February 1665, endorsed by Clarendon. PM, R of E Box 08, CII, Part 1, 019

23 THE ITCH OF HONOUR

1 Norrington 115, CII to Minette, 8 April 1665

2 Jusserand 140, The ambassadors to Louis XIV, 20 April 1665

3 Evelyn III 412, 22 June 1665

4 Rochester, *Letters* 247

5 Marshall, *Intelligence* 136–7, 151–2. Her instructions are printed in W. J. Cameron, *New Light on Aphra Behn* (1961) 34–5

6 Janet Todd, *The Secret Life of Aphra Behn* (1996); *The Works of Aphra Behn*, ed. Janet Todd, 7 vols (1992–6). See also Sara Helen Mendelson, *The Mental World of Stuart Women: Three Studies* (1988)
7 Evelyn III 407, 21 April 1665
8 Ibid. 44–5, 5 April 1665, note added *c.*1683

24 LORD HAVE MERCY UPON US

1 Clar. *Life* II 352
2 Ibid. 253
3 Evelyn III 416, 7 August 1665
4 Richard S. Westfall, *Never at Rest: A Biography of Isaac Newton* (1980) 143
5 Pepys VI 130–1, 17 June 1665
6 Vincent 32
7 Evelyn III 418, 7 September 1665

25 FORTUNES OF WAR

1 Harris, *Sandwich* I 293, in *POAS* 25 n.
2 Clar. *Life* II 386
3 Fox 29–30
4 Harris, *Sandwich* I 304–5
5 Norrington 120, CII to Minette, 8 June 1665
6 Clar. *Life* II 394
7 Pepys VI 123–4, 9 June 1665
8 *The Second Advice to a Painter*, 1666, attrib. to Marvell, *POAS* 44 (Smith 336)
9 Norrington 124, CII to Minette, 13 July 1665
10 Jusserand 143, The ambassadors to Louis XIV, 24 May 1665
11 Dispatches, 9 July 1665, in Hartmann 82; also *Painted Ladies* 97
12 Jusserand 142, Courtin to Lionne, 24 May 1665
13 Clar. *Life* II 417; see also Harris, *Sandwich* and C. H. Hartmann, *Clifford of the Cabal* (1937) 75–80
14 Rodger, *Command of the Ocean*, 70. See also Arthur Tedder, *The Restoration Navy from the death of Cromwell to the Treaty of Breda* (1916, 1970 edn)
15 Rochester, *Letters* 46–9
16 Burnet, *Some Passages* 180–1
17 Sandwich, *Journal* 281
18 Pepys VI 300, 16 November 1665
19 Milward 266–70, 20–21 April 1667
20 Pincus 335
21 Pepys VI 305, 22 November 1665
22 Norrington 130, CII to Minette, 29 January 1666
23 Sir John Holland to Sir William Gawdy, 30 January 1666; HMC *10th Report*, 200

26 THE LONG HOT SUMMER

1 Pepys VII 365, 10 November 1666
2 Roth 175
3 Hutton, *CII* 232
4 Evelyn III 429, 29 January 1666
5 Josselin 525, 4 March 1666
6 Pincus 334

7 Sir John Mennes to the Navy Board, 18 August 1666; Rogers 50
8 *Gazette* 26 April 1666
9 Norrington, CII to Minette, 2 May 1666
10 Lieut. Jeremy Roch, of the *Antelope*, quoted in Rodger 72
11 Pepys VI 141, 2 June 1666
12 See *A True Narrative of the Engagement between His Majesties Fleet, and that of Holland* (1666) 5; also the contemporary accounts in J. R. Powell and E. K. Timmings, *The Rupert and Monck Letter Book 1666* (1969)
13 Powell and Timmings, *Rupert and Monck*, 254; Rodger 74
14 Evelyn III 441, 16/17 June 1666
15 Josselin 528, 3 June 1666
16 R. Parsons, *A Sermon preached at the funeral of . . . John Earl of Rochester* (1680), 20; Burnet, *Some Passages* 177–8; Frank Ellis, *ODNB*
17 Burnet I 421
18 Pepys VII 159, 10 June 1666
19 Pepys VII 199–200, 10 July 1666
20 *Cal. Clar. SP* V 546
21 *Savile Corr.*, Henry Savile to Sir George Savile, 2 August 1666
22 *CSPV* 1666, 49
23 See Marshall, *Intelligence* 133
24 Clar. *Life* III 80
25 Wood, *Life and Times* II 82

27 CONFLAGRATION

1 James Malcolm, *London Redivivum* IV (1807) 73; Tinniswood, *Wren* 147
2 Bell 29; for the Fire see also Adrian Tinniswood, *By Permission of Heaven: The Story of the Great Fire of London* (2003)
3 Pepys VII 269, 2 September 1666
4 Bell 160
5 Gideon Harvey, *The City Remembrancer*, quoted in Neil Hanson, *The Dreadful Judgement* (2001) 118
6 Pepys VII 271, 2 September 1666. See *Gazette* 3–10 September 1666. For poems, see R. A. Aubin, *London in Flames, London in Glory* (1943)
7 See *CSPD* 1966–7, 94–5
8 Le Fleming MSS 42; Bell 313–14 and Appendix I
9 Vincent 45
10 Evelyn III 453, 3 September 1666
11 Vincent 50
12 John Rushworth, 'A Letter Giving Account of that Stupendious Fire which consumed the City of London, 1666', *Notes & Queries* V (15 April 1876)
13 Evelyn III 457, 6 September 1666
14 Hanson 208
15 Lisa Jardine, *Ingenious Pursuits: Building the Scientific Revolution* (2000) 302
16 Baxter, *Reliquiae Baxterianae* III 16
17 *Autobiography of William Taswell, DD, Camden Miscellany* II (1853) 10–11, 14
18 BL Add. MS 11,043 ff. 117–18; Windham Sandys to Viscount Scudamore, Bell Appendix

28 BLAME

1 *CSPD* 1666–7, 99–100, 104
2 Vincent 58; see also Evelyn III 458, 7 September, and W. Sandys to Viscount Scudamore, Bell 317
3 Leo Hollis, *The Phoenix: St Paul's Cathedral and the Men Who Made Modern London* (2008) 118; *Autobiography of William Taswell, DD, Camden Miscellany* II (1853), 18
4 Clar. *Life* III 85
5 Ibid. 87
6 Hutton, *Restoration* 249
7 Clar. *Life* III 88–92, 92–6. See Hastings MSS II 370–2, HMC Eliot Hodgkin (*15th Report*) 306; *CSPD* 1666–7, 99, 127–8; Burnet I 403
8 Bell 318
9 Clar. *Life* III 92
10 Locke, in Robert Boyle, *The General History of the Air* (1692) 106; see also Wood, *Life and Times* II 85
11 *CSPD* 1666–7, 140
12 Newsletter, Bod. Carte MS 72, f. 105v; Pincus 382
13 For the rebuilding see Jardine, *Wren* and *Hooke*; Cynthia Wall, *The Literary and Cultural Spaces of London* (1998); Hollis, *The Phoenix*
14 Fraser 247
15 Burnet I 421
16 Margoliouth II 42–3
17 Ibid. 53
18 *CSPD* 1666, 188, 107, 100
19 Evelyn III 464, 10 October 1666
20 Pepys VII 324, 15 October 1666; Evelyn 465, 18 October 1666. See Ribeiro 230–8
21 Ribeiro 230
22 Evelyn III 476, 18 February 1667
23 Pepys VII 379, 22 November 1666

29 THE TRICK TRACK MEN

1 *Last Instructions*, Margoliouth I 150 (Smith 371); see Pepys VII 356, 5 November 1666
2 Buckingham Commonplace Book, Hester Chapman, *Great Villiers* (1949) 129; C. Phipps, ed., *Buckingham, Public and Private Man: the prose, poems and commonplace book of George Villiers, second duke of Buckingham, 1628–1687* (1985)
3 Clar. *Life* III 133
4 Carte III 326
5 Burnet II 250; for context see Harris, *Politics*
6 Pepys VII 343, 27 October 1666; *LJ* XII 18–22
7 Carte III 336
8 Pepys VII 399, 8 December 1666
9 Ollard, *Clarendon* 273
10 Clar. *Life* III 153–4
11 Pepys VII 426, 31 December 1666
12 *Letters* 198; *LJ* XII 81
13 *CSPD* 1666–7, 490, 541

30 BREATHING SPACES

1 Evelyn III 474, 24 January 1667

2 Ibid. 476, 18 February 1667
3 *Gazette* 17 September 1666; Hollis 136
4 Clar. *Life* III 101
5 Jardine, *Hooke* 151–9, *Wren* 259–315. For the rebuilding see also Michael Cooper, *A More Beautiful City: Robert Hooke and the Rebuilding of London after the Great Fire* (2003) and Wall, *Literary and Cultural Spaces of London*
6 Pepys VIII 81, 24 February 1667
7 Ibid. 148, 29 March 1667
8 Ibid. 595, 29 December 1667
9 Ibid. 562–3, 3 December 1667
10 Picard 30
11 *Gazette* 24 October 1667
12 Pepys IX 317, 25–26 September 1668 and n. 2. For the New Exchange see also Peck 59–60
13 Evelyn III 473, 8 January 1667
14 Ibid. 478, 27 March 1667
15 Pepys VIII 163, 11 April 1667
16 Margaret Cavendish, *The World's Olio* (1655); Whitaker 294
17 Whitaker 304. For Margaret Cavendish see also Worsley, *Cavalier*
18 Cavendish, *Life* 312
19 *Grammont* (1888 edn) 153–5
20 Kate Lilley, ed., Margaret Cavendish, *The Blazing World and Other Writings*, (1994) 124
21 Pepys VIII 362–3, 1 May 1667
22 Ibid. 183–4, 26 April 1667
23 Anthony Hamilton alleged that Castlemaine waited until they were together and, at a signal from Bab May, informed the king that Frances was not ill but with her lover. *Grammont* 315–16
24 Burnet I 462; Pepys VIII, 18 March 1667. See *CSPD* 1666–7, 91
25 *Grammont* 315–16; Le Fleming 46, Newsletter 12 April
26 Pepys VIII 167–8, 173, 15 and 21 April 1667
27 Ibid. 185, 26 April 1667
28 J. Milton French, *The Life Records of John Milton* (1949–58), IV 392; A. N. Wilson, *The Life of John Milton* (1982) 222

31 THE DUTCH IN THE MEDWAY

1 Aphra Behn to Halsall, 14 Sept 1666, PRO 29/171.120
2 Figures from Hutton, *Restoration* 259
3 This is the argument of Pincus, 379–93
4 *LJ* XII 81; Speech at Prorogation of Parliament, 8 February 1667
5 Samuel Tucker to Arlington, 1 February 1667, State Papers 84, 184; Rogers 62
6 Pepys VIII 257, 10 June 1667
7 Rogers 64
8 Clar. *Life* III 249
9 Smith 385; see *Journal of the House of Lords* 165, 16 June 1666
10 Pepys VIII 268, 14 June 1667
11 *CSPD* 1666–7, 186: *CSPD* 1667, xxxv–viii
12 Clar. *Life* III 265
13 Le Fleming, newsletters 46–7
14 See Pincus 410–11
15 Pepys VIII 354–5, 27 July 1667

16 Ibid. 362–3, 29 July 1667
17 *Annus Mirabilis* 1057–64, Dryden, *Poems* I 192
18 See Martin Delzainis, 'Andrew Marvell and the Restoration Literary Underground: Printing the Painter Poems', *Seventeenth Century* XXII no. 2 (Autumn 2007) 395–410; also *CSPD* 1667–8, 363, and 1670, 486
19 *Savile Corr.*, 18 June 1666
20 Barbour 109; Rodger 164
21 Pepys VIII 489–92, 20 October 1667; *CJ* IX 85–6, 21 April 1668
22 *CJ* IX 10; Milward 92–3, 22 October 1667
23 Milward 128, 14 November 1667; see also 107, 31 October 1667
24 Marvell, *Last Instructions*, *POAS* 92 (Smith 389)

32 THE BLOWS FALL ON CLARENDON

1 Sometimes attributed to Marvell, the poem continues 'The grand affronter of the nobles lies,/ Grov'ling in dust, as a just sacrifice/ T' appease the injur'd King and abus'd nation./ Who could expect this sudden alteration?' *POAS* 158
2 Marvell, *Last Instructions*, *POAS* 137 (Smith 392)
3 Pepys VIII 427, 8 September 1667
4 Carte II 351
5 Col. Cope to Edward Weston, 28 May 1737, Weston Papers, HMC *10th Report* 267
6 Burnet I 463; Hartmann, *La Belle Stuart* 124–8
7 Bod. Carte MS 35 f. 461. Quoted in Ollard, *Clarendon* 279
8 Carte II 349
9 Pepys VIII 342, 17 July 1667. See BL Add. MS 27,872: 13, 'The Examination of Buckingham by Arlington'
10 Clar. *Life* III 272–3
11 Pepys VIII 331, 12 July 1667
12 Clar. *Life* III 282
13 Ibid. 283
14 'The King's Vows', *POAS* 160, often attrib. to Marvell, but possibly by Buckingham or Buckhurst
15 Clar. *Life* III 291
16 Pepys VIII 404, 27 August 1667
17 *Savile Corr.* 21, Henry to George Savile, 5 September 1667
18 Clar. *Life* III 324–6
19 Evelyn III 502, 9 December 1667

33 THE TRIPLE ALLIANCE

1 Marvell, *Last Instructions*, *POAS* 138 (Smith 394)
2 Evelyn III 490, 17 August 1667. See also Keay 147
3 Many of the letters from Ruvigny and his successor Colbert are transcribed in Mignet, and can also be found in the 'transcripts from French archives' PRO 31/3/106–125 (1660–70). The responses of the foreign minister Lionne and Louis himself are in CA.
4 Ruvigny to Louis XIV, 6 December 1667; Barbour 125
5 T. P. Courtenay, *Memoirs of Sir William Temple* (1836) II 381–2. See also K. H. D. Haley, *An English Diplomat in the Low Countries: Sir William Temple and John de Witt, 1665–1672* (1986) 162–82
6 Instructions to Sir William Temple, 25 November 1667; Pincus 434
7 Hutton, *Restoration* 255
8 Norrington 143, CII to Minette, 23 January 1668

9 Reresby 75
10 Reported by William Temple in a letter to his father, 22 July 1668, Temple, *Works* (1750) I 434–8

34 BUCKINGHAM'S YEAR

1 Norrington 146–7, CII to Minette, 5 March 1668
2 Pepys VIII 512, 31 October 1667
3 His Commons allies included Osborne, Sir Thomas Gower, Sir Henry Belasyse, Sir William Lowther, Sir Richard Temple, Sir Robert Howard, Charles Sedley, Edward Seymour and William Garaway. Buckingham I xxxiv; Alan Marshall, *The Age of Faction* (1999) 41–5
4 Halifax, in Ollard, *Image* 158
5 Ailesbury I 146
6 Hutton, *CII* 506, citing Maurice Lee, *The Cabal* (1965)
7 Burnet I 183–4
8 *Absalom and Achitophel*, Dryden, *Poems* I 495–6
9 Buckingham I xl
10 Pepys IX 27, 17 January 1668
11 Norrington 139, CII to Minette, 17 October 1667
12 See Pepys IX 27, 17 January 1668 and Le Fleming 55
13 *CSPD* 1667–8, 192, 193, 400; *Gazette* 27 February
14 Commonplace Book; Chapman, *Villiers* 148, 149
15 Pepys IX 201, 15 May 1668
16 Burnet I 453
17 February 1668; see Miller, *CII* 138. Charles also dismissed the bishops of Winchester and Rochester from court and appointed Herbert Croft of Hereford, the sole anti-Clarendon bishop, as the new dean of the Chapel Royal.
18 Buckingham II, Appendix I, 3
19 *CSPD* 1667, 437, 451, 454–5, 457, 484
20 Magalotti 25
21 See Shapiro 170–5
22 See D. R. Lacey, *Dissent and Parliamentary Politics in England 1661–1689* (1969) 56–8. Sir Matthew Hale drafted the comprehension bill; Dr John Owen, leader of the Independents, drew up proposals for toleration of sects outside the Church.
23 *LJ* XII 181
24 Milward 179, 6 February 1668
25 Ibid. 216–22 for the lengthy debate on the King's speech, 11 March 1668, also 248–50
26 Keay 133, citing BL Add. MS 36,916, f. 103r
27 Quoted in Nicholas von Maltzahn, 'Andrew Marvell and Lord Wharton', *Seventeenth Century*, XVIII no. 2 (Autumn 2003) 255–6
28 *Paradise Lost* XII
29 Sir Charles Wolsely, *Liberty of Conscience, the Magistrate's Interest* (1668), quoted in Gary S. de Krey, 'Radicals, reformers and republicans', Houston and Pincus 84
30 Grey, *Debates* I 71, 14 February 1668
31 Bod. Carte MSS 46, f. 600, Arlington to Ormond, 18 February 1668
32 Pepys IX 71, 14 February 1668
33 Milward 190, 19 February 1668
34 Pepys IX 178, 29 April 1668
35 Grey, *Debates* I 95–6, 93–7; Milward 200, 27 February 1668
36 *CJ* IX 44

37 See Harris, *London Crowds* 82–91
38 Pepys IX 129, 24 March 1668
39 Ibid. 132, 25 March 1668
40 *The Poore Whore's Petition. To the most Splendid, Illustrious, Serene and Eminent Lady of Pleasure, the Countess of Castlemayne* (1668); MSS reply, Bod. MS Don b.8, 190–3; *The Gracious Answer of the Most Illustrious Lady of Pleasure, the Countess of Castlemayne . . . To the Poor-Whoores Petition* (1668), reprinted in Steinman, 101–11
41 *The Gracious Answer*, Hamilton 120–1
42 *State Trials* VI 879–914; *CSPD* 1667–8, 310–11
43 Pepys IX 373, 23 November 1668

35 LOVING TOO WELL

1 Pepys IX 192, 9 May 1668
2 *King's Works* 215–16
3 Evelyn III 555
4 Reresby 259
5 Magalotti 27; Weiser 19
6 Magalotti 27
7 'A Satire on Charles II', Rochester, *Poems* 11–15
8 Pepys VII 368, 30 July 1667
9 Ibid. 368, 355; 30 and 27 July 1667
10 Etherege, *She Would If She Could* I ii, ed. C. M. Taylor (1973) 25
11 Downes 55
12 Burnet 483
13 Pepys IX 81, 20 February 1668
14 Pepys IX 186, 5 May 1668
15 Hamilton, *Castlemaine* 121
16 Pepys IX 398, 21 December 1668
17 Quoted in Weiser 21
18 Norrington 151, CII to Minette, 7 May 1668
19 Pepys IX 210, 31 May 1668
20 Mary married the Earl of Derwentwater, and by a heartbreaking turn of fate, two of their three sons – Charles's grandsons – were executed in the Jacobite risings of 1715 and 1745.
21 Norrington 138, CII to Minette, 26 August 1667
22 See *Hatton Correspondence* I 52
23 Norrington 143, CII to Minette, 23 January 1668
24 Pepys IX 205, 19 May 1668
25 Norrington 151, CII to Minette, 7 May 1668
26 Ruvigny to Lionne, 28 June 1668, Hartmann 158
27 Norrington 154, CII to Minette, 14 June 1668
28 Fraser 261; Shapiro 219, 288

36 SWEET LADIES

1 Pepys IX 335–6, 338–9, 23, 25 October 1668
2 Anon. (attrib. Etherege), 'The Lady of Pleasure: a Satyr', see James Thorpe, ed., *Poems of Sir George Etherege* (1963)
3 S. M. Wynne, *ODNB*. Several different versions appear in the biographies, including J. H. Wilson (1952), Roy MacGregor-Hastie (1987), and Derek Parker (2000). The most recent is Charles Beauclerk, *Nell Gwyn: A Biography* (2005).
4 Pepys IX 91, 2 March 1667

5 Winn 183. Dryden had recently lent Charles £500, returning an instalment of his wife's dowry.

6 Dryden, *Secret Love* I ii, *Works* IX 187

7 Ibid. V i, *Works* IX 182

8 Ibid., *Works* IX 199

9 *The Mad Couple*; Summers 116

10 Beauclerk 128

11 Dryden, *An Evening's Love, or The Mock Astrologer* IV I, *Works* X 273

12 Ibid., *Works* X 280

13 PRO 31/3/121, Colbert de Croissy to Lionne, 31 January 1669; S. M. Wynne, 'The Mistresses of Charles II and Restoration Court Politics', *Stuart Courts* 180

14 Beauclerk 138–40

15 Pepys IX 415, 417; 15, 16 January 1669

16 Dryden, *Tyrannick Love* V I, *Works* X 178

17 Evelyn III 560, 28 August 1670

18 Magalotti 39

19 *Grammont* 101

20 Beauclerk 154; PRO 31/3

21 Burnet I 484

22 The first mention is the *Supplement* to James Granger's *Biographical Dictionary*, 1774.

37 TROUBLESOME MEN

1 Thirsk and Cooper, I 520–24; PRO SP 29/247, no. 15. The members were Arlington, Robartes, Buckingham, Lauderdale, Clifford, Carteret and Ashley. In 1670 a new Council for Plantations was created, followed by Ashley's Council for Trade and Plantations of 1672.

2 Burnet I 170

3 Ralph Montagu to Arlington, 19 October 1669, Montagu–Arlington letters, Buccleugh MSS 442

4 Pepys IX 386, 7 December 1668

5 Hartmann, *Madame*; Chapman, *Great Villiers* 153

6 Pepys IX 462, 467, 471–91; 1, 4, 6–20 March 1669; PRO/31/3/121 ff. 198–200, Colbert de Croissy to Lionne

7 Buckingham I 249–54

8 Pepys IX 469, 4 March 1669

9 Ibid. 346, 4 November 1668

10 Harris, *Restoration* 380

11 Le Fleming MSS 61; Carte, *Ormonde* III 69

12 Burnet I 489

13 Ibid. 432

14 September 1667. See *Lauderdale Papers* II 49–90

15 *Lauderdale Papers* II 168–71

16 Mary K. Geiter, *William Penn* (2000)

17 *Lauderdale Papers* II 163–4; Harris, *Restoration* 121

18 Margoliouth II 221, ascribed to Marvell but authorship unknown. MS dated 1680

19 Burnet I 448

38 CHARLES AND LOUIS

1 Norrington 155, CII to Minette, 22 June 1668

2 Hutton, *CII* 262

3 Norrington 16, CII to Minette, 14 September 1668
4 Pepys IV 21, 25 January 1665
5 Norrington 169, CII to Minette, 20 January 1669
6 Miller, *CII* 162
7 Pepys IX 451–2, 17 February 1669
8 Sandwich's journal, in Richard Ollard, *Cromwell's Earl: Edward Montagu, First Earl of Sandwich* (1994) 250
9 Pepys IX 451–2, 17 February 1669
10 Norrington 172, CII to Minette, 12 March 1669
11 Pepys IX 427–8 and n. 473, 26 January, 7 March 1669
12 Norrington 171, CII to Minette, 7 March 1669
13 Pepys IX 474, 8 March 1669
14 Norrington 175 (code removed in current text), CII to Minette, 25 April 1669
15 *Letters* 236, CII to Minette, 24 May 1668
16 *Letters* 239, CII to Minette, 7 June 1668
17 Barbour 163; HMC Verney, *7th Report* 487
18 *Letters* 242
19 Colbert de Croissy's despatches, PRO 31/3/125
20 Hartmann 310, Colbert to Louis XIV, 24 April, 2 May 1670
21 Arlington, *Letters* 423–30
22 Norrington 209
23 This story, from *Memoirs of Madame Montpensier* IV 107–14, in Hartmann, *Madame*, repeated in Norrington. See also Paul Sonnino, *Louis XIV and the Origins of the Dutch War* (1988) 108
24 Sandwich MSS *Journal* c 274; Harris, *Sandwich* 207

39 DOVER AND BEYOND

1 Schellinks, *Journal* 39
2 Hartmann, *King My Brother* 311
3 *CSPV* 1669–70, 187, 201
4 Barbour 168
5 Text of Treaty, John Lingard, *History of England*, 10 vols (1819) IX, Appendix 503–10
6 Mignet III, 256–67
7 For Lingard's text of the Treaty, see Browning, *Historical Documents* 863–7
8 Le Fleming 70, newsletter 17 May 1670
9 Ibid. 71
10 *CSPD* 1670, 233–5
11 CA 97 ff. 250–5, Croissy to Louis, 30, 31 May 1670
12 CA 101 ff. 66–8, 8 October 1671, Colbert to Pomponne; Barbour 181
13 Burnet I 617
14 Norrington 170, CII to Minette, 7 March 1669
15 Hobbes, *Leviathan*, Part I, Ch. 3, 81

40 SAILING

1 Norrington 213, Minette to Thomas Clifford, 21 June 1679
2 Madame de Lafayette, *Historie Secret de Madame Henriette d'Angleterre*, ed. G. Sigaux (1988) 89
3 Hartmann, *King My Brother* 39
4 Ralph Montagu to Arlington, 30 June 1670, *Bath Papers*, HMC *4th Report* 144. See also M. B. Curran, ed., *The Despatches of William Perwich, English Agent in Paris*, 1669–1677 (1903)

5 Rochester, *Letters* 57, July 1670
6 Fraser 257–8
7 See Miller, *James* II 58–9 and Sir John Dalrymple, *Memoirs* (1773 edn) I 32–3
8 *Absalom and Achitophel*, Dryden, *Poems* I 495–6
9 Andrew Marvell, *Account of the Growth of Popery and Arbitrary Government* (1677)
10 Barillon's testimony in H. D. Traill, *Shaftesbury, the first Earl*, ed. Andrew Lang (1888) 179
11 Ollard, *Image* 158
12 In 1684 he made no move when Robert Baillie, accused of conspiring, was taken from London to be questioned in Scotland, where no law existed against torture. Aidan O'Neill QC, Scottish Human Rights Commission Conference, Strathclyde University 2008.
13 Fraser 412
14 Evelyn IV 403, 413–14, referring to 25 January 1685
15 Ibid. 455, 15 July 1685
16 Burnet II 461; Evelyn II 206; Lady Anne Mason, 'Account of the death of Charles II, by a wife of a person about Court at Whitehall', *Household Words* IX (1854)
17 Burnet II 473, S. M. Wynne, *ODNB*

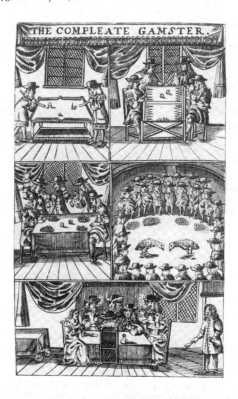

List of Illustrations

LIST OF ILLUSTRATIONS

Index

Académie des Sciences, 241
Act of Oblivion and Indemnity (1660), 103, 105–7, 110, 118
Act of Uniformity (1662), 186, 191–3, 446
The Adventures of Five Hours (Tuke and Calderón), 281
Africa, 308–10, 314, 316, 320, 412
agriculture, 169–70, 238
Ailesbury, Thomas Bruce, 2nd Earl of, 135, 437
Aix-la-Chapelle, Treaty of (1668), 431
Albemarle, Duke of *see* Monck, George, Duke of Albemarle
alchemy, 219, 223, 240, 244
Alexis, Tsar of Russia, 246
Algiers, 152, 298, 493
Allen, Sir Thomas, 49
Allestree, Richard, 9
Allin, Sir Thomas, 318, 493
Amalia von Solms, Dowager Princess of Orange, 92
ambassadors, 144–8, 246, 341; *see also individual ambassadors by name*
America *see* North American colonies; South American colonies
Amsterdam, 294, 307, *307*
Anglesey, Arthur Annesley, Earl of, 104, 255, 385, 447, 480
Anne, Queen, 497, 523
Anne of Austria, Regent of France, 30
Annesley, Arthur, Earl of Anglesey *see* Anglesey, Arthur Annesley, Earl of
Annus Mirabilis (pamphlets), 190, 413; *see also* Dryden
Argyll, Archibald Campbell, Marquess of, 23, 108
Arlington, Henry Bennet, 1st Earl of: portrait, *plate 19*; 201–2, 205–8, 210, 261, 295, 299, 311, 356, 387, 407, 415, 437, 444–5, 475, 476–7, 492, 509, 512, 516, 524; Keeper of King's Privy Purse, 202; made Secretary of State, 203; and

spy network 315–16, 324–5; made Baron Arlington, 336; rivalry with Buckingham 385, 387–8, 421, 498; Clarendon's fall, 422, 423, 425; Cabal, 428–30; Treaty of Dover, 500, 506–7
Arlington, Isabella, Countess of, 429
Armstrong, Sir Thomas, 512
Arran, Richard Butler, Earl of, 99, 137, 140, 383
Arundell, Henry, 3rd Baron Arundell of Wardour, Lord, 492, 493, 506
Ashley, Lord *see* Shaftesbury, Anthony Ashley Cooper, Lord Ashley, 1st Earl of
Ashmole, Elias, 223, 229
astronomy, 228, 231
Aubrey, John, 54, 222, 256, 271
Audley End, 450
Avebury, 256

Backwell, Edward, 204, 295, 296, 457, 515
Bacon, Sir Francis, 224, 237, *243*
Badminton, 166–7, 256
Baillie, Robert, 556
Baltimore, Lord, 73
Bank of England, 291
bankers, 293–6
Barbados, 74, 303, 355
Barbon, Nicholas, 394
Barlow, Francis: artworks by, *24*, *141*, *168*, *451*
Barrow, Isaac, 178
Bath, 256–7, *257*
Bath, Earl of *see* Grenville, John (later Earl of Bath)
Batten, Sir William, 337
Bawdy House riots 447, 448
Baxter, Richard: 78, 181–2, 183, 191, 192, 365, 442
Bayley, Charles, 212
Beauclerk, Charles, Duke of St Albans (son of CII and Nell Gwyn) *see* St Albans, Charles Beauclerk, Duke of

[561]